Walking Out, Speaking Up

This book makes me realise the full import of how street theatre confronted concrete issues through public reasoning, contributing powerfully to the growth of the women's movement in India. Deepti Mehrotra's work offers important insights from the past, and is an essential tool for all democratic rights activists and creative artistes in the struggle against pervasive patriarchies, old and new.

– Professor Manoranjan Mohanty, Political scientist and teacher

A valuable contribution to our knowledge of an essential strand of our collective history, the multi-faceted women's movement. This significant volume revisits and analyses a variety of sources, from the deeply personal to the highly public, to enhance our understanding of how activist theatre helped bring about changes of perception, action and legislation with regard to women's lived realities in contemporary India.

– Anjum Katyal, Theatre critic, writer and editor

A warm and wonderful introduction, by an insider, to the rich tapestry of feminist street theatre in India. The author captures the ecstasy, anger, creative outpouring, exhaustion and exhilaration that marked street protest and street theatre, in the churn of the 1980s and 1990s. Essential reading!

– Feisal Alkazi, Director, playwright and educationist

A marvellous record of the important cultural resistance that feminist street theatre of the 1980s embodied. Women spoke up in crowds, sensitising people to think and engage with radical change. The plays were very creative, with brilliant dialogue, songs and stories, and they made an impact. This book recovers that history, affirms and brings it alive, thus filling a critical gap in the literature.

– Uma Chakravarti, professor of history, writer and filmmaker

Walking Out, Speaking Up

Feminist Street Theatre in India

DEEPTI PRIYA MEHROTRA

zubaan

ZUBAAN
128 B Shahpur Jat, 1st floor
NEW DELHI 110 049
Email: contact@zubaanbooks.com
Website: www.zubaanbooks.com

First published by Zubaan Publishers Pvt. Ltd 2025

India Foundation for the Arts and South Asia Women's Fund supported part of the research for this book.

10 9 8 7 6 5 4 3 2 1

ISBN 978 81 97673 02 3 (paperback)
ISBN 978 81 97673 01 6 (ebook)

Zubaan is an independent feminist publishing house based in New Delhi with a strong academic and general list. It was set up as an imprint of India's first feminist publishing house, Kali for Women, and carries forward Kali's tradition of publishing world quality books to high editorial and production standards. *Zubaan* means tongue, voice, language, speech in Hindustani. Zubaan publishes in the areas of the humanities, social sciences, as well as in fiction, general non-fiction, and books for children and young adults under its Young Zubaan imprint.

Typeset by in Adobe Text Pro 10/12 by Jojy Philip
Printed and bound at Raj Press, New Delhi

Contents

SECTION FIVE
STREE MUKTI: SCRIPTING WOMEN'S LIBERATION, IN MAHARASHTRA AND GUJARAT

SECTION SIX
MANY PLACES, MANY PLAYS: FOR VOICE AND CHOICE

SECTION SEVEN
FEMINIST STREET THEATRE AS CONTEMPORARY HISTORY

SECTION ONE

PERFORMING THE MOVEMENT

> You cannot have any activity without song and dance, in the Indian women's movement.
>
> – *Gouri Choudhury (interview 2015)*[1]

> Thousands of eyes are staring at you, while you are out in the open, not surrounded by protective darkness... There is an active audience, street noises you have to fight against, say your lines, project your voice, it's not easy.
>
> – *Rati Bartholomew (Seagull Theatre Quarterly 1997a: 45)*[2]

> When we come together to make a play, we become friends—who have a common vision. The togetherness unfolds variations of group activity while allowing [one] to see oneself better. As partners we become each other's mirror and all our qualities merge to give the group its unique tint. And even when we need to disperse, the group's imprint remains on all of us.
>
> – *Tripurari Sharma (Sharma and Krishnamurty 2000: 27)*

Feminist street theatre came into being in India in association with the autonomous women's movement. We explore this theatre in the present volume, a labyrinthine journey down memory lane. The most

[1] Gouri Choudhury (1938-2022) was an activist in the women's movement. She co-founded the women's groups Saheli, Jagori and Shakti Shalini, and was chairperson of Action India, where she worked for nearly five decades.

[2] Rati Bartholomew, Tripurari Sharma and Lakshmi Krishnamurty are pioneers of feminist street theatre. Rati (1927-2021) was a guest faculty member at the National School of Drama; director, actor, and co-founder of Theatre Union, a Delhi-based theatre group; she taught at Indraprastha College, Delhi University. Tripurari (1956-2023) was a playwright, director, screenwriter and professor at the National School of Drama. Lakshmi Krishnamurty is a social anthropologist, researcher, and theatre facilitator.

vibrant phase in the development of feminist street theatre unfolded in the late 1970s and 80s, but its legacy continues, in many avatars.

In the first section, we will revisit the atmosphere of the times and probe the politics and aesthetics of this form of theatre. The opening chapter provides brief glimpses into one particular play performance, held at an iconic public site. It foregrounds the trope of women questioning, challenging, and walking out of unjust, hurtful patriarchal structures. Similar plays were produced and performed across the country, signifying the tremendous churning in women's hearts and minds, and indeed in much of society. Documenting and reviewing this theatre has meant retrieving diverse scripts, scattered stories, and multi-layered histories of resistance.

Feminist street theatre developed a unique aesthetic, even as inspired dramatists joined forces with radical politics. To understand the terrain better, in Chapter 2 we will trace some of the contexts, sources and participants, as well as identify characteristic features of this theatre. Its content was in sync with issues occupying the women's movement, and the form developed in ways that were quite distinct from conventional norms. Feminist street plays tended to be imagistic, teeming with voices and vignettes. And they were open-ended, inviting audience participation in the adventure of resolution and transformation.

1

Where Kanchan Walks Out

Scripts, Stories, Histories

February 1981: A young woman lies dead on the Boat Club Lawns at India Gate, in the heart of New Delhi.

Normally, no woman would dare lie sprawled in such a public spot, the quintessential venue for protest demonstrations.[3] Government employees from Udyog Bhavan and sundry loiterers basked in the winter sun with peanuts to pass the time. A few hundred people gathered around the play as it unfolded—agog, incredulous as they witnessed murder.

It was *Om Swaha* that was being performed, a play based on the life and death of the very real Hardeep Kaur. Hardeep was abused in her marital home, set on fire in October 1978, and died in hospital, of third-degree burns.

Hardeep's father-in-law thundered: 'I'll deal with the police. You will marry again, my son...a second dowry!' Hardeep's husband whooped with joy. Four pall-bearers picked up the corpse, chanting '*Ram naam satya hai*', and dumped it in a corner. The police were eminently bribable, and Hardeep's parents and brother elected to focus on the living and forget the dead.

---

[3] The Boat Club at the lawns of India Gate was, for several decades, India's 'resistance square', hosting enormous public gatherings. It is located in the midst of government offices where some 1,50,000 personnel were employed at the time, and is close to the presidential residence. By the early 1990s, rallies and protest gatherings were banned at the Boat Club with imposition of Section 144 of the Indian Penal Code. In July 2018, the Supreme Court of India ordered lifting of this blanket ban, but the Boat Club is no longer a venue for protests. Rather, it is a manicured tourist spot, now a part of Delhi's revamped Central Vista.

Om Swaha, India Gate, 1981. First photo: family members harassing Hardeep; Actors (Left to right): Ein Lall, Maya Rao, Gouri Choudhury, Anand Swamy, Deepti Mehrotra, E. Theophilus, Sharda behn, Jyotika Virdi, Chhaya Sharma, Runu Chakraborty. Second photo: Hardeep being killed; Actors: Deepti, Anand. Third photo: Husband and father-in-law talk over Hardeep's corpse; Actors (Left to right): Theophilus, Anand.

The drama continued at a brisk pace. Hardeep's friend Kanchan sensed that the death was a murder, not an accident, and spoke up. But her family hustled her into wedlock with a 'good' boy from a well-to-do family. Eerily enough, Kanchan was also subjected to abuse at

Om Swaha, Mehrauli, 1980. Kanchan abused. (Left to right) Urvashi Butalia, Maya Rao, Anuradha Kapur. Kanchan decides to walk out.

her sasural. Her parents advised her to adjust; she feared she would be killed, the same fate that befell Hardeep.

Kanchan invited the audience to intervene, and help her take a decision. Onlookers were persuaded to reflect, and take a stand. As it turned out, nobody insisted she continue staying with her husband and in-laws, thereby submitting to torture and death. Walking out of her marital home was daring, almost unthinkable, yet clearly it was the only humane option possible.

Society was on the cusp of change. Kanchan walked out, suggesting that it was possible for women to live independent of men. That nobody ought to suffer helplessly within violent family situations. That human dignity and integrity were of the highest importance.

The women's movement of the time sparkled with creative modes of expression and resistance—plays, songs, posters, sketches, poetry, reportage, music, dance, journals, leaflets, slogans, and more. While the issues and contexts were deadly serious, there was an exhilaration in these oppositional politics.

Women from various sections of society, working-class, elite, homemakers, professionals, rural, urban, young and elderly, contributed to the mélange. Plays were replete with energetic movements, dialogue, film music and folk songs, familiar tunes deployed in novel settings, adapted with new lyrics. Theatre groups exuded joie de vivre as they traveled and performed; they also experienced sorrow, anger and empathy.

Drawing crowds was easy. The streets were not yet clogged with automobiles. You could comfortably walk or cycle. Most people used public buses, only a few were proud possessors of a Vespa or Lambretta scooter, an Ambassador or Premier Padmini car. Today's traffic jams, flyovers and underground metros were as yet unimaginable. There were trees aplenty, birdsong, clean air, skies blue by day and star-studded by night. Fresh fruit and vegetables were wheeled on hand-carts, right up to customers' doorsteps.

Itinerant traders called out their wares—toy-sellers, bangle-sellers, candy-floss-sellers—while the snake-charmer, *bandar-wala*, and *bhalu-wala* provided entertainment. Nats (acrobats) performed somersaults and pole-vaults, bodies flexible from training since infancy. Circuses came to town, with acrobats, clowns, elephants, and a lion or two. Popular travelling theatres, Nautanki, Khayal, Therukootu and many others performed every now and then.

People conversed at home, in buses, at tea-shops and vendor stalls; no computers, mobiles or iPads leached away attention. Grandparents might tell stories to children huddled around them, listening with big eyes. Doordarshan ran over only a few evening hours, featuring black and white news, Krishi Darshan on crops and fertilisers, and the Sunday film which was eagerly awaited, neighbours gathering in any home that boasted a TV set. Vividh Bharati's *Vande Mataram* woke children up at 6 a.m., nudging them to dress up for school; languorous Bollywood numbers wafted across long, lazy afternoons; Hawa Mahal offered dramatised radio skits every evening. Seeing a movie in a cinema hall was an exciting family outing; picnics were popular, with hampers of home-cooked food.

The immediacy of encounter, of face-to-face interaction, remained the major form of communication. Electronic media hovered on the margins of lives—an exciting margin. Phone meant landline, index finger turning the dial, digit by digit. The idea that one day one could see the person at the other end, thousands of miles away, was in the realm of science fiction. Someone with a Kodak camera would take the rare photograph, adjusting focus and aperture, and negatives would be developed in a studio. In the 90s, clunky computers began appearing on our desks.

In the non-digital era, petitions couldn't be endorsed online, nor were protests channeled via Twitter or X. One had to be physically present: sit-in outside bride-murderers' homes, demonstrate against sexual harassment, sati, domestic violence, communal killings. It was in this scenario that feminist street theatre shot into prominence. It brought cutting-edge perspectives into the public domain. Ideas were played out and stories told at busy thoroughfares, inner-city by-lanes, parks, colleges, schools, courtyards, marketplaces, neighbourhoods, and outside police stations.

Street plays were a novelty. Fiction merged with documentary, making for searing content, and rich aesthetics. The play was like a Trojan horse—the rhythm of the tambourine, drum, song and movements won entry into people's consciousness. As the play unfolded, feminist analysis unfurled, challenging patriarchal mindsets. Actors were speaking truths they often couldn't as lone individuals, describing discrimination and violence, a denial of mobility and autonomy. Strong messages got across. And the messengers survived, for here they were together, not alone and isolated.

These were 'new women', who refused to adapt, adjust, tolerate the intolerable; they were part of a trend, and among the trendsetters. Street theatre offered a means to initiate multiple conversations across society. It drew attention, sparked discussions. The women's movement surged along with hundreds of plays, touching countless lives. It spread from one to another, ripples that grew into waves. Actors immersed themselves, as did audiences, and courage developed as women stepped further into the unknown. Horizons broadened, and choices were made.

Much of this remains hidden from history. The specific is often lost behind broad labels such as 'second wave feminism'. But feminism is deeply rooted in the local; the personal is political, and infinitely varied. My masi, seeing a performance of *Om Swaha,* remarked with wonder: 'In my time, we challenged many things, but never came out on the streets!' She'd fought to attend school, and persisted, becoming a well-respected educationist.[4] And here I was, enabled to study as much as I wanted, yet stepping out to act in a street play. There's a continuum to women's struggles, sharpening with each generation; a logic of its own though the path might zigzag. The changes manifest in open dissent, shifts in policy, law, public discourse, and infinitely subtle transformations of the personal.

Recovering Scripts, Stories, Histories: A Brief Note on Methodology

Telling our stories is important: it facilitates the interplay between inner and outer worlds. Yesterday's stories of resistance remain relevant today. Like Hardeep and other women characters from the 80s, today too women face sexism, and aggression. Often, in meeting demands and expectations, we lose track of our own stories and priorities, forget what matters most deeply.

This, then, is a history from below, sharing narratives of women, a movement, and a time. These pages recreate some of the colour and magic of street theatre during that long moment, when women laid claim to power: to speak, to sing, and to imagine a transformed world. Testimonies unfolded, and new, disruptive ideas entered, even invaded, the public sphere. Feminist street theatre of the time was insistent and audacious as it transgressed beyond designated boundaries and brought alternative imaginations to life.

Though theatre has a unique significance, it might leave behind few traces. Its live and ephemeral aspects render documentation difficult. India's rich history of theatre is, in general, insufficiently documented. Cultural studies tend to focus on print commodities and genres such as the novel for recovery of dissenting voices, neglecting performative genres. Thus despite 'the utter centrality of theatrical activity, in its varied forms, to subversive cultural practices,' much of it remains undocumented and un-theorised (Bhatia 2010: 118-19).

---

[4] Surad Pyari Sukhia (1911-2002), Principal of Women's Training College, Dayalbagh, Agra, and Vice-Chancellor of Agra University, was my mother's eldest sister. Her early struggles involved individual strategising to continue her schooling at every stage beyond Class 2; eliciting quiet support from her mother and maternal grandmother. She balanced her studies with housework and sibling-care (as she was the eldest of ten children), and was often the only girl/woman in her class.

In the case of feminist street theatre, there are next to no systematic records of plays and performances; of shows, casts, days, dates, venues, and audience reactions. This paucity of documentation may seem baffling. The fact is, participants were already overstretched, juggling theatre with their regular work, leaving little energy for record-keeping. There were typically no funds for doing or documenting plays. Cameras were uncommon, videography rare. In the urgency of action, the significance of documentation was overlooked, and neglected.

The historian Uma Chakravarti[5] (interview 2015) describes how *Patan,* a powerful street play by students of Miranda House, Delhi University (DU), performed a few times, packed up after a few shows: 'The students had to sit for exams. I said to Anuradha [Kapur, director of the play], "It's terrible that it has to end." She said, "This is the nature of street theatre, it is ephemeral, it cannot last." She was reconciled to that, but I wasn't, and I'm still not'. Uma has no copy of the script, nor does she know if it exists at all, and rues the fact.

Oral History: Interviews and Conversations

In the tradition of critical feminist ethnography, this work elicits memory, using oral history methods. It builds on approximately 25 interviews which took place largely between 2014 and 2017, with actors, directors, activists, and academics, all of whom were part of, or closely associated with, street theatre.[6] Generous with their time, they recalled events, discussed experiences, conversing with pleasure, nostalgia, regret, joy, yearning and satisfaction: indeed a kaleidoscope of shifting emotions.

---

[5] Uma Chakravarti is an eminent historian who taught at Miranda House, Delhi University, in addition to being a human rights activist and documentary filmmaker.

[6] Interviewees included Maya Rao (whose full name is Maya Krishna Rao), Gouri Choudhury, Amrita Chhachhi, Sheba Chhachhi, Runu Chakraborty, Savita Sharma, David Devadas, Sanjoy Roy, Shanti, Vidya Thapa, Gyanvati, Veermati, Moloyashree Hashmi, Anjali Deshpande, Anand Kumar, Renuka Mishra, Dilip Simeon, Rukmini Rao, Parveen Garewal, Jyoti Mhapsekar, Uma Chakravarti, Urvashi Butalia, Anand Swamy and Jyotika Virdi. In addition, Vibhuti Patel shared memories over email; and I had conversations or informal discussions with Harsh Kapoor, Ein Lall, Manohar Khushalani, several Sabla Sangh/Action India activists, who added to the pool of memories and testimonies. Conversations during theatre workshops and post-performance discussions provided additional sources of information. When I approached Anuradha Kapur for an interview, she expressed willingness (via an email exchange in 2015), but was busy with one thing and then another during the relevant time span. The case with Vrinda Grover was also similar.

When I began this research, the plan was to write about early feminist street theatre within Delhi. But the idea took on a life of its own, and expanded to other geographies. The bulk of the narratives and detailed descriptions in this book are still from Delhi, but we explore kindred stories from elsewhere as well. The writing draws upon my multiple interactions with street theatre over the decades, in Delhi, Chhattisgarh, Uttar Pradesh, Rajasthan, Madhya Pradesh, Maharashtra, Manipur, and some other parts of the country.[7] My active participation in *Om Swaha, Ehsaas* and *Teen Behenon ki Atmahatya* during the 80s,[8] and documentation (Priya 1995) of a series of theatre workshops in the 90s,[9] melds with a collage of collective memories. Being an insider in the world of women's street theatre as well as a documenter and researcher, has meant that I have been a participant, at other times a participant observer, in theatre workshops and theatrical performances. It has afforded me multiple entry points and perspectives—ranging from immersed swimmer to ringside viewer. Tactile, physical and emotional immersion in feminist theatre, especially during the 1980s, has helped guide my understanding of its meaning and its power. During the 90s, I documented street theatre and began writing about it, and of course kept watching, hearing and reading about street theatre performances. And then, research for the present volume (from 2014) led me to dip into a pool of the older street plays, and inspired a public performance of 'vintage play readings' which I co-developed (described in Chapter 25).

All this has allowed an expanded scope for ethnographic inputs and insights than is usually available to a researcher. Auto-ethnography, the participant observer stance, and oral history methods have all contributed to the present volume. Apart from formal interviews, there have been numerous conversations. These conversations included informal personal exchanges (face-to-face or over email), discussions during theatre workshops, as well as post-performance audience

[7] This volume makes no claim, however, to a comprehensive coverage. The states comprising South India, most states of the North-east, as well as Odisha, Bihar, Uttarakhand, Jammu and Kashmir and Himachal Pradesh, for instance, are almost entirely left out. Much more work is needed, ideally by a team of researchers and writers.

[8] I was a participant in the theatre workshop that created *Ehsaas* in 1979, and was an actor in the play between 1979-80 as well as 1982-87. I was an actor in *Om Swaha* between 1980-85. While both these plays were Delhi-based, in 1988 in Kanpur, I turned playwright for the street play *Teen Behenon ki Atmahatya,* facilitated the theatre workshop that produced the play, and acted in it.

[9] This series of workshops is described in Chapter 21 of the present volume.

responses. These multiple voices weave through the book, forming its veins and arteries.

Play Scripts and Photographs: The Text and the Visual

A rich pile of data gathered, including material from interviews and conversations as well as textual material and a few photographs. This volume delves into a number of plays, though these form only a fraction of the corpus of street plays that the Indian women's movement of the time generated.

Overall, I was able to locate 23 play scripts in their entirety. Seventeen are in Hindustani/Hindi, and the rest are in English. Several of these are translations from the original Bengali, Marathi, Gujarati, and other regional languages. I closely read each script, and mapped its theme, storyline, plot, dramatis personae, approach and treatment, including imagery, songs, dialogue, and movement. I translated selected excerpts from the Hindustani/Hindi scripts into English. All this textual material was synthesised, with material gleaned via oral histories, media documents and academic literature.

Film scholar Jyotika Virdi[10] (interview 2017) recalls an effort to gather play scripts way back in 1986-87: for 'the same reason as what you're doing now—these plays shouldn't get lost.' Jagori, the women's resource centre with which she then worked, collated scripts and published them as an anthology called *Nukkad Nukkad Angan Angan* (Jagori Samooh 1988). The publication included a note by Jyotika on the significance of the documentation, which reads:

> These scripts are witness to the creativity of the women's movement. Groups from distant places, often unknown to each other, raised similar issues, in their own ways, through the medium of theatre. This book helps to win recognition for their efforts. It reflects the voices of women coming together and surging forward. Various groups can use it, to perform plays, or initiate discussion. Hearing others' stories makes it easier to share one's own feelings and experiences. We aim to value and preserve the contribution of each tiny bubble rising from this wave of the women's movement. Each play has a special place in the history of the movement. (Virdi 1988: vii-ix)

---

[10] Jyotika Virdi is Professor of Film Studies at the University of Windsor, Canada, and specialises in cultural and postcolonial studies. She was an actor in the street plays *Om Swaha* and *Ehsaas* in Delhi during the 1980s.

Malini Bhattacharya's *Giving Away the Girl* (2003), translated from Bengali, is a compendium of three plays. This book made it possible for me to revisit and reconstruct specific play histories. The following booklets were useful too: Jyoti Mhapsekar's *Beti Aayi Hai* (2010), and *Two Street Plays for Women* by ASTHA (1988), a project of the Xavier Institute of Communications, Mumbai. Each of these offers play scripts, along with introductory notes.

Sheba Chhacchi's photos of *Om Swaha* help provide a visual connect to the ambience of performance spaces, aesthetics of the plays, and audience reactions. These are precious for their archival value, also because photos of feminist street theatre are so very rare.

There are no photos, for instance, of *Ehsaas* during its major innings (1982-87), when it was performed perhaps hundreds of times. I have a hazy memory of a set of photos from *Ehsaas* performances during a street theatre meet in Bhopal in the mid-80s, but have found it impossible to trace them.[11] We had a rather cavalier attitude towards documentation at the time, so when someone suggested video-recording *Ehsaas*, the group ignored the suggestion; it seemed unnecessary. This was, and is, a real loss.

A feature of street plays was flexibility: the actors memorised their parts during improvisation and rehearsals, and ad-libbed if the situation so demanded. Thus, variations were introduced over time. There was often no need for a written script; writing would also lend a false fixity to one particular version. Sometimes a script may be hand-scribbled, as was the script of *Teen Behenon ki Atmahatya,* of which I have preserved the only surviving copy. The script of *Pyramid,* probably never published, is fortunately accessible in PDF form—sent to me by academic-activist Vibhuti Patel, who composed it in 1982; she also shared brief details about its production. Many scripts are lost forever, as are many photographs. And sometimes I found a script, but was unable to trace its genesis or performance history. At other times, I could access memories of making and doing a play, but no accompanying script, as with *Patan.*

Secondary data includes some insightful scholarship on feminist street theatre of the 80s. Mangai (2015) devotes a detailed chapter to the theme in her vivid account of gender and theatre in India. Nandi Bhatia's (2010) discussion of theatre and politics in colonial and

[11] Rahul Roy is a documentary filmmaker, and was an actor in *Ehsaas*. He confirmed (in an email dated 1 March 2015) that he probably has photos of *Ehsaas* somewhere, and promised to track them down, but despite his efforts and my reminders, it has not yet happened.

post-colonial India includes a few succinct pages relevant to feminist street theatre, so do Radha Kumar's (2011) classic work on the Indian women's movement and Subhadra Butalia's (2002) book on the anti-dowry movement. Each of these is immensely valuable, as is Lakshmi Subramanyam's edited volume *Muffled Voices* (2013). Tripurari Sharma and Lakshmi Krishnamurty (2000) vividly describe workshop processes which led to the production of street plays, particularly with women. Additionally, I was able to locate a few articles and papers focused on the feminist street theatre of the time, and scattered reports of workshops and performances held in different parts of the country.

Writing: Reconstructing History Out of Fragments

Rustam Bharucha (2000: 33) calls attention to 'the extraordinary power of the fragment'—aware that, often in trying to reconstruct a moment, all that the researcher has are fragments, perhaps not even a date or place, only a memory, a slogan or song. The task for the writer is to give each fragment due attention, discover linkages with other fragments, without attempting to synthesise a falsely complete picture. Nor can the researcher afford to be sanguine about the task; it is best to be on guard, slightly ill at ease with the control derived through the acts of writing and documentation.

Critical reflexivity requires listening to data with openness, without arrogance; acknowledging emotion and subjectivities. Rather than false detachment or indifference, there is a sense of involvement. Writing such as this hopes to enrich our understanding of the past, as well as trace links with the present.

The Scope of this Book

The old feminist plays resonate, even today, with women's experiences. The present book focuses on this theatre, which has consciously identified with the women's movement.[12] Section 1 provides an

[12] This focus necessarily excludes a close study of plays by Jana Natya Manch (Janam), Jagriti, Nishant Natya Manch and other street theatre groups which at that time neither identified as feminist, nor were women-predominant. It was a hard decision to make, since these groups do have plays on women's issues offering diverse perspectives on gender. I also have powerful interviews with Maloyashree Hashmi of Janam, and Anjali Deshpande and Anand Kumar of Jagriti, but they could not fit within the scope of this book.

overview and an introduction to the politics and aesthetics of this theatre.

Sections 2, 3 and 4 dwell upon feminist street theatre in Delhi. Specifically, Section 2 situates and describes the play *Om Swaha*, which was an integral part of the anti-dowry movement throughout the 80s. Section 3 explores *Ehsaas,* and the autonomous university-based women's group that performed it over several years. Section 4 looks closely at a spate of plays by activists in Delhi's working-class *bastis*; this grassroots theatre was the most widespread in terms of sheer numbers, performances and outreach, yet is barely visible in the literature.

Section 5 explores street theatre by women's groups in Maharashtra and Gujarat. From Maharashtra, the play *Mulgi Zali Ho* occupies a place of its own, as the longest-running feminist play known to the public. Another set of plays was closely associated with Mumbai's autonomous women's groups, especially campaigns against rape, domestic violence, and discriminatory personal laws. Yet another lot of plays, exploring popular culture, symbols and myths, emerged from within an academic institution. From Gujarat, we have three plays produced by women's and youth groups, which brought out aspects of gender stereotypes, violence against women, and women's resistance.

Section 6 looks at plays from many places: Chhattisgarh, Bengal, Rajasthan, Uttar Pradesh: all from the 80s. These plays deal with various aspects of violence against women, including dowry, sati, suicide; they too focus on women's refusal to submit and conform. We also look at a particular set of plays from the mid-90s by women activists from across the country, made in intensive cultural workshops, performed locally and globally.

Section 7 probes the significance of feminist street theatre for critical education, theory, and increasingly complex understandings of gender. It traces continuities, ruptures, and much that is new, breaking through and evolving. The concluding chapter draws together various threads, coming full circle: it describes creative presentations of some vintage plays and the responses of contemporary audiences, indicating a startlingly strong relevance across the decades.

2

Feminist Street Theatre
Politics, and Aesthetics

Feminist street theatre was very much about dissent: sharply political, anti-establishment, with social commentary, struggle and the element of solidarity. Plays critiqued prevailing structures, and emphasised the possibility of rebuilding lives along with creating democratic spaces.

Theatre and Dissent

Theatre has long been a site for dissent. Plays came under strict surveillance in colonial India, with the banning of the play *Nil Darpan* (1860), and passage of *The Dramatic Performances Act* (1876). The colonial government sought to stamp out nationalist plays which questioned state policy. Nationalist, anti-colonial plays raised several issues, including the rape of working-class women by British officers. However, they tended to define normative Indian women as 'good' mothers, daughters and wives, chaste, and self-sacrificing. Women who were raped might die by suicide while men protested on their behalf; the ideal woman was one who lived within her household, excluding public performers and most other working-class women.

Performing in public entailed a life of struggle, whether for Jadumoni or Binodini Dasi in Bengal's public theatre, Latifa Begum or Jahanara Kajjan in Parsi theatre, Gulab Bai or Radha Rani in north India's Nautanki. At the same time, theatre offered a measure of autonomy, income and mobility, as actors travelled widely. Many actors came from traditional singer-dancer backgrounds, such as tawaifs, devadasis or the Bedia caste, all of which were renowned for their artistry, and had developed genres like thumri, kathak, sadir and rai. Successful women actors sometimes set up drama companies, as in the case of

Kumbakonam Balamani in Tamil Nadu, Gulab Bai in UP, and Tamasha artiste Kantabai Satarker in Maharashtra. Despite winning acclaim, stigma usually clung to their personae, especially with the ascendance of nationalist notions of ideal womanhood.

Women's cultural practices often subverted such ideals, critiqued conventional morality and patriarchal norms. In Bengal, Bihar and Andhra Pradesh, women's folk retellings of the Ramayan have depicted Ram as a weak character and spineless husband, and positioned brave, suffering Sita as the central character.

The tawaifs of Lucknow, who earned by entertaining select male patrons with fine singing and dance routines, considered themselves much better off than married women. In private, they had 'a secret repertoire of satirical and bawdy songs, dances, informal miming, and dramatic representations aimed at the institution of marriage and heterosexual relations' (Oldenburg 1992: 39). Within themselves they might, for instance, enact a typical family scene showing the married woman crushed as workhorse and sexual object.

Some Nautankis, such as *Virangana Veermati* and *Bekasur Beti,* showed oppressed daughters and daughters-in-law battling for justice. The heroine might go a step further and take up cudgels against the colonial state. Popular travelling theatre was often expressly anti-colonial, such as the Nautankis *Jhansi ki Rani, Gandhi Haran* and *Shaheed Bhagat Singh.* In *Bahadur Ladki,* the central protagonist was a flower-seller with nationalist leanings, and in Kanpur in 1942, the audience broke into anti-British sloganeering when she (played by Gulab Bai) slapped a lascivious British officer. The Kanpur administration banned the Nautanki troupe from the city, invoking *The Dramatic Performances Act, 1876* (for more details, see Hansen 1991; Mehrotra 2006; Morcom 2014; Sai 2007).

Interestingly enough, in Britain, the Actresses' Franchise League (AFL), which had over 900 members by 1914, produced and performed a huge number of 'suffrage plays', such as Beatrice Harraden's *Lady Geraldine's Speech,* and Cicely Hamilton and Christopher St John's *How the Vote Was Won.* These were unapologetic propaganda plays, meant to communicate ideas, and inspire action (Paxton 2013). A wave of suffragette theatre sprang up in the USA too, with plays such as Charlotte Perkins Gilman's *Something to Vote For* and Inez Milholland's *If Women Voted* (Erminia Thompson Fulsom Collection).

In the Soviet Union and Germany during the 1920s, agitprop theatre developed, aiming to raise revolutionary consciousness amongst the proletariat. A portmanteau term combining 'agitation' and 'propaganda', agitprop presented political analysis with the goal of mobilising the masses. It was widely performed, in outdoor settings, and profoundly influenced oppositional cultural practices around the world.

During the 1940s and 50s, the Indian People's Theatre Association's (IPTA) travelling troupes performed radical anti-imperialist plays. Performance was a grey area for middle-class women, but the IPTA provided an enabling space and many broke the mould, becoming theatre actresses: Dina Pathak, Shanta Gandhi, Sheila Bhatia, Sneh Sanyal, Sarla Sharma, Gul Zaveri, Zohra Segal, Tripti Mitra and Reba Roychoudhury among others (Banerjee 2021, Bhatia 2010, Kaushal 2005, Segal 2010).[13] However, despite this and the fact that one of the founder-members of the IPTA was a woman, Anil Marcia De Silva,[14] its agenda marginalised women's perspectives and undercut their autonomy and personhood. Neither the organisation nor its archivists were entirely free of 'puritanical morality and casual misogyny', which expected women to be 'safe' and 'non-threatening'. The figure of the woman was acceptable, not as a leader and an organiser, but only as an actress 'dedicated to the words and actions of a male cultural leader' (Banerjee 2021: 87, 95).

Plays written by Rasheed Jehan and Ismat Chugtai in and beyond the 1930s sharply delineated women's subjectivities, family dynamics and personal politics. As such, they, prefigured some of the concerns of feminist street theatre. Around the same time, Norah Richards staged nationalist plays in rural Himachal Pradesh. During the 50s, Sheila Bhatia began to bring women's concerns onto the Delhi stage; Vijaya Mehta, Dina Pathak and Shanta Gandhi did the same in Mumbai.

Street theatre combining traditional forms with Brechtian devices became popular in Bengal during the 1950s and 60s, with plays by Utpal Dutt, Tripti Mitra and others. These plays focused on agricultural labour and factory workers' lives and concerns. Habib Tanvir and Moneeka Misra's 'Naya Theatre' worked with Chhatisgarhi actors, in the 60s and beyond. Gursharan Singh's radical street theatre was performed extensively in Punjab, especially during the 80s and 90s.

---

[13] These women led fascinating lives, making diverse contributions to stage and screen.

[14] Anil de Silva was a Sri Lankan writer and art critic. She was extremely active in the IPTA between 1941 and 1946, as an organiser.

Badal Sircar's 'free theatre' or 'third theatre'[15] used the bodies of actors with minimal props in plays like *Juloos*, which were performed in the open, though usually to a cultivated audience. During 1978-79, Sircar held several performances of *Bhoma* in Delhi, and a theatre workshop at Delhi's Shri Ram Centre, which inspired the city's theatre enthusiasts (Ein Lall 2019).[16]

The first street plays in Delhi can be traced to the early 70s. Mukti (later renamed Jagriti, and then Aahvan), formed by students and teachers from Delhi College (now Zakir Hussain Delhi College), performed plays questioning anti-people state policies. Nishant Natya Manch (NNM) began doing street theatre in the mid-70s. Jana Natya Manch (Janam) performed proscenium (stage) plays from 1973, and street plays from 1978 onward. These theatre groups have always had both women and men in them, though invariably more men than women. Members have included exceptionally talented actors such as Moloyashree Hashmi (Janam), Anjali Deshpande (Jagriti), and Neelima Sharma (NNM). In the late 70s, Rati Bartholomew, Anuradha Kapur, Maya Rao, Manohar Khushalani, Vinod Dua[17] and other serious theatre-persons set up Theatre Union, and made some powerful street plays.

The Lokdoot cultural troupe performed plays and skits in working-class settlements from the mid-70s, focusing on social and legal issues, including health, livelihoods and women's rights. The troupe was set up within Mobile Creches, a non-governmental organisation committed to providing daycare to children of migrant construction workers.[18] Lokdoot plays were colourful and creative, incorporating Rajasthani songs, puppets and phad (scrolls), which were traditional media that the construction labourers brought with them. Initiated by dramatist Mina Swaminathan and her colleagues in Mobile Creches, this radical theatre directly supported working-class self-organising.[19]

---

[15] 'First' being traditional theatre and 'second' being modern proscenium theatre.

[16] Ein Lall (well-known documentary filmmaker, video artist and theatre-person) notes how important seeing *Bhoma* and attending Sircar's workshop was for her and several others, including Manohar Khushalani (an actor and teacher) and Mira Kaushik (the Director of Akademi, a South Asian Dance Collective in London).

[17] Vinod Dua (1954-2021) was a pioneering journalist in Hindi media, anchor and political commentator. Manohar Khushalani is a Visiting Professor at the Indraprashta Institute of Information Technology.

[18] Mobile Creches (1933-2022) was an NGO initiated in the early 70s by Meera Jacob Mahadevan (a social worker and author).

[19] Mina Swaminathan (1933-2022) was an educationist, dramatist and child rights activist, and co-founder of Mobile Creches and the Centre for Women's Development

Habib Tanvir described the 1970s-80s as pioneering days for street theatre, with no clear-cut models. It was propelled by enthusiasm and energy: 'No amount of public concern alone can push you to theatre, unless it is also combined with zest' (Tanvir 2013, 71).

Feminist Street Plays: The Stuff of Politics

Autonomous women's groups, alert to the politics of the personal, made the earliest feminist street plays we know of: *Om Swaha* and *Ehsaas,* both Delhi, in 1979. Street theatre quickly mushroomed in various parts of India, embodying a radical egalitarian politics.

Specific circumstances enabled feminism, and with it, feminist street theatre. During the Emergency (1975-77), democratic rights were severely curtailed. People's movements burgeoned, aware of the need to be proactive, to defend basic freedoms. The heydays of feminist street theatre and the early vibrant phase of the autonomous women's movement were sandwiched between the Emergency and the economic liberalisation of the early 90s.

We have long, rich histories of women's struggles: spirited campaigns for education, suffrage, employment, land rights, political rights, and against sati and child marriage. Women participated in public agitations, pickets, sit-ins, processions, peasant and working-class movements, the freedom struggle, civil disobedience, Quit India, the list goes on. In the early 70s, women led Chipko movements to protect Himalayan ecology, brandished rolling pins and empty tins in Maharashtra to protest rising prices, and joined the mass agitation in Bihar for 'sampurna kranti' (total revolution).

An influential and well-researched report titled *Towards Equality: Report of the Committee on the Status of Women in India* (Government of India 1974) revealed the abysmal conditions of health, education, violence, employment and political participation amongst women in India. The then Prime Minister Indira Gandhi said she'd been unaware of these realities. By the late 70s, a country-wide movement built up to end violence against women sparked off by two cases of gang rape by policemen—that of Rameeza Bi, a working-class woman in Hyderabad, and Mathura, a young Adivasi in Maharashtra.

Studies. She developed methods for using drama in education, and in 1993 set up Voicing Silence (within the MS Swaminathan Research Foundation in Chennai) to link women's experiences with women's expressions.

The issue of 'dowry deaths' also became prominent. During the Emergency, despite clampdowns on the press, frequent newspaper reports appeared; a tiny, bland paragraph mentioning that so-and-so's clothing caught fire when her kerosene stove burst. Authorities considered the issue apolitical.

The nascent women's movement investigated some cases, and realised that such 'accidental' deaths were usually murders, or else suicides. They demanded police investigation into all such cases, and simultaneously took the issue to the people. In that moment of fervour and anguish, street theatre was adopted as a form of public engagement.

The lines depicted here were chanted by the chorus in Om Swaha*: 'Zara tum bhi socho Zara hum bhi sochein, Ladke ladki mein Koi bhed na rakhein, Dono ki padhai Hum ek si rakhein, Jayedaad mein hissa Dono ka rakhein, Padh-likhkar bachche Ho jaayein sayaane, Hai yehi sab kuchh Hum sab yeh maane.'* (*Think a little, So will we, Let's treat girls and boys equally, Provide similar education, Equal division of property. Let children study, Become mature and wise, That's all that's needed, Let us all agree.*)

The issues taken up by the women's movement provided content for street theatre: domestic violence, male alcoholism, rape, personal laws, communal violence, oppressive customs, economic policies, price rise, gender stereotypes. This theatre reflected and demonstrated women's protests and resistance. The concerns were grounded and, to some extent, intersectional. Early formulations drew eclectically upon liberal, socialist, and radical feminist thought, local histories of women's struggles, and miscellaneous sources including left, Gandhian and Freirian perspectives. Women's agency was emphasised and considered imperative to change.

Theatre opened up elements of the personal, in public, for political ends. Mangai (2013: 45) comments that women's street theatre of the 1970s and 80s was concentrated, euphoric and linked to the possibilities of action. In a sense, 'being visible' constituted a form of political action in itself. The sheer presence of groups of women, performing in the open, was startling; the street (as well as parks, marketplaces, police stations) were quintessential male spaces.

Arriving at a public spot, the actors would demarcate a circular performance space. Women have long been familiar with circles of confinement, a 'lakshman rekha' beyond which they cannot step, promising the illusion of safety. But here women were reinventing circles as spaces of freedom, from where they could step in and out. In *Ehsaas*, women expressly reclaimed the public realm, the wide world as it were, defying patriarchal diktats which tried to keep them within a ghera, circle, defining limits, enclosing and confining them.

> A man (addressing women): Stay inside, further inside *(andar, aur andar)*! Hide away, do not show yourselves!
>
> One woman (women jostle around, restless): Why?
>
> Man: Because my gaze can harm you.
>
> Second woman: Then why don't you remain inside?
>
> Man: To see that you don't get out.
>
> Third woman: What if we do?
>
> Man: Stay inside!
>
> Fourth woman (surges out): You harm us inside too! We will not stay!
>
> (Several women step out.)
>
> Man (agitated): Hey, get back in!
>
> All the women: No!
>
> Man: Streets are male territory. You can't move around here.
>
> Fifth woman: Why is our coming here making you nervous?
>
> Man: Why have you come into my area?

Sixth woman: The world is for everyone! (*Duniya sabke liye hai!*)

Man: Don't know why they've come!

Women together (walking freely): To study, to learn, to see, to earn!

They head off in different directions—and the line of containment loses all meaning.

Woman emerging—beyond the circle of containment.

Plays like *Ehsaas* projected no unreal fantasy of easy liberation. But they affirmed the significance of women's protests and acknowledged both private and public spheres as sites of conflict and contestation. Writing of the freedom struggle, Thapar-Björkert (2006) describes women in Kanpur and Aligarh locked up by families to prevent them from joining demonstrations; yet many managed to step out, join protests, distribute subversive literature. 'At such moments of heightened political resistance, the street is seen as the site of righteous battle, with liberatory potential for both self and society.' Once again, feminist theatre configured the streets as spaces for subversion, where intense conflicts were played out, compelling the audiences to engage and introspect.

Anuradha Kapur recalls: '[M]any of us in Delhi did street theatre which was directly connected to visibilising issues. I, along with many women in Stree Sangharsh, dealt with rape laws and dowry problems and that was a very direct connection...' (Subramanyam 2013b: 217). Kapur's expertise was integral to making several feminist street plays, including *Om Swaha*.

At a workshop with women's groups in North India, Seema, a member of Sakhi Kendra, a women's group in Kanpur, improvised, playing the role of a submissive woman who is tortured by her alcoholic husband until she finally walks out. It was her own story; she wanted to tell it to the world, and the sequence got included in the play *Gumraah*. Seema

Zimmedar Kaun, Red Fort grounds, 8 March 1991. Activists portray humane, collective ways to resolve conflicts. (Left to right) Gyanvati, Bimla, Vidya Thapa, Reshma Sonkar, Susheela, Sudha, Devi Kripa. (Second picture) Sudha, unidentified actor, Maharani, Devi Kripa, Shanti.

shone as an actor, and was happiest when she performed in Pahlepur, her natal village, where she now worked to support other women.[20]

Participants in feminist street theatre cut across class and caste: students, community workers, activists, teachers, homemakers and sundry others. Challenging the status quo, problematising gender, marriage and the patriarchal family helped prepare the ground for the open politics of sexuality, including the LGBTQ movement which developed subsequently in Delhi and elsewhere.

Most participants understood patriarchy and capitalism as interlocking systems that reinforced one another. They were deeply concerned about economic inequality, and the class differences between women. At the same time, a collective politics was sought, emphasising women's common issues, for instance around gender-based violence. The theatre, and indeed the women's movement, was an attempt to listen to one another, and build a radical politics from the ground up.

Rati Bartholomew (in *Seagull Theatre Quarterly* 1997a: 44), who facilitated numerous women's theatre workshops across the country, noted that there was tremendous sincerity and conviction amongst the participants. The theatre was sharply political, even when several participants were paid workers in non-governmental organisations (NGOs). That many women required some remuneration in no way undermined their contributions: it would otherwise have been impossible for them to engage regularly. Essentially, feminist theatre helped them to reflect deeply on their own lives and aspirations, and understand the social forces they were up against. It facilitated the development of closer personal bonds as well as an exposure to various social milieus. Ultimately, women participated in the theatre because they believed in it; they found that it enabled them to say what they wanted to.

Feminist Aesthetics

Gifted dramatists facilitated theatre workshops and directed feminist street plays in different parts of the country. These professional theatre-folk, Rati Bartholomew, Anuradha Kapur, Tripurari Sharma, Maya Rao, Madhusree Dutta, A. Mangai, Aditi Desai, Ein Lall and their ilk were largely responsible for the stunning quality of plays.

---

[20] See Chapter 21 for more on this workshop and play.

A special kind of creativity, as well as feminist perspectives, spurred a unique internal development. Meaningful, pithy dialogue melded with music, dance, colour and humour—elements drawing from popular travelling theatres, films, and women's traditional sub-cultures. Many participants, especially those who were rural or first-generation urbanites, carried within themselves rich repertoires of song, dance and expressive enactment, learnt and practiced during festivals, marriages, and humdrum tasks like planting saplings or pounding rice.

Participants carried within themselves traditions of song, sung while performing humdrum tasks and during festivities.

These, along with exercises, games, experiential sharing, thematic discussion and improvisations in participatory workshops led to the development of new play scripts.

Uma Chakravarti (interview 2015) describes a theatre workshop held in Miranda House, led by Anuradha Kapur, soon after the 1984 anti-Sikh carnage in Delhi: 'A small group improvised upon the national symbol of the four lions. They sat still, back to back, then suddenly started getting active, flexed, got up, raised their arms, and began killing. The state was killing; and people chanted "Hatyamev jayate!" instead of "Satyamev jayate".[21] Thinking about it gives me goose pimples even now.' The sequence was included in the play *Patan (Downfall)*. Their college principal was horrified by the sequence, and feared it was seditious. *Patan* was about two friends, from two communities, who gradually turned into enemies. It was performed successfully in half a dozen colleges, and at a joint women's movement event at Lal Qila on 8 March 1985. The last show was at Tilak Vihar, performed for survivors of the carnage.[22]

---

[21] 'Satyamev jayate' translates to 'Truth alone triumphs', and 'Hatyamev jayate' as 'Murder alone triumphs'. During 1984-85, Professor Uma Chakravarti was the staff adviser to Miranda House's English theatre society.

[22] Nearly a thousand widowed survivors of the anti-Sikh carnage were alloted small flats in Tilak Vihar, a colony in west Delhi.

The aesthetics of feminist street theatre evolved through creative exploration, seeking forms that could fit with women's experiences. Some conventions were shared with agitprop and earlier street theatre, distinct from proscenium theatre. Performing in the open, in found spaces, frequently amid large crowds, prompted a need to project, achieved by making large, emphatic movements, using loud voices, short phrases, repetition, choruses, collective singing, drum-beats and tambourines.

Rati Bartholomew (*Seagull Theatre Quarterly* 1997a: 45-47) notes that street theatre is far more difficult than stage theatre, performed as it is in the open, surrounded by street noises, large and active audiences, and no protective darkness. In the face of orthodox critics who might say that street theatre has cardboard characters and situations, she asserts, 'Characterisation and subtlety—can you put them in a street play? Of course you can.' The impact can be incredibly powerful, for 'there is an electricity between the audience and the performers.'

Street theatre relies on the body, with barely any props. Moloyashree Hashmi muses (in *Seagull Theatre Quarterly* 1997a: 45): '...body movements in any theatre are larger than life. In street theatre, it has to be a little more than that.' In a street play, the actors' positioning and movements form dynamic patterns which vibrate with energy.

The aesthetics of street theatre, differing from conventional theatre, are in some ways closer to cinema. Jyotika Virdi (interview 2017), recalling *Om Swaha* and *Ehsaas*, reflects, 'It was like using cinematic techniques and edits with just bodies, hardly any props: making circles, swirls, various formations—and just cutting to the next scene. The aesthetic resembled film in the way you morphed from one scene to the next, and the use of body formations, minimal script, dialogue or a narrator.' She adds that street theatre differs from film in that its staging and setting rely largely on suggestion, leaving the viewer to fill in the rest with their imagination; whereas in film and conventional theatre, scenes are mimetic.

In the early 80s, Tripurari Sharma (in Katyal 1998-99b: 109) found that street theatre by groups like Janam was marked by 'the black uniform and the choral speech and more about information and facts, with snippets of dialogue.' She was interested in evolving something quite different. Her aesthetic approach concerned itself with finding appropriate expression for women's experiences. Seldom did women have just one major dilemma that could be neatly resolved, as in a conventional play.

Their multi-tasking, dwelling simultaneously in several worlds, was reflected in the feminist plays. Rather than pushing towards a resolution, these plays adopted open-ended exploration, suggesting the need for complex change. Linearity was replaced by diffuse, disjointed narratives.

A density of familiar associations, like games, dupattas...

The feminist street plays evolved with rich imagery. These images connected organically, not necessarily through a linear story: 'When I find the connection between form and content, a lot of things make sense. If there is a knotted cloth, then the opening of the knot itself can make a structure. You can dramatically conceive it and convey it—that can become the structure, that you undo the knot and open the piece of cloth,' (Sharma in Katyal 1998-99b: 109). The plays held a density of familiar associations and allusions; a piece of cloth, flourish of a dupatta, sindur, ghunghat, clinking utensils, a children's game, a plate passed around, each of which, imaginatively deployed, could convey many different meanings.

The content and design were often intense, as participants brought in the dimension of dreams and longing, layering their experiences. There were heavily laden images sometimes very personal to the actors. Unlike agitprop and most extant street theatre, the feminist street plays often conveyed very heart-felt, intimate feelings.

In a conversation between siblings in *Ehsaas,* the sister reaches home from college later than usual; her brother shouts, 'You know what can happen to you, the dangers...' He sees himself as keeping her in order. She fixes him with a stare and says, 'Why don't you stay home—all the problems arise from your side!' As Uma Chakravarti (interview 2015) remarks, a whole history is encapsulated in that one line; we have all been upbraided for returning home late. She herself recalls being harassed on her way home and her brother, who was in the Air Force, saying, 'Why did you go out?'

Madhusree Dutta (2003), directed *Bandor Khela* and *Meye Dile Sajiye* in Calcutta in the mid-80s, and found them ambitious in form and scale. She writes: 'Those churning of images, metaphors and forms, that restlessness, were part of a broader (and not very visible) excavation for women's narrative forms.' In *Bandor Khela*, the depth of depravity in human relationships was starkly conveyed, using the ploy of a monkey pair; the male wanted to get rid of his wife and marry again for dowry, but wasn't up to killing her; the play made the chilling comment: '[H]e says he can't set his wife on fire!... Would it have been a problem, had he been a man?'

The feminist street theatre gave form to complex ongoing debates on women's rights. In the play *Farq*,[23] a rope was used to show property, with shares going, or not going, to women. Four persons would hold a rope to form a square, symbolising a house. When they dropped the rope, the house vanished. This simple device brought out women's lack of property rights, under different personal laws. Such creativity became the hallmark of feminist street plays. More than text, images became significant, disturbing conventional ways of grasping reality.

In the context of the ongoing nation-wide anti-rape campaign,[24] Theatre Union made *Dafa 180 (Statute 180)*, a play on custodial rape and anti-rape legislation. Anuradha Kapur (in Erven 1992: 119) recalls that the rape scene was the hardest to devise, because there was always the question of what you're doing to the audience—are you titillating them? They decided upon an abstract representation. Uma Chakravarti (interview 2015), who saw the play on 8 March 1981 in Ajmal Khan Park, Karol Bagh, found the abstraction worked very well, even amid a huge audience: 'There was a women's rally, crowds in the park, and policemen all around. The play team wanted to suggest gang rape but didn't want to show anything crude. So, they had a sequence, where a ghunghru was passed around between the gang of men. I think it was a fantastically creative way of doing it. The woman was lying there and the men threw the ghunghru to each other over her body.'[25]

---

[23] Chapter 12 has a brief description of this play.

[24] In 1979, the Supreme Court of India acquitted two policemen of the 1972 custodial gang rape of Mathura, a 16-year-old Adivasi from Gadchiroli district, Maharashtra, citing previous sexual experience and an absence of marks of injury to allege that sexual intercourse was consensual. Four law professors wrote an open letter to the Chief Justice protesting this miscarriage of justice. Several cases had come up during the 1970s of sexual violence against Adivasi, Dalit, Muslim, working-class women, including gang rapes by police, military and paramilitary personnel. Sporadic protests had taken place. In 1980, women's movement and human rights activists took up the cause, generating a nation-wide anti-rape campaign, raising public awareness and pushing for legal changes.

[25] *Dafa 180*'s team of actors included, among others, Anuradha Kapur, Maya Rao, Ein Lall, Urvashi Butalia, Ragini Prakash, Vinod Dua and Manohar Khushalani.

Interestingly, a year earlier, on 8 March 1980, four anti-rape plays had been staged, by the theatre groups Jagriti, Janam and Ruchika, at a huge women's demonstration in Old Delhi.[26] In three of the plays, one by Jagriti and two by Janam, the woman lay prone while men bent over her; throughout the play she was either silent, or weeping. In the audience, some men responded with gratification; women giggled uneasily. Ruth Vanita (1980: 26-27) pointed out that such plays strengthened the 'strong man helpless woman' stereotype, and wondered, 'what is the use of talking about rape, if we only strengthen the stereotypes?'[27] Ruchika's play showed the woman protesting; yet overall, it too strengthened the 'strong man helpless woman' stereotype.

The feminist street plays, on the other hand, were highly sensitive to the politics of gender, body language and representation. It is pertinent to note that women directors were involved with feminist street plays such as *Dafa 180,* but not with any of the 1980 anti-rape plays. This fact needs interpretation, sans essentialism! Most women directors of the time (including some, like Vijaya Mehta, who worked in proscenium theatre) were perhaps responding viscerally to feminism, which was in the air, reflecting and thinking intensely about gender. They thus began relooking at standard archetypal characterisations, and narrative modes so naturalised that they seemed universal. As Anuradha Kapur notes (in Subramanyam 13b: 217-18), that sort of awareness has informed women directors at the level of content, finding things which might be discomfiting and being constantly alert to the problem of the male gaze. This awareness gave rise to some common concerns of women directors, such as 'figuration or how to present a woman on the stage..., a kind of head-on thought about sexuality, the meaning of presenting a sexualized persona which is not just sexualised as an object.'

Feminist street plays moved away from naturalism and overturned canonical notions of structure and characterisation; they tended to be episodic rather than linear, multiple voices representing diverse

---

[26] Hundreds of women, from various organisations as well as many concerned individuals, marched through Old Delhi chanting 'Supreme Court, Supreme Court, against you where can we report?', singing songs, and distributing leaflets.

[27] Anjali Deshpande (interview 2016) from Jagriti acknowledges Ruth's comment, and has an interesting reflection: 'Partly, it was my fault. We wanted to show how the woman responds, but it didn't come out properly. It was easy for me to act quiet—we girls were used to suffering quietly! I could do a victim's body language!' She adds that Jagriti's thinking on and depiction of women's issues gradually matured.

gendered locations, rather than fixed characters enacting a standard story. Instead of having climactic resolutions, the plays were usually open-ended, reflecting the imperative of wider social change, with many people participating in efforts to transform situations, and work towards resolution.

Street theatre, unlike most proscenium theatre, was open to everyone; there was no commercial transaction, selling or buying of tickets. Actors travelled to diverse locations, and performed without masks, lighting, green rooms or wings. They made eye contact, exchanged energy with the audience—an audience who remained very visible, rather than vanishing into a darkened hall. Boundaries blurred, distances shrank; people responded, and were invited to join discussions, to explore difficult situations together.

However, street audiences were inevitably more male than female. To ensure that women, too, watched the plays, troupes performed in non-street venues as well, such as home courtyards, terraces, women's colleges, and at meetings and community halls. The feminist street theatre thus came to be called not only 'nukkad natak' but also 'angan natak', courtyard theatre. In each distinctly different venue, the plays usually managed to forge a strong connection with their audience.

In an article, journalist Ayesha Kagal (1986) graphically described two performances of *Mulgi Zali Ho*, performed for very diverse audiences:

> That night in Miraj more than 14000 people collected at the main cross-road of the town, a sea of heads stretching as far as eye could see. Squatting, standing, perched on vegetable carts, balanced against bicycles, packed close against each other around the raised, flood-lit podium, expectant and then enthralled. Their attention riveted, their response palpable as they watched the play *Mulgi Zali Ho* (A Girl is Born)—the 152nd performance in the last two years.

And, at a Dalit girls' boarding-school, in rural Maharashtra:

> [A] small, dark classroom with peeling walls and rows of washing hanging up to dry, becomes an impromptu theatre.... And as you watch the flash-fire interaction you feel the seeds of 'streemukti' germinate. You see the ideas of male-female inequality grasped instantly, at a day-to-day level, not abstract ideology.... In the small classroom *Mulgi Zali Ho* bursts forth in all its potency... a flexible, adaptable vehicle with infinite opportunity to communicate—simply and directly, with humor and song—what it means to be born female.

Each performance of a street play was different, because the audience, and entire setting, was different. The theatre had a meaning and a special place in the lives of those who participated in it, whether as performers, or as members of the audience; it was not just a passing moment.

The New Woman

The feminist street plays of the time may be theorised as dramatising the new, aware woman. Aesthetic and political radicalisms aligned; the medium was part of the message. The plays demonstrated that women can cross limits, break out of enclosures, and perform womanhood differently. It was a radical political vision, which coincided with the advent of such women in real life. Actors on the frontlines of public interaction, as well as the roles they enacted, shattered the mould of docile, invisible women. They spoke their minds, asserted independent identities.

Play after play showed women rejecting the status quo, questioning normative submissive, secondary roles, refusing indignity and violence. This was a huge shock to the establishment. Nor was it just about a handful of feminist activists, who could be conveniently marginalised. Countless women, in cities, towns and villages, seemed to resonate with the sentiments expressed in the plays.

The new woman, portrayed in feminist plays, was no stern revolutionary with impossibly high ideals. Rather, she was confused, vulnerable and inconsistent. She could laugh, love, fool around, grieve, rage—exist at several levels. She wished to maintain relationships, but not at the expense of her self-respect. She was somebody most women could identify with, at least partly. She was one of them, braving circumstances, hurting, keen to improve matters. Lines of division between actors and women in the audience often blurred, as common cause was established. This was not superficial or merely strategic: feminist actors, too, were part of society, facing its onslaughts.

Indeed, feminists in the 80s were routinely attacked and stereotyped as shrill, frustrated, man-haters and home-breakers. Feminist playwrights and actors sometimes went the extra mile to defend themselves against such negative labelling. One strategy was to emphasise their participation in common female concerns and activities. Thus, protagonists in the play *Mulgi Zali Ho* declared, 'We too marry, run our households, bring up our children; the only difference

A woman speaks up, in a street play in Delhi, 1980s.
Actor: Parvati.

is, we are angry about certain things.' (Mhapsekar 2010). *Mulgi Zali Ho* strongly championed collective struggle across differences; at the same time its protagonists underlined the reality of a continuum rather than a break from conventional roles.

Women street play actors were vulnerable: fathers, mothers, brothers, husbands or other family members might taunt, insult, emotionally blackmail and impose restrictions on them, even prohibit their participation in the theatre. This was because women acting in public, that too out on the streets, was not considered respectable. Even apart from this, it was difficult for actors to combine street theatre with their studies, housework, marriages, jobs, activism; it was time-consuming, exhausting, nerve-wracking and sometimes impossible. Thus the attrition rates were high—most actors dropped out after a short stint.

At times, onlookers were riled by the spirit and politics of the plays, the issues raised, and they threatened the performers. Actor-activist Vidya Thapa (interview 2015) describes taking the play *Zimmedar Kaun* into areas where communal violence had taken place. The actors faced hostility, threats and open aggression, and their families wanted them to withdraw. She says, 'We did not give up. We were not afraid...' And she adds, with a gleam in her eyes, 'We also had a lot of fun! We chatted, laughed and teased each other. We were friends from different bastis and it was an occasion to be together!'[28]

The theatre was liberating. It was hard work, heart's work, shot through with pleasure. In the warm atmosphere of a theatre workshop, tensions were released amidst talking, tears, laughter, buffoonery, the sharing of confidences: a rare space of exploration and discovery. In moving out and performing the play there was the whiff of freedom, and the taste of sweet power. Some fundamental core within the participants changed: how they felt about their bodies and minds, about who they were, their lives, friends, families, studies, work, relationships, their futures; all these were deeply affected.

Vidya initially felt nervous about acting, and was embarrassed to wear the kurta pyjama required for her role in the play *Zimmedar Kaun*. But seeing the phenomenal impact that the play was making, she quickly gained confidence. If some members of the audience opposed the message conveyed, there were many others who appreciated it, who wanted to see, learn and understand. At their core, the feminist street plays were about educating people, and influencing attitudes; the actors too were learning, growing and changing.

Tripurari Sharma reflects (in Sharma and Krishnamurty 2000: 115-116):

> Apart from the satisfaction of communicating with people, and being part of a process of change, there is a unique joy in performing without barriers and drapery—of being in the open and yet amidst people. To unite with the earth, the sky and the human breath all at the same time, connects with one's roots—both with nature and with the human race. As performances increase there is a sense of adventure and abandonment in performing in different locations.... It soaks away tiredness and gives you strength—for many many more such occasions that liberate you from your limitations and bind you with something that is bigger, wider, more encompassing and universal.

Soni (conversation 2016), a community worker with Action India, mused: 'The plays showed the pain women went through. They experienced sexual harassment, but there was no name for it. Today, we are able to name it. This is a triumph of the movement. The older generation's history is our strength. We join, and move ahead.

[28] Vidya Thapa was a senior Community Worker with Action India and a member of Sabla Sangh, New Seemapuri until her retirement in 2018. For more details about the play, see Chapter 12.

Sometimes we feel we are scattering, breaking, but then, we get up and start walking again.'[29]

Getting up, walking on. *Zimmedar Kaun*, Red Fort, 1991. (Left to right) Vidya Thapa, Devi Kripa.

[29] This conversation with Soni occurred during post-performance discussions as part of the Vintage Play Readings Programme, *Zindagi ke Natak, Natakon ki Zindagi*, held in the Action India office on 8 April 2016. Chapter 25 details the Play Readings Programme and its significance.

SECTION TWO

OM SWAHA, THE ICONIC 'ANTI-DOWRY' PLAY

Na das lakh, na chheh lakh, na teen lakh, na ek lakh,
Na fridge, na TV, na press, na mixie... Ha ha ha ha... Ha ha ha ha...

–*Om Swaha, 1979*

The *Om Swaha* experience was phenomenal... In the first year, we did a hundred shows!

– *Gouri Choudhury (interview 2015)*

We held regular theatre workshops, especially for activists. Acting is not just about talking and giving a speech, it's about using your body. And we were doing street theatre, which is about using all of your body! It was great fun, and it was all kinds of things.

– *Maya Rao (interview 2015)*

All of us did everything ourselves at that time–making placards and posters, writing, acting, agitating. There were no professionals—that was very special about that time... From the moment we formed the circle, we knew there was audience around us whom we had to convince. After a performance, we broke into small groups and started discussions right away.

– *Amrita Chhachhi (interview 2015)*

This section explores various dimensions of *Om Swaha,* one of the most significant plays associated with the Indian women's movement. As the first feminist street play we know of, it occupies a unique place in the history of both street theatre and the Indian women's movement.

We begin with a glimpse into the issues the play dealt with: bride-burning or dowry murder, the people affected, and their linkages with the nascent women's movement. We describe the groups that responded to the situation on the ground, and the accompanying analysis, of chronic violence, power and powerlessness within the patriarchal family.

The process of transmuting anger and analysis into theatre is explored: many people participated in making *Om Swaha* the phenomenon that it was. Its aesthetic qualities and the fluid collective of activists, academics and theatre-persons involved in its production were rather unusual.

Performances of *Om Swaha* were integral to the anti-dowry campaigns of the 80s. The play challenged domestic violence and a range of callous practices taken as normal and routine, within families and society. Responses to the play initially surprised the actors, especially the scale of problems shared by audience members. As we shall see, all this churning led some of the actor-activists to set up organisations, women's groups and shelter homes, in order to support survivors of domestic violence.

The play went through various iterations over the years. It was taken up by groups in different parts of the country, achieved remarkable popularity, and exceptional longevity. Media and academia, too, were impacted.

3

Bride-Burning
'Just Another Incident'

As a child in the 60s, one sensed hope in the air, the hum of people working to build a new India: modern schools, universities, steel foundries, hydro-power plants, high-yielding seeds. Gramophones, television, geysers, air-coolers, gas-stoves, refrigerators and mixies were proudly entering middle-class homes. In school, teachers were earnest and so were we, improving our English, neglecting Hindi (and other mother-tongues), studying maths, science and social science, embroidering handkerchiefs and knitting mufflers, playing basketball and table-tennis. During high school in the 70s, I diligently read the daily newspaper, yet had a limited understanding of the issues that were shaking up the world. Revolution, Emergency, Congress, Janata, factories, forestry, feminism, dowry deaths, communalism, human rights, were all on the distant horizon.

In 1979, upon joining university, the shell cracked open. Once I found my feet, I attended some classes and selectively bunked many, spending usefully the time thus saved—with friends, performing street plays, organising against sexual harassment, joining health work in resettlement colonies, participating in study circles, and making trips to Bastar, Singbhum, Champaran, to learn the country. Immersed thus in the school of life, having plunged into women's and human rights movements, one learnt nitty-gritty intricacies of issues swirling around in the world. One understood that, across India, hope was giving way to anger, despair and frustration.

We discovered there was violence scattered across our own city, in homes not entirely different from ours. Young women, dreaming of love and happiness, were instead subjected in some marital homes to abuse and worse.

Nur Jehan, of Nangloi, north-west Delhi, was killed by her in-laws in 1977; Rakesh Kumari, from Punjab, was killed in Karol Bagh, west Delhi, in 1978; Hardeep Kaur, burnt in Jangpura, south Delhi, died November 1978; Shashi Bala, in Gandhi Nagar, east Delhi, in March 1979; Kanchan Mala Hardy, in Tagore Garden, north Delhi, killed in April 1979; Tarvinder Kaur, in Model Town, north Delhi, May 1979; Kanchan Chopra, killed in Patel Nagar, west Delhi, June 1979; Sudha Goel in Ashok Vihar, north Delhi, in December 1980.

Premkumari was murdered in Kanpur, in 1978; P. Valsala of Kerala, killed in Ranchi in April 1979; Gayatri was killed in Chhattisgarh in 1981; Pushpa, Lalita, Shobha, and thousands more, known and unknown. Typically, in-laws proclaimed that her clothes caught fire while she was cooking. Neighbours remained quiet, the police took bribes. That is, until the women's movement came along and took the lid off the family, which had previously been a closed box. 'Bride-burning' was not even recognised as a crime. It had no settled name: earlier it was usually called 'dowry death', a euphemism which left the cause of death ambivalent. Later, the term 'bride-burning' came into common use, and sometimes, 'wife-murder.'

In June 1982, Dr Shakuntala Arora of S.P. Mukherjee College was battered to death by her husband Dr Subhash Arora, of Hansraj College. When her colleagues protested, the District Commissioner of Police, West Delhi, told them, 'This is not a case, it is an incident...I have 5,000 incidents like this, it is just another incident, a very ordinary matter.' (Deepti and Shobha 1982: 45-46.)

Married, Tortured, Murdered

Nur Jahan, 18: Her corpse lay outside the police station...

Nur Jahan [if she could speak]: My mother worked in a factory. We lived in Nangloi. In 1975, she arranged my marriage in Nangloi itself.

Shahjahan Begum: A few days later, Nur Jahan wept, saying her in-laws were troubling her for Rs. 7,000. I took a loan, kept feeding my family and repaying the loan.

Nur Jahan: They tortured me to get Rs. 30,000. I asked Ammi. I did not tell her how much they tortured me. I felt, Ammi works so hard, the strain will be too much for her. One afternoon, my in-laws began to brawl, they threw kerosene at me and lit a match...

Shahjahan Begum: People called me, I ran to their house. Her devar prevented me but my sister went in, saw our girl burning and wrapped a quilt around her. My 12-year-old ran to the police station, but they wouldn't come. I became crazy with grief. I brought my daughter's lifeless body, and placed it in front of the police station. I didn't know any women's organisations. In my fury, I just sat there, others sat with me. It was a gherao. Traffic stopped, everyone got to know. Then the police had to register a case. After that we took her, for burial.

Shahjahan Begum at Shakti Shalini, early 1990s.

I fought the case, but her in-laws had bribed the police. One day in court, I met a young lawyer, Nandita Haksar. She became one of us, and helped fight my case. I learnt so much from her.

Nur Jahan: Because of me, my mother's life changed. She began helping women. People started coming to her for help and advice.

Shahjahan Begum: I threw aside my burqa, stepped out, leaving my younger children with the older ones. My husband would shut me out of the house, but there was no way I could return to my old life. In 1986, when Shakti Shalini,[30] the shelter home opened, Gouri Choudhury and others asked me to join. I ran Shakti Shalini for twenty-five years. What happened to my daughter must not happen to anyone else![31]

Shashi Bala, 24: 'Just a twisted black bundle'

Shashi Bala was the first woman graduate in her family. Soon after she graduated from Lakshmibai College, Delhi University, in May 1978, she

---

[30] The organisation was called Shaktishalini up to the end of the twentieth century, and probably a few years beyond. It was then renamed Shakti Shalini. I have not been able to trace exactly when or why this change occurred. I have standardised the name to Shakti Shalini throughout.

[31] Based on 'Shahjahan Apa', a documentary film by director Vishnu Mathur, as well as the author's interview (2002) with Shahjahan Begum and several informal interactions between 1991 and 2010.

was married to Subhash Bhasin. On 15 March 1979, Subhash visited his mother-in-law, Satyarani Chaddha, and demanded a scooter. She said she would give it to him after her grandson's birth—Shashi Bala was four months pregnant at the time. On 17 March, around midnight, Satyarani was told that her daughter had sustained burn injuries. She rushed to Gandhi Nagar, where Shashi Bala's mother-in-law Krishna, brother-in-law Naresh, and sisters-in-law Chanchal and Aruna all claimed that Shashi Bala had poured kerosene on herself, and set herself on fire. She said, 'I had never seen anything like it...there were no eyes, no mouth. Just a twisted black bundle lying in a corner, and the mother-in-law refused to give me even a kafan (shroud) to cover the body. She told me to pick up my rubbish and clear her courtyard.' (Vyas 1979: 19)

Satyarani was distraught and felt helpless. She was an ordinary housewife, a mother of five. And then, in June, she found a newspaper report of an anti-dowry demonstration.[32] She tracked down activist Subhadra Butalia,[33] whom the article had mentioned, and went to meet her. Satyarani pursued her daughter's case, briefcase stuffed with legal documents and pictures of Shashi Bala. For years she ran from pillar to post, yet justice remained elusive (Butalia 2002: 26-30).

Satyarani: 'Now I am not afraid of anyone... I have met everyone, Lieutenant Governor of Delhi, Home Minister, Prime Minister... I want justice... I want to loudly proclaim the culprits' names, for I know my former son-in-law is planning to marry again.' (Vyas 1979) When the women's shelter home, Shakti Shalini was set up in 1986, Satyarani joined it and ran it along with Shahjahan Begum. Both steadfastly supported a stream of battered women, helping them survive, revive, and move towards self-reliance.

Hardeep Kaur, 21, and Tarvinder Kaur, 24: Similar or different?

Hardeep Kaur and Tarvinder Kaur were childhood friends. Hardeep, married into a business family in Jangpura, was admitted to hospital with severe burns in October 1978 and died on 2 November. Tarvinder, married in February 1979 into a business family in Model Town, died

---

[32] The demonstration was in Model Town, on 1 June 1979, and was organised by Stree Sangharsh, a women's collective.

[33] Subhadra Butalia (1921-2011) taught English Literature at Dayal Singh College, Delhi University, and set up the organisation Karmika, to support victims of dowry and domestic violence.

on 17 May 1979. In her dying declaration, made in Jai Prakash Narayan Hospital, Tarvinder stated that while she was watching television on the evening of 17 May, her mother-in-law poured kerosene on her clothes and her sister-in-law set her afire. Despite Tarvinder's dying declaration, the police registered a case of suicide (Das 1979, 15).

Tarvinder's brother, H.S. Bhandari, alleged that her in-laws, the Anands, tormented her, demanding a two-wheeler, gold, and cash to expand her husband's spare parts business. A few days before her death, she went to meet her father and brother in their shop in south Delhi. She was desperate and wanted to return to her parental home. Her brother confessed: 'If only we had realised how serious the situation was! We thought it was just another case of marital adjustment and in a few days everything would be normal.' (Sethi 1979)

Kanchan Mala Hardy, 19: Left her husband, took up a job, yet...

Kanchan Mala burnt to death on 2 April 1979, in the bathroom of CA 1/34, Tagore Garden. She'd been studying in S.P. Mukherjee College when she happened to meet Sunil Hardy; after a brief romance, they married. She objected to his seeing other women; he thrashed her with a belt. Shocked at the battering, she returned to her parents, and found a job. A few days later, Sunil came, apologised, and persuaded her to return with him to celebrate their first wedding anniversary. Soon after, Kanchan Mala's mother was summoned to Lohia Hospital. She saw her daughter's terribly burnt body: 'It didn't look like her. I couldn't believe it was my daughter.'

Her parents, the Kapoors, received anonymous letters from the Hardys' neighbours, saying they had heard Kanchan Mala screaming, and had banged on the door, but it was opened only after ten minutes. They tried to rescue the burning woman; however, being scared of the Hardys, nobody was prepared to give evidence in court (Singh 1979: 18).

Kanchan Chopra, 24: A 'family matter'

Kanchan Chopra, who worked as a stenographer in the Union Public Services Commission (UPSC), was being harassed in her marital home, in Patel Nagar. On 29 June 1979, after office she went to her parents' house in Malviya Nagar, and told them she felt unsafe at her in-laws' place. Her husband arrived the same night, and forced her to return with him. Her brother went along, but as soon as they reached the Patel Nagar house, her husband began beating Kanchan. Her brother rushed to the police station, but the police refused to intervene in a 'family matter'. Around midnight, Kanchan's parents were informed that she was badly burnt and had been admitted to Lohia Hospital. By the time they arrived, she had passed away (Das 1979: 16).

The First Protest Demonstrations Against 'Dowry Murder'

As concerned women became aware of the crimes being committed by countless ordinary families, in spaces considered sacrosanct, they brought the phenomenon to public attention. Thus it was that the media, government, legal system and people at large began to recognise 'bride-burning', 'dowry murder', or 'wife-murder'.

Stree Sangharsh, a feminist collective, was formed in Delhi in 1977 by a small group of academics and activists. They were among the first to expose and denounce dowry deaths as being, in fact, murders. Other women's organisations, Mahila Dakshata Samiti (MDS) and Nari Raksha Samiti, also challenged the routine dismissal of such deaths as accidents.

Protesting the Death of Tarvinder Kaur

On 1 June 1979, Stree Sangharsh held a spirited demonstration to protest the death of Tarvinder Kaur. This was a milestone in the women's movement. About 50 protesters assembled in the Model Town market. These were Stree Sangharsh members and others they had mobilised, including students and teachers from the Indraprastha College Women's Committee and the Progressive Students' Organisation (PSO). The enraged women marched through the residential area shouting anti-dowry slogans: 'Punish the murderers of Tarvinder', 'Stop burning brides', 'Women will not put up with any more atrocities'. They put up hand-made posters and distributed leaflets, 'Women Are Not for Burning', which carried facts and figures about dowry deaths; people read these with keen interest.

By the time they reached F3/7, Model Town, Tarvinder Kaur's in-laws' house, the numbers had swelled, with about 200 local residents, domestic workers, passers-by, spontaneously joining the protest. They took out buckets and paintbrushes and painted slogans; the family cowered indoors. It was a very hot day, and the women had spent several hours marching and shouting. Local residents offered them some water and cold drinks. Newspapers, television and news-magazines covered the protest sympathetically. Stree Sangharsh members felt that a good beginning had been made (Das 1979: 15; Butalia 2002: 46-47).

A Spate of Protests

A spate of protests followed: it was as if a dam had burst. Such concerted action was unprecedented. Much of the groundswell consisted of bystanders, especially women, joining wherever a demonstration was held. They vented long-simmering anger, and demanded justice. Documentation by the MDS showed that some 350 women were burnt to death in Delhi in just one year, 1975—ironically the International Year of Women. Delhi's Police Commissioner acknowledged that the actual number of cases was likely to be at least two times those reported.

On 12 June 1979, Nari Raksha Samiti held a demonstration in the alleys of Old Delhi against a bride-burning in the area. Protesters, including working women, housewives, mothers with babies, burqa-clad women, walked from Chandni Chowk to Parliament Street, and presented a memorandum to the Home Minister. They carried placards that read: 'Arrest the Killers of Women', 'We Will Never Let Women Burn', 'All Marriages Must Be Registered', and 'Severely Punish Bigamists'. Press and television reported on the event enthusiastically (Das 1979).

An anti-dowry protest, Delhi, early 80s. Satyarani Chaddha laments her daughter Shashi Bala's murder; other protesters listen attentively.

On 26 June, the Delhi State Mahila Federation passed a resolution at a public meeting attended by hundreds of women, urging the government to make dowry a cognisable offence, and make a post-mortem mandatory if a woman died within seven years of her marriage.

Protesting the Death of Kanchan Chopra

On 1 July 1979, two days after the death of Kanchan Chopra, about 200 people held a three-hour dharna outside the Patel Nagar police station, demanding the arrest of Kanchan Chopra's husband and in-laws. Protesters included residents of Malviya Nagar, where Kanchan's parents lived, and where she had grown up. They went to the Chopras', house, E-205 West Patel Nagar, shouted slogans and wrote on the walls that the killers would not be spared. The Chopras' neighbours were sullen and uncooperative. The police had registered the case as a suicide, but under public pressure, they changed it to murder. The local Station House Officer (SHO) was transferred, and the case was handed over to the Special Cell (Das 1979).

In early July 1979, various women's organisations, with the family members of a number of murdered women, met Delhi's Police Commissioner and Lieutenant Governor to complain about the inefficiency and corruption of the police and administration, and demanded immediate action in all such cases.

From private tragedy, 'bride-burning' was rapidly escalating into a collective, public, even national, issue. But as Subhadra Butalia noted two decades later: 'Little did we know then that it takes more than a few demonstrations and newspaper reports to change things.' (Butalia 2002: 27).

4

Collective Theatrical Production
Delhi, 1979

Soon after the first protest demonstrations in mid-1979, Stree Sangharsh initiated the making of a street play on bride-burning/dowry murder. The aim was to reach wider spectrums of society, so that there may be a collective recognition of abuse and violence, pervasive within many families. Such awareness, they felt, was a necessary step in what would be a long battle for ending violence against women.

Stree Sangharsh had an extraordinary set of thinkers, active in workers', human rights and peace movements: including Radha Kumar, Amrita Chhachhi, Gita Sahgal, Urvashi Butalia, Ayesha Heble, Subhadra Butalia, Gouri Choudhury, Bharati Roy Chowdhury and a few others.[34]

---

[34] Radha Kumar is an academic and peace activist. She has been head of the Mandela Center for Peace, Jamia Millia Islamia University, Director General of the Delhi Policy Group, a member of the Foundation for Communal Harmony, Ministry of Home Affairs, and Chair of the United Nations University Council.

Gita Sahgal co-founded the Centre for Secular Space, and Southall Black Sisters, London, headed Amnesty International's Gender Unit, and is on the editorial board of *Feminist Dissent.* She has made documentary films on themes including dowry murders and sati. In the 70s, she worked for some years with farm labourers and quarry workers in Mehrauli, Delhi.

Amrita Chhachhi has taught Women, Gender and Development Studies at the International Institute of Social Studies, The Hague, Netherlands. She researches and writes extensively on gender and labour, social policy and sociological theory.

Ayesha Heble taught at Zakir Hussain College, Delhi University, during the 70s, and worked part-time with farm labourers and quarry workers in Mehrauli. She has taught English language and literature in several countries, and currently teaches World Literature, Modern Drama and Academic Writing at Sultan Qaboos University in the Sultanate of Oman. She is a novelist and short story writer.

Bharati Roy Chowdhury (1953-2011) was a grassroots organiser and leader in Action India and Vikalp Social Organisation (Saharanpur), and a founder-member of the

Some of them came to women's activism via an involvement in left movements, and they were all guided by a strong sense of social justice. In its short, intense life, Stree Sangharsh contributed to strengthening the foundations of feminism in India. It was never registered, most members being opposed to state intervention, official ratification and hierarchical organisational structures.

Stree Sangharsh drafted a manifesto, socialist feminist in tone, which analysed dowry in contemporary India, in relation to private property. The manifesto pointed out that dowry was a kind of 'bridegroom-price' which augmented the consumable capital in the hands of a groom and his family, who then used it to finance business ventures, educate younger sons, furnish dowry for their own daughter(s), and so on. The bridegroom was apparently 'sold', but in fact acted as a conduit for the transfer of liquid capital. The transaction was similar to that of blood money, with the bride held hostage. Dowry thus manifested as a form of ransom, blackmail and extortion. By harming and threatening to further harm her, the groom's family could milk the bride's family dry. After that, their purpose served, they got rid of her. Bride-burning allowed the groom to remarry and fetch another dowry.

Traditionally, parents gave a dowry to their daughter at the time of her marriage, but it belonged to her as *stridhan*, a safety-net providing her with some security and status. During the colonial period, dowry began to transmute into wealth belonging to the groom's side; rather than being given to the bride, it became something given to the groom and his family. In the original sense, it was a source of women's power; in the modern sense, a sign of her disempowerment. Veena Talwar Oldenburg (2002) traces this change in the meaning and definition of dowry to new property laws, which recognised only male ownership of agricultural land, denying women's customary rights. Since a woman had no rights to any property, the groom's side began treating her as a poor dependent whom they could abandon, harass, or kill; dowry demands became a way of blackmailing her parents.

Over the years, the disempowerment of women within the family structure intensified, and dowry demands spiralled, spreading into different communities. Most women caught in violent marital situations were too scared to speak up in self-defense, dreading the escalation of conflict. If a woman tried to return to her parental home,

---

National Forum of Forest Working People (NFFWP) and New Trade Union Initiative (NTUI).

her parents generally advised her to adjust and sent her back to her husband and in-laws.

Stree Sangharsh members researched the issue, interacted with many families, held protests and discussions with other women's groups. They created a mobile poster exhibition on violence against women, and put it up in public venues to bring awareness. It was an innovative medium, with an element of street art: they would put it up anywhere, simply using rope and clothes pegs. People looked at the exhibition carefully, there was interest. Stree Sangharsh found in their audiences an eagerness to learn, question, and converse face-to-face.

Making *Om Swaha*: The Process and the Participants

Realising how relevant creative media was for effective communication, Stree Sangharsh members thought of making a street play. They invited two young, sensitive theatre-persons, Anuradha Kapur and Maya Rao, who agreed to script and direct a street play. Both of them were part of Theatre Union, a recently founded group for innovative, radical theatre.

Stree Sangharsh invited many more people concerned with women's issues to participate in the process of devising a play. Thus, *Om Swaha* was developed by a fluid collective, including activists Amiya Rao, Renuka Mishra, Primila Lewis, Manmohan Dayal, Rukmini Rao, Kalpana Mehta, university teachers Sudesh Vaid, Kumkum Sangari, Pankaj Butalia, and others. Regular intensive meetings were held, debating and discussing the story, characters and plot. Maya and Anuradha participated in each meeting and, on the basis of the discussions therein, would later write up a drama sequence. At the next meeting they would present the sequence to the group, absorb the group's responses, and proceed to rewrite the script on the basis of collective feedback. It was a very unique collaborative process. They drew on real events to build the plot: the script they evolved had elements from the life-and-death of, in particular, Hardeep Kaur, Tarvinder Kaur, and Kanchan Chopra.

Hardeep's story in *Om Swaha* closely followed that of the real Hardeep Kaur, while Kanchan's was an amalgam of Tarvinder Kaur and Kanchan Chopra's stories. The script altered details, fictionalised for dramatic flow, depth and impact. Events were imaginatively reconfigured, transmuted into public spectacle, to inspire reflection and critical thinking. However, the original version of *Om Swaha* was faithful to reality in showing that both Hardeep and Kanchan were killed by their respective in-laws. (It was in the second version that Kanchan's story was further fictionalised, showing her making an active choice to survive, even if it meant walking out of her marital family.)

Once the script was ready, Anuradha and Maya held workshops, training the activists to act. There were no professional actors available for this venture, so willy-nilly the members of Stree Sangharsh and some others became actors. They threw themselves into the task at hand; rehearsals took place in earnest and within a couple of months, the play was ready!

To give a lively sense of how *Om Swaha* evolved, I juxtapose here the voices of four women involved in its making: Subhadra, Amrita, Gouri and Maya.[35] Subhadra describes how Hardeep Kaur's death affected her, Amrita provides a connect with socialist feminist politics, Gouri conveys the viewpoint of a grassroots activist, while Maya speaks as a full-blooded theatre-person. We see how a mélange of these influences went into making the play.

You might like to imagine each of the four women coming up one by one, and speaking her dramatic monologue—within a circle of viewers!

Subhadra: 'We Have to Do Something!'

At the time, Subhadra Butalia was teaching at Dayal Singh College, Delhi University, and lived with her family in Jangpura. Across the road was a big house where a joint family of industrialists lived; Hardeep Kaur was the daughter-in-law.

> I shall never forget the afternoon Hardeep Kaur was set on fire. I came out on to the small balcony of our house shortly after lunch. I registered smoke coming out of Hardeep Kaur's house. Suddenly, her screams rent the air. The husband and wife often had noisy arguments and confrontations which, as neighbours, we ignored. But this was different. The girl was burning, screaming, and people from houses around rushed out. It was as if we were all paralysed, still standing and staring when a taxi drew up in front of the house and Hardeep was brought out, wrapped in a white sheet. She needed support to make it to the taxi and was rushed off to hospital. The neighbours who had collected in small groups to talk gradually dispersed and quietly filed back to their homes (Butalia 2002: 4-5).

[35] The narratives of Amrita, Gouri and Maya are based on the interviews I conducted with them in Delhi between 2015 and 2017. Subhadra's narrative is largely based on her writing (2002).

Hardeep sustained 70 per cent burns, and died within two weeks, on 2 November '78. She gave a dying declaration, in the presence of a magistrate, stating that she was burned by her mother-in-law and grandmother-in-law. Meanwhile, the neighbourhood seemed indifferent, and the general opinion was: it's best not to interfere in domestic affairs.

However, Mahila Dakshata Samiti began to investigate the death. Two women from MDS came to Subhadra Butalia's house, to enquire if she knew anything; they also asked other people in the neighbourhood. Perhaps under pressure from them, the police began an investigation. On the basis of Hardeep's dying statement, a charge-sheet was filed and the case was sent to court. Most neighbours told the police they saw and knew nothing. Only Subhadra Butalia testified, describing what she had seen.

Even Hardeep's brother was unwilling to testify against her marital family. He said that Hardeep was gone anyway; he needed to look after his own family, and his business. If he kept chasing the case, all that would fall by the wayside. The talk was that Hardeep's in-laws had paid him off. They did certainly bribe people in the neighbourhood. Hardeep's father-in-law actually visited the Butalias and offered to gift Subhadra any item of her choice from his shop, if she were to retract the statement she had made in court. She refused, of course. Members of Hardeep's marital family were convicted of the crime. The family promptly filed an appeal in the High Court, and deployed a common trick: the mother-in-law and grandmother-in-law were admitted to hospital, claiming they were ill.

Subhadra Butalia (2002: 8, 24) writes, 'The more I tried to get Hardeep out of my system, the more her story clutched at my heart [...] At some stage, those of us who were getting more and more worked up about these incidents began to think we could not just sit around feeling angry. We had to try and intervene in some way.'

It was soon after Tarvinder Kaur's death that Stree Sangharsh organised the first-ever anti-dowry-death demonstration, on 1 June 1979, in Model Town. The protest was far more successful than they had anticipated, with people responding spontaneously, and appreciative media coverage. This inspired their decision to build up an intensive public campaign. They had already observed how the poster exhibition created a stir wherever it was put on. During discussion, the idea of a street play came up and there was tremendous excitement, for they thought a play had great potential. But none of them knew how to make a play:

> So we got in touch with a friend, Anuradha Kapur, and she brought in another friend, Maya Rao. Anuradha and Maya scripted the play we eventually put up on the basis of real-life stories of dowry deaths that we told them and those they were familiar with, and we began rehearsals in the house of another friend, Lakshmi Rao,[36] in central Delhi.
>
> We would assemble there every day, travelling across the city by bus or scooter riksha—none of us was rich enough to take taxis and few of us had cars. Anuradha and Maya would take us through a series of improvisations on the stories we had told them, and bit by bit a final script began to take shape. We were all dedicated and fully committed—I think none of us even felt the tiredness of travel or of the long hours we spent discussing, enacting and writing this or that scene. As I look back on that period today, I wonder how I managed with my job and my household responsibilities and all the time taken for travel. It seemed that in no time—though in reality I know it was at least a month or two—we had our play ready. We called it *Om Swaha.* (Butalia 2002: 49-50)

Amrita: 'How Enthusiastic We Were, So Intense'

Amrita Chhachhi, a research scholar at Jawaharlal Nehru University at the time, was working on labour issues, and experimenting with meaningful action on the ground. She recalls her initial turn towards feminism, and intense involvement with Stree Sangharsh, Om Swaha and the women's collective Saheli, as follows (interview 2015):

> In the mid-1970s, a whole bunch of us were broad left in JNU, and also in Bombay, Bangalore, Kanpur.... But when there was an actual worker-management conflict, the guys told us we couldn't come, it wasn't safe for us. The struggle was in Faridabad. That was our first moment of saying—'What is this, we are all comrades but suddenly we are women!' Three of us began to discuss this, and we became a women's caucus within the wider group. Then Emergency happened. On International Women's Day, 1976, we organised a big exhibition, with posters and messages on huge boards, at JNU and Lalit Kala Akademi. There was a section on encounters and torture, Rosa Luxemburg, people's movements. We were socialist feminists, discussing surplus value, housework, the working class.... How enthusiastic we were, so intense!
>
> ...Stree Sangharsh was a coming together of diverse people. Meetings were held in homes—Radha's, Subhadra's, Gouri's. We had

[36] Lakshmi Rameshwar Rao is an educationist, social science teacher, writer, poet, and spirited activist; she took active part in the women's movement in Delhi in the 1980s.

ideological debates, trying to define Stree Sangharsh. We were building it as a socialist feminist group but Subhadra was more practical—'This is the purpose and I don't want any of this ideology.' She was [a] clear-cut liberal feminist, concerned about rights for women, and very brave. When the virginity test issue came up, there was discussion how Simone de Beauvoir and other French feminists had publicly said they'd had abortions; Subhadra said we need to have some unmarried women speaking up, saying they're not virgins. That's radical thinking!

That moment we were really doing a lot of things. When people talk of intersectionality today, I often say, 'Excuse me, from the very beginning the women's movement in India has been intersectional!' Women's issues were always intersecting with class, so from the start the perspective was very strong. We had huge discussions on rape. Radha made a trip to the Santhal Parganas, and we brought out a report and leaflet, 'Rape in the Santhal Parganas'. It was very strong, bringing out the dimension of state versus working-class and tribals. Our thinking was international—we supported Solidarity, Polish workers and mothers,[37] linking all these things.

We took up the anti-dowry campaign. Stree Sangharsh grew around that, and was very active for three or four years. We brought out a newsletter on the dowry campaign, and worked out definitions of feminism. We applied a socialist feminist analysis to dowry—we said dowry death was murder, linked to the commodification of women, capitalism and consumerism. Now everyone says this, but that was the first time the link was made: we made that link.

We created an exhibition—cut out stuff from newspapers, marriage advertisements, dowry reports etcetera. We showed it all over, hung on laundry lines, in JNU, Hindu College, Delhi University, many other places. I remember fantastic posters we made on dowry, rape, with Sheba and Jogi[38] in my grandfather's verandah in Jorbagh. All the intersectional feminist thinking was in those posters. All of us did everything ourselves at that time—making placards and posters, writing, acting, agitating. There were no professionals—that was very special about that time.

Om Swaha evolved over many meetings. We got in touch with Maya and Anuradha, and they wrote the play. The play was written in discussion with all of us, so in effect it was multi-authored. Initially, I think, there was no set script, rather a sequence of events, a story.

---

[37] Solidarity was the first independent trade union in Poland, which mobilised an extraordinary citizens' movement between 1980 and 1989. Women's participation for workers' rights, including the rights of women workers, was integral to the movement.

[38] The artist Sheba Chhachhi, with designer Jogi Panghaal, created iconic posters, sketches and artwork within the early women's movement.

I don't remember memorising lines. I remember the household scene—early morning, coughing, sabjiwala and kabadiwala calling, Hardeep being harangued by her in-laws. Each person who came into a performance would add some new words or gestures, ad-lib. The basic structure remained, but what happened inside was improvised a lot: we developed nuances and speeches as we went along. Shettyji[39] joined, and played the damru to call people, he was fantastic: it was a wonderful way to gather people. We had practice sessions at Buchy's[40] place in Canning Lane.

I threw myself into *Om Swaha* and enjoyed it very much. During my BA at Stella Maris in Madras, I had been very much into theatre, with the Madras Players. Of course, street theatre was very different compared to college theatre—that was just theatrics. This was very charged, intense. We were communicating a message. From the moment we formed the circle, we knew there was an audience around us whom we had to convince. After a performance, we broke into small groups and started a discussion right away.

Day and night we were involved—with no funding, no money!

Gouri: 'You Could Change the World...'

Gouri Choudhury was working with marginalised communities on issues of education and citizenship when she got drawn into Stree Sangharsh and the making of Om Swaha*. Here she describes her involvement with* Om Swaha *and the initiation into feminist politics (interview 2015):*

I came to Delhi in the early '70s, with my husband and children. I joined Mobile Creches, and participated in a weekly study circle that Action India was running. The whole concept of a better world, of revolution, was mind-boggling. I was in my mid-thirties, not a young student, but the fact that you could change the world, was overwhelming. I joined Action India and began organising a school, and health work, in an unauthorised colony below the old Yamuna Bridge. They had no ration cards, were not on the voters' list. My first march on the streets was for ration cards! We managed to get them on the voters' list. About that time, Mrs Indira Gandhi declared the Emergency. I continued working, but in August '76, the Yamuna bridge settlement was demolished. It was the height of the monsoons. Half the people were sent to Jahangirpuri, half to New Seemapuri. We began working in Jahangirpuri and New Seemapuri; with me were Sharda behn, Bharati, Runu.

---

[39] A steady actor in *Om Swaha* over several years, Shettyji was employed as a chauffeur by Gouri Choudhury's family.

[40] Buchy is Lakshmi Rameshwar Rao's chosen name among friends and colleagues.

One day in 1979, I got a phone call from Stree Sangharsh, saying a young woman had been burned for dowry, and we want to hold a protest. We joined that protest in Model Town. That was the beginning of feminist ideas coming into Action India. It was a journey from Marxism to Marxist feminism, with an emphasis on gender, class and caste. I immediately became a part of Stree Sangharsh, all the discussions and demonstrations, and then we thought of doing a street play.

The *Om Swaha* experience was phenomenal. Bharati[41] and I were part of the discussions on plot, storyline. Maya and Anuradha developed the script, and were the directors. We met at Mrs Butalia's house for discussions, and at Jessica's[42] house in Lajpat Nagar, before she left for Bombay. I was part of the very first team that performed the play, in the chorus. We practiced at Buchy's house, in the garden and the back verandah.

Our approach in Action India was to educate people, men and women, to fight for their rights, enable them to organise for collective action. After the Stree Sangharsh influence, we began looking at women's issues. The feminist thinking and approach grew stronger with *Om Swaha.* From then on, more of our time and attention went into working on violence against women, at the grassroots.

You cannot have any activity without theatre, song and dance in the Indian women's movement! For us, that began with *Om Swaha,* and it carries on today!

Maya: 'Thinking Up Dialogues, Making Up Songs'

Maya Rao, the well-known and exceptionally talented theatre-person, recalls the process of scripting Om Swaha, and directing and acting in it:

In 1979, I was teaching political science in Kamala Nehru College, but most of my time was spent doing theatre with the girls. Then Anu and I got a call from someone in Stree Sangharsh, saying, there are all these dowry deaths coming to the fore, and some of us want to find a way to start a public discussion around this—so will you do a street play?

At that point, we didn't have any actors. It was probably a blessing in disguise, because we told them, 'We don't have any actors. If you people will act, we can think of doing it!'

None of them were actors, but all of them were activists, and thereby hangs a tale. We spent evenings and evenings together at

---

41 Bharati Roy Chowdhury, a core member of Action India.

42 Gouri did not remember Jessica's full name, nor did others in the original group whom I interviewed.

meetings. There were many women, each differed from the other in terms of ideology, politics, personal tendencies, everything. It was a great learning curve for me. When you're in it you want to tear your hair out, because you can't get a sequence, you can't get one-tenth of a sequence, because already there are ten opinions before you can even design the play!

We would say—now we've got all these views, now we're going off to write some sequences. We did a bit of writing, but then of course we had to go back and open it for everybody. There was all this going to and fro. We would make blocks and the dialogues, and take it back to them, and they'd say, 'No, how can it be like this?' There was a lot of all that!

Anu and I kept thinking up words and dialogues. We're hopping in and out of three-wheelers, and making up songs. That's how we made '*Na das lakh, na teen lakh, na ek lakh, na ye na vo, karoon main kya...*'[43]—it was made in a three-wheeler! This was the song chanted while killing Hardeep, and it was incredibly powerful. It became popular and quite famous. We'd sit in Anu's house or mine, and keep perfecting the songs. We felt top of the pops, what fabulous lines we're creating, when we made a song, and it all fell into rhythm. After thirty years, people still remember some of those lines!

Then we held workshops, regular actors' workshops, especially for activists. Acting is not just about talking and giving a speech, it's about using your body. And we were doing street theatre, which is about using *all* of your body! It was great fun, and it was all kinds of things.

The meetings and rehearsals were held in different people's homes. There would be hangers-on, some people who'd just sit and watch us rehearse, discuss and chat. There was a core of people, but there were these others too, a floating population. One day you think they're doing a role, but the next day they're not there!

Anu and I thought we'd be directing, but found ourselves doing roles too. I acted as Hardeep, and at some point I acted as Kanchan. Apart from Anu and me, the initial cast were all activists. At some point a number of boys joined, Vinod Dua, Manohar Khushalani from Theatre Union. People would come, do a show or two and move on. It touched various people and they touched the play—it was like that.

---

43 The refrain of a song chanted ominously by Hardeep's in-laws while surrounding, beating and burning her; it translates as: '*Neither ten lakh, nor three lakh, nor one lakh, nor this nor that, what am I to do...?*'

Om Swaha, Karol Bagh, 8 March 1981. (Left to right) Harsh Kapoor, Theo, Malika Virdi, Deepti, Sharda behn, Maya Rao, Anand Swamy.

It Came Together, and Continued to Grow

It came together: content and form. Home, neighbourhood, events, and emotions were evoked through familiar sounds, images and actions—the morning rush of breakfast and tiffin boxes, marriage rituals conveying absurdly harsh injunctions, a two-wheeler dowry demand vrooming in so that the wedding nuptials could continue; abuse, murder, the disposal of the corpse, All India Radio announcing another death... Yet, soon, one more woman is married off, into a similar household.

The structure was set by Maya and Anuradha, but they encouraged the actors to innovate. While improvising the wedding scene, somebody began singing '*Kala Doriya*', the popular Punjabi wedding song, and it stuck because it was so appropriate. When the bride was to leave for her sasural, Subhadra started singing the heart-wrenching film number, '*Babul ki duayein leti jaa*', and it too became a permanent fixture. Similarly, after the wedding and early-morning household scenes, when her in-laws berate Hardeep, somebody picked up a dupatta, and the directors felt, let's use this (Butalia, interview 2016). Thereafter an orange dupatta, or else shawl, was essential to every performance of *Om Swaha*, to collectively flail and flog Hardeep, and then simulate flames, rising and engulfing her.

5

'A Hundred Shows in One Year'

Some Early Performances

The very first performance of *Om Swaha* was at Indraprastha (IP), Delhi's oldest women's college. It was held in the expansive open space in front of IP's graceful and stately main building in Civil Lines, a stone's throw from Delhi University's main campus. It was late 1979. The IP College Women's Committee, which had been formed in 1978, invited the group to perform.

A few hundred college girls gathered around, and were amused by the sutradhar's opening spiel: 'Namaskar, Sat Sri Akal, Walekum Salaam, Welcome, Hello, Hi! Come, you will find what you want! I am Professor Shetty M.B.—Marriage Broker! I have IAS boys, right up to peons. Unemployed boys demand just Rs. 2 lakh as dowry, to open factories after marriage. Doctor, engineer, businessman, officer, professor, clerk, I have boys AtoZ. Girls, fathers, brothers of girls, bring your cash, pick a groom! The girl must be fair, good-looking, pleasant and caring. If she is a working girl, a 2 to 10 percent special discount is available!'

A radio announcement changed the mood to sombre: 'Hardeep Kaur, 20, wife of Gurpal Singh, was admitted to Jayprakash Narayan Hospital with severe burns. She died on 2 November 1978.'

Her neighbours say they saw nothing.

Then her friend, Kanchan, shares, 'After marriage, whenever I met her, she wept. Her in-laws tortured her for dowry! She has been killed!'

The young women in the audience were tense by now; their own dreams of marriage mixed with dread as they watched Hardeep's story in flashbacks. Women sang *'Kala doriya'*, the bride and groom were about to circumambulate the sacred fire, but the groom's father shouted, 'Stop the wedding! Where is the scooter you promised?!' The chorus appealed, 'Don't stop the wedding! The girl's life will be ruined,' and a two-wheeler, mimicked by two actors, arrived. The pandit chanted verses, a satire on the routine rites: *Om Swaha!*[44] Om Govindayanam, Om Gopalayanam, Om Scooterayanam! Beti, worship your husband, be suhagan forever! Whether or not he is Ram, you will be Sita... Even if he insults your parents, you must serve his! Let them mould you as they want, like wet clay!' The chorus sings, '*Babul ki duayein leti ja, jaa tujhko sukhi sansar miley...*'

Rather than the happy future she wished for, Hardeep frantically cooks, cleans and serves, yet is constantly harassed by her husband and in-laws. Their complaints built up and morphed into something sinister as they closed in around her, chanting:

> *'Na das lakh na teen lakh na ek lakh, no fridge no TV, no press no mixie, ha ha ha ha.*
> *No ear-ring no bangle, no toe-ring no nose-ring, no shoes for sasur,*
> *No suit for brother, no jersey for Pappu, no sari for nanad, ha ha ha ha...*
> *No this, no that, got nothing, what do I do? Ha ha ha ha,*
> *Hah, ha hah ha, hah ha, hah ha, ha ha ha hah hah hah hah hah haaaa...!'*

Frenzied voices built into a crescendo as her in-laws battered and finally burnt Hardeep.

No action was taken against Hardeep's killers. And soon, Kanchan was forced into marriage, and similarly abused by her in-laws: 'I, Kanchan, am still alive, but everyday a new demand, insults, taunts, and beating.' Kanchan's parents insisted she try to adjust in her sasural; the sutradhar said: 'Kanchan, what can you do all alone? This has been going on since centuries... At least you did not keep quiet. You tried to fight your battle.'

The play closed with a helpless Kanchan screaming: 'Yet my situation hasn't changed! So long as people keep giving dowry, taking dowry, we women will keep on suffering! I have expressed my feelings, but what has everybody been doing? Simply watching the fun?' The chorus exhorted the audience: *'Na dahej lena, na dahej dena... Do not take dowry, do not give dowry!'*

---

[44] *Om Swaha* is a ritual chant in Hindu wedding ceremonies. 'Om' signifies Ganesh, remover of obstacles, while goddess 'Swaha' bestows Agni, the fire god, with the power to burn.

The audience was pensive; the play affected them powerfully. Shettyji recalls, 'People in the audience had tears in their eyes when they heard *Babul ki duayein,* sung beautifully. Even we would get goose-pimples!' (conversation 2018). Subhadra Butalia recalls: '...As Maya's screams rent the air, it was almost as if everything, even the traffic on the roads outside, came to a standstill. Even we, who were familiar with every line and nuance of the play, were moved.' (2002: 50-51)

For the actors, the first show was reassuring. They had rehearsed often, but didn't know how audiences would respond. Students spoke frankly during the post-performance discussion, as was the case in other women's colleges too. Questions and contradictions seemed to sharpen within their minds. Seeds were sown, some of which would likely take root and grow over time. It was, for some, an introduction to feminism as a way to engage with the conditions of one's life, and take courageous action.

The group also performed in mixed colleges, such as the Delhi College of Vocational Studies (DCVS). It made a huge impact there. Students got inspired and three college boys joined the group, becoming part of the chorus for a few shows. Sheba Chhachhi, freshly returned to Delhi from the National Institute of Design, Ahmedabad, vividly remembers seeing the performance at DCVS: 'I'd heard so much about the play, so I went along. I stood there watching it, feeling tremors run through my body. I was really very powerfully affected by that performance. I can still feel it—a sudden flash of *Om Swaha*!'

There were hostile responses too. Maya distinctly remembers performing at a mixed college, either Venkateshwar or Deshbandhu, which had only a tiny percentage of girls. The actors made a circle with dupattas, to mark the performance space, but some boys crossed the circle and kept coming closer, in a threatening sort of way: 'In the end we had a space not more than four feet in diameter. It became a contest: "Will you have the last word, or will we?" As we did the last line, we picked up our props, made a beeline for the van, and left. It was all very exciting!'

Scripting Change

At various places, members of the audience suggested that the play should end on a positive note. Kanchan was struggling, but her struggle was futile; it seemed as if there was no way out for women. The *Om*

Swaha team, after a few shows, decided to change the finale—so as to portray hope, rather than the misery of a dead-end.

In subsequent versions of *Om Swaha,* Kanchan was determined to live; towards the end, she would assert: 'Today, dowry is not just a personal family matter... Today, we refuse to die! We will not burn to death! Nor will we be forced into committing suicide. We want justice! We want your support, all of you!' She took her issues to the public, and elicited their participation.

She became the change, through the alchemy wrought by theatre. With this, the play indicated that women could exercise agency; society would move forward, with women in the lead.

The play changed in another equally significant way. The first version of *Om Swaha* focused on dowry as the major factor implicated in bride-burning; the audience was urged to 'stop taking dowry, stop giving dowry'. From the second version onward, the emphasis shifted to a gamut of factors responsible for women's powerlessness; at the end, the audience was exhorted to educate their daughters and sons, encourage both to be independent and progressive, to build a better future.

The drama collective's ideas evolved as the group immersed itself in debates, and heard dozens of personal narratives during post-performance discussions. It became clear that along with dowry, a number of factors were implicated in 'bride-burning'. Girls and boys were brought up very differently; they faced unequal expectations, and emotional and sexual problems were rife within couples. In most cases, newly married women were terribly isolated, in alien homes; all this, and more, made them vulnerable to extreme violence.

Building Campaigns

Amrita Chhachhi recalls performing *Om Swaha* mostly in relation to particular campaigns, in localities like Model Town, where there had been cases of bride-burning. This was during the height of the anti-dowry campaign, 1979-81. Often several friends, co-activists, accompanied the play troupe, and distributed leaflets amongst the audience and passers-by. Occasionally, the group also put up the Stree Sangharsh poster exhibition on dowry and bride-burning. People in the audience would watch, read, absorb, and then engage in intense discussion.

Sometimes the play was performed in a very charged atmosphere:

I'll never forget the day in Shahpur Jat.[45] There'd been a dowry death in a local upper-caste family. We did the play right there, near their house. We held a demonstration too. For me, those were the high moments. People from the area joined us and we all wound our way through the village, and held a dharna outside the police station.

We thought we should follow up, maintain a relationship, go back and discuss issues. We tried to do so. After we did the play in Malviya Nagar, I went back once or twice and held meetings, because I lived close by, in Press Enclave. But I wasn't able to carry on for long.

Then there was a big case in Mathura. The guy had burnt his wife, and married again. The dead woman's family must have approached us. We decided we must protest. So we went all the way to Mathura, did the play and held a demonstration. It was very difficult, because we knew hardly anybody there. All the same, we didn't face any hostility.

Doing the play in the context of demonstrations was the most powerful experience for me. We did face silence or hostility at a few places—but I don't remember aggression. Today you see aggression all

Nangloi, 1980, women's sit-in demanding justice. Placards: *Jaswanti mari nahin, maari gayi, hatyaaron ko sazaa do* (Jaswanti was killed, punish the murderers); *Adha bharat nari hai, phir kyon bechari hai* (Women are half of India, yet so exploited).

---

[45] Shahpur Jat, originally a village, was gradually surrounded by posh south Delhi colonies. Along with its original inhabitants, it is now home to new settlers and commercial establishments.

waha, Nangloi, 1980. 'Neighbours saw nothing, will say nothing' (left to right, sitting) Gita Sahgal, rita Chhachhi, Renuka Mishra, (standing) Bharati Roy Chowdhury, Ayesha Heble. Second scene ng protest song (left to right) Ayesha, Amrita, Bharati, Sharda behn, Gita, Gouri Choudhury, Maya Renuka. Placards held up by protesters: *Bahut saha hai, ab na saheinge, apne adhikar lekar raheinge* (We've suffered too much, now no more, we will wrest our rights!). A woman gives testimony.

> around, so I wonder what people would face today if they were to do this kind of street theatre (Amrita Chhachhi, interview 2015).

In Nangloi, a sprawling resettlement colony in west Delhi, the group performed *Om Swaha* in 1980, to protest the murder of a young woman, Jaswanti. Hundreds of local women sat on dharna outside the Nangloi police station, demanding that the murderers be punished. They shouted slogans against police inaction. Jaswanti's mother was part of the dharna. This performance of *Om Swaha* aroused a lot of emotion, and many women spontaneously shared their stories, testimonies of survival and loss. They detailed harassment, domestic violence, death—of loved ones, a sister, a daughter, a neighbour or niece. The atmosphere was explosive as women shed their habitual silence in that moment of solidarity. Even some policemen, batons in hand, seemed to get drawn into the circle of human caring and concern.

During 1980, the group performed *Om Swaha* at Karol Bagh Central Park, amid a huge crowd (Runu Chakraborty, interview 2015). Radha Kumar, Ayesha Heble, Gouri, Anuradha, Maya and others were acting in the play, and several co-activists who had accompanied them distributed leaflets and initiated dialogue with the audience.

Art Meets Reality

The group performed *Om Swaha* at Malviya Nagar, where Kanchan Chopra's parents lived. Her mother was in the audience. Kanchan had been killed by her in-laws in Patel Nagar; her parents, brother and neighbours had held demonstrations at her in-laws' house and the local police station, demanding justice.

Maya Rao (interview 2015) recalls Kanchan Chopra's mother's response to the play:

> I'll never forget that day. I was acting as Kanchan, the second girl in the play, who decides she will live, not die. I didn't know that the real Kanchan's mother was in the audience. As the play ended, this woman came up and grabbed me. She took hold of me, pulled me down, put my head on her lap, and kept thumping me. Can you imagine?
>
> She must have felt I'm her daughter! She acted out her feelings. I couldn't retract myself from her. I stayed there. It was as if her girl, or the spirit of her girl, had come to life. So I just kept quiet, let her do what she had to... She let me go after a while. It was the first and last time I saw her. I remember this very distinctly—in my bones I remember it.

Fact and fiction merged, in this surreal encounter. A bereaved mother, as if in a trance, caught hold of her lost child, back from the dead. Her grief and anger underwent a metamorphosis, during one charged moment, into searing love, and impossible hope. In her own way, Kanchan's mother replayed and rewrote history as in a psychodrama.[46] Perhaps for her, it proved cathartic.

---

[46] Psychodrama is a method of extempore dramatisation within groups, in which people enact scenes from their own lives, dreams and fantasies. The process is often designed to help individuals recover from trauma, and express and integrate blocked emotions.

Maya realised afresh the awesome power of theatre, the impact it can have:

> It totally shook me. I think that was the day the hugest penny dropped, for me. We keep talking of the social responsibility of theatre. We think, there's this real world, and then there is the imaginary world, and you're putting a bridge between the two. I was suddenly yanked from that imaginary. One starts wondering, what is it I'm saying in the play? I hope I'm responsible for every action and statement I make in the play!

Each Performance Was Different

Each performance was different. At the busy Patel Chowk roundabout in central Delhi, a number of men, mostly government employees, saw the play. Afterwards they dispersed, without much discussion, sharing of thoughts or experiences. At another show, performed at a workers' meeting in Hissar, Haryana, the male audience was very

Om Swaha, at Mazdoor Mela, Mehrauli, 1980. Kanchan walks out of her abusive marriage. Actor: Maya Rao

responsive. The workers, and sympathisers such as Dilip Simeon,[47] had invited the group to perform. There was a huge shamiana that housed a large gathering. The actors travelled there in a bus, and performed the play. Afterwards, the workers talked a lot, said that protests should be built up around dowry and domestic violence, and that such plays should be performed (Urvashi Butalia, interview 2016).

The play was performed in Mehrauli for farm workers, quarry workers, and their families. It fitted in well with the Mazdoor Mela organised by the Dilli Dehat Mazdoor Sangh, an independent union with which Primila Lewis, Renuka Mishra, Manmohan Dayal and Gita Sahgal were deeply involved. Action India put up an exhibition at the Mazdoor Mela called *Aurat ka Chamatkar*, on women's health and reproductive rights. With almost all union members being men, there was a need to raise questions about women's rights. Workers and their families were very interested, in the play as well as the exhibition. Theatre Union members Vinod Dua and Manohar Khushalani also acted in this show, as did a few college students.

When the play was performed in residential colonies, there was usually immediate connection and empathy. Many people reacted as if the play was presenting their reality, reflecting it back at them. At a south Delhi performance, parents of various girls began relating their stories. In Mukherjee Nagar, north Delhi, residents started talking about what was going on in their homes and in the neighbourhood. In Sujan Singh Park, an upscale neighbourhood in central Delhi, very few residents came out, but bystanders (mostly domestic help, drivers and guards) stopped to see the play, and began sharing some of their problems.

Renuka Mishra (interview 2015) realised that the play filled a critical gap: 'Strangers would begin talking to us, opening up issues they never spoke about to anyone else. I think there was no feeling of community in the city, and people missed it. We filled that vacuum without consciously intending to. We provided people with a sense of community.'

[47] Dilip Simeon is a labour historian. At the time, he taught at Ramjas College, Delhi University.

Om Swaha and Stree Sangharsh, Karmika and Saheli

Gouri recalls being overwhelmed by the response to *Om Swaha*: 'We'd do a show, and people would relate personal stories to us, about how their daughter was suffering, or a relative or neighbour, and appeal for help. They needed help and support.'

In the initial years, the group distributed a leaflet during their play, which had several phone numbers on it. They began receiving many distress calls, people in various crises needing urgent intervention. This was much more than the group had expected; there was no way they could cope.

Stree Sangharsh was a motley group, not in favour of institutionalising. For a few years they had done many things together, and made a success of it: protesting 'dowry deaths' and rape, picketing police stations, bringing out newsletters and leaflets, putting up poster exhibitions, and performing *Om Swaha*. As Subhadra muses, 'Despite the fact that we argued and fought internally, for quite a while we held together and as a group we worked on different issues with an enthusiasm and commitment which would be rare to find today.' (Butalia 2002: 48) But by 1982-83, Stree Sangharsh was fading out.

Two organisations, Karmika and Saheli, developed organically from the Stree Sangharsh and *Om Swaha* experience. Subhadra Butalia founded Karmika, which dealt with dowry and bride-burning cases; she ran it for the next two to three decades. Saheli was collectively established, with Gouri Choudhury, Bharati Roy Chowdhury, Amrita Chhachhi, Lakshmi Rameshwar Rao, Amiya Rao, Sheba Chhacchi, Sharda behn, Runu Chakraborty, Kalpana Mehta and Rukmini Rao among the co-founders. They were soon joined by Prabeen Grewal, Vidya Rao, Savita Sharma, Ashima, Davinder, Shonu and several others who volunteered their time to carry on Saheli's work.

These zealous activists retrieved dowries, rescued battered daughters-in-law, gheraoed (surrounded) police stations, and urged social boycotts. Amrita recalls: 'We began Saheli and did what had to be done: counselling, legal aid, demonstrations. We took direct action, went ourselves to retrieve dowry. There's conservatism now, or cautiousness, people are shocked when they hear what all we did. We put everything at risk, heart and soul.' Rukmini Rao (interview 2015) recalls physically rescuing a woman who was locked up in her parental home. Another time, they helped a young mother by bringing her baby out of her abusive in-laws' home. There was a stream, or torrent, of real-life situations, 'cases', which they handled strategically. Some of this direct action may seem naive today or impossible. But its impact was enormous, and its energy helped shake up the status quo.

As for *Om Swaha,* by late 1980 or early 1981, most of the original performers had left, moving on to other pressing commitments. Amrita, who had enrolled for a PhD in Sociology, went to Bombay for research, where she got further involved with trade union work and a socialist feminist group which was setting up a women's centre.[48] She muses: 'Our activism was part of the radical spirit of the time. We broke a lot of rules, crossed many barriers, political and personal. My parents were upset. My father kept trying to bring me back home; my mother didn't speak to me.'

Others too were handling cutting-edge work alongside personal challenges: negotiating with families, recalibrating relationships, speaking out. Women activists were always doing too much, because too much needed to be done.

Om Swaha survived, with a bunch of new actors joining in, and some of the older ones sustaining their involvement.

---

[48] The Forum Against Oppression of Women and the Women's Centre, Bombay, are described a little more in Chapter 15.

6

The Long Haul
Om Swaha through the 80s

Maya Rao (interview 2015) recalls: 'I was part of *Om Swaha* for many years, though most actors kept changing. Gouri, Bharati, Sharda behn and Shettyji were in it from the first round and they continued. Most of the others had to leave the play after some shows, or a few months.' She herself took a break when she went to Leeds, to study theatre:

> I saw many people come and go. Sometimes I get the faces mixed up! There were activists doing *Om Swaha* in the first year. Theatre Union did a few shows: Manohar, Sushil, Vinod Dua, Ragini Prakash[49] and some other women, I can't remember who. Vinod Dua played the damru, got people together.
>
> Then, you students joined. Before I left for Leeds, I remember rehearsing you into Hardeep's role, and rehearsing Malika into Kanchan's role. This whole thing about handing over a role was quite a big thing. Those were non-video times, so you had to be there physically.

Om Swaha: Many Versions, Many Actors

Delhi University was the major catchment area: among those who joined *Om Swaha* in 1980 were Malika Virdi and Theo from the Delhi School of Social Work; Anand Swamy, Kavita Ramdas, Harsh Kapoor and Suvritta Khatri from Hindu College; and Jyotika Virdi, David Devadas, Sanjoy Roy and myself, from St Stephen's College.[50]

---

[49] Ragini Prakash was then studying Psychology at IP College. She continues to work on social issues.

[50] At the time, Malika and Theo (E. Theophilus) were studying Social Work; Anand, Economics; Kavita, Political Science; Suvritta and Harsh, Sociology; Jyotika, History; David, Literature; Sanjoy, Philosophy; and Deepti (myself), Economics.

Vivek, a young actor from Yatriks Theatre, also joined *Om Swaha*; so did social activist Lalita Ramdas, co-founder of Ankur, which focused on non-formal education in schools and low-income neighbourhoods. Because of Ankur's association with Abner Memorial School,[51] we secured the school grounds for *Om Swaha* workshops and rehearsals. This was wonderfully located, in the centre of town, the Mandi House area.

Runu Chakraborty[52] and Chhaya Sharma, both from Action India, also joined the play. They had already seen several early performances of *Om Swaha,* sitting with the audience, distributing leaflets, and Runu had sometimes filled in for absent actors, as part of the chorus or other roles. Runu recalls,

> I had no stage fear, but this was not the stage, it was the road! We performed in front of strangers, not family or relatives. Sharda behn, Chhaya and I were working at that time in east Delhi's Sunder Nagri, Nand Nagri. Chhaya lived in Sunder Nagri. We three would come by bus to reach for rehearsals at Abner Memorial. Rehearsals were at 2-2.30 in the afternoon.
>
> I acted in five versions of *Om Swaha*—from the second right up to the sixth. We must have done 300 to 350 shows over the years (interview 2015).

Malika and Theo later became pioneers of ecologically sustainable livelihoods in Uttarakhand: Malika with Maati Women's Collective, Theo with the National Tree Growers' Cooperative Federation; Malika also co-founded Himalayan Ark, based in Sarmoli village, Uttarakhand.

Kavita Ramdas has been CEO of the Global Fund for Women as well as Director of the Open Society Foundations' Women's Rights Program.

Others have joined academia or the media: Jyotika teaches Film Studies; Anand, Economics; Harsh currently edits the journal *Mainstream*; Suvritta teaches History at Deshbandu College, Delhi University; David is an author and political journalist; and Sanjoy is director of Teamwork Arts and the Jaipur Literature Festival.

[51] Lalita Ramdas and Feisal Alkazi started a Non-Formal Education project at Abner Memorial School. As their work and vision expanded, they set up the Ankur Society for Alternatives in Education (registered in 1983). This continues to be active today, in Delhi working-class localities. Lalita was later with Greenpeace and remains active in ecological and social movements.

[52] Runu was pursuing a BA in Economics from Ramjas College alongside her work with Action India, and Saheli. Later she worked with Jagori, Mahila Samakhya, and as an independent resource person. More recently, she and I enacted a few portions of *Om Swaha* for Action India members, as part of a memorial programme in Millenium Park, New Delhi, on 15 December 2022. When Runu sang in her powerful voice, everyone joined in!

Jyotika performed in *Om Swaha* through 1980-84, taking over the role of Kanchan in later shows, after Malika left. Jyotika recalls Maya training the group and getting the play off the ground—conducting theatre sessions, getting new actors into the script, working with bodies and movement. Ein Lall came too, to facilitate rehearsals. Previous *Om Swaha* group members came and did a performance for the new group, with Ayesha Heble in Hardeep's role, Maya as Kanchan, Pankaj Butalia as Hardeep's husband. Jyotika recalls (interview 2017),

> The theatre exercises and rehearsals at Abner were very cool... We were interested in theatre. College theatre was there, but this, street theatre, was very new. I remember being awed by this new form. It was so different from stage performances, which were really linear. I didn't have the words then, to understand or describe it.
>
> We weren't in it for theatre as much as for activism... When we performed, people would tear up—those dealing with the same issues.

David Devadas (interview 2015) recalls the workshops and rehearsal at Abner as being very powerful experiences. He found the brainstorming, sharing and trust exercises very impactful. David had been active in theatre right from school, in one-act play competitions. But *Om Swaha* was different: 'It was not about acting so much as about the purpose. It needed to be done, as our own little contribution to making a difference in society. It wasn't just entertainment, though that happened too.' He saw it as an effort at social reform, sensitising people to the plight of victims in conservative parts of society, especially middle-class joint families. It didn't connect to his own reality at all, since there was no dowry or oppression related to that in his family.

He recalls the marvelous group process, integral to *Om Swaha*:

> It was a cohesive organic group, impervious to some extent to social milieu and class. We could all relate—that was the best part of it. Imagine Sharda behn and Lalita Ramdas—Admiral Katari's daughter—together, thick as thieves! We all became like a group of friends. Sometimes we just hung around together and after rehearsals or a show, we'd go off to somebody's house. Lalita was older, so at first I called her Aunty, but she was firm she didn't want that. Gouri was always Gouri. Sharda behn was always Sharda behn.

He remembers, during stage productions, a great deal of nervousness and lots of management, people keyed up, going on and offstage, changing costumes, worrying about difficult lines. The *Om Swaha* experience was a contrast: 'Here, there was none of that.

There was a continuous flow without feeling any pressure of going on-stage or getting off. There was fluidity: we were continuously communicating, reaching out, touching the minds of the audience.' He found it fascinating, too, to be performing for completely unknown audiences—'Who knows who it was that stopped by?'

Sanjoy Roy (interview 2017) vividly remembers many people and lots of workshops: 'I remember all of us sitting on the floor in someone's house. We used to meet, discuss, rush off for protests; I remember standing in front of a big house with high gates in East of Kailash, where somebody had been burnt.' *Om Swaha* introduced him to a different world, and it was a revelation; he had grown up in London and Bombay, his Hindi was non-existent. He felt that he was fighting the establishment, rebelling against everything he came from. He got that sense from the conversations, discussions and camaraderie, learning Hindi, being part of a social process and getting to know people like Sharda behn.

Feisty older women led us down the garden path into activism. Here was an engagement with wider concerns, in some ways far more educative than what college was providing.

On 8 March 1981, the group performed *Om Swaha* at Karol Bagh Central Park. Theatre Union also performed the anti-rape play they had just made, *Dafa 180*. Several women's groups and independent feminists marched through Karol Bagh that day, marking International Women's Day with slogans, posters and leaflets condemning violence aginst women. The demonstration culminated at the Central Park. A large crowd of residents and passers-by gathered there, and watched the two plays. The atmosphere was electric: the plays made a tremendous impact.

The *Om Swaha* group performed in several localities where there had been incidents of 'dowry deaths'. In Jangpura, Tilak Nagar, Patel Nagar, performances were held in parks near houses where a woman had recently died of burns. Neighbours came out to see the play. In Patel Nagar, some of them spoke up about the frequent ill-treatment they had observed. Though earlier reluctant to get involved, the play had moved them and they prepared to give witness, testifying in court if needed.

The group performed in Pilakhuwa, a town some 75 kilometers from Delhi, where there had been a dowry death. Invited by local activists, the group traveled by public bus and stayed overnight in the activists'

Om Swaha, Karol Bagh, 8 March 1981. (Left to right) Malika Virdi (as Kanchan), Kavita Ramdas, Deepti, Jyotika Virdi, David Devadas, Lalita Ramdas, Runu Chakraborty.

Dafa 180, Karol Bagh, 8 March 1981. (Left to right) Ragini Prakash, Manohar Khushalani, Maya Rao, Anuradha Kapur.

homes. The performance was held in an open space in a residential colony, but it was a very different milieu and idiom; communication was poor, the response lackadaisical.

In Jahangirpuri, Sunder Nagri and other Delhi localities, people gathered, watched attentively, and discussed the issues thoughtfully. In Delhi University's Law Faculty, Arts Faculty, in various colleges, the Delhi School of Economics and so on, students and teachers would convene, and engage in animated discussions. The play was performed in bazaars, Nehru Place, outside police stations. Sometimes the response was palpable, at other times barely perceptible.

Audiences of *Om Swaha*. Intently viewing a performance; animated discussions post-performance; reading the accompanying leaflet; donating a one-rupee note.

A performance at the Boat Club drew a massive audience, of people who had been hanging about there. A middle-aged man was visibly moved, tears trickled down his cheeks. After the play ended, he shared, 'I have three daughters. I keep thinking: what will happen to them after marriage?' After a show at Central Park, Connaught Place, a woman in the audience wept, saying, 'My daughter recently returned from her sasural and didn't want to go back. But my husband sent her back. Next time my daughter comes and wants to stay, I will not let her be sent back. She will live with us if she wants to.'

Harsh Kapoor recalls (conversation 2022) that after the same show, 'There was a bandar-wala in the crowd. After we finished, he came up to us, his pair of monkeys in tow, and gave us some money. It was incredible. We probably used it up having samosas and chai!'

He notes that the audience of the time had a kind of innocence, which perhaps isn't possible today. There was an authenticity, their emotions were not trained. They weren't people who paid to come and see theatre; the actors went to them, and addressed them directly.

Harsh further remarks: '*Om Swaha* was spectacular. You don't get that quality today, in street plays that I've seen. What we experienced as theatre did something to us. We weren't out to make money, there was no brand we were promoting; it was a certain passion that drove us. We raised a wider social issue. It was very special.'

A Joint Anti-Dowry Front—While Dowry Carries On, So Does *Om Swaha*

In the early 80s, an anti-dowry front named Dahej Virodhi Chetna Manch was formed by several oganisations including Ankur, Action India, Karmika, Saheli, Mahila Dakshta Samiti, the All India Democratic Women's Association (AIDWA), All Indian Women's Conference (AIWC), Young Women's Christian Association (YWCA) and National Federation of Indian Women (NFIW). The joint front lobbied for appropriate legal changes and police investigations, along with public campaigns against dowry and bride-burning. It frequently called upon the *Om Swaha* group to perform in order to raise awareness, especially at venues where an incident had recently taken place. The play was staged at Masjid Moth in 1984, where a woman had been killed.

The anti-dowry front drew attention to the dereliction of duty on the part of law and justice agencies. In December 1980, Sudha Goel, nine months pregnant, was burnt in Ashok Vihar, north Delhi; she

Masjid Moth DDA Colony, Delhi, 1984. Parents of murdered women, *Bhookh Hartal—Shaheed betiyon ki maaon ki pukar, hamein insaaf chahiye* (Hunger Strike—Mothers of martyred daughters demand justice). *Jala Diya* (Burnt Her) painted by women activists on the Masjid Moth culprits' house. People sign a memo demanding justice. *Om Swaha* actors (left to right) Malika Virdi and Sharda behn hold post-performance discussion with neighbours, Sanjoy Roy (on right) spreads a shawl to collect donations.

stated that her husband, mother-in-law and brother-in-law set her on fire. She died at St Stephen's hospital, of second-degree burns. In May 1983, the Sessions Court pronounced death sentences for Sudha's husband Laxman Goel, her mother-in-law Shakuntala Devi and brother-in-law Subhash Goel. The Delhi High Court, however, subsequently acquitted them, observing: 'It is customary for Hindus that on the delivery of a first child, particularly the birth of a male child, the parents give presents. The in-laws or husband may have felt the need of a scooter and a refrigerator and therefore, wanted the deceased to demand a frigidaire and a scooter [from her parents]' (Shakuntala & Ors vs the State 1983).

The *Om Swaha* team added a section within the play including quotes from the High Court judgment and testimonies from neighbours who bore witness:

> Neighbour 1: Sudha Goel was burning. I took a blanket from my house to wrap around her and save her.
>
> Neighbour 2: We took her to hospital.
>
> Neighbour 3: We went to court, spending our money, and gave witness.
>
> Neighbour 4: But what did all this achieve?
>
> Neighbour 5: On 27 May 1983, the Sessions Court awarded a death verdict to Sudha's mother-in-law, husband and brother-in-law, thus making history.
>
> Sutradhar: Hey stop! On 3 November 1983, two honourable judges of the High Court overturned this judgment, and released all three criminals. According to them:
>
> Judge: A married man, father of children, can never kill the wife of his own brother. Therefore, I consider Sudha's brother-in-law to be innocent....
>
> Judge: While boiling milk, Sudha died due to [the] stove exploding.
>
> Sutradhar: What kinds of stoves are being manufactured nowadays, that explode as soon as young women, daughters-in-law, touch them!
>
> Chorus (song): *Andher nagri chaupat nyaya, hatyaare parivaar ko judge bachaaye!'* (Dark city, no justice here, A family of murderers, the judge their saviour!)

This updated version of *Om Swaha* was performed in Ashok Vihar in early 1984. Among the cast was a new member, Savita Sharma. She recalls (interview 2015): 'We did *Om Swaha* in the park in front of Deep

Cinema, near Sudha Goel's in-laws' house. Neighbours were so worked up about the judgment that we all held a spontaneous demonstration, in front of Sudha Goel's husband's shop. It was nearby.'

Delhi State as well as the Indian Federation of Women Lawyers filed an appeal in the Supreme Court, challenging the High Court judgment. During these hearings, women's groups often held meetings outside the Supreme Court, sang songs, got *Om Swaha* to perform a couple of times, and once formed a people's chain surrounding the court. Subhadra Butalia was arrested during a meeting in the court premises, along with Suman Krishna Kant of Mahila Dakshta Samiti, and Brinda Karat of AIDWA; all three were charged with contempt of court. This was stressful and scary. They were summoned separately by a panel of judges, to explain their points of view. In her defense, Subhadra asked, 'When you acquit those who are accused in dowry cases and we feel hurt, what can we do except protest? I simply gave vent to my resentment which is my fundamental right in a free society' (Butalia 2002: 111). Eventually, all three were cleared of the charge.

In September 1985, the Supreme Court held Laxman Goel and Shakuntala Devi guilty of Sudha Goel's murder, and meted out life imprisonment to both, noting clear evidence that the deceased had been subjected to physical and mental torture for quite some time; dowry demands had been made, kerosene was sprinkled on her clothes and she was set on fire. Her husband and mother-in-law were held responsible for the killing (Delhi State vs Laxman Goel & Ors 1985).

Like the rest of Delhi's women's movement and human rights activists, *Om Swaha* members were shocked by the anti-Sikh carnage that followed Indira Gandhi's assassination on 31 October 1984. Most got involved with relief camps and rehabilitation work, resulting in a long break from the play. Runu remembers reaching Abner for a rehearsal the day Indira Gandhi was killed—she didn't know about it yet. Nobody else came. That same evening the carnage began in many parts of Delhi, and the activists plunged into dealing with the terrible tragedy.

After some months, the group picked up *Om Swaha* and began performing again. Usually they performed in response to an urgent need that came up in their work with communities, or when somebody requested a show. The Dahej Virodhi Chetna Manch was active up to 1990 and a little beyond. Meanwhile, several erstwhile *Om Swaha* actors got involved in other street plays, as we shall see in Sections Three and Four.

Tracing Impact

Following *Om Swaha,* scores of plays on dowry and bride-burning were produced and performed across the country by women's organisations, colleges, schools, youth clubs and informal associations. This flurry of plays was an emphatic declaration of outrage: business as usual would no longer be tolerated.

Dowry demands and bride-burning became recognised as issues in the public domain. The understanding continued to evolve; today, dowry is no longer seen as *the* central issue per se: feminist activists now emphasise daughters' (women's) rights to inheritance, and continue to battle the widespread prevalence of gender-based violence.

Sheba Chhachhi, who co-founded Jagori, a women's resource centre, in 1984, recalls that when, in 1986, they put out a call for scripts of women's street plays, groups across the country responded. At least 80 of the scripts that they sent were patterned on *Om Swaha*! They may have been adapted to local idioms and contexts or carried a different name, but most were presented almost as if independently produced by that small group somewhere. There was need for such a play, and many people simply adopted *Om Swaha* and made it their own.

Scouring the net in 2015, I found a video recording of *Om Swaha* performed by students of the Indian Institute of Technology (IIT), Mumbai on 8 March 1983.[53] It was their debut performance, done with great energy and passion. Directed by Ravindra Shevade, actors included Chayanika Shah, Rekha Hatakanagalekar, Deepti Pradhan, Paritosh Dhavale, Vinay Sane, Abhay Patil, Ajit Gaunekar, Sujit, Jagriti (among others); the subjects they were studying included maths, physics, electrical engineering and chemical engineering. Their play faithfully

[53] Video recording of *Om Swaha* (1983), cinematography by Shaibani, performance by IIT Mumbai students, posted by Abhay Patil on 13 July 2014. Available: www.youtube.com/watch?v=3C-U2Vk99hc (last accessed 12 August 2015). Chayanika Shah studied and taught Physics, and is a writer and activist with LABIA Queer Feminist LBT Collective. Rekha Hatakanagalekar studied Maths. Deepti Pradhan studied bio-organic chemistry and researched and taught at Yale, where she also runs a science café. Paritosh Dhawale studied engineering, and is at GE Healthcare. Vinay Sane studied electrical engineering, worked as an engineer, and is now a full-time artist. Ravindra Shevade studied chemical engineering, and is an independent technology consultant. These brief bios give us some sense of the diversity of the young people who performed *Om Swaha.*

followed the script the Delhi *Om Swaha* group was then performing; they credited the script to Theatre Union. However, the production lacked some of the vivid imagery, quicksilver moves, rhythm and music of the original. On the other hand, the Mumbai group was far more advanced in recognising the value of video recording, than the Delhi crowd!

When I elicit Anand Swamy's recollections of *Om Swaha*, in a flash he recites lines he, as Hardeep's husband, used to chant while battering her: '*Na das lakh na chheh lakh, na teen lakh na ek lakh...*' (interview, 2014). The entire, long litany seems etched in memory; Runu, too, replays the ominous chant, and also belts out songs from the play. For many of the actors, when we jog our memories, the old words come spilling out. Such recall across the decades speaks volumes about the extraordinary quality of the lines, and the indelible impact of the play on its youthful performers.

The power of the medium, its quality of engagement with a wide public, taught confidence. Reserved young women in particular, brought up within norms of polite feminine behavior, gained confidence, buoyed by passion for a cause. As they became more assertive, spoke their minds, stepped out at odd hours to remote places, families reacted variously. My parents, like those of several others, were a tad uncomfortable with our performing in public spaces such as streets, parks and marketplaces. Though they both appreciated the social reform agenda, my father sometime felt that I had been 'given too much freedom'. Years later, however, he proudly introduced me as a feminist 'active in dowry cases even when she was a student, going to help at night if needed!' Personal change happens in unpredictable ways; as one woman changes, people close to her might start changing too.

Manohar Khushalani, who acted in *Om Swaha* several times, says: 'The play affected me so much that later, when we had a daughter, I made sure we named her Kanchan!' (conversation 2019). He wanted his daughter to grow up strong, a person who stands up for her rights, walking out if need be, from any oppressive structure.

Om Swaha merged with activism, and helped influence mass media. David Devadas notes (interview 2015), 'When I became a journalist, I tried to cover dowry, domestic violence. I found that by the late 80s there was awareness. Dowry and violence were being talked about, written about, in magazines, at seminars, lectures. That conscientisation was achieved in part due to the street plays. They reached segments of society that may not have been reached otherwise.'

SECTION THREE

EHSAAS: CHALLENGING EVERYDAY SEXISM

> Girls: ... this year too, no girls' hostel will be made?
> Principal: No, no, no! Girls' hostel has many problems. Who wants to take risks?
> ... Announcement: Girls are hereby informed that they must reach their hostel rooms before 7 p.m. If any girl does not do so, all kinds of accusations will be leveled against her!
>
> – *Ehsaas*

> 'The conditions at home have not changed. But there is a definite change in me.' She was learning to assert herself more.
>
> – *Ancy et al. (1979-80: 24)*

> The street theatre is not trying to please, but it is more of a fight. In that there is dignity.
>
> – *Tripurari Sharma (Sharma and Krishnamurty 2000: 16)*

> The line between self-enjoyment and performance is very thin, but distinct. To cross over implies first and foremost an awareness of being watched, observed by a circle of onlookers. To remain relaxed and skillfully competent in their presence is a demanding task and it requires a level of concentration and discipline to accomplish.
>
> – *Tripurari Sharma (Ibid.)*

The word *Ehsaas* means perception, awareness, or a strong feeling based on experience. There is a sense of the direct cognition of reality, something we feel in our bones, as it were. It may be an emotional truth that we realise, or a fact about society. Made in 1979, *Ehsaas* (the play) brought out women's everyday experiences of discrimination and abuse, and the process of their growing awareness and feelings of pain and anger, interspersed with glimmerings of protest.

This section documents the journey of *Ehsaas*—how the play was created and performed, and its significance as the first street play we know of that explores chronic, everyday sexism. We will see how the play was made, based on women's sharing within a feminist theatre workshop held at Delhi University, which included participants from outside the university as well. The first performances were held in late 1979 and early 1980, but due to time and other constraints, the group soon fizzled out.

The next two chapters trace how and why *Ehsaas* saw the light of day again, and the long, adventurous path upon which it then embarked. Chapter 8 traces a group of students from Delhi University coming together and building an anti-sexual harassment campaign during the first three months of 1982. Chapter 9 shows how this context provided a new lease of life to *Ehsaas*: the group found the play, adapted and performed it for several years (1982-87). It became the fulcrum around which they continued to meet, work together and reach out in an effort to deepen and expand their campaign for women's rights. A self-organised informal student's group, their journey with *Ehsaas* was meaningful, in some ways more than formal education. It afforded real learning, as understanding evolved through autonomous action, and interaction with multiple audiences.

The *Ehsaas* group was invited to perform in university spaces and outside, in Delhi and elsewhere. The performances contributed to a growing critical awareness of gender. They helped sensitise audiences, encourage dissent, and spin some of the early threads that got intertwined into future active struggles, as well as feminist studies.

7

Sharing Experiences, Shaping a Play

Ehsaas developed from actual sharing by a group of women in a safe space: a skillfully designed feminist theatre workshop. It was experimental and participatory, pioneering an approach that encouraged interweaving of collective personal experience, yielding an original theatrical production. The play produced by the group underlined oppression, and indicated revolt.

Feminist Theatre Workshop

November 1979: On my college noticeboard, a small notice appeared, announcing a women's theatre workshop to be held in Miranda House (MH).[54] Having been in St Stephen's college since July 1979, I was reeling under the impact of its overly masculine ethos: male-only hostels, a six-to-one ratio of male to female students in my Economics class, our teachers all men. A women's theatre workshop would be a huge relief!

The workshop was held at Ruth Vanita's[55] room in the MH hostel, organised under the aegis of *Manushi,*[56]a pioneering feminist journal

---

[54] MH, situated within the main DU campus, was founded in 1948. It has a proud record of student activism and activist teachers. Uma Chakravarti taught there, and *Om Swaha* actors Anuradha Kapur, Maya Rao, Urvashi Butalia and Ayesha Heble are MH alumnae.

[55] Ruth Vanita was co-founder and co-editor of *Manushi* (1978-1990). She is now Professor of Liberal Studies and Women's Studies at the University of Montana, and a prolific writer.

[56] *Manushi* was a key part of the women's movement in the 80s, carrying reportage and analysis on dowry, domestic violence, sexual harassment, protests, theatre, films, and much more. Its politics changed from feminist and secular to right-wing by the late 90s.

launched in January 1979. Ruth, who taught English Literature at MH and co-edited *Manushi*, participated in the workshop. Several young women joined the workshop, of whom around ten remained up to the end—including a student from IIT Delhi, some from MH, and a couple of women from outside the university. The youngest participant was 18, the older ones were in their late twenties.

Tripurari Sharma, recently graduated from the National School of Drama (NSD), facilitated the workshop. Ruth co-facilitated while Madhu Kishwar,[57] *Manushi's* co-editor, participated occasionally.

Workshop sessions commenced in early December. It was an intensive, immersive experience—three or four hours every afternoon. Our initial trepidation soon melted away; we relaxed, enjoying the theatre exercises and games: walking on cotton-wool, on scorching sand, crouching into tight balls, opening up, reaching towards the sky, walking dwarf-like, expanding into giants, breaking through the roof. We slithered, bumped, laughed, as tension flowed out of our bodies. Hearts lifted, imaginations soared.

Spontaneity emerged, amidst laughter and tears. We played Trust: one person stands with the others around her; she falls, limp, and the rest must hold her. Fear and distrust gave way, for nobody ever fell down: the person falling was always held by the group. The game became pleasurable as we recognised generosity, caring, and a sense of responsibility in one another. Perhaps some deep disturbance shifted, and something more tranquil began clicking into place.

We played Mirror: dividing into pairs, one reflects the other, becomes her mirror image. It requires total attention; each one learns to follow, and to lead. We played Action-Reaction: one person carries out an action, her partner 'reacts' to it, performing an action that complements the first, and so it flows on.

Voice exercises took us through highs and lows—whispers, screams. We made O, AA, EE vowel-sounds, felt vibrations in the pit of one's stomach, chest, throat, the hum in one's head. We chuckled, cackled, and were surprised at the sounds we could make. For some it was difficult to laugh aloud, for others it seemed impossible to shout. We did what we were comfortable doing—and then a little more.

The activities helped us shed inhibitions, stretch fingers, torsos, limbs in new ways, loosen up. We interacted, gelled as a team, and took

[57] Madhu Kishwar has been a Fellow at the Centre for the Study of Developing Societies and is currently a professor at the Indian Council of Social Science Research.

our exploration into the realms of emotion and mind. We talked about our lives, each day. We learnt of diverse backgrounds: Ruth's puritanical upbringing, Asha's battles in the male-dominated IIT, another's battle against discrimination vis-à-vis her brother, yet another overworked, fending for her whole family. My frustrations weren't easy to articulate—restrictions on mobility, sexuality, a prescriptive moral code of behaviour, taboos forming invisible boundaries, psychological shackles.

We were all sick of sexual harassment—of men leering and grabbing in DTC buses, on the streets, in parks, cinema halls, anywhere. It was terrifying. One of the students spoke of travelling by public bus a couple of years earlier, when she was still a schoolgirl, of a hand suddenly groping beneath her school skirt, touching her thighs... her blood froze. She had never told anybody about it—she felt ashamed, as if filth from dirty hands, eyes, minds, had rubbed off onto her skin.

We hinted at experiences for which we didn't have a name: terms like 'child sexual abuse' were not in circulation at the time. We had the experiences but not the words to describe them, nor the skills to deal with them, or to care for ourselves. It turned out that we lived in fear, all of us. Each one was on her guard, wary of insult or molestation by a man on a motorcycle, in a crowded bus, on a dark road.

A mountain of experiences gathered: discrimination, neglect, hurt and humiliation. Several of us spoke of our mothers slaving from morning to night, cooking, cleaning, caring, perhaps doing a job too, unwell, unfulfilled—and a circle of pain flowed between us.

We felt our words being valued, and self-confidence reared its head. We began to recognise negative patterns which leech self-esteem, clip the soul. Growing up 'sheltered' could translate into cultivated ignorance; denying our desires, downplaying our rights. A process of self-exploration was sparked. Simultaneously, we began to role-play, improvise: it was a seamless move into theatre.

Shaping the Play

An article titled 'A Women's Theatre Workshop', by Ancy, Anita, Asha, Deepti, Fatima, Seema, Sanjeevani, Ruth, Madhu and Tripurari (1979-80: 24), describes the powerful workshop process:

> ...a group of us in Delhi came together in an attempt to evolve a play out of our concerns. We decided not to work on any social issue,

> however important, unless it was also a personally felt issue. So we began by talking to each other about our lives, our problems, our anger. This was difficult, often painful to begin with, but even though we are women from very different backgrounds, gradually we began to see commonness in our predicament. At some point or other, we had all felt constrained and imprisoned by the fact of being women in this society—whether it was in the family, on the roads, in college or school, in male-dominated professions or with male friends.
>
> As we began to see this commonness, we developed a script which expressed our feeling of oppression and our need to break out of it, by coming together in struggle. The experience of making the play was a unique one because most of us had never acted before. We improvised and acted out situations from our own lives in our mother tongues, ranging from Malayalam to Punjabi, and then translated them into Hindi. The play was a collective creation with no 'director' or 'script writer'.
>
> Most significant was the fact that we, who were absolute strangers to each other, could in 15 days develop a sense of sisterhood and become intimately involved with each others' personal problems. We were able to see that these problems were not peculiar to any individual but were our common problems as women.
>
> We did face many difficulties because some of us were prevented from participation by our parents and had to confront traumatic situations at home. At times, it seemed near impossible to complete the project but we carried on. And amazing as it may seem, we too began to change in this short period. As one of us put it, 'The conditions at home have not changed. But there is a definite change in me.' She was learning to assert herself more. We had begun to analyse and question what we had been taught to accept, we began to see that it was possible to challenge unjust authority, that other women had challenged it. And we began to do things we had never imagined we were capable of doing, even if it was just a quiet girl learning to sing and speak loudly, or to find her way home alone...

Immersed in the experiential, we role-played, enacting family scenes, dialogues with friends, street scenes, using prompts such as, 'It's a dark road, you're walking alone' or 'You reach home late one evening'. Varied backgrounds helped bring in a width of experiences: from the thoughtful Asha of IIT-Delhi, to first-year students just out of their homes, to hard-pressed working women. Each one added her bit, and quite spontaneously we collectively built up a dramatic sequence.

Tripurari noted, 'A theatre workshop is not judgmental—it makes and provides space for divergent views and people. But one thing that these girls had in common was an urge to shape their lives themselves and not be shaped by the existing moulds or role models'. There were, of course, differences within the group: 'Some brought their strengths to the workshop, others their doubts. There was sharing and there was disagreement, but the differences did not pull us adrift'. She discovered layers of creativity within each person, and a sensitivity to speech, comment and gaze: 'they spoke of "vibrations" at home when they reached late, and being jostled in the bus by passers-by who intruded into their privacy by the way they looked at them.' (Sharma 2013: 140-41)

Some of this got transmuted into dialogues, lyrics and dramatic sequences. Our improvised sequences stitched together like a patchwork quilt. Tripurari, with Ruth, gathered voices, words, to mix, blend and distill into a rough script. A structure emerged, stabilised. It became a fledgling play, a montage of vignettes, words and images. Characters were not given names, rather they were familiar archetypes—mother, daughter, school-teacher, school-girl, father, brother, girlfriend, boyfriend, wife, husband, and finally the perceptive, outspoken woman, emerging out of a morass of ascribed roles, determined to carve out her own identity.

Improvisation merged into rehearsal. Drama, in this mode, is born three-dimensional, in the form in which it is performed rather than as a two-dimensionsal written script. Even while rehearsing we added words, honed gestures. Absorbed in the moment, most of us were barely aware that soon an audience might sit around us. Caught in a flurry of blocking, moving, cues, our lines and bodies fell into a coordinated rhythm.

We chanted rather than sang. A little later, when we rehearsed outside MH, Tripurari invited her colleague Ravi Baswani to help us sing; he couldn't be invited into MH since it was out of bounds for men.

We called the play 'Ehsaas'—a living-breathing word, expressing some of our collective feelings and growing awareness. The play held fragments of different lives, like colourful shards in a kaleidoscope. The art of theatre made a whole, a pattern, out of these shards. Each fragment had a place, sparkling with meaning.

Most of the participants were new to theatre. Nor had we seen or even heard of street theatre. We had little idea what we were heading towards. Had we known, some of us may never have joined the workshop, daunted by the prospect of acting amid huge crowds, out in the open!

Performing: The First Shows

The first performance was on 19 December 1979, held in the large open ground within the MH hostel. In the early evening about a hundred hostellers gathered, buzzing with excitement, and settled around us.

The play opens with a schoolteacher asking little girls what they want to be when they grow up; she frowns at ambitions like doctor or pilot, instead teaches them: 'I will be a good girl, ... good wife, good mother'. They recite, in a sing-song chant:

Ooncha mat bolo, ooncha mat hanso,
Ooncha mat dekho, bas neeche hee neeche,
Duniya tumhari...

(Don't speak loudly, laugh loudly,
Don't aim high,
Your world is down, down, down...)

The next scene portrays women: washing clothes, chopping vegetables, making pickle, calling out to each other:

'I am a good wife.'
'I follow my husband, walk behind him wherever he goes.'
'Eat after he eats.'
'Do what he says.'
'Never answer back.'
'He beats, I suffer silently.'
'I look after his relatives, have forgotten mine.'
'I let him sleep beside me, gave birth to the child he wanted!'

One woman dreams of wafting through closed doors, away from the dark house, and spreading, a free spirit... But her frenetic reality holds: rushing home from office in a crowded bus, going straight into the kitchen while her husband reads the newspaper... Her daughter laments her mother's chronic ailments: a disease called 'goodness' has eaten into her, like white ants; she neither sings nor laughs; her body aches, her feet burn.

A street scene, women's bodies taut, defensive: '*Sambhal kar chalo, dekh kar chalo...*' (Be cautious, protect yourself, be alert...). A woman: 'Hands crept, groping wherever they could... I was alone in the crowded

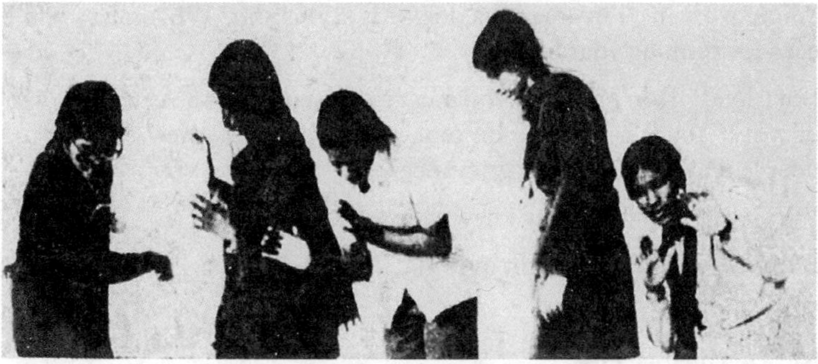

Ehsaas, Delhi, 1979-80. Street Scene: '*Sambhal kar chalo, dekh kar chalo*'. (Left to right) Ancy, Deepti, two unidentified actors, Fatima.

bus as they closed in, eyes, hands, arms, legs, private parts, greedy, ruthless. To save myself from their assault I became small, smaller; if I only could shrink and vanish! I regretted my very existence. What most hurt was that all this was deliberately thrust upon me!' A woman suggests, 'Can't we get together and confront such men? Instead of watching silently, paint their faces and leave them in the back-alleys?' A third says, 'This can happen. But usually it doesn't!'

A young woman returns home 'late'; her brother hurls accusations, her mother advises her to suppress herself and learn to adjust to a male-dominated world. She has secured admission in IIT; the mother is proud of her, but the father insists on marrying her off. A stranger blindfolds her, and leads her 'home'; he claims to love her, and will therefore not allow her to go out alone or take up work. The entire situation gnaws at her self-esteem. She wants to see the world with her own eyes. She pushes limits a little further each day, realises she is capable of much, and decides to live out her dreams, even if they don't fit with the man's.

A parallel scenario: A young woman studies engineering. Her boyfriend insists she give it up, declaring the profession is too demanding for a woman.

Blindfolded and taken 'home'.

Young woman: 'I'm amazed a doctor is saying this! What salary will I earn for running your house?'

Boyfriend: 'Don't be silly! You must understand, it is a very tough line of work. You'll have to go on tour, inside factories, meet all kinds of people. Labour problems, grievances...'

YW: It's tough, that's why I have chosen it!

BF: Do I not have any right over you?

YW: Not in this matter!

BF: Do you love me?

YW: Yes...

BF: Then I will not let you go!

She decides to pursue her own path; every day her world expands.

'I looked out, and saw the world with my own eyes.'

The final scene has two women:

One: I've come a long way. Could I rest here for a while?

Two: Yes sure, come, sit! Let's talk...

One: ... There was a man. He said he loves me...!

Two: ... That's why he stopped me from doing anything.

One: I chiseled a tiny hole in the wall. Every day, it grew. I looked out, and saw the world with my own eyes. I stepped out. He had lied, that I'm delicate, I'll lose my way. I went everywhere! I read lots, I understood everything!

Two: He kept saying don't go! I stepped out, on my path... There used to be a window, through which we exchanged sweet nothings. Now, there's no window—there's only the road!

The play closes with a collective song, reiterating the themes of pain and resilience, as well as solidarity and friendship:

'Vo ehsaas bataati hoon,
Raat raat bhar lambi baatein,
Paas hamein jo layeingi—
Sapne jo vo le gaye,
Sapne jo jee utthe hain,
Tere mere jeevan me,
Vo ehsaas sunaati hoon!'

[I tell of those experiences, many stories over many nights, which will bring us close—dreams they stole away, dreams that have awakened, in your life and mine, I speak of those realisations.]

The audience watched intently. Questions hung in the air. Some students commented hesitantly, others confidently. Young women came to MH from different parts of the country; it meant a lot to study in this highly reputed college. Every evening they were locked up, like precious commodities; hostel authorities claimed that that's what parents wanted. But what did these young women want? The play touched a raw nerve; some of their own emotions were mirrored back to them. Many felt it as a welcome shock. There was a strong sense of connection; they began to verbalise similar experiences. Thoughtful teachers welcomed the intervention, the conversations initiated.

For the actors, this first-time performance was momentous. Stunned by the response, we realised the incredible power of the medium: alert eyes surrounding us, empathy writ large. We shared our experiences via the play, and emerged feeling stronger, rather than more vulnerable. A tiny group of women had made the play, and the performance drew in a wider circle. The gravity of this work, which we had taken up almost unknowingly, began to sink in.

For the second performance, we thought of the Central Institute of Education (CIE), which is adjacent to MH. We performed in the spacious grounds of one of the staff quarters at CIE, by the side-garden, with tall jamun and mulberry trees overhead.

CIE faculty members came—teacher educators Drs Jain, Katiyar, RP Sharma the philosopher, Hindi scholar Anand Prakash Vyas, psychologist Saradamani Devi, my mother who specialised in language, and my father who specialised in maths.[58] Hostel residents gathered: Jayshree Mathur, pursuing her PhD in the philosophy of education, Ranjana Srivastava, who was working on educational policy, and several others. They settled on the grass with a handful of day students, while most staff members sat on chairs.

The audience was serious, absorbed. Dr Sharma was impressed by the form, finding it powerful and impactful. Saradamani Devi was enthusiastic about challenging gender discrimination; she herself was single by choice—'because once you're married, you can't read a word!' The performance held a special charge for me, since the audience included my family and de facto extended family. There was some consternation amongst the more conservative, whose notions of women's roles, gender and family life didn't accord with ours.

My mother was intensely supportive. Not so long before that, she'd written and directed a docu-drama called *SHE*, depicting the lives of several women and staged in the CIE hall. She enjoyed hosting the *Ehsaas* performance, and readily opened up the space as a venue for rehearsals. Thereafter, we would gather in the side-garden, and perfect our act. Ravi Baswani came a few times, set the songs to music, and tutored us in singing.

We performed next in the Post-Graduate Women's Hostel, just across the road. Hostel residents were appreciative and articulate. They were subject to restrictive rules, similar to the MH hostellers, despite being older. 'How long is curfew supposed to carry on?' one asked. 'Until we marry and are docked safely in the sasural!' answered another.

---

[58] My parents taught at the Central Institute of Education and we lived in this particular house.

With the academic term drawing to a close, the university campus began to empty out. As winter vacations began, *Ehsaas* decided to shift to Lajpat Nagar, a middle-class colony in south Delhi, where *Manushi* worked out of a rented house.

In Lajpat Nagar, the actors encountered a completely different audience. *Ehsaas* performances were held within homes—sometimes in an angan (courtyard), at other times on a chhat (rooftop terrace). These were homes inhabited by Punjabi families, who had typically come into Delhi as Partition refugees. During the day, while the men were out, the angans and chhats were quintessential woman-space: here they chopped vegetables, prepared pickle, washed clothes, chatted and rested awhile, basking in the winter sun, gazing at the open sky, dreaming a little.

The audience, homebodies clad in baggy salwar kurtas, seemed to be very different from the university audience. They watched as intently though, eyes shining with tears, empathy or horror. The performance seemed to melt the distance between us, it stirred their emotions and they too had stories to share, from their own storehouses of experience. It was a shock to listen to their broken narratives. Beneath robust practicality festered grief, their suffering stretching across the decades, wove into the minutiae of daily life.

Satya Kaur told us she married at 13, and spent her entire life since then serving a man who hardly ever looked at her or smiled, but who ordered, and criticised. Munni spoke of a daughter harassed by in-laws, and how she had dreamt that her daughter would lead a better life than her own. Gurpreet said she'd been taught girls shouldn't speak too much—*zubaan nahin chalaani chahiye*, it only gets them into trouble.

Such sharing allowed us a glimpse into their lives, revealing a continuum between their experiences and ours: the expectation that girls should be quiet and docile, for instance, was shared. Discussion continued over tea, which the hosts would prepare, a milky sweet broth with ginger and cardamom, very welcome in the December-January chill. We, too, wore baggy salwar kurtas, wrapping sweaters and shawls around ourselves.

It was an extraordinary learning experience. These women described their daily grind, and it felt like it was out of our play: unceasing thankless drudgery, the tearing pain of sending away one's daughter, rage at violence inflicted, aspirations crushed. *Ehsaas* effectively created an atmosphere of trust, where confidences could be shared. We were much younger than most of them, and yet this intimate woman-talk ensued. Perhaps it was that conveying emotions so frankly in the play touched a raw nerve throbbing in their bodies. Though they did not speak of the trauma of Partition, it lurked beneath their anguished words; a deeper engagement would perhaps have helped elicit those memories.

After university reopened in January, we resumed performances there. We presented the play in MH and CIE again, for the entire college body each time; and at Daulat Ram College, Delhi School of Economics, the Arts Faculty lawns and a couple of other spots. Everywhere, the response was positive, and discussion sparked off.

In February, there was a lull, since several members were unable to spare the time to participate. In the joint article referenced earlier, the *Ehsaas* team wrote that a few performances had been held, followed by discussions, adding, 'We hope to expand the group through such discussions and gradually to develop a women's theatre which can be a means for women to reach out to each other.' (Ancy et al. 1979-80: 24)

However, the group never met again, it just seemed to fizzle away.[59] Ten to twelve performances of a play, and then closing down may not seem unusual. Much of theatre is done with fewer performances, and then the production winds up. Yet it felt sad to put aside a play so lovingly made, its potential barely tapped.

Happily, another set of people, two and a half years later, picked up the script and adopted it. They took it to heart and performed it for quite a while. Thus the first stint, between 1979-80, was only the beginning of the *Ehsaas* story: almost just a prelude to its larger, longer playing out.

[59] Manushi made a street play, *Roshni,* in 1986, which had a defined set of characters, a central problem and a resolution, unlike *Ehsaas* and most feminist street plays, which are open-ended, and do not provide any neat resolution. *Roshni* depicted a spirited girl who questions discrimination at home; she later takes up a job, and rejects marriage, asserting that her priority is to become strong and capable. Feisal Alkazi facilitated the theatre workshop, and Ruth Vanita scripted the play on the basis of group improvisations. It was performed by a team of eleven women, and evoked a positive audience response (Manushi Collective 1987).

8

#MeToo of the 80s
Women Students Organise

In the summer of 1982, a group of students discovered *Ehsaas*, made it their own, and performed it over the next few years. This group did not begin as a theatre troupe; it was first formed spontaneously, to rally against sexual harassment. A number of women students got together, January 1982 onward, and built up an anti-sexual harassment campaign in Delhi University, bringing some core issues into the public eye and winning considerable solidarity and sympathy. In July 1982, they took up and adapted *Ehsaas*, seeing it as a way to expand conversations on sexual harassment, and a range of women's issues.

We will trace, in this chapter, the genesis of this feminist students' group within the crucible of the anti-sexual harassment campaign. The next chapter will track the youthful group's journeys with *Ehsaas* over the next few years.

Sexual Harassment

On Friday, 20 March 1981, a gang of about sixty ruffians walked into St Stephen's College, drumming on tin cans, shouting 'Holi Hai!' They entered from a side gate into the nimbu-pani stall and then the college café, the main college building visible across a large open ground. It was a holiday, since the next day was Holi. The Principal, a handful of staff members, and plenty of male students, predominantly hostel residents, were on campus. Two extra classes had been scheduled that day, for which a few women students had come, some travelling by family car for the sake of safety. Most women students kept away, rough play in the name of Holi being a menace in buses and on roads for several days preceding the festival.

But here was rough play, within the college itself! The ruffians quickly isolated the women they found and forcibly rubbed gulal on them, groping bodies, tearing clothes. The assault was devastating, that too in a space that was supposed to be absolutely safe. The women were surrounded and overpowered by the gang, despite resisting, screaming and hitting out in self-protection. Male students, teachers, and the Principal were unable to prevent the assault. Perhaps they were too taken aback to do anything effective: neither did they physical defend the women, nor did they call the police. Who could imagine such a scenario within one's own highfalutin college? One male student, who was in the café when the goons came bursting in, explained later that he tried to intervene, but backed off when they threatened him.

The gang carried neither knives nor guns, only rough-hewn tin drums and dry Holi colors; yet they were able to freely waylay and molest women students. One student later narrated, on condition of anonymity:

> They rushed into the café and in a flash, yanked me from my chair, and pulled me outside. They pushed me to the ground. I have never been so terrified in my life. They were laughing raucously. I felt they will rape me. They dragged me to the nimbu-pani stall; then suddenly left. Thank god! I was in a complete state of shock. (Student, interview 1981)

The goons obviously realised there had to be some limit: after all, it was broad daylight. One lot had rushed into the main building, where they caught hold of a few women students in a classroom. After about half an hour of wreaking havoc, the entire gang left on their own, triumphantly beating drums. Nobody intercepted or tried to apprehend them.

The violated students were traumatised. Some were brave enough to want to file a police report. The Principal forbade them from doing so, declaring it would mean further trouble. This seems to have been his sole contribution to protecting them. They were invited to teachers' homes, to borrow clothes from wives and daughters. Many survivors never told their parents about the assault: 'My parents would simply pull me out of college' (Student, interview 1981).[60] They tried to forget, and carry on with their lives.

---

[60] The interview was given on condition of anonymity. It was a relief for her to speak about the traumatic incident, but she was clear her identity should not be disclosed.

The incident might have remained concealed had some women not made an effort to expose, record and protest it. On Monday 23 March, students and teachers from the IP College Women's Committee organised a demonstration in conjunction with a handful of Stephanian women. Within Stephen's, a shroud of silence prevailed, yet quite a few joined the protest. It felt tremendously strengthening. We wound our way through Stephen's, in and out of several streets, colleges, faculties and university grounds, holding placards, shouting slogans, 'Women's Safety Women's Right', '*Nari Ekta Zindabad!*' (Women's Unity Will Live Forever!) and '*Har zor zulm ki takkar mein, Sangharsh hamara nara hai!*' (In every battle of power, of exploitation, Struggle is our motto!). Many more students and teachers joined all along the route.

To protest was a relief; at least the assault was being challenged. But later that day, in the college café, one of the waiters, Jagdish, confided, 'Some men in the demonstration, walking with you all, were in the gang that day, they harassed women. I saw them then and again today!' This revelation was deeply disturbing. A few hundred persons had joined the demo, and it would be impossible to get them together again for Jagdish to identify.

Hardly any of the survivors had joined the demonstration; most were trying to forget about the episode. Through word of mouth, I tracked down some survivors, and elicited their testimonies. I think they were relieved to simply talk, on condition of absolute confidentiality. I asked some male students who had been present on campus to narrate what they had witnessed. It is on the basis of these testimonies of survivors and witnesses that it became possible to roughly reconstruct this sequence of events (Priya 1985).

College authorities, as well as the Students' Union, maintained a studied silence on the entire ugly episode of 20 March '81. It was as if it had never happened. Even earlier, several women students were uneasy about aspects of gender discrimination and sexism within the college. They now felt anew the strong undercurrents of misogyny, condoning male aggression and trivialising violence against women.

Our experiences at university resonated with the wider women's movement. After repeated incidents involving the sexual harassment of students and teachers in DTC (Delhi Transport Corporation) buses, on 23 February 1979, the IP Women's Committee mobilised 800 women, largely from women's colleges, who marched through Daryaganj and Bahadur Shah Zafar Marg in central Delhi (Vanita 1979). They gave a memorandum to the Police Commissioner and DTC, demanding the setting up of appropriate preventive mechanisms. As a result of this protest, the issue was discussed in parliament on 27 February 1979. Thereafter, every DTC bus put up signs saying 'Eve-teasing is an offence'. Of course, this was not sufficient, but at least it was incipient official recognition of the criminal nature of sexual harassment.

IP College set up a sexual harassment committee with two students, a teacher and a karamchari, to follow through on complaints of harassment. This was a pioneering move, the first such committee at a time when sexual harassment was hardly recognised as a crime. It was a precursor to the presence of such mechanisms today; sexual harassment committees are now mandated by law, in all public institutions. After IP College's initiative, several women's colleges began setting up such committees.

In December 1980, an investigation team went to Jharkhand to record the testimonies of Adivasi women in villages near Gua, a mining township; many of these testimonies related to assault by members of the Provincial Armed Constabulary (PAC). The PAC, in 'helping' the mining company sort out a dispute with workers, fired at (male, Adivasi) workers and raped women with impunity.[61] Back at St Stephen's the hoodlums of March 1981 assaulted women, got away with it, enjoyed impunity. The parallel was uncanny: in common was a rapacious mentality that perceived women as objects to be violated. In violating women, perpetrators sought to shame the community, or institution, to which the women 'belonged'. It's quite likely that the hoodlums, irked by Stephanian elitism, justified their assault: 'You Stephanians think you're superior, see what we can do to your girls!' But college authorities too stood by while women students were assaulted, and later proscribed legal redress; in Jharkhand, the perpetrators were actually agents of the Indian state.

Feminists of the time redefined sexual assault as a crime of power: men harass and rape to establish or reinforce their power over women, and over those to whom the women 'belong'—men, families, communities, institutions, nations. In violating her, they shame the men who 'own' her. In multiple conflicts between men, women are

[61] Madhu Kishwar, lawyer Rani Jethmalani, journalist Neerja Chowdhry, and I were part of the investigation team. We never wrote up a formal report.

attacked and violated. The men of their own communities often try to conceal the fact, refusing to acknowledge their own inability to protect women, nor the suffering the women undergo: indeed, they often reject the violated women as 'spoilt goods'. Women's identities, their safety and integrity are unimportant in the patriarchal scheme of things.

Launching A Campaign

In January 1982, with Holi again approaching, a notice appeared in the Ladies' Common Room, recalling the harassment of the previous year. It noted that no steps had been taken to prevent a recurrence, and suggested that we needed to pool our pain and anger, and devise creative solutions. If we didn't do this, nobody would; nothing would change. I think some of us had learnt and been inspired by the anti-sexual harassment protests that the IP Women's Committee had organised, and the anti-rape movement raging across the country; we took up cudgels in St Stephen's.

A meeting was held. Women came, joining what soon ballooned into a full-blown campaign. Although Stephen's wasn't an activist student body—there was a kind of premium attached to being apolitical, noncommittal—yet strong feeling crystallised around this issue. After discussing and refining our ideas over several meetings, we invited the entire student body and our teachers to a larger meeting. I recall two women teachers in college at the time, Nandita Narain and Upinder Singh, and they came, as did a few male students.[62] The ideas women had generated were shared, and suggestions invited; thus the women garnered wider support for the campaign.

The plan of action encompassed reaching out to countless women across the university. We went about it with enormous enthusiasm, enjoying every minute of purposeful action.

> During the months preceding Holi 1982, several of us actively campaigned against sexual harassment. We had come to see it as a widespread problem, solutions to which could only lie in the direction of concerted struggle, and thus we extended the campaign to many other colleges.
>
> Joining hands with women from other colleges, we participated in a

[62] Including Anirudh Deshpande, Promatesh Acharya, David Devadas and Amit Tandon

> wide-ranging campaign. Through discussion, we devised action which included sharing of experiences, general body meetings and assembly addresses in colleges, lessons in self defence, a television program on sexual harassment, and leafleting in several colleges. Suggestions from women of different colleges were collated and given to the vice chancellor, police and DTC. Steps were taken to form joint vigilance committees of students, administrative staff and teachers, which were active before Holi day (Priya 1985: 33).

We printed a leaflet, pooling our pocket money: 'Apathy Is a Crime Too!' A group of ten to fifteen women began trooping out in the mornings,[63] heading to Daulat Ram College, MH, IP, Khalsa, Delhi School of Economics, Kirori Mal, Hans Raj, Hindu, Ramjas, CIE, Law Faculty, DSSW—and further into town, Mata Sundari, Lady Shri Ram, Gargi, Kamla Nehru... everywhere, the group distributed leaflets and stirred up discussion; at places, we spoke in college assemblies. Animated discussions ensued: women everywhere were extremely angry about pervasive sexual harassment and desperately wanted it to stop. In Khalsa College, men were indignant about male apathy: 'We would never stand by; we would protect our women with our lives!' It was a refreshing approach, though not quite our idea of a definitive solution.

We invited a team that taught feminist self-defense to come to Stephen's and hold some sessions for us. The team was led by Asha, who had been in the original *Ehsaas* group; she learned feminist self-defense in an intensive workshop in IIT Delhi in December 1981. We enjoyed the self-defense sessions in Stephen's, and later some of us attended a longer workshop held in IIT.[64] In these sessions, we learnt to punch, kick, break-fall, and practice verbal self-defense: rehearse confident responses to comments, leers and insults. Learning feminist self-defense can be extremely empowering: one day, a few of us from the course were travelling by DTC bus when somebody harassed one of us; we made the driver take the bus to the nearest police station,

[63] Active campaigners included, amongst others, Shobha Aggarwal, Vrinda Grover, Jyotsna Kapur, Bishakha De Sarkar, Shrabani Basu, Jyotika Virdi, Sangeeta Bhalla and Alpana Shah from Stephen's, Aditi Phadnis from Miranda House, and Suvritta Khatri from Hindu College.

[64] G. Asha, Anju, Cath and G. Arunima were instructors at the three-week workshop in IIT Delhi, May 1982. Lawyer Nandita Haksar and journalist Sujata Madhok held sessions on law and media during the workshop. Asha and Anju, both students of IIT Delhi, were pioneer feminists, creating space for women in that male bastion.

Daryaganj, where we registered a complaint, and handed over the miscreant. Doing this was a really big deal: it was usually impossible to take any action, in cases of harassment.

As we did the rounds of different colleges for the sexual harassment campaign, students shared specific problems and made concrete suggestions. They demanded more University Specials (dedicated public buses), lighting on dark roads, and a system for reporting harassment, including by male teachers. During Holi, women police should be deployed, and Vigilance Committees formed in each college. We mulled over the question: what does security mean for women? We tried to develop a common understanding, a feminist perspective on security, to define what was needed to be safe.

'We should do a TV programme on sexual harassment,' someone suggested, and off we went to Delhi Doordarshan. The producer incharge of youth programming liked the idea, but the word 'sex' was taboo in Indian television, so we couldn't use the term 'sexual harassment'! He suggested we switch to 'eve-teasing', which we refused, since the term trivialises harassment and misrepresents women. We chose, instead, to use 'harassment of women' and 'molestation of women'.

The programme, a panel discussion, turned out to be very lively, with Professor Uma Chakravarti, lawyer Nandita Haksar, social worker Malika Virdi, me, and probably one or two others. It created quite a stir, for everybody watched Doordarshan in those days, and this was the first ever programme on sexual harassment on Indian television. The discussion ranged across harassment on streets, in buses, colleges and workplaces; apathetic bystanders; how boys were being socialised; what girls and women could do in self-defense; and the role of authorities and the police. I happened to mention that sometimes a man in a crowded DTC bus would rub against the shoulder of a seated woman, 'masturbating'. Since the programme was live, Doordarshan couldn't excise the word. A colleague of my mother's (from another campus college), frothing in anger, accused her of harbouring a daughter who used obscene language; my mother retorted: 'I'm very proud of her and her friends! They will reform all these obscene men!'

As Holi came closer, small boys would aim water-filled balloons at women passers-by, causing considerable discomfort, sometimes injury; their families laughed it off as 'harmless fun'. Alone or in pairs, we walked through Kamla Nagar, adjoining Delhi University, and, as expected, got hit. We climbed up, to first- or second-floor homes;

mothers stoutly defended their boys. Soon, however, they appreciated our point. 'Teach your son to respect women,' we'd request. 'This is not innocent play.' A mother would then cajole her son out from hiding, and ask him to apologise: 'Sorry, Didi. I won't do it again.' We felt satisfied with this small-scale experiment; it needs repeating, on a large scale, even today!

It became clear that sexual harassment was no stand-alone crime, rather a product of the entire toxic social ethos, which had little respect for women's rights. Harassment was common, casual, trivialised and justified. Only when women persistently, publicly questioned it, did it begin to be perceived as a significant concern.

Entrenched male domination was most clearly visible in mixed colleges. Stephen's Students' Union was all-male, except one 'Member for Women's Affairs'; Union members were hostellers and held Union meetings late at night, without even bothering to inform the sole woman member. There were six hostel wings, for over 300 male students; but no women's hostel. Moreover, women weren't admitted into college unless their parents lived in Delhi.[65]

As part of the sexual harassment movement, we organised a signature campaign, demanding a women's hostel run on lines similar to the men's hostel, without curfew timings and draconian rules. Over 400 students signed, more women, but also men. When handed to the principal, he brazenly tore up the sheets, saying: 'I can collect 500 signatures from boys who don't want a women's hostel.'[66]

We demanded at least a proper space within the college campus where women students could rest and relax, instead of the miniscule 'Ladies' Common Room.' We zeroed in on a large independent room, which could accommodate a few dozen persons. We won this struggle and were allotted this room, which we dubbed the 'Women's Common Room' (WCR).

We further demanded the provision of sanitary towels (STs), which were not just unavailable but also apparently unmentionable in the college. The principal treated this demand as a joke and asked us in a bantering tone, 'These things are kept in educational institutions?' We educated him on sanitary towels being a basic necessity and told

---

[65] In 1984, a case was filed against college authorities by Malika, a young woman who was denied admission to St Stephen's College on the grounds that her father was posted out of town.

[66] A women's hostel finally came up in 1997.

him they were stocked in many schools (including ours) and colleges that we knew about. For once he went silent; we obtained official permission to stock STs in the WCR.[67]

In Stephen's admission interviews, women were often subjected to questions like, 'Which perfume do you use, young lady?' Scandal sheets *Kooler Talk* and *Spice* were brought out by a team of male students and staff advisers. 'Chick charts' were put up on official notice boards, rating women students, reducing them to sex objects: 'It's a cool, cool experience', 'big surprises in small packets', and distorting names (for example Menude instead of Meenu). Authorities condoned all this and justified it as 'harmless fun'.

The sexual harassment campaign demanded that such charts and scandal sheets be discontinued: they were insulting and misogynist. Space for dissent opened up, the issue began to be discussed. Women from different institutions began to speak up, sharing their discomfort and rage. It turned out that IIT Delhi had similar chick charts; Sri Ram College of Commerce (SRCC) produced equally demeaning 'uglies charts'.

The sexual harassment campaign organised meetings with women students in more than twenty colleges, eliciting their issues and demands. By late February 1982, these were collated, and a memorandum of demands was prepared. We submitted this to the Delhi Police, the DTC authorities, and the Vice-Chancellor of Delhi University. We held meetings with them to explain the need for gender training for college staff and students, the police, bus drivers and conductors. There was a need for more University Specials, and changes in specific DTC bus routes and timings. Demands pertaining to different colleges were put forward. For instance, LSR hostellers objected to a host of draconian rules; Mata Sundari College students required police presence on a lonely stretch of road near their college. Most students wanted women police, since policemen themselves often leered at and harassed women. We also suggested that colleges form Vigilance Committees during the Holi season.

Some of our urgent collective demands were met. During Holi, women police were deployed on campus. Some were in uniform, others in plainclothes, acting as decoys. They were able to identify and nab miscreants. Women students and teachers felt safer having the policewomen around: it was an idea that worked.

---

[67] The next year, the spacious WCR was snatched away.

As Holi approached, some colleges formed Vigilance Committees. In Stephen's, an informal committee was set up with student, teacher and karamchari representatives. Committee members were posted at various college gates during the days preceding Holi, with an agreed-upon system of communication, should there be any hint of harassment. This arrangement gave women a palpable sense of security. Holi, 10 March 1982, was peaceful, with no untoward incidents. This was no mean achievement!

The sexual harassment campaign had generated a strong network of women students across multiple colleges, who actively mobilised against other forms of blatant violence as well. In Ramjas College, on 18 February 1982, the principal's henchmen brutally assaulted a teacher, Dilip Simeon, who had been questioning corrupt practices; he was hospitalised with a broken leg and smashed teeth. Ramjas students spontaneously protested. Women students, especially from Stephen's, MH and IP, joined the 'Ramjas movement' in unprecedented numbers. Students held meetings and dharnas outside the Vice-Chancellors' office and residence; and outside the homes of Ramjas 'lalas', businessmen on the Ramjas College Managing Committee. There was a memorable dharna (sit-in) outside a Managing Committee meeting in Daryaganj. Students, as many women as men, walked 7 kilometres from the university to Daryaganj, and crowded into an open courtyard, which had a staircase leading to the Managing Committee's meeting room. The lalas were effectively held captive, since students blocked the only route by which they could leave! The students chatted and sang songs, in high spirits and perfectly happy. After several hours, as night fell, the Managing Committee asked to meet a student delegation. Thus it was that a proper investigation committee was constituted, with members chosen by the students; this led in due course to the principal, Kartar Singh, being suspended.[68] As one fallout of all this activism, democratic-minded students and teachers from different colleges formed the Committee Against Goondaism, Goonda Virodhi Abhiyan, which was active for a few years.

The sexual harassment campaign of 1982 was an important milestone in women students' struggles. Women asserted their rights

[68] The investigation committee included Professors Jit Uberoi (sociologist, then at the Delhi School of Economics) and Upendra Baxi (then at the Law Faculty, Delhi University).

to safety, dignity and freedom in powerful and creative ways. In addition, by expressing solidarity with and by participating in joint struggles such as at Ramjas, they won more male allies to their cause.[69] Of course all these positive developments could not put an end to the deeply entrenched culture of violence, discrimination and misogyny in the university.

In St Stephen's College, there was a backlash as well. Authorities cracked down on students who were active in the sexual harassment campaign and denied some of them admission into postgraduate courses despite excellent academic records. In 1983, the spacious Women's Common Room was locked up and women students were again relegated to the poky little Ladies' Common Room.

But the anti-sexual harassment campaign had broken barriers, and opened the door to feminist protests—that door could never be shut again. In 1984, Stephanian women students reiterated their opposition to chick charts, as well as the freshly minted 'hen charts'. The authorities ignored the women's protests and dubbed them as troublemakers. On 31 January 1985, some Stephanian hostellers raided women's lockers in the Ladies' Common Room, pulled out clothing, including undergarments, and hung a bra on the cross atop the college tower, visible from all sides. They painted threatening graffiti on college walls. The authorities brushed off the episode saying, 'Boys will be boys', taking the stance that this was a 'prank'. Journalists got wind of the matter, but the principal said it was 'a domestic issue' (Bhargava 1985). Stephanian teachers Nandita Narain, Tanika Sarkar and Sunil Kumar criticised this attitude, and over a hundred university teachers issued a memorandum expressing shock at the attempt to conceal the sexual humiliation of women students and privatise an essentially social problem.

In February 1985, hundreds of students and faculty members from MH, IP, Jesus and Mary College, Daulat Ram College, Stephen's, Ramjas and other colleges held a huge protest at the St. Stephen's gate, in solidarity with the struggles of Stephanian women, and demanding punitive action against the miscreants. They sang songs and raised slogans—'We're neither pretty nor ugly, we're furious!' and '*Hum Bharat ki Naari hain, Chick nahin chingaari hain!*' (We, the women of India, are sparks, not chicks!)

---

[69] The anti-sexual harassment campaign of 1982 helped lay the foundations for conscious feminist activism at the university, especially in St Stephen's.

Demonstration against anti-women practices in St Stephen's college, demanding action against miscreants. Banner reads 'An Insult to Women of Stephen's Is An Insult to All.'

The authorities were alarmed by the bad press they were getting. They called in the Central Reserve Police Force (CRPF) and Section 144 was imposed in the college (Bhargava 1985). Armed personnel guarded the newly-installed college gates, to 'prevent militant women's organisations and riffraff students from other colleges' from entering the premises. Women students were forbidden from holding meetings or gathering in groups of more than two. Gangs of male Stephanians stalked the women students and eavesdropped on them (Dewan 2012).

Some active women students were charged with indiscipline and acting against college interests, and were threatened with expulsion. These included Saba Dewan, Sukhpreet Bhinder, Uma Gokale, Dipta Bhog and Vrinda Grover. Their parents were called in. However, the parents stood by their daughters, and took the authorities to task for their regressive attitudes (Dewan 2012). This unnerved the authorities. Under pressure, they put a ban on 'chick charts', *Spice* and *Kooler Talk*. Three miscreants who had raided the women's clothes were rusticated, though they were allowed to come into college to take exams (Priya 1985: 35).

In St Stephen's, a women's hostel was finally built in 1997. However, its rules are discriminatory to date, and there are women students who have launched protests on the issue (Gautham 2014).[70]

Back in 1982, by mid-April, university exams grabbed everyone's attention. The next academic year began in July, after a two-month-long summer break. Several of those who had been active in the sexual harassment campaign got together to take stock. They had been really very deeply involved and felt energised by the experience of autonomous organisation. At the same time, they knew it was only the beginning. It was important to consolidate and carry on, but how exactly was this to be done?

That's when *Ehsaas* came to mind, and it soon entered the picture in a big way: to help keep up the momentum, and widen the ambit of change.

[70] Most of the issues that women students have raised in Stephen's are not particular to that college. Hostel rules are discriminatory across the board. There have been protests elsewhere too. Beneath the veneer, almost every college is a hotbed of conflict. Women students from various colleges have been active over the years, including the extraordinary group Pinjra Tod (literally, Break the Cage), which has broadened and deepened the struggle across universities, with a consistently intersectional approach, taking on the state as well as society.

9

Youthful Drama

More Educational Than Education

An Autonomous Feminist Theatre Group

An important legacy of the anti-sexual harassment campaign, which raged in the first three months of 1982, was the experience of autonomous organisation. The campaign was steered by a loose group of women students who had connected with and mobilised many more. It had made a palpable impact, and group members were keen to carry on the movement against sexual harassment within a broad feminist understanding.

This is what led to *Ehsaas* being resurrected, in a new avatar, in July 1982. We felt that the play might be able to reach out across society, raise questions and carry forward some of the work begun during the anti-sexual harassment campaign. I dusted the script lying on my shelf. We read it together. Its dialogues, straight from the heart, resonated with our own feelings. The play drew attention to gendered social norms, how these play out in life and how women respond, conform, resist.

Thus, the Ehsaas Play Group was formed, mostly comprising of women who'd been involved with the anti-sexual harassment movement. Doing the play was a freely chosen activity: we were seeking to somehow defeat or at least deflect patriarchy, and the play became a companion as we transgressed beyond the bounds set by family, university, society. I think it helped us gain an education which was meaningful in ways that our university courses could never be. Rather than dry, detached teaching, which several formal courses seemed to specialise in, street theatre brought us face-to-face with live contexts, in vibrant communication with diverse realities. It provided an opportunity to develop life-skills such as empathy, creativity, self-confidence, critical thinking, resilience; it was constructive, artistic, empowering social engagement.[71]

We began meeting regularly to work on the play. Tripurari Sharma came by a few times, to oversee and support the group's adaptation of the original script. Initially there were over a dozen participants, all DU students—Aditi Phadnis from MH, Suvritta Khatri from Hindu College, Rahul Roy from Ramjas, Shobha Aggarwal, Alpana Shah, Sangeeta Bhalla, Jyotsna Kapur, Vrinda Grover and Sanjoy Roy from St. Stephen's, Jyotika Virdi from the Delhi School of Social Work (DSSW), Jashodhara Tripathi and myself from the Arts Faculty, and some others.[72] Everyone took to the play. Images and emotions built bridges of connection. There were experiences in common, and a similar ground reality.

During the original theatre workshop, of December 1979, Tripurari had infused the play with fine dramatic qualities; Ruth Vanita's participation ensured a sharp analytic edge. They had picked the raw material from sharing and improvisations, moulding a play suffused with meaningful symbols and ideas, which aligned well with our group.

Few plays, at the time, articulated women's thoughts and self-perceptions. Tripurari had been consciously exploring the possibility of women defining content: could they sift, recreate and enact something born of experience? The enactment in *Ehsaas*, abstracted from the actors' collective experience, went beyond realism. For instance, sexual harassment was presented in *Ehsaas* as a bare scene in which men were conspicuous by their absence and only the women stood stiff

[71] Also called socio-emotional learning (SEL), or 21st century skills, life-skills are being promoted vigorously in educational institutions across the globe today, as essential elements missing in formal courses. SEL is promoted even by the New Education Policy, 2020, framed by the Ministry of Human Resource Development, Government of India; and by organisations including UNICEF, WHO, the Harvard Life Skills Taxonomy Project and Quest Alliance.

[72] Aditi, Suvritta, Rahul, Shobha, Alpana, Sangeeta, Jyotsna, Vrinda and Sanjoy were pursuing undergraduate courses; Jyotika had joined a Master's in Social Work and I had joined an MA in Philosophy; Jashodhara was pursuing a PhD in Political Science. Aditi, Alpana and Sangeeta were there for quite a few shows, and Rahul, Sanjoy and Jashodhara were there for another year or so; the rest—Suvritta, Shobha, Jyotsna, Vrinda, Jyotika and I—carried on longer.

School-teacher: 'Come girls, what do you want to be when you grow up?' She dismisses dreams of becoming pilots or doctors, and instructs them to chant, instead, 'good daughters, good sisters, good mothers'.[73]

and straight, their bodies tense and defensive as they spoke urgently: '*Vo aa rahe hain, ghoor rahe hain, ek haath idhar se, ek haath udhar se...*' ('They are coming, they are staring, one hand from here, one hand from there...'). Panic built up, the tempo increased and they walked faster, telling one another to hurry, to escape. After this one woman asked, 'Can't women get together and confront such men?' Another woman replied, 'Yes, this can happen. But it usually does not happen!'

The *Ehsaas* opening scene, of a school teacher with little girls, conveyed gender socialisation, roles and stereotyping—the transmission of repressive conditioning from one generation to the next. Through conversation and poetry, the teacher taught the little ones that 'good' girls must clip their ambitions and desires.

The next scene, with women working and sharing morsels of their lives, indicated a pervasive lack of control over their own labour, sexuality and fertility: the very definition of patriarchy. Such analytical terms and definitions had barely entered academia even in our universities, yet in the play the analysis was already there.

---

[73] The illustration accompanies the script of *Ek Thee Achhi Ladki* (ASTHA 1988) and is a replay, with variations, of the opening scene of *Ehsaas*. Jyotsna Kapur worked with girls in Bombay to make *Ek Thee Achhi Ladki;* she had been part of the *Ehsaas* team in Delhi during 1982-86. It was very common for popular lines, songs and sequences to be carried from one play to another, and it was quite wonderful. There was no question of copyright, rather it was acceptable and the original writer/writers/director/actors usually felt pleased rather than put out.

Improvising, Adapting *Ehsaas*

Ehsaas had a fluid structure, showing varied women, personal snippets interspersed with social comment. Power circulates through the capillaries of daily life, as indicated in evocative dialogues, soliloquies and choral statements. The scenarios were so familiar: there was the contrived dependence of women and everyday resistance. The new actors inhabited similar experiential worlds, and voiced the words spontaneously. Where there were differences, they could add, delete, recalibrate. So, for instance, a new sequence was improvised:

> Announcer: Some girls made an application. You can meet the principal, in 15 minutes.
>
> Principal: Come, sit down. What is it?
>
> Girls: Sir, Holi is coming up. How are goondas to be prevented this Holi?
>
> Principal: Why are you making a noise? What's new about this?
>
> Girls: What's new is that we are asking questions.
>
> Principal: The more noise you make, the more you attract goondas. Just don't come to college three days before Holi!
>
> Girls: But classes, library, exams... Will the college be shut?
>
> Principal: No, no. Girls won't come. It's they who have problems.
>
> Girls: Oh! And this year too, no girls' hostel will be made?
>
> Principal: No, no, no! Girls' hostel has many problems. Who wants to take risks? You may go!
>
> (The girls leave, disconsolate.)

Frustrated, they wonder what to do, how to organise further, for their basic rights. The play continues with multiple vignettes, a patchwork quilt of conflict and contestation. They win some, lose some. At another place, another announcement is made: 'Girls are hereby informed that they must reach their hostel rooms before 7 pm. If any girl does not do so, all kinds of accusations will be leveled against her!'

Ehsaas underlined the importance of women speaking up and taking action to transform the future. We usually began our performances with a song popular in the women's movement of the time:

Hum apni awaz uttha rahe hain, vo naraaz kyun, vo naraaz kyun?
Khamoshi todo, vakt aa gaya!
Hum kehte hain ki azadi ho, hum kehte hain ki pyar ho
Hum kehte hain milkar,
Azadi todo vaqt aa gaya...!
(We lift our voices high, why are they angry, why are they angry?
Break the silence, it's time!
We speak for freedom, we speak for love, we speak together!
Break the silence, it's time...!)

Tripurari Sharma (2013: 140-141) recalls that the college women she worked with were breaking stereotypes in their personal life, and participating in the politics around them: '[O]ne thing most of these girls had in common was an urge to shape their lives themselves and not be shaped by the existing moulds... A salient undertone was the concern for their mothers... The pervasive desire was to see them less tired and happier.' As she helped the play get going, Tripurari herself found the collective process energising. Group members talked of extreme tension at home when they reached late, and were sensitive to words and moods.

Some sequences felt incredibly powerful in the doing: the mother-daughter scenes, embroiled in sentiment, the street scene, confronting harassment.

Adapting the play, taking up roles, the group rehearsed regularly, and within a month or so, was ready to perform. Jyotika Virdi (interview 2017) recalls:

> We began rehearsing *Ehsaas*—in Stephen's, the DSSW lawns, and in your house. A bunch of girls joined, angry about harassment during that horrible Holi episode. Alpana and Sangeeta were there for quite a while. Aditi Phadnis acted in a few shows. Initially Tripurari watched us rehearse. Your mom played the harmonium to set tunes for the lyrics and get us to sing in tune. It all fell into place. We did a few performances at PGW[74] and some other spots in DU. The group that finally coalesced and stuck it out was Suvritta, Shobha, Jyotsna, Vrinda, you and me.
>
> All this resonated very well with the phase we were going through—feminism, Saheli,[75] *Manushi*, campus politics, our Study Group[76]—it

[74] Post Graduate Women's Hostel, Delhi University.

[75] The *Ehsaas* team worked alongside Saheli in the women's movement overall.

[76] A group of students organised a Study Group, which met frequently during 1980-83; it included Gaurav Dutt and Raman Nanda from the Delhi School of Economics,

was all rolled together. This format made sense; doing street theatre helped us do something that made sense.

It became our Identity Card. We chose it over conventional theatre. Stephen's had the Shakespeare Society, and lots of folks who took theatre very seriously participated. Then street theatre came along. There was no glamour, none of stage theatre's competitive norms of auditioning, winning roles etcetera. Its language was different. Commitment to a cause was important, and that's what kept us going.

There was some unconventional theatre around at the time: Barry John's theatre with Xavier's school-kids was innovative and thought-provoking. But we had made a choice—we were interested in doing activist theatre, street theatre. Some of us had been doing *Om Swaha,* too.

Sanjoy Roy, who acted in *Om Swaha* as well as *Ehsaas*, says (interview 2017):

> I found *Ehsaas* a mature play. *Om Swaha* focused on the dowry issue. It was more like a debate, black and white. *Ehsaas* was about how you perceive things, how we look at each other, gender, how society is structured. It had much more difficult messaging. I think audiences were far more moved by it.

Performing: In Delhi

The group performed *Ehsaas* in diverse women's colleges, on-campus and off, with students ranging from elite to lower middle-class: MH, Janki Devi, SP Mukherji, Maitreyi, LSR, Gargi, Kamala Nehru, Lakshmi Bai, Kalindi, Daulat Ram, IP. A very strong connect got established everywhere, and there was always a lot of discussion.

We performed in mixed institutions, and found the audience receptive, whether it was Hansraj, KM, Stephen's, Hindu, Ramjas, SRCC, Dayal Singh, Khalsa College, DSSW, or the Law Faculty, Arts Faculty, CIE, Delhi School of Economics, IIT, Jamia Millia, JNU.

Over the years, we performed more than once at several sites. Initially, to fix a show, one or two of us would go across, meet the principal, tell her about the play and offer to perform in the college. As word about the play got around, we were invited. It could be a group

---

Anand Swamy, Nikhil Roy and Harsh Kapoor from Hindu College, Jyotika and I, and several others who came for a while.

of college students, or motivated teachers, who felt gender issues needed to be raised. We were on a roll, doing the play, our own specific contribution to raising awareness.

Sometimes particular incidents of sexual harassment called for urgent awareness and action. Dilip Simeon invited *Ehsaas* to Ramjas College after a woman student's harassment came to light: a male student had pursued her, with requests for 'friendship', and finally with a knife. As a result, she had stopped coming to college. We performed amid a sizeable crowd, mostly made up of deeply attentive young men. I suppose this was how the whole idea, and significance, of 'gender sensitisation' began to dawn upon people. The play set into motion a process of learning and gradual 'training', and clearly there was a need for such a process.

Performances were held in lawns, central courtyards, parks, in the open-air. Audiences were moved, and post-performance discussions were usually intense. Young women asked questions about restrictions on mobility, curfew timings, discrimination, harassment, pressures to marry. In schools and women's colleges, principals and teachers often recognised the concerns as genuine, and spoke of their own experiences. There was a deep need to articulate, and no forum to do so: no recognition of gender at the time, in syllabi or curricula. Women's Development Cells (WDCs), Sexual Harassment Committees, and setups such as Delhi University Women's Study and Research Centre came up several years later.

Schools, NGOs and women's movement collectives invited *Ehsaas* to perform in diverse neighbourhoods. We performed amid protests, dharnas and meetings and at theatre festivals, cultural programs.

People shared real problems and wanted to know what to do. While we enjoyed the interactions, and there was a great deal of mutual learning, we felt besieged by the sheer volume, like a landslide wherever we went, and the wretchedness of situations. Many times, girls would come up after the collective discussion to share a personal problem with one of us. We responded as best we could, made suggestions, and surely that might have helped some. We encouraged self-organising, and informal networking; referred them to nascent women's organisations for counselling or legal aid; spoke to their teachers about creating formal support structures. We tried to keep in touch, but systematic follow-up was needed, which we weren't in a position to provide.

We missed classes to do *Ehsaas*, but that hardly bothered us; we caught up somehow, and invariably did well academically. We traveled by DTC buses, sometimes three-wheeler auto-rickshaws, shaking and rattling towards our destination. There were no special costumes, but the salwar kurtas we selected from our ordinary everyday wear were bright and colourful. Post-performance, there would be animated discussion. We'd spread out a shawl and accept small donations for local conveyance; sometimes tea, samosas and barfi were arranged for us, and we felt amply rewarded!

The NGO Ankur invited *Ehsaas* to several schools. Whether it was Victoria Memorial School, Bharatiya Vidya Bhavan, St Thomas, Abner Memorial or Springdales, students watched rapt, bright-eyed, as a whole new world of possibilities opened up. Perhaps they began to observe the workings of gender in their lives, and in society. Hopefully, the teachers and Ankur facilitators took forward this learning.

With organisations like Saheli or Action India, we performed in shanty and resettlement colonies, working-class areas where large crowds gathered, including excited children who babbled incessantly but also listened with big eyes. Women watched empathetically, and during post-performance discussions brought up experiences of repression, harassment, the desire to study, family pressures, overwork, ill health and marital violence. We did *Ehsaas* in middle-class colonies like Defence Colony, Lajpat Nagar, Kotla Mabarakpur, in women's homes, on rooftop terraces; they responded, '*Ye to hamaari kahaani tumne bataa di,*' (You have related our story.)

Ehsaas was performed at the Boat Club and in Parda Bagh in Daryaganj, an all-women space; and in a large compound within the Kasturba Hospital, Daryaganj, watched by nurses, doctors, patients and their families (the hospital specialises in maternity services).[77]

Ehsaas was invited to perform within Saheli, at its Nizamuddin office. The atmosphere was upbeat, hopeful; Gouri Choudhury enthusiastically dubbed the actors 'young Sahelis'. We invariably performed on and around 8 March, at joint rallies held by women's groups, and at sundry smaller events.

---

[77] Earlier called Zenana Victoria Hospital, it was renamed Kasturba Hospital in 1975, and is popularly known as Machhliwala Aspatal (the hospital adjacent to a fish market). Its clientele is huge, ranging from working-class to lower-middle class, and it is one of the largest hospitals offering maternity services in Asia.

In May 1983, a week-long feminist festival of the arts, 'Kriti', was held at Aurobindo Ashram, organised by Saheli and Women's Centre, Bombay, with some 170 participants from Bombay, Pune, Delhi, Madras, Maharashtra, Bangalore, Chandigarh and elsewhere. We performed *Ehsaas* amid an appreciative, excited audience; some of us were in the *Om Swaha* performance too. We watched the play *Mulgi Zali Ho,* from Maharashtra. There were many workshops and, in the theatre workshop, participants made a skit showing women's double burden of work. Dancer Chandralekha articulated Kriti's central thematic: '*She* understands vital areas of life... But she is not able to see herself. Every woman is a capacity. But unless she first recognises this, she cannot link it to awareness, action...' (Anonymous 1983: 34).

Once, *Ehsaas* was performed in an upscale setting, perhaps a living-room in Gulmohar Park: 'A well-known Hindi writer was in the audience, she criticised our Hindi diction.[78] Our Hindi accents were appalling, enunciation terrible—reeking of our convent school education! I remember this vividly. I look back and think, that's what feedback should be like. Teji Bachchan was at the same show; she had a conservative sort of response, got testy and argumentative.' (Jyotika, interview 2017)

An amateur group, we definitely fell short on several counts, including diction, and singing. My mother tried to get us to sing tunefully; Rashmi Pant, then doing a PhD in History at JNU, coached us a couple of times. Sadly, all us *Ehsaas* actors were tone-deaf. Yet we enjoyed belting out songs, and they were effective in reaching out to audiences thanks to their powerful words, excellent tunes, and our infectious youthful enthusiasm.

We'd chosen to begin the play with a feminist adaptation of the Turkish poet Najim Hikmet's song '*To Paul Robeson*':[79]

Vo hamare geet kyun rokna chahte hain?
Khamoshi todo, vakt aa gaya...

(Why do they want to stop us from singing our songs?
Break the silence, the time has come...)

---

[78] I recall the writer mentioned by Jyotika as being Mridula Garg, but my memory is hazy on this. Jyotika agrees that it might have been Mridula Garg, but she too is not sure.

[79] Najim Hikmet's 1949 song 'To Paul Robeson' begins: 'They don't let us sing our songs, Robeson...' Kamal Sarkar adapted it into Bengali as '*Amar Negro Bhai Paul Robeson*'.

And we'd sing, within the play, original songs:

Ye sadkein jo har subho jaati hain
Phir laut aati hain
Hame bulaati, kuchh kehti hain
Ye sadkein...

(These streets, wander away every morning,
Then later, return,
Beckon to us, tell us something,
These streets...)

Suvritta, as a quintessential mother-figure, would appeal to her daughter, '*Itni der kyon kar di beti, tumhe maloom hai tumhari maa darwaaze pe khari intezaar kar rahi hogi*!' ('Why so late, daughter, you know your mother would be standing at the door waiting for you!')

Rahul, acting the part of the patriarch, would try to control women, menacingly: '*Andar, aur andar!*' *(Stay inside!)*

Women, breaking out, sang:

Ek ghera hai,
Isi mein rehti hain hum...

(There's a circle,
Within which we live...)

We faced rough questioning sometimes, and allegations like 'feminists are anti-men', 'women are women's worst enemies'. We learnt to counter such warped comments with patience and logical arguments. Post-performance discussions helped sharpen our skills of persuasion; we grew more at ease, and more articulate in the process.

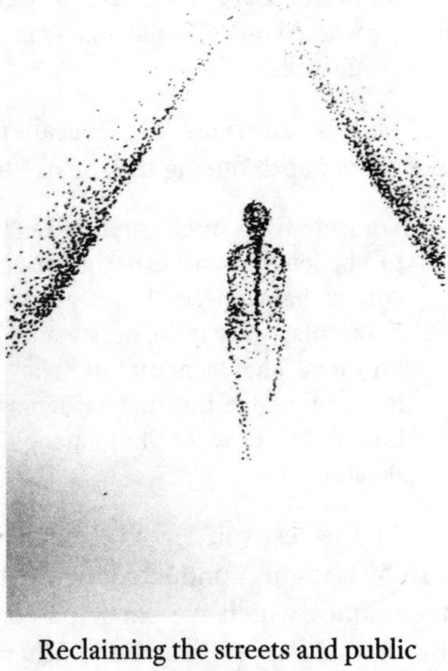

Reclaiming the streets and public space, for women.

Performing: Outside Delhi

In Bhopal: A Theatre Festival

In 1983, *Ehsaas* participated in a National Street Theatre festival at Bharat Bhavan, Bhopal, organised by the Sangeet Natak Akademi in collaboration with the Bharat Bhavan Rangmandal. We were conspicuously the only women's troupe in this gathering of dozens of drama troupes.

Performing for the theatre fraternity was a novel experience. Stalwarts of street theatre and cutting-edge experimental theatre were there—Gursharan Singh from Punjab, Sanjoy Ganguly from Calcutta, Habib Tanvir, Tripurari Sharma, Safdar Hashmi, Rajendra Nath, Neelam Mansingh, Bansi Kaul, BV Karanth and several more. Sanjoy Roy recalls (interview 2017) that for the *Ehsaas* team, it was a very successful foray into the world of theatre:

> There was a workshop inside with a lot of action. After that, we performed *Ehsaas* in the outdoor space. Everybody loved it. I thought we were the stars of that whole festival. There was a huge discussion after our play. They were struck by the performance.
>
> We performed the play at several places in Bhopal. I remember we went to the walled city and did *Ehsaas* in a Muslim mohalla. You girls told Rahul and me, we have to be conscious; the show was being done for women only. We did a show in another basti, and in a girls' school, inside walls.

Jyotika (interview 2017) recalls the Ehsaas group as being somewhat out of its depth during the theatre festival at Bharat Bhavan:

> We were fish out of water there. They were theater-people, wedded to challenging and experimenting with theatre forms... It's true of course that we were the only woman-predominant group. The issues in our play were more personal. We did perform in the theatre space for them. That went off fine. They assumed we shared their concerns in cutting-edge theatre. But it was like we were undergrads thrown into a PG crowd. These people were eating, sleeping, thinking theater.

At the festival, Habib Tanvir's Naya Theatre troupe performed. Sanjoy Ganguly conducted a workshop using Theatre of the Oppressed techniques which we participated in. We watched performances by Bansi Kaul, Naya Theatre and others. Several of these seasoned artistes were able to go into the city streets, bazaars and bastis and perform spontaneously, improvising on the spot. The *Ehsaas* actors weren't prepared or equipped to do that.

We performed *Ehsaas* several times while in Bhopal. I recall one show organised by Anjali Noronha, of the NGO Eklavya;[80] she had studied in Delhi University and knew us from there. The performance was in the large, green campus of Maharani Lakshmi Bai College. Students and teachers were enthusiastic, even wanting to do the play themselves. We later sent across a copy of the script.

Back in Delhi, the *Ehsaas* group continued performing. After the anti-Sikh carnage of November 1984, the play was put on hold, as most of us became deeply involved with relief and rehabilitation work. In the summer of '85, we got back to *Ehsaas*. Gouri Dey joined the group; a wonderful singer, she had earlier worked with people's movements in Chhattisgarh and Maharashtra. Shobha, Suvritta, Jyotsna, Vrinda, Jyotika and I rejoined. Neither Sanjoy nor Rahul were able to continue giving time to *Ehsaas*. Two students from Ramjas College, Amar Kanwar and Praveen Kumar, joined instead—we had met them during relief work with Sikh survivors.[81]

Jyotika started working with the NGO Jagori, and rented a place in Jangpura. We often rehearsed there. Doing *Ehsaas* had brought us close, as a group. Some had been friends earlier; other friendships began, and ripened. We'd help each other skirt curfew timings and mobility limits, offering strategic support to counter family pressures. We'd rehearsed in almost everyone's home at some point or the other: Shobha's in Asaf Ali Road, Vrinda's and Jyotsna's in Patel Nagar, Rahul's in Bharati Nagar, Suvritta's in the Janki Devi College campus where her mother taught Sanskrit. Over the years, there were ups and downs, we had fun and we had fights. We quarrelled, somebody was hurt, irritated, exhausted, took time out, and came back. A strong sense of purpose sustained the group, and a politics that intermeshed with the personal.

[80] Eklavya, set up in 1982, is a leading NGO working to democratise school education.

[81] Amar was studying for a BA in History and Praveen for a BA in Economics. By that time, Shobha and Vrinda had joined LLBs in Delhi University's Law Faculty; Suvritta, an MA in History at JNU; Jyotsna, MA in History at Delhi University; Rahul, Mass Communications at Jamia Millia Islamia University; Jyotika had worked in Madhya Pradesh from May 1984 to July 1985 with the NGO Kishore Bharati, and with Bhopal gas tragedy survivors; Sanjoy was pursuing further work in theatre and the media; I had joined an MPhil in Political Science at Delhi University.

Again we performed in a number of colleges, and diverse neighbourhoods. As Jyotika recalls (interview 2017), 'The shows were by arrangement. We connected with people, and put the word out. It was all part of the movement. It was good, it was voluntary. We had the passion and spirit, and we were interested in doing this.'

In Lucknow: With Women's Groups and NGOs

Then a young woman named Vandana Singh wrote to us from Lucknow, keen to know whether we would travel to perform there.[82] Vandana was associated with Suraksha, a women's group in Lucknow working against dowry and domestic violence. We exchanged a few letters, and the plan firmed up. Off we went by train, stayed at her home, and got busy doing a series of performances. Suraksha arranged most of these. Suraksha was headed by Mrs Kumar, a social worker who was very committed and serious about the mission of empowering women, as was Urvashi Sahni, a member of the organisation.[83] Another organisation, Kshitij, organised a few shows.

Everyone who hosted us and arranged the shows in Lucknow was warm and enthusiastic. In those days a group like ours was treated with enormous respect and affection, put up in homes with simple hospitality, offered wholesome home food, and mattresses were spread out on the floor for us to sleep on. We travelled by train, and locally by three-wheelers and local buses, with the occasional luxury of somebody's car. There was no culture of being put up in hotels or hiring expensive taxis or travelling by air. There was never any talk, offer or expectation of payment. The joy and excitement of performing, the attention our play received, and the feeling that we were helping inspire change were reward enough.

Lucknow was a whirl of activity: performing at several colleges including Isabella Thoburn, Mahila Vidyalaya Degree College, City Girls' College and Avadh Girls' Degree College. As elsewhere, there emerged a spontaneous rapport and sharing of experiences as well as a deep the yearning for freedom, for change. Our being a women's group,

---

[82] I don't remember how Vandana knew of *Ehsaas*. But I do recall learning at some point that she was a granddaughter of Chaudhary Charan Singh, the Indian Prime Minister during 1979-80. I have not been able to trace her presently.

[83] Mrs Kumar's son, historian Sanjay Kumar, taught History at Delhi University. Her daughter Nita Kumar is a fine academic too. Urvashi Sahni currently heads the Study Hall Educational Foundation in Lucknow, which works on gender and education.

self-motivated, self-organised, seemed to be a source of inspiration, perhaps the stuff of dreams.

We performed in some schools too. Of the schools, I remember a Balika Vidyalaya located within a crowded basti, schoolgirls in striped uniforms and neat plaits looking out at us through metal grills, their eyes puzzled. There was no opportunity for discussion. As we walked through that basti, some young boys catcalled and hooted, and I remember feeling distinctly out of place.

Kshitij organised a show where the audience had four or five young men who were very serious about women's liberation. They were running a study group on women's issues. During the post-performance discussion, the question of why their group didn't have any women became a point of contention. The unspoken sub-text was gender segregation: that culturally it just wasn't easy to form non-segregated groups. But, did they have any right to speak on behalf of women? They, however, didn't think that this was what they were doing; they were simply doing what they believed in (Virdi, interview 2017).

We went from Lucknow to Kanpur and performed on a stage in IIT Kanpur, in front of a hall packed with male students. A college festival was on, and they were probably expecting entertainment. Most members of the audience leered at the actors, rather than listening seriously. It was terribly uncomfortable and after the performance, we quickly left. I can't recall how the show was organised, but it was obviously a mistake. Elsewhere in mixed settings, including at IIT Delhi, the play had gone well.

In Aligarh: In and Around the University

We went to Aligarh, in 1986 or 1987, invited by an activist a few years older than us, recently returned from Nicaragua. He had grown up in Aligarh, and we stayed in his parental home.[84] Several university teachers whom he contacted welcomed us with enormous warmth. They arranged a number of performances. These were held in Aligarh Muslim University, Aligarh Women's College, and another in the college hostel; its tall walls are still vivid in my memory—tall walls seemed to be characteristic of all women's hostels at the time.

The *Ehsaas* shows in Aligarh went off very well, with animated discussions, the sharing of experiences and bits of history. Students and teachers also expressed an interest in doing a play like *Ehsaas*.

[84] His name was Anurag Gupta (as reminded by Nandita Jain, conversation, 2024).

Dreams and Dilemmas

We continued performing up to 1987. We carried on for nearly five years, an unusual length of time for an amateur group. We were quite in love with the play, and closure was difficult.

An autonomous women's theatre group is a rarity even today. As such we occupied a niche space: visible, in-your-face feminist and footloose. Our very existence was, for many who saw us, an eye-opener. People were startled to find a group of young women travelling, performing, just like that, of our own free will. Doing so helped forge our identities, deepen our convictions. Through the gravitas of social commitment, it anchored us.

Doing the play held a touch of magic; this was our season in the sun. It was subversion, a bid to remake the world. The experience greatly enriched our understanding of gender, finding themes that recurred across locations, with infinite variations. As in the rest of the autonomous women's movement, there was much discussion on basic rights and transforming the status quo, discourse which would gradually enter media and academia.

We hung on to *Ehsaas* both for the camaraderie and the sense of purpose it provided amid nebulous career plans, roller-coaster love lives, and the hurly-burly of family negotiations. The drama we enacted blended with the drama in our lives. We supported each other in our explorations, vagabonding, breaking taboos and engaging in subterfuge to defeat societal dictats. During that long moment, the play group was a trustworthy, empathetic, non-judgmental space. As young adults, we grappled with difficult choices. The group held us through rough patches, sometimes by quietly listening, through gentle acceptance, or just by letting one be.

In tune with the times, we were idealistic and upbeat. We were wary of the temptations of big funding, of the name and fame that began to rear their heads as the women's movement institutionalised, recreating hierarchies and altering priorities. The *Ehsaas* group remained informal, trying to build authentic politics, maintain integrity and solidarity, with responsibility as much as freedom. As actors in the street theatre, every performance was an end in itself, a reaffirmation of meaning and connection.

Our families were scared for us, wondering where our lives were headed. While our mothers intuitively understood a lot of our struggles, they too faced major dilemmas: as middle managers of patriarchy, their job was to keep us in line. We were subject to surveillance, just like other young women. It was humiliating, and intolerable. Resisting establishment norms tied us up in knots. The tug-of-war with family was exhausting and continuous. Within our circle, we inhabited a dream-world of social revolution, love and friendship; our conditioning and family pressures pointed one way, and our aspirations beckoned elsewhere.

One memorable evening, six of us *Ehsaas* women invited our mothers to a meal at Jyotika's place in Jangpura. We felt we were sowing the seeds of a different kind of community, against the grain of patriarchal dominance. Our mothers had diverse backgrounds and interests, some full-time homemakers, others professionals, but they relaxed together, and chatted as their daughters cooked rajma chawal and kheer. We had fun pampering them and the atmosphere was light-hearted. For once, tensions and stress receded.

We enjoyed our collective strength and our day-dreams, hardly realising how ephemeral it all was. We thought about stabilising the group, setting up steady work to take forward what we had begun: this was the imperative of so many interactions, discussions, questions which needed urgent answers. But we ourselves were transitioning into new roles. Our circle of theatre didn't quite fit the squares of a career or of marriage. The choices each of us confronted were neither black nor white, but shades of grey.

After two core members, Jyotsna and Jyotika, left Delhi, the group finally folded up.[85] As the 90s approached, for most of us, interests became careers, lovers became spouses; worlds shifted and distances grew—geographical, experiential and emotional. As Vrinda Grover put it, in response to my request for an interview for this book, 'All those plays, those days, sometimes it seems like another lifetime!' (email 2016).

In our different lives, *Ehsaas* left its mark. Maybe we are actors still: in the drama of law courts, classrooms, film studios, and the activist worlds some of us still occupy.[86] As actors, we were truly speaking our minds and doing what we believed in: I hope we can still say so, for whatever is done today. In a more mundane sense, street theatre trained

[85] Jyotsna went to Bombay, and Jyotika left for a PhD in the US.

[86] Jyotsna is Professor of Cinema and Media Studies, Southern Illinois University, USA; Vrinda is a leading human rights lawyer, Shobha is a lawyer and co-founder of AIDS Bhedbhav Virodhi Andolan, Suvritta and Jyotika are academics, Praveen is a filmmaker, and Amar a multi-media artist.

its actors to communicate clearly, be participatory and democratic, facilitate rather than impose, keep learning, and present ideas simply, de-jargonised, in a way that feels immediate. Perhaps most of all, it taught us to have fun, with action mixed in; to be light-hearted and serious as two sides of the same coin.

SECTION FOUR

'THOUSANDS OF PLAYS': WORKING-CLASS PERSPECTIVES FROM DELHI BASTIS

A girl is born. Rukma beats a thali to celebrate.
Neighbours question: 'Who beats the thali when a girl is born?'
Rukma and Jethani reply: 'We do! We are really happy to have a girl! We are the ones who give birth, yet when we're born, nobody celebrates!'

– *Aurat aur Dharm (1985)*

We made the play *Aurat aur Dharm* after working with survivors of the 1984 riots, Sikh widows. At that time, we used to go in juloos, jathas, with every sangathan. Today, there is none of that.

– *Susheela (conversation 2016)*

We made thousands of plays—we kept making plays—on housing rights, PDS (the public distribution system), child rights, how little girls do so much housework, on domestic violence, untouchability... If there's an issue, we could just make a natak, songs too. That was the situation. On every issue, we'd make a play! We showed plays in bastis and all over. I remember doing a play on housing rights on 8 March. We did a lot of 'angan theatre' too, 'courtyard plays', performed only for women.

– *Runu Chakraborty (interview 2015)*

I stepped out of purdah, then out of my home, lane, neighbourhood, and out into the world!

– *Gyanvati (interview 2014)*

During the 80s, working-class women activists rooted in Delhi bastis made street plays on a host of issues. This section explores the dynamics of this theatre, focusing mostly on plays made by members of the NGO Action India and associated local women's collectives, called Sabla Sanghs—often in collaboration with like-minded organisations and individuals.[87] Embedded within the bastis, the core activists connected with cutting-edge feminist thought, leading to ground-breaking initiatives on health, gender-based violence, education and access to basic amenities. Street theatre, songs, dances, posters, and exhibitions were designed to reach out to thickly populated constituencies.

As grassroots activists' understanding of issues and interventions grew, this theatre spread out from bastis to the world beyond. That Delhi's autonomous women's movement of the time was intersectional owes much to such activists and their theatre. They were inexhaustibly productive; a play would be created, performed and the specific issue discussed threadbare. They would then make another play, on another relevant theme. They integrated theatre with their daily work; it was a way to share concerns with a vast public, helping shape and strengthen people's struggles. It became a favoured mode of communication within the fairly radical self-help approach, combining social work with a critical political perspective.

This theatre was charged with the energy of feisty grassroots activists: Gyanvati, Ramzan, Manorama, Veermati, Reshma, Devi Kripa, Vidya, Bhagwati, Susheela, Bimla, Shanti, Sumitra, Maharani, and more. Over time, some left, others joined. Their skills and talent in identifying issues, analysing, improvising, creating scripts, directing, and acting were honed over time. Action India organisers Runu Chakraborty, Gouri Choudhury, Bharati Roy Chowdhury, Sharda behn and Chhaya played their part, as did theatre-persons Rati Bartholomew, Tripurari Sharma, Maya Rao, Ein Lall and Anamika Haksar.

This section explores how grassroots activists became performers, the nitty-gritty processes involved and the contributions their theatre made. We begin the section with Shanti's life-narrative, tracing some of her journeys as an activist and actor, with street theatre as well as intimate theatre. While street theatre reached out to large numbers,

---

[87] Ankur was a frequent collaborator in the early years, as was Jagori a little later. Members of Alarippu and Shakti Shalini contributed to some of the plays, as did Disha and Vikalp, organisations based in Saharanpur district, Uttar Pradesh. University students also participated occasionally.

Shanti introduces us also to some remarkable experimental theatre performed within small circles of women.

The next two chapters describe a few plays in some detail, their contexts, actors, storylines and performances. These plays emerged from personal sharing as well as research, thought and discussion. Runu, Shanti and Devi Kripa were able to run workshops independently and generate plays. Within the hurly-burly of the movements of the 80s, these plays were performed for hundreds of thousands of people. The history of this extraordinary theatre definitely needs to be told, for it was among the most effective and productive.

Parivar ki Gaadi, Nand Nagri, Delhi, 1986/87: a play on domestic violence. Runu Chakraborty as husband, Rama as wife. Runu facilitates post-performance discussion with audience.

By the 90s, many more young women and men from working-class backgrounds were doing street theatre.[88] The organisation Nav Srishti set up a street theatre group as an integral part of its efforts to educate and empower girls in working-class bastis. We will discuss this initiative, its internal dynamics and impact. In Action India-Sabla Sanghs, street plays are still performed, though in keeping with the times, their radical content is diluted. Street theatre in general has transitioned to being more instrumental, a conveyer of messages rather than a space of discovery and transformation.

[88] This includes several members of the NGO Alarippu: Zarina, Nisha, Yavar, Salim Salmani, Raju, Pinky, Rati Singh, Gouri Dey, Shiv, Bhanwar Gopal and some others. Rati Singh (interview 2015) describes her experience in Alarippu during 1990-92: learning to act, making several plays and performing on streets and in bastis, on issues such as drug addiction. She herself learnt a great deal from post-performance discussions with audiences. She went on, between 1992 and 1999, to set up street theatre teams in Disha and Vikalp, both rural organisations in Saharanpur. In the early 2000s, Rati made street plays and performed as part of the Sangwari theatre troupe, established with All India Students' Association (AISA) activists Nishi Saxena, Kapil Sharma, Himmat Singh and others. She is the founder of the NGO Abhudaya, which works for women's social and economic empowerment. Gouri Dey (conversation 2023) describes acting and singing in many plays, including *Farq* and *Ek Adalat Aur Bhi*, during her stint with Alarippu from 1987 to 1993.

10

An Actor's Life

'Mere Dukh Khareedogi?'

Shanti grew up working in stone quarries in Rajasthan; she also absorbed rich folk traditions of music and dance from her family and community. Later, in the Delhi women's movement, multiple talents unfolded, including the theatrical. She learnt to read and write; and produce plays, acting, co-directing, co-scripting, often composing songs and music. The intimate plays *Mere Dukh Khareedogi?* and *Suhagan Abhagan* are Shanti's creations, imaginative, emotive, and intense. Here is Shanti's story (conversation and diary 2015),[89] focusing on her forays into the world of theatre:

> I recall plays in the thousands...! On a banyan tree in the dense jungle, sit two birds, Chakva-Chakvi.[90] Chakva says, "Tell a story! It will help pass the dark night." Chakvi replies, "Listen! One friend said to another, 'Write down your memories, of performing plays!'"
>
> Here are my memories! My experiences were like thread through a needle. Amid jungles and hills, we lived each season. In bitter cold, wearing lehnga odhni, rubber chappals, my Ma and I walked two hours, leaving home at dawn. We worked in the quarry, breaking stones. My body throbbed with pain, until the chulha's flame pierced through heavy fog. That warmth still lives within me!

---

[89] Shanti responded to my questions about her recollections of street theatre by writing a narrative (or diary), which I translated and edited for this book, weaving in additional information from conversations with her.

[90] Chakva and Chakvi, a bird pair, are stock characters: storytellers in the folklore of North India. They are spectacular orange-coloured birds, called ruddy shelducks, or Brahminy ducks. The birds have a loud honking call, and inhabit inland water bodies. Ruddy shelducks form long-term breeding pairs and are seasonal migrants from Central Asia.

After joining the movement, I had similar experiences. I went for training to Sevapuri near Banaras. Datta Savle, the facilitator, said, "Make a play! Select your theme!" There were 20 women. The educated ones prepared plays. I couldn't figure out what to do.

Everyone presented plays on water, sanitation, unemployment... When my turn came I became Hanuman, and created havoc: grabbed and flung people, made them run, teased and tricked them! Everyone laughed so much, our tears flowed! For half an hour I didn't breathe, nor let anyone breathe. I caught hold of Dattaji's feet and spun him, people screamed but I kept twirling him round! Gradually I slowed down, gently let him down!

He asked me how I got this idea. I said, "As a child sometimes my Dadi, grandmother, took me to the Ramlila. I saw Hanuman behave like this. I'm not educated, couldn't think of anything else. My life was spent among stones, rocks, hills and jungles." Datta Savle said, "Who says you are uneducated? You are a brave woman!" He praised me with great respect, in front of everyone. I was thrilled and inspired to forge ahead. I learnt a lot in theatre workshops.

We made several plays in Action India. Once, I became the earth—that was a very powerful play. We performed thousands of plays! I joined Action India in 1982-83, and worked for eight years. For every issue, we made a play. Every day we worked on plays and performed continuously. Here I tell of a few; we did many more. There was a strong wave; lots of transformation took place. Now everybody talks of government, but in those days we tried to do everything ourselves.

At a workshop in Saharanpur, we made a play on Babri Masjid. One day,Devi Kripa and I gathered bhang (marijuana grew wild there) and made pakodas. Everybody else ate them! Everybody went crazy, speaking nonsense, anything that came into their heads, utter rubbish. Watching them, we laughed and laughed! Years flew by. Sadly, several members of that theatre group are no more in this world—Sharda behn, Devi Kripa, Bharati, Sudha.

In 1990, I joined Jagori and curated a theatre team. I trained Naurati, Sheila, Ragina, Shabnam, Jenu, Lilavati, Lachhmi, Bano's daughter, my son Shyam Babu, and some others. We performed in many places, like Gujarat, Saharanpur, Banaras, but mostly in Delhi bastis. We did many plays jointly with Action India; and with Alarippu.[91] For some plays, women from Shakti Shalini shelter home joined. Three or four traveled with us, shared their stories, we became very close. One was raped by her father. Another's husband used to sell her to his cronies.

---

[91] Alarippu, an NGO set up by Tripurari Sharma and Lakshmi Krishnamurty in 1983 to work in people's theatre.

We often held theatre training and rehearsed in Jahanpanah Forest, adjacent to Dakshinpuri. Songs, dholki, tambourine were always with us. We made merry in the jungle! Policemen would come and question us. We made such a commotion, improvising. That time was something else! We were in high spirits. I went for theatre workshops to Orissa, Udaipur... In Borunda, Vijaydan Detha was there and so were Ramlal from Tilonia, and Karanthji.[92] I've forgotten some of the plays we made there. But I remember we ate plenty of bajra rotis!

Some of the Plays We Made

Aurat aur Svasthya (Women and Health)

In Action India, we made a play on health. There is a landless labourer, her child has diarrhea. There's terrible poverty, hunger, the roof leaks. The landlord refuses to give her half a day's leave. She buys medicine from the village shop, but there's no relief. She goes to Dai Ma, the midwife, who gives the child ghutti to drink. There's no improvement. Finally, somehow she takes the child to hospital. The husband asks people for a loan. But the child dies.

We performed it in women's homes, courtyards. Tears would flow, copious tears. Never was there a show in which those watching the play did not cry! You see, these things actually happened—many in the audience had experienced the death of their small children.

Mere Dukh Khareedogi? (Will You Buy My Sorrows?)

I made a play for one of the national-level women's conferences. Some 30-35 women sat in a circle. A basket in my hand, I visited each woman and asked, 'Sister, will you buy my sorrows?' Whichever woman I asked, answered, 'I have plenty already'. One said, 'I have so much sorrow it will cling to me over seven births!' Another said, 'I am full of pain, to the brim.'

Answers kept coming, from women in the circle. The atmosphere became heavy with grief. Tears flowed, like rivers. All the women, poor or rich, became one. That play was *Mere Dukh Khareedogi?* It was unforgettable.

---

[92] Vijaydan Detha (1926-2013) was a celebrated writer and folklorist, Ram Lal Bhatt is an actor and puppeteer from Rajasthan now based in Dehradun, and BV Karanth (1929-2012) was a well-known dramatist and film director who worked in Kannada and Hindi. Vijaydan Detha founded Rupayan Sansthan in 1960 in his own village, Borunda to preserve Rajasthani language, folklore, arts, culture and music.

Shanti narrating stories of women's lives, with visuals painted on a phad. Dakshinpuri, Delhi, 1990.

Suhagan Abhagan (Married Woman, Single Woman)

I did *Suhaban Abhagan* many times. I made three tiny dolls, one in white, one colourfully dressed without ornaments, one wearing colourful clothes and ornaments. Women sat in a circle with their eyes closed. Softly I sang *Teen gaz ki odhni...*[93] and placed the dolls in the centre. Gently I touched each person, saying, 'Open your eyes.'

She would see the doll, and share her feelings—about being *suhagan, abhagan*. Sharing experiences, emotions, with lots of discussion, some women became strong and challenged society. One who was widowed young insisted on still wearing bangles, toe-rings and colourful clothes; after three years her mother-in-law got her married again, just as if she were her own daughter.

But some women said, 'How can we leave our customs and rituals?' Some women raised doubts, saying, 'You are creating divisions between woman and woman; single woman and married woman.' There was little understanding at the time, of the politics of difference. We introduced this, the thinking about differences between woman and woman.

---

[93] *Teen gaz ki odhni* was a song composed in a theatre workshop. It plays upon the three-yard-long odhni, whose four corners are like the four corners of a room, within which one suffocates. This is counterposed against following one's heart, to freedom, flying the odhni like a flag.

Aurat aur Hinsa (Women and Violence)

We made a play on domestic violence, *Aurat aur Hinsa*. The man comes home drunk, beats his wife. One day, she hits back! We used puppets. I went to Darya Ganj and bought the puppets. Bano's daughter became the wife, Shyamu the husband. They made the puppets dance, showing the husband-wife thrashing one another!

We performed this play at the Tirupati National Women's Conference.[94] Women from all over saw it. There we didn't use puppets. I acted as the husband, Jenu as wife. I come home drunk, beat Jenu. Jenu got scared! She left the stage; Bano came and took her place. Somehow, we completed the play. Such weird incidents have happened among us! Later, we talked, and realised she got reminded of some of the violence she'd suffered in her own life.

Aurat aur Panchayat (Women and Panchayats)

I held a theatre workshop with women's groups from villages around Itarsi, Madhya Pradesh. Sharda behn was with me. Some women from Vanangana participated.[95] We made a powerful play, *Women and Panchayats*, based on their experiences, issues.

When we did the play, we'd ask one or two persons from the audience to join us, to act as the bania in the grocery shop, or moneylender. The play showed the corrupt functioning of Panchayats, and how women Panchayat members were trying to bring about change.

We performed in many villages, for thousands of people. Pradan[96] organised workshops, and the shows. Wherever we did it, people responded strongly, with stories about their Panchayats. The local women's groups kept performing the play after we left.

Multiple Audiences

Usually when NGOs arranged shows, more women saw our plays. When we performed without pre-arrangement, there were more men in the audience. Maximum plays we performed in Delhi bastis, in courtyards and homes, on streets and in bazaars.

In bastis, most people supported our views, but some disagreed. When we did our play on communalism, men said, 'You are right—

---

[94] The National Autonomous Women's Conference, Tirupati, was held in 1994.

[95] Vanangana, a women's group in Banda, UP, has a strong theatre group, to date; this is further described in Section 7.

[96] Pradan (Professional Assistance for Development Action) is an NGO that was set up in 1983 to build livelihoods through action by rural communities.

nobody should indulge in fighting and rioting.' But if we did a play on violence against women, some men said, 'You are creating conflict in the home!'

We performed in China in the mid-90s, a play on the women's movement. It had 25-30 people in it—Bhanwri Bai of Tillonia,[97] Kishwar Shirali,[98] and others from different parts of the country. To make the play, we stayed in Sanskriti Kendra,[99] and connected strongly with each other. The play raised many issues that was its strength. We performed at Beijing on a large stage, thousands of women from all over the world saw it![100]

Currently, I provide oversight for the FLP (Feminist Leadership Programme) at Azad Foundation. The trainees, all basti women, are learning to become chauffeurs. Recently, I made a street play with some trainees, on the importance of skills-training, so women can earn. We performed in Govindpuri, Jahangirpuri, Malka Ganj and several bastis. After seeing the play, some more young women got motivated and joined Azad, to learn driving!

When you and I prepared our programme of readings, of old plays like *Aurat aur Dharm* and *Ehsaas,* often my granddaughter Rhea was with us. She learnt many dialogues! I took her to Jaipur to visit my elder son. All along the bus journey she chanted dialogues, '*Beti ke paide hone pe kaun thali bajata hai?' 'Hum bajate hain!'* ... Everybody's ears pricked up. Now that is really educating the public! It was so much fun.

---

[97] Bhanwri Bai is a senior village activist associated with the Tilonia Social Work and Research Centre, Rajasthan.

[98] Kishwar Shirali is a feminist psychotherapist who taught at the Psychology Department, Punjab University, Shimla and set up Atma Svasthya Kendra (ASK) to work directly with disturbed and distressed women and children. She presently lives in Sidhbari, Himachal Pradesh.

[99] Sanskriti Kendra, Anandgram, is a centre of art and craft with space for workshops and residencies. It is located in Aya Nagar, on the Delhi-Gurugram Road, New Delhi.

[100] See Chapter 22 for more details.

11

Grassroots Theatre
Contexts and Concerns

Action India began working in Delhi's resettlement colonies in the mid-70s: these were bastis set up by the Delhi Development Authority (DDA). During 1975-77, the DDA forcibly relocated some 1.5 million people, demolishing shanty colonies in central parts of the city, and sending their inhabitants to some 24 locations, on the outer edges of the city. There was no infrastructure there, no amenities. Gyanvati describes how her home in Gud Mandi, near Delhi University, was bulldozed, her family transported in trucks to Jahangirpuri, which at the time was open scrubland, flood-prone, lacking potable water, toilets or indeed plots for people to build homes on. There was great distress, and a struggle for basic survival (interview 2014).

Action India had been working in a slum at the Old Yamuna Bridge, and continued working with people who got evicted and relocated. In Sunder Nagri, where some of the evictees resettled, Action India worked with weavers, in a bid to help protect their livelihoods. During the late 70s, the organisation shifted its focus to work with women.

By 1980, small groups of women formed, with the intention of helping themselves and the neighbourhood. The early women's group in Jahangirpuri, including Gyanvati, Bhagwati, Reshma, Bimla, Bano, Lakshmi, Suresh, Sudha and Veermati, approached government officials and pressured them to provide basic amenities. They formed a self-help group and used their skills of needlework to earn an income. As they began to understand the ropes better, they took up work on a range of issues: health, hygiene, domestic violence. They gave themselves the name 'Sabla Sangh'—Collective of Empowered Women. Soon, groups in Sunder Nagri, Nand Nagri and Dakshinpuri took on the same name. A few Sabla Sangh women subsequently began working full-time with Action India, on a small salary, as Community Health Workers (CHWs).

Action India-Sabla Sanghs created many street plays. Ankur, Saheli, Shakti Shalini and Jagori collaborated with them from time to time, jointly holding theatre workshops, making plays, posters, exhibitions and phads. As Sheba Chhacchi recalls (interview 2015), organisational boundaries were porous during the 80s, there was a lot of overlap. In many ways, it is a shared history of a movement, rather than separate histories of individual groups.

Posters, Plays and Processes

Aurat ka Chamatkar *(The Wonder that is Woman)*

Women began bringing their health problems, particularly reproductive issues, to Action India-Sabla Sangh women. With support from epidemiologist Dr Sathyamala,[101] the local teams carried out a survey on health facilities and women's reproductive issues. Based on their research, sharing and discussions, in 1980 they made *Aurat ka Chamatkar,* a poster-exhibition on women and reproductive health. Close associates in the movement such as Sheba Chhachhi were also involved in making *Aurat ka Chamatkar.* The exhibition questioned women's lack of control over fertility and childbearing, and provided information on the body, sexuality, menstruation, conception and contraception.[102]

The exhibition was put up at the Mazdoor Mela in Mehrauli, where another branch of Action India had been unionising farm and quarry workers. Union members and their families formed the bulk of the audience during the two-day Mela. For sharing sexuality-related information, the exhibition had two enclosures, one for women, the other for men. This was a skilful ploy, accommodating people's

---

[101] Christina Sathyamala (currently a Research Affiliate at the International Institute of Social Studies, Academic Staff Unit) is an epidemiologist with decades of work in community health.

[102] A documentary film called *Period. End of Sentence,* made with Action India's field support, indicates the organisation's persistent efforts to support women's menstrual health, and fight menstrual taboos. The film won an Oscar: the Academy Award for Best Documentary of 2018 (Short Subject) at the 91st Academy Awards, Los Angeles, 2019.

inhibitions on these issues, within segregated setups. It was a radical set of posters for its time, opening up incredibly important themes which were usually taboo for women. There were flip-charts and booklets as well, providing a range of information.

The explicit diagrams and information in the exhibition embarrassed and shocked many women who were in the audience. But beneath the embarrassment, they were very curious, keen to learn and understand. Sabla Sangh-Action India women guided them and answered their queries. The women responded positively, thoughtfully absorbing new perspectives, which would help them make informed decisions regarding childbearing and related matters. Finding the exhibition very effective, the team took it to other places in Delhi, and outside as well, such as Kanpur.

Processes: Making the Plays

A play's theme would come from the ground, usually when local activists felt the need to take forward their work on a particular issue. Sometimes a play was made within a particular field area, while at other times participants from different areas met and made a play together. To initiate the process of devising a play, a resource person such as Rati Bartholomew or Ein Lall was invited to facilitate a workshop. During the workshop, through discussions and spontaneous improvisations, a storyline would emerge. Actors would take up roles, and rehearsals would begin.

By 1983, Runu Chakraborty picked up enough skills and confidence to facilitate workshops independently, so plays began to be made totally in-house. By the mid-80s, Shanti and Devi Kripa too became adept at facilitating and directing plays. Runu had joined Action India in 1978 as an organiser in Sunder Nagri and Nand Nagri. In 1983 she participated in a month-long theatre workshop in Sonebhadra, Mirzapur, facilitated by Tripurari Sharma and Lakshmi Krishnamurty.[103] That was a memorable workshop, with some 30 to 35 participants, all NGO workers and activists from around the country, including, among others, Nandlalji, Ashwin and Kanhaiya Lal from the Sunder Nagri weavers' group, and Ram Lal, Shiv and Bhanwar Gopalji from Tilonia.

For Runu, that workshop proved transformative. She recalls, 'We made 42 plays in that workshop. I could see the power, of bringing

[103] The workshop was held in the campus of a Gandhian organisation, Banvasi Seva Kendra.

change within a person and the power of communicating it to others.'[104] Back in Delhi, she started doing things differently:

> I shared with other women, and we started making plays at once. Everything was integrated, in those days. We lived it. It showed in our lives, our families, our plays and songs.
>
> We made thousands of plays—we kept making plays—on housing rights, PDS [the public distribution system], child rights, how little girls do so much housework, on domestic violence, untouchability... If there's an issue, we could just make a natak, songs too. That was the

Grassroots activists made 'thousands of plays' and composed and sang many songs during the 80s and 90s. The images above show one such performance.

[104] *Intezaar* was one of the plays made at the Mirzapur workshop; more on this in Chapter 20.

> situation. On every issue, we'd make a play! We showed plays in bastis, and all over. I remember doing a play on housing rights on 8 March. We did a lot of 'angan theatre' too, 'courtyard plays', performed only for women. (interview 2015)

Among their early plays that came out of the workshop was *Ek Rikshevale ki Maut (The Death of a Riksha-Puller),* which focused on the situation of intense poverty so common in the bastis. The protagonist, a riksha-driver, was evicted from Yamuna Pushta and dumped in one of the resettlement colonies. He lost his livelihood, and was driven to an untimely death. All the team members felt strongly about this story. They related real-life stories, composed dialogues and songs, improvised and wove together sequences. Thus they made a play, with no need to write down the script: everyone already knew the words by heart.

They would step out of their handkerchief-sized homes, typically built on 22.5-square-yard plots. Living in frontier colonies, running families in miniscule spaces, these women evolved into never-say-die activists and grassroots theatre-persons. They would meet, rehearse their plays, and perform. Approaching issues from the ground up, they developed sharp critiques of aspects of patriarchy and capitalist-led development, and suggested means by which society may reorder itself. These women were full of ideas, contentious, quarrelling, laughing, enjoying each other's company.

Rakku ki Kahani (Rakku's Story)

In 1984, the Action India-Sabla Sangh women made a play, *Rakku ki Kahani,* which exposed the links between ill health and poverty. Primarily involved in this were community health workers. They based the play on what they saw around them, and the books *Where There Is No Doctor* (1983) and *Rakku's Story* (Zurbrigg 1984), which they read with Bharati Roy Chowdhury. Their understanding of salient issues sharpened during workshops with a few medical doctors.[105]

The play showed a family of construction labourers, unable to access medical care for their little child, Rakku. Ill health and death were traced to inadequate nutrition, a lack of clean water, pitiful health services, misinformation, poverty and powerlessness. Children worked

---

[105] A number of workshops were held, with Drs Sathyamala, Raj Gupta, Ritu Priya Mehrotra and Mira Sadgopal. Early support for health workers also came from the Boston Women's Health Collective.

rather than attending school, their families living hand-to-mouth, with insecure employment, low wages, arduous and back-breaking labour. The play was simple, fulfilling its aim: to communicate, stir thought and discussion. It emphasised people's knowledge and collective struggle to improve matters.

Rakku's Story was performed at different spots within the bastis, to raise awareness and encourage people to prioritise health, understand the root causes of disease, and demand accessible public health services. Most basti families were migrants from various parts of India, economically challenged yet with rich traditions of food, healing remedies and bodily knowhow. A few doctors who saw the play were appreciative; they were reminded of the role of socio-economic factors, which were routinely overlooked and obscured by the modern medical establishment (Vidya Thapa, interview 2015).

Parivar ki Gaadi (The Family Omnibus)

Parivar ki Gaadi was made in December 1985, in a theatre workshop with about 15 women, including seven or eight from Sabla Sangh-Action India, two or three from Jagori, and four students from Lady Irwin College. The theatre workshop was held in Lady Irwin College, located centrally in the city; its principal Dr Anandalakshmy supported the venture. Tripurari facilitated the workshop. The group chose to work on the theme of violence. Some of them had been reading about violence against women, and engaging with issues on the ground. But everyone felt that rather than begin with stories from elsewhere, it would be meaningful to explore their own lives. Over the course of a few days, there was a deep sharing of personal experiences. It turned out that everybody in the group had experienced some

A graphic portrayal of the Family, *Parivar*, displayed on cloth held up by two actors.

form of violence in their families at some time or another, emotional or physical.

This was a shocking realisation. Somebody asked, 'Why do we continue to live in the same families?' There were many answers: we live within our families for security, love, out of habit, just because it is convenient, or for izzat. What are the alternatives? How committed are we to creating alternatives? These were the broad questions the play raised. Much of it was based on incidents that were shared within the group. Raw emotions came into the play. It showed how commonly

Parivar ki Gaadi, Seemapuri, 1986/87, Runu as husband, Rama as wife. Group surrounding Rama includes (left to right) Vrinda Grover, Jyotika Virdi, Parvati, [unidentified], Rajrani (sitting), Susheela, Devi Kripa, Nisha. Post-performance discussion facilitated by Rama, Susheela, Runu and another [unidentified] activist.

women are subjected to insult, abuse and violence, in ordinary life. Myths were shattered—that wife-beating happens only in poor families, or only when a man is drunk, or that men are naturally prone to violence.

Vignettes from different homes were presented. One was of a very wealthy woman whose husband frequently beat her, and wanted her to flirt with his boss so as to help him get a promotion. Another was of a very poor woman, just skin and bones, being dragged on the road and abused by her husband, who was cursing her and calling her useless. Finally, the play showed women coming together to create alternative families, free of violence.

Some in the group felt that the play should be shown in the open, but most felt it should be shown only to women. Among men, especially if done on the streets, it could arouse hostility. Performing for women in courtyards, homes, terraces, women's meetings, it proved to be an excellent play for initiating discussion. It created a charged atmosphere, and opened up a space for women to relate their suffering, which was usually kept hidden within. This was a big relief, for many. Women became very emotional and got involved in helping one another. Those in the play also understood things better, from listening to so many women (Runu, interview 2015; Jagori Samooh 1988: 22).

Over the years, Action India-Sabla Sangh women became adept at counselling and para-legal work. Their Mahila Pachayats helped bring a measure of resolution and justice in situations of domestic violence. They trained others, too. And in later years, there was focused outreach to sensitise men and boys as well.

The Actors: Profiles of Working-Class Activists

Action India-Sabla Sangh activists evolved into frontline feminists, thinkers and doers. They took part in workshops, trainings, study circles, surveys and plays, and worked daily as community organisers. Their learning curve was steep, and they developed feminist perspectives incorporating an intimate understanding of ground realities. These were gentle, angry women, from diverse social backgrounds—Hindu, Muslim, Sikh, Christian; Koli, Khatik, Chamar, Jat, Valmiki, Rajput, Brahmin... These women worked hard within their homes as well—lifting heavy pots, bucketsful of water, kneading mountains of dough, making piles of rotis for multi-generational families, cooking early in the morning before setting off for work, then again at night... Sometimes they walked rather than take a bus or riksha, to save a rupee or two.

Gyanvati (interview 2014) grew up in a weavers' family in old Delhi, and remembers walking miles as a child almost daily, to deliver finished goods and pick up raw material from wholesalers, along with attending school. Her organisational skills came to the fore in Action India. She sang, played the dholak, and added immense value to the many plays she took part in. After Gouri Choudhury's passing (in September 2022), Gyanvati became Chairperson of Action India. Alongside her work for women's empowerment, she brought up four children with progressive values.

Reshma (conversation 2022) battled with her family to step out of home and work with Action India. After her marriage, she moved back to Jahangirpuri, where she set up house, so that she could continue working in the community. A Dalit feminist, she took part in many plays, bringing sharp, incisive analysis to bear upon issues of the day. She later left Action India, invested in three-wheelers, hired drivers for them, and managed all the household finances, as well as saving for old age.

Ramzan (conversation 2016) rebelled against purdah restrictions: she needed to earn. Her family and community, in New Seemapuri, felt it was unsafe for her to go out to work. Persisting in her career, Ramzan became one of the finest health workers. An empathetic, affectionate person, she is quick to grasp new ideas, make changes, and convince others around her to do the same.

Veermati (interview 2014) married into a family in rural Haryana. After her husband's sudden death, she was forced to marry her devar, as is customary in her Jat community. She finally walked out, physically and emotionally traumatised, and returned to her parental home in Jahangirpuri. She managed to bring her elder daughter with her, and later fought for, and won, custody of her younger daughter. Immersing herself in her work with Action India helped her heal, and grow as a person and an activist. She took part in many plays, contributing valuable insights that were both practical and philosophical, and enjoying the learnings and interactions the plays facilitated.

Devi Kripa (interview 1998), a Tamilian Dalit Christian, developed an in-depth understanding of health work over the course of her life. Wise, patient, and an excellent leader, she headed the Community Health Program at Action India for several years. She lived in Sunder Nagri, where she brought up her children and looked after her mother, who had contracted leprosy. Devi Kripa facilitated many workshops within Action India and acted and directed plays from the mid-80s onward. She passed away from cancer in the late 90s.

Vidya Thapa (interview 2015) was born into a family that had migrated from Nepal. She grew up in Dehradun, and moved to Delhi's New Seemapuri after marriage. Here she joined Ankur, imparting functional literacy to women. Soon she shifted to Action India, where she proved an energetic organiser. Vidya was a vibrant presence, a born singer, her voice carrying amid large crowds, and a natural actor.

Manorama (conversation 2016) came from rural Bihar to stay with her brother in Sunder Nagri. She was single, having been widowed at the age of 19. In Delhi, she began going for Sabla Sangh meetings, which were held near her house. Despite her brother's opposition, she joined Action India. She gained knowledge and experience, participated in many street plays, and emerged out of the taboos and restrictions imposed on widows. She later chose to remarry, making a success of it despite opposition from her family. Today she is held in respect by members of her family and community for the help she extends to anyone in need.

Susheela (conversation 2016) of Dakshinpuri was the first woman in her (high-caste) family to step out for work. She faced barbed comments and outright hostility. Later, when she gained knowledge, taught and advised others, everybody grew to respect her. She is a seasoned activist who recalls many plays which she helped create, and that she acted in. She comments that there were many protests (dharnas) during the 80s and 90s. And that this is no longer the case.

I got to know some of the Action India-Sabla Sangh women when I began visiting them in their office at Jahangiripuri, in 1980-81 (soon after joining the *Om Swaha* team). I would take along material to share, help prepare posters, and so on.[106]

This was a Delhi I never knew existed—rows of matchbox homes, community toilets, barren parks, slushy lanes, hole-in-the-wall shops, people and more people, children playful, snotty, ragged and bright-eyed. Gyanvati's, Reshma's and Veermati's homes and the tiny G-block

[106] For instance, I picked up booklets, flip charts and videos on menstruation from the Voluntary Health Association of India (VHAI) in south Delhi, and shared these with the Action India-Sabla Sangh activists, in their tiny office in G-block Jahangarpuri (which is in north Delhi). I worked on preparing communication material with them too; Reshma recalls (conversation 2022) my making illustrations of ringworm, tapeworm and other worms, posters which she and the rest of the team used for years as part of their health education programme in Jahangirpuri.

office room were vibrant learning spaces, teaching me more about society and economy than my college classrooms did.

Sheba Chhachhi interacted with Sabla Sangh-Action India women during the 80s, and participated in several theatre workshops with them. One of these was an intense, experimental theatre workshop with Deepak Mazumdar,[107] held in Bharatpur, with influences from Grotowski's Poor Theatre, which dispensed with lavish props, elaborate settings and costumes.

A theatre workshop was held in Naukuchia Taal in the late 90s, facilitated by theatre-person Anamika Haksar.[108] One of its aims was to develop women's narratives, of 'my identity'—personal stories, woven into the social fabric. Sheba proposed fictionalised documentation, which would allow certain things that couldn't be said in a pure documentary to be woven in. Though this wasn't taken up at the time, Sheba herself took the idea forward in photographic art: she invited several activists to recreate how they would like to be seen. The staged portraits that resulted were fictional and captured a deeper self. Contemplating her own life-journey, each activist carefully selected her role, props, costume, settings; the resultant images were dense and multi-layered. These staged images were theatrical: silent mono-acts, akin to installations, suggestive of the multiple dimensions of a life, a person, a feminist.[109]

The Action India-Sabla Sangh women held their own in the thick of the feminist movement. They lived in tough conditions, and as they

Theatre workshop, Naukuchia Taal, late 1990s, (In circle, right to left) Sumitra, Devi Kripa, Ramzan, Maharani, and others; (second image, left to right): Gouri, Maharani, Prem, Vidya.

---

[107] Deepak Mazumdar was a director and poet from Calcutta, and an important influence on his work was Jerzy Grotowski, the Polish theatre director.

[108] Anamika Haksar is a well-known theatre writer, director, and filmmaker.

[109] Some of the staged portraits are available on www.tate.org.uk/art/artworks/chhachhi-seven-lives-and-a-dream-130204 (accessed 12 June 2023).

emerged they broke many barriers, personal and political. As Gyanvati says (interview 2014), 'I stepped out of purdah, then out of my home, lane, neighbourhood, and out into the world!' As they emerged, they questioned class, caste, the privileges of the elite, including within the movement; those challenges remain alive, and relevant.

Continuing to have deep roots in rich oral cultures, even as they came into literacy and became creative writers and composers, it is not surprising that many of the Sabla Sangh-Action India activists took to theatre, immersed themselves in it, and became adept. The medium was well suited to their talents and their purposes. Rather than writing long tomes, they narrated stories, their own and others', showing rather than telling, communicating directly and face-to-face. Each play represented a slice of reality—in fact fictionalised documentation of the grim realities they knew so well.

There were the 'Chhoti Sablas' too—a next generation, beginning in small ways with activists' daughters, spreading to hundreds of girls in the bastis. Runu began making plays with girls in Jahangirpuri, during the mid-80s. She would tell and listen to stories, they would take up roles. The first play the Chhoti Sablas put up was about animals helping one another. Everybody enjoyed it tremendously. Runu muses (interview 2015), 'Little girls in the bastis, mostly daughters of Sabla Sangh women to begin with, and then many more, started becoming very creative. Those girls have grown up with different ideas. It shows in their lives!'

Children were always in the audience, engaged, curious, learning, expressing.

12

How Religions Divide Us

Women Against Bigotry and Hate

Action India-Sabla Sangh activists worked on issues concerning gender, religion, and fundamentalism, developing campaigns against religious bigotry, prejudice, and hate. As part of this work, they made and performed a number of street plays. Two important plays were *Aurat aur Dharm* and *Zimmedar Kaun: Dharm ke Naam pe Dange Kyon?*

Aurat aur Dharm (Women and Religion)

Aurat aur Dharm debuted in February 1985, just a few months after the anti-Sikh carnage that rocked Delhi following Indira Gandhi's assassination on 31 October 1984. The city erupted into violence. The sprawling bastis of Trilokpuri, Nand Nagri, Seemapuri and Sunder Nagri in east Delhi, Mongolpuri, Sultanpuri, and Nangloi in west Delhi, and Jahangirpuri in north Delhi were among the worst affected. Devi Kripa, Veermati, Vidya and other Action India-Sabla Sangh activists engaged with survivors, Sikh women and children, some of whom had seen fathers, sons, husbands and brothers humiliated and killed. Survivors were traumatised and grief-stricken.

Secular-minded people and organisations including Sabla Sangh, Action India, Ankur, Saheli and many others formed Nagrik Ekta Manch (NEM), a citizens' group, to provide urgent relief. NEM set up a number of relief camps in different parts of the city. Gyanvati recalls a big relief camp that NEM set up in Jahangirpuri, where activists distributed food, clothing, blankets, and talked with survivors. Those from Jahangirpuri A-block were very angry: many people had been killed, women raped, their homes burnt. Activists tried to help survivors come to terms with what had happened and think about the future. Testimonies were taken down, to help track down perpetrators. After the camps dispersed, Ankur and Action India continued working in Tilak Vihar, where many of the survivors were relocated. They wound up a few months later, when Sikh community organisations took over, and the government provided menial jobs to some of the survivors.

As activists tried to understand and help survivors grapple with many difficult issues, a process of reflection was sparked off. They saw the blatant use of religion, by families, to control women's sexuality, mobility and property. Widowed Sikh survivors were expected to wear only white, and shed all their ornaments. Some were pressured to marry a younger brother-in-law, the 'chadar odhna' custom sanctified among several communities in Punjab and Haryana. Several activists had faced similar taboos and pressures in their own lives: for instance, Veermati had been forced to marry her devar. When some of the widowed survivors were provided monetary compensation and a small house in Tilak Vihar, families scrambled to grab these. Activists intervened as much as possible, but survivors were in a tricky situation; it was not easy to fight family elders and community patriarchs.[110]

Mulling over their own lives and what they found happening with Sikh survivors, activists saw how religion was being used to oppress women. Seething over the injustices, Sabla Sangh-Action India and Ankur activists realised it was important to go deeper, and spread public awareness on underlying chronic issues.

In February '85, a group of activists met regularly, with Ein Lall as their resource person. The group, including Gyanvati, Veermati, Maharani, Sumitra, Reshma, Shanti, Jenu, Devi Kripa, Runu and Malika, were all very shaken by the riots. They had worked in relief camps across the city. Discussing their experiences, and the continuing experiences of Sikh survivors, they felt the need to build wider understanding on the role of religion in women's lives, the way it is used to crush and control. They began to role-play, improvised scenes, characters, songs, movements. Within a few intensive weeks, they had a play ready; they called it *Aurat aur Dharm*.

The play made a strong bid for women to come together, across

[110] Lalita Ramdas (1985; 2015) describes some of the work with survivors which she, Jaya Shrivastava and others of Ankur engaged in, alongside Action India activists in Tilak Vihar, well into 1985.

religious boundaries. In a brief introduction, they explained, 'We realized that no religion accords women equal rights. Rituals and beliefs reinforce our position as slaves of men. Why should we women suffer, due to an ascribed identity? It divides us. Why don't we create another, more basic, identity, a new set of values, uproot and discard this hollow exploitative facade?' (Jagori Samooh 1988: 94).

Shanti recalls:

> We made a play, *Aurat aur Dharm*. Young men had been killed by mobs—in some houses two, four, six. The government distributed forms. Women's tears were still flowing, but they ran around to offices, filled forms: name, address, the data of dead men. When money started being distributed a worse calamity befell them. They were married by elders, the biradar, without their consent, to brothers-in-law. To control her and her money, they forcibly put bangles around her wrists!
>
> Mobs took men's lives, then the government didn't intervene! Now, this new assault on women, under the pretext of custom and tradition! All her life she bears mountain-loads of pain, but why? Our play showed the women's new perspectives. They needed homes to live in, education for their children, food to fill their bellies, and a halt to atrocities.
>
> The play had a scene which showed a widowed woman wrapped in a white chadar, weeping. Hundred of rituals for women, not one for men! Why so many restrictions on women, controlling her desires, body, food, drink and dress? It so happened that some of us in the play group lost our husbands around the same time—to a heart attack, TB or an accident. My husband had died. We shared issues connected to our lives. This helped widen the discussion.
>
> We performed all over Delhi. It stirred up discussions on single women's issues. Those discussions saved many women from forced marriage. We achieved this not by fighting, rather through dialogue and persuasion. Women's thinking changed and they grew stronger.

The team began performing *Aurat aur Dharm* in the first week of March 1985. The earliest shows were in their own bastis. Those who had made the play acted in it; two men from Action India joined them.

4 March 1985: The team arrived in Jahangirpuri, women in salwar kameez, saris, kurta pyjama, beating a rhythm with the tambourine (daphli) and dholak, singing loud and clear. People gathered in a jiffy, at the slight open space where the play was performed. It showed women rejecting bigoted religious injunctions, menstrual taboos, celebrating the birth of a daughter, challenging the biases against single women, wearing what they want. Two characters, Ustaad and Jamura,[111] discussed how men rule the world, insisting it's the natural order. Women like Rukma and her sister-in-law Jethani refused to be quiescent victims; so did Harjeet, a young Sikh survivor.

Some people in the audience were jolted by the challenge to religious authority, and words like 'menstruation' being openly spoken. Girls and women felt a sense of relief: they were supposed to be ashamed of 'dirty' blood—but here were didis saying there's nothing to be ashamed of. Rather it's a matter to take pride in. They found the idea of celebrating the birth of a girl wonderful and liberating!

Coming together to challenge patriarchy across religions.

8 March 1985: Many women's organisations came together to celebrate International Women's Day just outside the Red Fort. It was a huge gathering. *Aurat aur Dharm* was performed as part of the programme.

Imagine performing in front of the Red Fort, a magnificent site, thick with centuries of history; here were the women of India stating their case for equality, liberty, and human rights.

> *The play opens: women sing about equality at the start of time, enact earth covered with water, plants arise, a forest, animals, and then human beings.*
>
> Ustad and Jamura: What nonsense! What do women know about the world?
>
> Jamura: The world was made by men—cities, streets, schools, colleges, police, law courts, guns, bullets, factories, radio, TV...

[111] A know-it-all man and his sidekick: stock characters in bhand, a traditional folk theatre form in North India.

Ustad: Every religion says, keep women within four walls. (*They throw shawls over the women, covering them.*) Our religion has no place for impure women!

...Jethani (holding an infant): Can you help us, Panditji, Mullah ji? My baby is dying!

Panditji (Hindu priest) and Mullahji (Muslim priest): We cannot help you. A menstruating woman has touched your baby. Nobody can save the child!

The baby dies; family and neighbours blame Rukma (Jethani's younger sister-in-law), because Rukma was menstruating at the time she helped Jethani look after the baby.

Jethani: My baby died of dehydration. We did not get proper advice, nor correct information. It had nothing to do with Rukma's menstruation!

...Jethani is about to deliver another baby, and calls upon Rukma to assist her. Rukma hesitates, for she is menstruating; Jethani urges her to come help. Rukma assists her during the delivery; a girl is born. Rukma beats a thali to celebrate.

Neighbours question: Who beats the thali when a girl is born?

Rukma and Jethani reply: We do! We are really happy to have a girl! We are the ones who give birth, yet when we're born, nobody celebrates!

... An elderly widow, bamboozled by her sons, signs away her property. A much younger woman, Harjeet, a Sikh survivor, begins working for a living. Her parents-in-law insist she marry their younger son; she categorically refuses. In the house where she's employed for domestic work, they ask why she wears colourful clothes.

She says: I wear what I wish!... Why should I dance to others' tunes? Nobody is going to feed me, I run my own life, in the midst of great hardship!

... Ustad: She's out to face the world! Let's see how long she can fight...

Jamura: By citing religion, we divide women, and rule!

Rukma: Religious heads and politicians use religion for nefarious ends! We lose our strength!

Harjeet: We grow weak, and cannot wage collective struggle, against common enemies like poverty and unemployment!

Jethani: Today we ask, in the people's court, how long will they get away with this?

Rukma: We women are uniting and asking questions!

Song: *Dheere dheere aayee hamein chetana... Ab poochheinge ham khoob savaal... (Gradually we grew aware... Now, we ask plenty of questions...)*

The show went off very well. Everybody watched intently, laughed at the humour, and grew thoughtful when issues and concerns were unpacked. Runu (interview 2015), who acted as Ustad alongside Mallika Virdi's Jamura, muses, 'People remember that performance to date.[112] We won a lot of respect and different groups asked us to perform, in different areas of the city. We did this play and other plays, so many times, in localities, rich and poor, at meetings and demonstrations.'

A play like this holds meaning at several levels. It indicated that women rebel; even in the space of the home they get together and quietly support one another. The women's movement is not something out there, external to the daily lives of women. Rather, it grows in and from the hearts and minds of ordinary women. Dissent is generated within complex daily dialectics; feminism builds on the struggles waged by countless ordinary women.

Wherever it was performed, the play evoked plenty of discussion. It dared to breach the silence around some very sensitive issues. Collectivity lent courage, to challenge religious norms and dogma. As women talked with one another and the actor-activists who worked with the community, issues were discussed, silences were breached, awareness grew, and for many, over time, quiet confidence gradually replaced confusion, shame and embarrassment.

Zimmedar Kaun: Dharm ke Naam pe Dange Kyun? (Who Is Responsible: Why Riot in the Name of Religion?)

Another street play was made around 1989-90, seeking to tackle religious bigotry head-on. Called *Zimmedar Kaun: Dharm ke Naam pe Dange Kyun?* (*Zimmedar Kaun* in short), it encouraged audiences to consider who was responsible for the murderous attacks on Sikhs in 1984; and analysed Hindutva politics.

---

[112] Runu recalls an odd incident during the Red Fort show: two women in the audience started hooting. She and Malika called them out by name, and they went quiet; the audience probably thought this was part of the play!

In the mid-80s, the Vishwa Hindu Parishad (VHP) had initiated a nation-wide campaign for access to the Babri Masjid in Ayodhya, allegedly built over Hindu shrines. Women activists found, in their own bastis, a growing polarisation between communities in response to fundamentalists and politicians, who were in effect drumming up hatred against minority communities.

Vidya, of Nand Nagri, recalls that not all perpetrators of the 1984 carnage were outsiders. Insiders were involved, people from neighbouring lanes and localities, who shared markets, schools and streets with the victims. In Nand Nagri, people from different religions lived in close proximity. Sikhs were concentrated in a few pockets. The mobs knew where the Sikhs lived, went straight there and committed murder and rape, burnt down houses. They caught Sikh men, chopped off their long hair, poured kerosene over them and burnt them. Vidya and her colleagues were aghast, horrified; they worked with survivors, women and children.

> Time went by. There was no justice. The survivors were facing enormous problems, and the killers were roaming around scot-free. We couldn't bear to see this situation. We felt we have to do something. We cannot sit silent. That is why we made the play *Zimmedar Kaun*, and performed it all over. Veermati, Sudha, Prem, Vidya, Susheela, Maharani, a lot of us were in that play. (Vidya Thapa, interview 2015.)

Rati Bartholomew and Runu Chakraborty ran a two-week workshop in Saharanpur, in which the play was made. Some 20 women from Action India-Sabla Sangh went for the workshop. There was intense discussion on the 1984 riots. Though they were no longer working with survivors, they could not forget what had happened, or that perpetrators were still roaming free.

Based on their deep involvement, together they analysed the phenomenon of communalism. They spoke about how ordinary people become pawns in deadly games played by the powerful. Unscrupulous politicians whip up negative emotions in ordinary people, and get them to kill, loot, rape, destroy people and property belonging to the 'other' group—all in the name of religion. Many people who join murderous mobs are misled; yet they too must be held accountable for their actions.

The activists discussed how propaganda around the Babri Masjid was inciting Hindu masses to violence. Hindutva politicians were spreading the message that the mosque should be demolished and a temple built on the spot, where Lord Ram was supposedly born millennia ago. This idea created havoc; it was designed to foment conflict and might lead to riots.

Out of all this churning, the group made *Zimmedar Kaun.* The play portrayed communalism very imaginatively. There was a beautiful forest with trees, flowers, a river, rabbits, deer and an elephant. Everyone sang a song they'd composed, set to the lilting folk tune, '*Lo basant aayo, phool khile, phool khile!*'[113] Suddenly, a monster appeared, roaring loudly. Animals took fright, ran helter-skelter and began fighting one another. That monster represented the ideology of communalism. Shanti (interview 2015) remembers, 'Reshma was the elephant, Bimla, Maharani and others were deer and rabbits. I was the monster!'

The play went on to ask, Ram and Rahim are one, so what is the fight about? If Ram is present everywhere, in every particle of this universe, what need is there to break a mosque and build a temple in its place? Mandir-masjid (temple-mosque) was just an excuse. The aim was to create riots! Ordinary people want food, jobs, education, not mandir or masjid. The play showed Ram, Sita, Lakshman, and Hanuman as ordinary people, who don't want any conflict.

The play turned out to be very powerful. Gyanvati (interview 2014) says, 'I will never in my life forget the training by Rati. It was stupendous. We learnt so much from that workshop. I didn't take any of the children with me: my saas took care of them. I could immerse myself fully in making the play.'

The team performed *Zimedaar Kaun* in their own neighbourhoods, in lanes and alleys, many other places in the city, as well as Ghaziabad and Gurgaon. Sometimes somebody asked them to perform it in their area, and they would go do it; they also performed in public spots, like the Boat Club and Lal Qila (Red Fort) Grounds. Sometimes they performed every day; they continued over the years to perform at least once a fortnight; later, once a month.

For Vidya, it was her first experience of playing a male role. She found it difficult at first; felt awkward wearing kurta pajama, and acting on the streets. Crowds would gather, more men than women, because more men were on the streets. But as they continued doing the play, everybody grew confident. Vidya felt comfortable in her white kurta pajama. People took the play seriously, watched it with full attention, and responded positively. They voiced their feelings. Many agreed

---

[113] Folk song sung at the advent of spring, Basant, when flowers bloom.

with what was being conveyed, supported the ideas and said that those responsible for the riots must be punished.

The theme was immensely sensitive and there was opposition, too, especially when they took the play into the heart of the violence, quarters where the rioters lived: 'We faced a lot of hostility and rage, a lot of threats. But we were charged up. We did not give up. We were not afraid. We were not bothered about any danger to ourselves. At home, our families were concerned; they said we should be careful.' (Vidya, interview 2015.)

Women protest bigotry and hate in the name of religion, and lay claim to peace and harmonious coexistence.

Their families were scared, and would often forbid the actors from doing the play. So, when going for a performance, or a rally on these issues, they hid it from their families, just said that they're going to work. Gyanvati recalls (interview 2014), 'My parents-in-law objected, but my husband understood. He read the newspaper and asked me, "You'd gone for this? Action India's name is in the paper." I said, "Yes, this is what I had gone for!" He didn't say anything after that.'

As Vidya (interview 2015) recalls, the actors came from different bastis—Veermati, Gyanvati, Reshma, Sudha and Bhagwati were from Jahangirpuri, Shanti, Rama and Susheela from Dakshinpuri, and the rest were from east Delhi, Seemapuri, Sunder Nagri and Nand Nagri. They enjoyed meeting and doing the play: 'We also had a lot of fun! We chatted, laughed and teased each other. We were friends from different bastis and it was an occasion to be together!'

Performing, whether in bastis or elsewhere in the city, was not devoid of danger; the actors were extraordinarily courageous, continuing to perform despite the real risks involved. They kept learning as they went along. When they performed in the Chandni Chowk-Old Delhi area, they often asked a person from Nishant Natya Manch[114] to accompany

[114] Nishant Natya Manch, a street theatre group set up in the mid-70s, had an awareness of gender issues from its early years. Take for instance the play *Gaddha*, composed by the group and performed innumerable times, especially during the 80s. The group is still active, and is helmed by Shamsul Islam and Neelima Sharma.

them; he was more aware of the local culture and politics of that area, and could confidently tackle any tensions that might arise.

Sometimes, a gang of rowdies would land up during a performance and shout, 'These people are anti-Ram. Throw them out... We will build the mandir there! We will kill or be killed!' They would gather suddenly, and instigate violence. The team decided that they would not after react in such situations. If the atmosphere deteriorated, they would wind up the play, form a circle, play the tambourine and sing, '*Mandir masjid girjaghar ne baant liya bhagvan ko, Dharti baanti, sagar baanta, Mat baanto insaan ko!' (Temples, mosques, and churches have divided god, the earth and oceans, Do not divide human beings!)* Then they would simply leave that place, and go elsewhere.

Occasionally, finding their threats were not working, the aggressive disrupters would slink away. Other people in the audience would feel relieved, and ask the group to continue the play. If the ground was clear, the actors would pick up where they'd left off, and complete the play. It inevitably led to a rich discussion.

One day, the group was performing *Zimmedar Kaun* in Palika Bazaar, Connaught Place. Section 144[115] had been imposed in the area, and there was an unusually heavy police presence. A huge crowd gathered. They had hardly performed for two or three minutes when policemen surrounded them, shouting, 'Stop the play! Section 144 is imposed, and you are doing a play!' Usually Gouri Choudhury and Bharati Roy Chowdhury, Action India organisers, accompanied the play group to public spots like this and handled situations, talking to the police and things like that, but that day they hadn't been able to come. Shanti recalls (interview 2015):

We spoke to the police, explaining everything. The play had Ram, Sita, Lakshman, Hanuman. Devi Kripa was Ram; after her role, she went and spoke to the police. Sudha was Lakshman; after her role, she called Devi, "It's time for Ram's role, come quick!" Then Sudha went and spoke to the police. I said, "Sudha, it's Lakshman's role now, come quick!" Then I went and spoke to the police. Devi would say, "Shanti, it's time for Hanuman's role, come quick!" One by one, we kept the police busy, talking and convincing them, and the play went on. People there supported us totally, some even spoke to the police—"Sir, they are giving a positive message, let them perform!"

---

[115] Section 144 Indian Penal Code prohibited the assembly of four or more persons.

Farq (Differences)

Zimmedar Kaun inspired many people to recognise and oppose communal ideologies. Another play which had a similar effect was *Farq*, made in 1987.

Farq powerfully showed the impact of communal violence on women's lives. Made by Alarippu, it was directed by Rati Bartholomew and its actors included Lakshmi Krishnamurty, Runu, Tripurari, Gouri Dey and Vrinda Grover. Tripurari, Lakshmi and Runu played a Hindu, Muslim and Sikh woman, all suffering from the trauma of Partition, as well as the travesties of daily life. After they met and got to know one another, they overcame stereotypical prejudices and realised how similar their pain and suffering was. This powerful play evoked a strong emotional response whenever it was performed (Runu, interview 2015; Gouri Dey, conversation 2023).

Despite the steady work being done by such theatre and people's organisations, fundamentalists carried on with their agenda of communal divide, spreading hatred quite successfully. Secular-minded grassroots organisations like Action India, Sabla Sangh, Alarippu, Ankur, and Shakti Shalini collaborated with progressive activist groups such as the Sampradayikta Virodhi Andolan (SVA, Movement Against Communalism), which had formed after the 1984 riots. SVA aimed to mobilise public opinion in universities and outside, in Delhi and some other places like Kanpur, to build a counter-force to communalism.

Dilip Simeon, a historian and activist, spearheaded SVA; he recalls the contributions of stalwart women activists as being a very important part of the concerted movement against communalism. On 30 January 1990, SVA held a demonstration through Chandni Chowk, and a Convention at the Delhi Town Hall. There were hundreds of people, and much excitement, in opposition to Hindutva politics around the Babri Masjid and Ram Janmabhoomi issue. Dilip remembers (interview 2015) how active the women's groups were; their vibrant participation, and the powerful theatre they performed:

> Ankur and Action India were there from the bastis, in considerable numbers. They did their plays during the demonstration too, on 30 January 1990, Gandhi's martyrdom anniversary. We held a huge march through Old Delhi, and then held a big Convention, at the Town Hall, a historical venue. The women were an enthusiastic and important part of SVA, of the whole movement against communalism. Whenever we organised something, they were sure to participate. Through the

> years, they were there. Their plays, songs, speeches, the energy they brought in, was very special. By the mid-90s, SVA lost steam, though the women's organisations kept saying we should keep it going.

Both feminist street plays were staged during the Convention: *Zimmedar Kaun*, and *Farq*. Runu recalls that when they did *Farq*, inside the hall, there was pin-drop silence. Everyone was moved and many in the audience had tears in their eyes.

The group performed the play again a few times, often for all-women audiences. The three lead actors took it to Pakistan too. The response there was much the same: people got emotional. That play was never actually done on the streets, simply because of the extremely sensitive subject matter.

On 8 March 1991, *Zimmedar Kaun* was performed at a huge anti-communal programme at the Red Fort Grounds, viewed by hundreds of people.

On 6 December 1992, the Babri Masjid was broken down, as per the rightist fundamentalist stratagem. The Action India-Sabla Sangh group continued doing *Zimmedar Kaun* and working on related issues with vigour.

Zimmedar Kaun, Red Fort Grounds, 8 March 1991. (Left to right) Reshma (back to us), Susheela, Veermati, Gyanvati, Shanti (all sitting). (Arms raised) Susheela, Maharani, Bimla, Veermati, Sudha, Reshma. (Standing, lone) Devi Kripa.

Women and Religion Group

In 1990, Action India, Ankur and Shakti Shalini set up a joint study circle named the 'Women and Religion Group' in order to strengthen and deepen understanding of these issues. Members were diverse: Afsha and Nafisa, from Ankur, lived in Chandni Chowk; Shashi, a Dalit feminist, was also from Ankur; Shahjahan Begum and Sudha Tiwari were from Shakti Shalini; Sudha, Veermati and Mary from Sabala Sangh-Action India; Sharda behn and Gouri Choudhury were from Action India; and Geetanjali Gangoli and myself were from Delhi University.

Each one shared personal experiences of religion. It turned out that most of us drew strength from spiritual-philosophical tenets, but felt oppressed by institutionalised religion. The group conducted a survey on purdah, finding many commonalities among Hindus and Muslims. Shahjahan Begum led the group into reading the Quran, especially its advice on women's rights. The group read Valmiki's Ramayana, and Dr Uma Chakravarti held a session on the Ramayana as myth and history.

The Women and Religion Group brought out a booklet called *Dharm Hamein Jodta Kaise Hai, Todta Kaise Hai* (1992; *Religion: How it Unites Us, How it Divides Us*). The booklet carried findings from the survey on purdah; a write-up on Sita and Surpanakha as voices of dissent; a note on women's rights in Islam; and reflections on the role of religion in our lives.

At a regional meeting of the National Women's Conference, in Kanpur in late 1992, the Women and Religion Group held a session titled 'Reinterpretation of Religious Texts', which explored feminist perspectives on figures such as Sita, Kaushalya, Kaikeyi and Surpanakha. Kaushalya (in one seldom-read chapter of the unexpurgated *Valmiki Ramayana*) insists that Ram obey her and stay on in Ayodhya, refusing Dashrath's command to go into exile: she reasons that mother-right precedes father-right. This interpretation would be anathema to the Hinduva brigade, but ordinary women connected deeply with the sentiment. At the session were many women believers from Kanpur bastis; they easily identified with Sita, as a single mother, as an immensely strong woman who braves all odds and, in the end, rejects her fickle husband.

The Religion and Women Group was active up to 1993. Its deliberations fed back into daily intensive work, in Delhi bastis. Insights developed in the small group were thus shared widely, forming a creative continuum with the theatre, and songs and campaigns against communalism.

13

The Limitless Work of New Creation
Nav Srishti

After the tragic death of her daughter Nur Jahan in 1978, Shahjahan Begum devoted herself to supporting women in crisis through the shelter home Shakti Shalini. She also keenly felt the need to educate young girls, so they could be self-supporting, build their lives on fresh lines, and escape the violence her daughter had suffered. This led to her setting up Nav Srishti, thus creating new opportunities for girls in Delhi's working-class neighborhoods.

In the lane where Shahjahan Begum lived, part of Nangloi resettlement colony, most girls were pulled out of school by Class 4 or 5. Ninety percent of its adolescent girls were not studying. In the early 90s, Shahjahan Aapa started a non-formal school in her tiny home: her daughters-in-law Shaheen and Shahida, and a young woman named Reena Banerjee, taught languages and needlework to girls from the neighbourhood, on a voluntary basis.

The effort was successful. Girls found a space where they could discuss their ideas and aspirations, grow mentally, as well as learn many skills. Parents were satisfied that their daughters were safe—a major obstacle to sending adolescent girls to the local school was sexual harassment along the route, and even within school. Soon there was increasing demand for admission into the classes Shahjahan Aapa had started. She ran around and got a small grant, so they could rent a slightly bigger room. As the organisation took root, they gave it a name—Nav Srishti, meaning 'new creation'.

Reena Banerjee worked as a typist in Shakti Shalini. She gave progressively more of her time to Nav Srishti, and finally took up the post of Director, a full-time commitment. Between them, she and Aapa secured grants, rented a larger space, took in more students and arranged to coach them in several subjects. Their first batch of girls passed Class 10, and then Class 12, through the National Institute of Open Schooling. Within a decade, Nav Srishti was teaching a few hundred girls, in seven working-class areas of Delhi. A few boys were taken in too—working children who had been unable to complete school, and were very keen to do so.

These young people made fast progress in their studies, and matured in terms of their life skills and understanding of social issues. Nav Srishti was concerned about so many other children and adolescents in Nangloi and other bastis, and wished to motivate the larger community to think on education, gender and social issues. That's when the idea of street theatre took shape—as a means to reach out. The group began doing street theatre, to take the change further and deeper.

A Girls' Street Theatre Group

Their work showed definite results. By the early years of the twenty-first century, Shahjahan Aapa said (interview 2002):

> There's change due to our work. Muslim, Hindu girls study in Nav Srishti; and a few boys too. Earlier, no parents would have dreamt of letting their girls do plays on the street! I told them, "You keep girls shut behind seven locks, yet they run away. Here girls are in the open, they understand what's good, what's bad. They have the power to think for themselves. Let them alone, let them think for themselves. Ask them sometimes what they want, what they don't want."
>
> They have done many plays, and they show these in Nangloi and several other areas. One of the first plays they made was on dowry and dowry deaths—like *Om Swaha* 20 years ago!

Nav Srishti's street theatre group was launched in 1998, with 20 adolescents, aged 14-18. These fourteen girls and six boys participated in an intensive workshop, run by theatre-persons from the NGOs Mehek and Alarippu. However, several of the girls' parents kept objecting to their girls mixing so closely with boys, saying it was giving them a bad name in the community. Nav Srishti tried to persuade them, but the parents gave an ultimatum—they would withdraw their daughters unless the boys left the group. Rather than let this happen, the boys had no option but to bow out. Some of them continued to provide support from the outside. The group itself became an all-girls group.

Mein Anpadh Kyun, Holambi Kalan, 25 January 2003. Nav Srishti theatre troupe gathers an audience, and then stages the play on the street.

Soon, the group of 14 girls was making plays, and performing these within Nangloi and elsewhere. They continued their studies alongside this. Within four years, they made 10 plays, all on issues pertinent to their own lives and neighbourhoods—education, domestic violence, child marriage, dowry, women's work, sexual harassment, rape, son preference, alcoholism, and drug addiction.

Girls' voices were not meant to be heard, their views were never taken into account. Through street theatre, they articulated their perspectives. Zeibun, Zarina, Varsha and Babita all experienced a process of growing confidence as they presented their issues and the concerns of their peers to large numbers of people. Crossing barriers and breaking stereotypes, they brought fresh possibilities alive. Varsha describes what this was like: 'Earlier I felt scared. But after I learnt to act, and we performed in our area, I have lost my fears. Now, I enjoy performing! I can go anywhere' (Mehrotra 2002: 15).

At a typical performance in 2003, the girls' team arrived in Holambi Kalan, a shanty colony in outer Delhi, wearing identical grey kurtas. They gathered a crowd by beating a dholak and singing '*Natak Dekho!*' Nearly 80 people watched the play intently. It was called *Main Anpadh Kyun (Why Am I Illiterate?)* and revolved around Meena, a girl who was denied schooling, married off at 16, and found it impossible to earn well after her husband's death in an accident. Most appreciated the message, that girls should be educated, and said that such plays should also be shown on radio and TV. Several women saw themselves or their daughters reflected in Meena. A few children said the play inspired them to study. Shabana, a Nav Srishti team member, said, 'People come for entertainment, but they go away thinking about the issues' (Ramachandran 2003: 53).

Doing these plays was incredibly empowering for the girls involved. In many ways, they embodied the change they were championing, making it persuasive, especially for other young girls. In communities where girls, Hindu and Muslim, were largely confined to their homes and married early, for girls to come out on the streets—singing, playing musical instruments, acting and speaking publicly—was an extremely radical step. Performances stimulated discussion, questions, and reflection.

Collaborating with other NGOs, the group performed in Vikaspuri, Najafgarh, Samaypur Badli and other localities. On Women's Day they performed at Talkatora Stadium, for dozens of women's movement groups. They performed in schools and colleges, and at meetings and conferences, like the National Convention of Education organised by several NGOs. These performances were highly appreciated.[116]

Initially, the girls faced nasty comments and barbed remarks, insults and humiliation. Zeibun's brother forbade her from doing plays because his friends laughed at him. But their mother, Khatoon Begum, said: 'If your friends don't like it, it's their problem. I like Zeibun doing this. I will support her!' Persistence paid off. Three years later, Zeibun says: 'Now, those same boys respect us. When we walk by, they make way!' (Mehrotra 2002: 16).

Shahjahan Aapa thoughtfully sums up the changes she has seen in the girls' lives:

> I have come from a time when we couldn't talk, and today we walk shoulder to shoulder with others. Looking at my own journey, I feel that girls will learn beyond what we have, they will do more and better than us. They will run families with equality and will teach others too.
>
> They are doing Open School, BA, MA, computer courses, and getting jobs. They have forged far ahead!
>
> But if we had not come out onto the streets and raised our voices, asked questions, these girls too would not have studied, nor done

---

[116] I observed the stunning impact these performances had on students from different colleges each time the Nav Srishti troupe performed at gender workshops for REACH, an inter-university programme. I conducted gender workshops for REACH between 2003 and 2007, and was able to invite the troupe, which was a joy all round.

street plays. They would not have come out into the world and become so capable.

The women's movement has been a very big word for us, but not just a word. Narivaad, narivaadi soch, [Feminism, feminist thought], is critical for me. We are not dividing—rather we are bringing everybody together. There is no limit to this work. If we reach one post, there is another ahead!' (Mathur 2003).

Women's movement gathering, 8 March 1991, Red Fort. Shahjahan Aapa addresses the huge gathering.

SECTION FIVE

STREE MUKTI: SCRIPTING WOMEN'S LIBERATION, IN MAHARASHTRA AND GUJARAT

With woman-power the yoke of housework mounts
And his advantages the capitalist counts (3)
Everyday...no rest, no leave, no overtime, no bonus,
no allowance, no medicines, no retirement, no remuneration...
Everyday...She works on
The capitalist does as he pleases
His profit everyday no doubt increases!

– *Pyramid (1982)*

Chorus: 'Today, we ask some questions... Who said god is a man, and woman a lowly creature? When the mother gives birth, why is the name the father's? Is religion more important than right to life? What is the point, if walking on these paths, we become half-human, hardly human?'

– *Agar Mariam Hoti (1988)*

Every woman should have education, work, and equal wage. Hostels for students and working women, Creches in every locality, every workplace!
Chorus: Women must organise, and win these rights, Fight shackles of religion, caste, class, realise our dream of equality, and spread new energy.

– *Mulgi Zali Ho (1982)*

One play doesn't bring revolution, but it can really help change people's mindset.

– *Jyoti Mhapsekar (interview 2016)*

The opening chapter in this section describes the iconic play *Mulgi Zali Ho,* which touched upon a range of women's issues linked with demands such as equal wages for equal work, daycare, and equality within marriage. The play, made by Stree Mukti Sanghatana, positioned the struggle for stree mukti (women's liberation) as integral to the liberation of all oppressed peoples.

Aamachya Aamhi Natya Manch, associated with the Forum Against Oppression of Women and Women's Centre, Mumbai, made two plays in the mid-80s: *Baara Gharachya Baara Jani,* which explored domestic violence, and *Hum Awaz Uthayeinge,* highlighting unequal personal laws. The same and overlapping sets of activists also made plays (in early 1982) dealing with working women's issues: *Rekha ki Kahani Usi ki Jubani* and *Pyramid.*

In the late 80s, two plays were created under the aegis of the media department of the Xavier Institute of Communications, St Xavier's College, Mumbai. *Agar Mariam Hoti* reinterpreted religion from women's perspectives, while *Ek Thee Achhi Ladki* expressed adolescent girls' thoughts and feelings about various customs impinging upon their lives, and their resolve to bring about change.

Two plays from the state of Gujarat made by the women's organisation Sahiyar are described in a subsequent chapter; both plays deal with violence against women. They are short, effective plays, simmering with rage, inspiring resistance. Another play on gender issues, made by a youth group from Gujarat named Udgar, is pitched at children.

There was of course far more street theatre activity linked to the women's movement in Maharashtra and Gujarat, than I have been able to explore. The Garib Dongri Sanghatana in Maharashtra, for instance, organised by 15 peasant women and two men in 1991, held discussions with abandoned women, and presented their exchanges in the form of a street play, *Social Trap* (Bhatia 2010, 117). A complete history of the theatre of these states would include such plays.

14

Mulgi Zali Ho
A Girl is Born

Mulgi Zali Ho is a living legend: written in 1982, the play is still going strong. This makes it one of the longest running plays we know of, in the women's movement, and in theatre history. Stree Mukti Sangathana has performed the play at least 3,000 times, in Marathi and Hindi. Performances by other groups and organisations, in eight different languages, would number several thousand. The play has been broadcasted on television, and many times on radio as well.

Mulgi Zali Ho was written in 1982, by Jyoti Mhapsekar.[117] Stree Mukti Sanghatana (SMS) activists, including Jyoti, began performing it in 1983. The play was on women's rights, within the home and family as well as in the workplace. It made a case for education, work, equal wages, creches and labour laws, as well as the right to live without violence. The play was strongly rooted in Dalit, left, women's movements. With stirring music, pithy dialogues, light-hearted humour, and determined stands taken by ordinary women, the play was able to forge connection with varied audiences.

To understand the genesis of *Mulgi Zali Ho*, we explore SMS and its cultural troupe, which has been active since 1975. They performed radical songs and, in 1980, staged a play concerning working women's rights.

Songs, and a Play, Prior to *Mulgi Zali Ho*

Jyoti and others in SMS were broadly leftist; though largely middle-class, they directed their energies towards working-class and Dalit

[117] Jyoti Mhapsekar (b. 1950) is a poet, singer, playwright, and co-founder of Stree Mukti Sanghatana.

women's issues. Jyoti came from a political family; her mother was a Teachers' Union leader and her father was a full-time member of the Lal Nishan Party. In her early twenties, Jyoti and a small group of women began meeting. They chose to define their interest as social work, not political. They participated in the 'Stree Mukti Sangharsha Parishad' (Conference for Women's Liberation Struggle) in Pune in October '74, meeting some 600 women—workers, teachers, landless labourers, Devadasis, trade unionists, women from left parties, Gail Omvedt, Sharada Sathe, Chhaya Datar, and more. After the conference, back in Mumbai, Jyoti and her comrades named their group 'Stree Mukti Sanghatana' (Women's Liberation Organisation). Sharada Sathe, a labour lawyer, became a guiding figure within SMS.

SMS was the first autonomous women's group in Maharashtra. To reach out to toiling women, the group formed a Kalapathak, a cultural troupe, in 1975. They performed songs in the popular Shahiri tradition: Daya Pawar's song on dam construction and Dalit problems; Narayan Surve's poem lamenting the water problem; Jyoti's mother Suman Kaatre's song on women workers; Madhav Chavan's songs such as '*Is desh ki ma behenon ko kehne jana hai ji, Milke sab sangram pukariye, kara todna hai ji' (Mothers and sisters of this country, come together and declare war, break the shackles).* Chavan also wrote songs based on the discussions that SMS women had, and the posters they made in small workshops and shared with him.

Jyoti Mhapsekar wrote her first song in 1979, on Jyotiba Phule. At a meeting, she sang about Ambedkar, and another speaker related Jyotiba Phule's work for women. Jyoti wondered why there were no songs on Phule, so she read his autobiography, and wrote a song. And in doing so she realised that she could write songs! Thereafter she wrote many songs, composing lyrics along with music, which became part of SMS Kalapathak's repertoire. SMS songs were published in a booklet which cost 50 paisa; it now costs Rs. 10. Nearly 1,00,000 copies of the song-book have been sold; several songs are widely sung, and included in diverse song compilations.

SMS performed its first play, *Ha Prashnacha Chukicha Aahe (The Question Itself is Wrong),* in 1980. It was based on the plight of women pharmaceutical workers who were thrown out of work if they married. This was a ploy by employers by which they avoided having to provide crèche facilities and maternity leave. The question itself is unfair—'Do you want a job or a husband?'. The play was written by Rajiv Kalelkar, and directed by Vinod Hadap. The actors were all women. There were only three performances: 'Our heroine got pregnant. Actually, in the group that year many of us gave birth to children. We kept meeting, but didn't do the play. We say that in that year, our organisation went on maternity leave!' (Jyoti Mhapsekar, interview 2016). Jyoti herself gave birth to a son in 1981; her daughter was born in 1971. Like most others at SMS, she held a job, and experienced enormous pressures performing multiple tasks.

During 1978-80, these young activists participated in the nationwide anti-dowry and anti-rape campaigns. They wanted to do a play on women's rights, but couldn't find any such play. Jyoti began thinking of a play like *Mulgi Zali Ho;* she had experienced the way people reacted when a girl was born, and how different it was from when it was a boy. She wrote a number of songs, weaving in many issues, and requested Vinod Hadap to write dialogues. He said he didn't understand all this feminism, and encouraged her to write the entire play herself. She started writing in 1981, and completed it by the end of 1982.

The SMS team rehearsed *Mulgi Zali Ho*—Sharada Sathe, Meera Adarkar, Neelali Mahesh, Chhaya Datar, Meena Deval, Kamal Phatak and Jyoti Mhapsekar; some of them had never acted before.

The first performance was in Delhi on 15 May 1983, at the Kriti Festival (organised by Saheli and Women's Forum-Mumbai). The actors left their children at home with their mothers-in-law, for a whole week. In Delhi, they performed amid a few hundred women's movement activists, in the spacious environs of Aurobindo Ashram.

Mulgi Zali Ho (A Girl is Born)

The play begins with a stirring song, paying tribute to Jyotiba Phule, Savitribai Phule, Pandita Ramabai, Gandhi, Ambedkar, and other pioneers, and pledging to fight for Nari Mukti and Dalit Mukti, 'to shatter the fort of orthodoxy'. A free-flowing conversation follows, with several women voicing the need for social change.

Kamal (an ordinary senior woman who comes up to the stage from the audience) demurs: 'Girls are studying, women work in different professions, the prime minister is a woman. But women's movement people still want to fight—against men!'

Meena emphasises that the fight is not against men, rather it is a struggle for equal opportunities. She adds, 'We are ordinary women, we work and run our households. But we are very angry about certain things!'

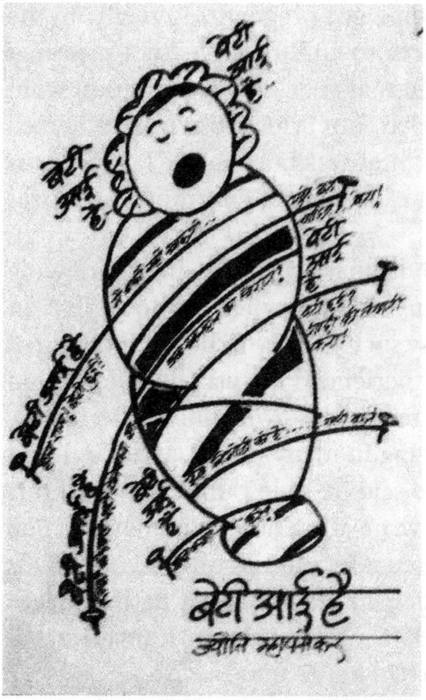

Beti Aayi Hai, Hindi translation of *Mulgi Zali Ho*; front cover.

Jyoti interrupts, unhappy because her daughter-in-law has given birth to a girl.

Meena tells her whether it's a girl or a boy depends on both the mother and father—modern science says so.

Jyoti wishes she'd known earlier; her husband and parents-in-law cursed her when she gave birth to daughters.

Mangla says, 'The world has changed! Educate your daughters to stand on their own feet.'

Meena grimly notes that girls' education is low priority; even if educated, she isn't free to support her own parents, after marriage.

A peppy song shows girls climbing into the 'shiksha ki rail', education train, but half of them drop out midway. A mother laments:

My darling daughter says, Ma send me to school,
I say, I'd love to, but who will look after the baby,
When I go to work? Bitti sobs, it tears my heart apart...

Girls who attend school are expected to return home directly, and involve themselves with housework.

Mangla berates her daughter for coming home late; the world outside is unsafe.

Sushma responds spiritedly: 'Ma, yesterday, a boy harassed Sudha. She tripped him, and he fell flat on his face!' She questions the curfew imposed on her, while her brother roams around.

Meena asks, 'Why are girls trained in housework only, rather than taught how to live with dignity and self-confidence?'

Kamal says, in Indian culture, men protect women. The chorus vehemently opposes this, giving examples—Manjushree Sharda died soon after her marriage into a rich Pune family, Adivasi girls in a Yavatmal hostel were raped by the Superintendent and cook, there have been rapes in police custody...

The play moves to a young woman, fantasising about interviewing her prospective groom, inverting the usual gender arrangement.

Neela: How much have you studied?

Boy: MA Pass.

Neela: Show your salary slip.

Boy: I forgot to bring it.

Neela: What division did you pass your MA?

Boy: I don't remember.

Neela: Can you make tea?

Boy: In our family, men don't make tea.

Neela: Do you fill your belly twice a day, never caring if enough remains for women?

Boy: This is what we are taught.

Neela: Does it say in the Manusmriti that woman should earn, and do all the housework...?

In real life, Neela fears that she will face a backlash if she challenges established norms; she marries this very boy. In their loveless marriage, he insults her daily, forbids her to meet her friends, and lounges around while she works. One day she informs him that she will return late from work, he forbids her. Neela brings up his drinking and gambling, upon which he rushes to beat her.

Sushma: Your mother taught you to be strong, but I see tears in your eyes...

Neela gradually makes up her mind to leave, Move out of this mental slavery, break these shackles... We are not weak... A girl is bright, brighter than the sun!

Chorus: Where will you go all alone?

Neela: I will not be alone. With me are Kamla, Vimla, Salma, Najma, Teena, Meena. We will walk together, sharing joys and sorrows; we will live with joy and dignity!

Chorus (singing): You call her Devi... She works in fields and factories, without maternity leave, crèches, proper wages. Works all day at home, but is unrecognised, unpaid, insulted, humiliated, in ads and media too...

Together, the women demand: Every woman should have education, work, and equal wage... Hostels for students and working women, crèches in every locality, every workplace...!

The chorus sings: Women must organise, and win these rights, Fight shackles of religion, caste, class, realise our dream of equality, and spread new energy, We struggle and bring all workers together, for human liberation, for a new society, Faith in our hearts, freedom for all oppressed people!

Performing: Thousands of Shows

The first show, at the Kriti Cultural Festival in Delhi, was an unforgettable experience. The audience didn't understand Marathi, but understood the spirit of what was happening. There was a great deal of discussion and excitement around the play.

The team kept performing in Mumbai, to all-women audiences; they were apprehensive about showing it to men. The 25th performance, however, was a big event with many people attending, including prestigious men. Journalists wrote about it, and the play became famous overnight.

Demands for performances poured in. The group was amazed by the runaway success of the play. They mostly performed in the open, in communities and local areas, but some shows were held indoors, in halls. Shows were always pre-arranged, and microphones used. Before the play, they sang two or three songs, relevant to the location, maybe on girls' education, alcoholism, or the abuse of women, and spoke about why they were performing the play. The entire programme would take one and a half hours. As Jyoti notes (interview 2016): '*Mulgi Zali Ho* is a musical, in the Shahiri tradition, which people love. The songs take the story ahead; they are not only to separate the scenes, but are interwoven into the script.'

Post-performance, some women from the audience would give their names, to volunteer for SMS. CDs of the play, its script and songbooks were sold, so these got widely dispersed and helped others perform *Mulgi Zali Ho*. Some people wanted a receipt when they

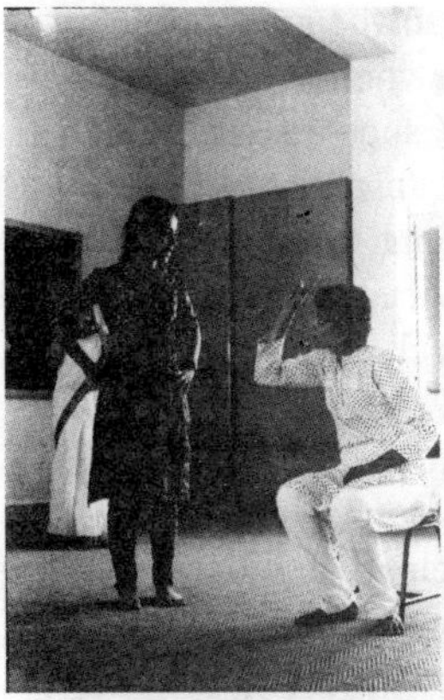

Mulgi Zali Ho, Kriti festival, Aurobindo Ashram, Delhi, May 1983. Actors: Neera Adarkar (standing), Neela Limaye (sitting). (In the circle): Meena Deval, Mangala Padhye (back to audience), Neela Limaye (centre of circle), Sharada Sathe (behind Neela), Neera Adarkar, Jyoti Mhapsekar, Chhaya Datar (behind Jyoti).

bought something. This pushed the organisation to register itself: Stree Mukti Sanghatana was formally registered in 1985.

During the discussions following a performance, women brought up problems of domestic violence, battering, and said, 'You are talking

Back cover, *Beti Aayi Hai*, Hindi translation of *Mulgi Zali Ho*.

so much, solve my problem also!' Overwhelmed by the volume of such cases, SMS started a counselling center in 1985. A young woman with a Masters in Social Work agreed to join as counsellor on a voluntary basis. The organisation was later able to raise funds and expand the counselling centre. The play helped build trust in communities, supporting SMS's intensive grassroots work on issues of health, education, livelihoods, and barefoot counselling.

The SMS team performed *Mulgi Zali Ho* continuously. They took no money for it; they earned a living from their day jobs. If somebody gave a bit of money when they performed, it went into the organisation's kitty, for travel and for accompanists' fees. Accompanists who played the dholak and harmonium were professional men, and not formally a part of SMS.

In 1985, the team went on a big tour, performing in Bhopal, Indore, Jhansi, Gwalior, Delhi, and elsewhere in north and central India, the Hindi belt, for Marathi people staying there. It was the 25th year of the establishment of Maharashtra state, and the state's Cultural Minister Sushil Kumar Shinde saw the play, got interested, and helped arrange this tour.

In Delhi, national TV, Doordarshan, interviewed the group and recorded their performance. The interview was shown right away, while the play was broadcast three months later in Marathi, on Mumbai Doordarshan. Lots of people in Mumbai watched the play on TV. The next day, when Jyoti (interview 2016) got onto the local train to go to work, 'Women embraced me, saying, "You are doing so much for women." Usually nobody knows a writer, but I got such a reception, because they saw me performing. Somebody gave me a seat—"Arre, call her, give her this seat!" Real love I have received, from people.'

In 1986 the group began performing the play in Hindi too, calling it *Beti Aai Hai*. Some non-Marathi people who saw the Marathi play, asked, 'Why don't you do it in Hindi?' Others said, 'How will you do it in Hindi, your Hindi pronunciation is not good.' The group requested Vasant Deo, who translated Vijay Tendulkar's plays into Hindi, to translate *Mulgi Zali Ho*. He had seen the play performed in college, and said it would be an honour to translate it. He translated songs in such a way that the music was retained. He organised rehearsals at his house, making sure the actors pronounced the Hindi words correctly.

In 1987, they did 20 performances in Delhi colleges. At a show at Delhi University, they were surprised to see only men in the audience, hundreds, all Sardarjis. Performing for only men was unusual. At another performance, in a textile mill in Mumbai, there was an all-male audience of some 3,000 millworkers.

For three consecutive years in the late 1980s, they performed at IAS Academy, Mussoorie.[118] Trainees said, 'We have heard lectures on feminism, but your play has given us an orientation, and energy to work.' The Academy invited them for two days, but they had to take a week off from work, due to travel-time. In 1990, they were forced to take a few more days off because of delays caused by the Mandal agitation.[119] In 1991 they performed in various cities in UP, but after that they didn't come to North India much. It was too troublesome.

Between 1985 and 1991, SMS organised 10-day 'Stree-Purush Samanta Yatras' (Journeys for Gender Equality), performing *Mulgi Zali Ho* in Marathwada, Vidarbha, Konkan, western Maharashtra. A busload would travel, including three or four groups of women performers, and accompanists who played the harmonium and dholak. They would stay in a small town, spread into nearby villages, and each group would perform in different places. Shows were announced beforehand, and somebody went ahead to set up the stage, microphone, and so on. At each venue, thousands of people saw the play. SMS kept records, and wrote about it in its magazine *Prerak Lalkari*. In the *Times of India,* journalist Ayesha Kagal (1986) graphically described some of the performances. Thousands of people thronged to the performance at a thoroughfare in the city of Miraj, for instance. There was an equally palpable response when the play was performed for Dalit schoolgirls in a down-at-heel classroom in rural Maharashtra: '*Mulgi Zali Ho* bursts forth in all its potency...a flexible, adaptable vehicle with infinite

---

[118] Lal Bahadur Shastri Academy, Mussoorie is where IAS (Indian Administrative Service) officers are trained.

[119] The agitation, in 1990, was against the implementation of the Mandal Commission's recommendation of caste-based quotas in government jobs and public universities.

opportunity to communicate—simply and directly, with humor and song—what it means to be born female.'[120]

These Yatras were unique, combining some of the flavour of traditional travelling theatre with contemporary ideas. In 2001, SMS organised similar Yatras, covering the Nashik, Jalgaon and Dhule districts of north Maharashtra. The audience connected strongly with many issues, such as dowry, violence, sex selection, sexual harassment, abuse. The words 'the sex of a child depends on men too, not only women, science says that!' made a huge impact; women would bring mothers-in-law or husbands just to hear it. The play helped women gain the confidence to speak out and articulate their demands; if they were facing violence, some got the courage to step out of marriage. Many men were compelled to introspect. Demands like crèches and working women's hostels became more acceptable. In 1989, SMS began a crèche called 'Aamche Ghar' (Our Home), and started adult literacy work with women in the slums of Chembur.

Mulgi Zali Ho was performed twice on international platforms, and was very well received. When they performed in 1994 in Adelaide, Australia at the 3rd Women Playwrights International Conference, one of them explained the main points of each scene to the audience in English. After the performance, some people commented, 'Yours is the only play talking about larger issues, common issues, like crèches, hostels and education. These are the demands of women all around the world.' Somebody came up to them and commented, 'You are so short. But when you perform, you look huge!' Indeed, Jyoti is less than 5 feet tall; others in the cast were 5', 5'1", and maximum 5'2".

When *Mulgi Zali Ho* was performed at the 1995 World Conference on Women in Beijing, China, the audience was mostly Asian, and in tune with what was being shown. They did it in Hindi, so women from Bangladesh, Pakistan and Nepal understood it to some extent; it also helped that SMS put up placards naming issues like dowry, alongside each scene. SMS booklets and CDs sold, and they were happy to hear that some women later performed the play in Pakistan.

In 1996, theatre-person Usha Ganguli directed the play in Kolkata, calling it *Beti Aai*.[121] She composed music for one of the songs, and the West Bengal government jointly awarded Jyoti Mhapsekar and

---

[120] See excerpts from Ayesha Kagal (1986), describing the two performances, in Chapter 2.

[121] Usha Ganguli, a pioneering theatre-person, set up Rangakarmee and produced Hindi-language theatre in Kolkata.

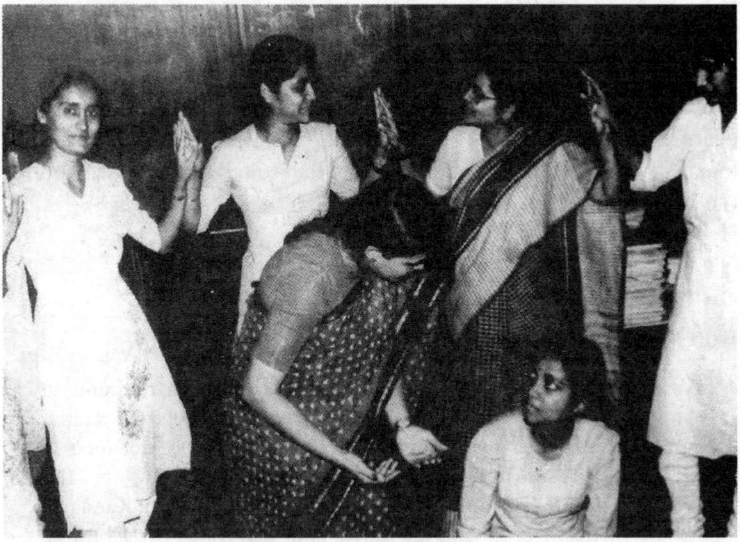

Mulgi Zali Ho, 1984. (Back row, Left to right) unidentified actor, Neela Limaye, Jyoti Mhapsekar, Sujata Khandekar; (Front row) Mangala Padhye, Sushama Pednekar (sitting).

Mulgi Zali Ho, Adelaide, Australia, June 1994. (Back row, Left to right) Alka Pawangadkar, Neela Limaye, Vrunda Godse, Sujata Khandekar, Kamal Phatak; (Front row) Jyoti Mhapsekar, Pradnya Saraf.

Usha Ganguli for 'Best Music Direction.' Ananda Lal (2020) notes that Ganguli took 'all-women Hindi theatre outside the proscenium with *Beti Ayi*, translated from the famous street play about the girl child by Mumbai activist Jyoti Mhapsekar. In Usha's words, it depicted "the everyday hell that rarely comes to light." She understood that to truly make an impact where it mattered, she had to take her message out of the comfort zones of auditoria.'[122]

The Long Haul

Jyoti Mhapsekar reminisces:

> We have performed *Mulgi Zali Ho* from 1983, every year a hundred shows or so; in 32 years, around 3,000 performances; 2,000 in Marathi, and 1,000 in Hindi. Apart from television,[123] the play was broadcast 40 to 50 times on radio in Marathi, and also in Hindi.
>
> *Mulgi Zali Ho* has been translated into Gujarati, Telugu, Kannada, Hindi, English, Urdu and Sanskrit, and performed in all these languages. At least 100 groups have performed the play. When people perform in these adaptations the music quality usually drops. We can't control that.
>
> I know at least ten groups in Maharashtra who have done 100 performances each of the play. Trupti Shah, from Gujarat, did 100 performances in Gujarati.[124] A group in Karnataka did 100 performances in Kannada. Sometimes people inform us, sometimes not. If we happen to hear of it, we say, 'Why didn't you inform us? We would like to know where the play is being done, we could keep a record.' Some groups ask for permission; yesterday I got a letter, somebody wanting permission to do the play for a competition. We never refuse permission.

---

[122] Soon after, Usha Ganguli directed *Mukti* (1999), in Bengali, based on a story by Mahasweta Devi. In it, the anti-heroine found mukti in herself, to do as she pleased—no 'happily ever after' holding her man's hand—much like the lead characters of many feminist street plays. Another production Usha Ganguli worked on thereafter, *Khela Gadi* (2007), had underprivileged Muslim women actors, one of whom enacted her own story.

[123] The video recording of *Mulgi Jhali Ho* (as spelt on the webpage provided below), produced by Vinayak Chaskar (2022) is delightful to see, with rousing music and spirited actors. It is 54.13 minutes long, placed online by Doordarshan Sahyadri at: www.youtube.com/watch?v=5kxDSubKECU. Credits include: writer, Jyoti Mhapsekar; actors, Jyoti Mhapsekar, Meena Deval, Mangala Padhye, Sharda Sathe and Others. The assistant producer is Shrikala Hattangaddi.

[124] Trupti Shah (1962-2016) was a founder-member of Sahiyar, Vadodara, further detailed in Chapter 17.

A teacher in a D.Ed. college, in a small Vidarbha town, saw the play during the Yatra in 1987-88, and was fascinated by it. He got every batch to do the play. For the hundredth performance, they called me. I was really amazed watching that performance. I felt, whatever I have written is meaningful. It was a fulfillment of one's wishes.

Last year, a young Indian woman in North Carolina wanted to do *Mulgi Zali Ho* there. She is my daughter's friend and saw the play while growing up in Mumbai. She discussed the production with us, over Skype. She did it in Marathi, with subtitles in English on the screen. Indians saw it and Americans too. Everybody liked it. After the performance she raised some donations too, for SMS.

SMS has grown. We have constructed a space in Navi Mumbai, with a crèche, shelter, and working women's hostel, putting everything, even our savings, into making that building. We run the counselling centre and five crèches, and work on livelihoods, especially with waste pickers. By now very few of the first team are with SMS, they did different work, formed new organisations. It was good, everybody was growing, stree mukti spread and expanded. Many others joined SMS, did the play too.

We still perform *Mulgi Zali Ho* sometimes. Till five years ago, I was acting. The play needs a set of good actors, thinking people who can also sing in tune. Professional actors charge for performing. No one funds plays. How do we fund it, then? We never had funding for the play, but earlier very devoted people were doing it.

There is still a lot of interest from colleges. It is on university syllabi, and performed in schools and colleges. A third generation is doing it now. Last year, we did workshops and rehearsals in 10 colleges. Right now, it's going on in one college. We train college girls continuously, and give them grounding in the women's movement, with slide-shows.

One play doesn't bring revolution, but it can really help change people's mindset. I loved performing because it gave me so much energy. I got so much happiness, looking at people, how they identified. Many women got a voice.

Mulgi Zali Ho has attained legendary status, occupying a unique place all its own. Its longevity is the result of a brilliant script, outstanding music, and the extraordianry commitment of its actors. Being part of a stable organisation has helped sustain the play. To date, more than 500 women associated with SMS have acted in it. SMS members refer to *Mulgi Zali Ho* as their flagship play, and are immensely proud of it.

The play turned 40 years old on 15 May 2023. During these four decades, it has reached out to millions through face-to-face performances, as well as through radio, television, the internet, CDs, script booklets, workshops and academic curricula. Its words and messages have drawn attention to women's issues and seeped into the social fabric, making an impact. Of course, the issues are still far from resolution and the play remains relevant even today.[125]

More Plays: Alongside *Mulgi Zali Ho*

During a Yatra in 1985, SMS presented a second play, which depicted the life of the radical social reformer Pandita Ramabai. It was written by a noted journalist, Sanjeevani Kher.

In 1986, SMS did a play called *Hunda Nako Ga Bai (No Dowry, Please),* written by Jyoti Mhapsekar. It was on marriage, caste, dowry, girls' dreams, and 'adjusting' after marriage. It was performed during Yatras and in colleges about 1,000 times, up to 1996, inspiring young girls and boys to take pledges against dowry.

Jyoti wrote *Baap Re Baap (Father Oh Father)* in 1994, a satire where men were granted the capacity to give birth instead of women. It needed ten men and five women actors. Only a few performances were held, as SMS didn't have enough men volunteers. All three plays were directed by Vinod Hadap.

In 2009, SMS along with the Academy of Theatre Arts, Mumbai University hosted the 8th Women Playwrights International Conference. Around 75 delegates from around the world and 200 from India, including 90 women playwrights overall, participated in the seven-day conference. There were 70 play readings, 17 performances by Indian women, and vibrant panel discussions (Stree Mukti Sanghatana 2012).[126]

Samatekade Vatchal (Towards Equality) was directed by Sushama Deshpande,[127] and written by Jyoti Mhapsekar in 2010. Over five years, they did some 30 performances of the 90-minute play. It depicts the history of the Indian women's movement. Colleges invited the group

[125] Strangely enough, there was a recent Marathi TV serial called *Mulgi Zali Ho*. It was a popular soap opera that ran from September 2020 to January 2023, with over 700 episodes. It was glitzy, completely different from the play. But it would be interesting to know how the name was chosen, and whether its producers wished to make a connection with the play.

[126] For more details, see Chapter 24.

[127] Sushama Deshpande is a well-known actor and director in Marathi and Hindi films and plays.

to perform. SMS charged a small fee, since they had to pay the actors, seven young women who were full-time theatre professionals.

A small musical street play *Ye Hai Mumbai Meri Jaan* (written by Jyoti, directed by Akshay Ahire) focuses on teaching people about waste segregation. It complements SMS's work with waste-pickers, the majority of them being women, and many being single mothers. Since 1999, SMS has organised women waste-pickers in six cities, encouraged self-help groups and the creation of a federation. The play is directed at people in housing societies so that they grow aware of issues surrounding waste and the waste-pickers. It has been performed in Hindi and Marathi more than 50 times (up to 2016), and broadcast on All India Radio.

SMS is considering making a play on girls like Malala, to inspire schoolchildren; and a play on women in different work-domains—waste-picker, factory worker, domestic help, and other trades. Jyoti says: 'I may not act now. But I will direct. And I will concentrate on theatre, songs, writing, and training younger people.'

From the birth of one daughter, SMS's theatrical journey has come a long way, giving birth to several daughters, each precious, and unique!

15

Twelve Women from Twelve Homes

Hum Awaz Uthayeinge

The autonomous women's groups Forum Against Oppression of Women (FAOW) and Women's Centre, set up in Mumbai between 1980-82, are very significant feminist organisations, and continue to be relevant today. Several members of FAOW and Women's Centre were also active in the Nari Sangharsh Samiti, which intervened in women workers' issues at trade union levels.

In 1982, members of Nari Sangharsh Samiti made and performed a play titled *Rekha ki Kahani Usi ki Jubani*. The same year, they also performed *Pyramid*, which had been made under the aegis of a cultural group in Mumbai called Jagruti Kala Pathak.

In 1985, several activists from FAOW and Women's Centre formed a street theatre group called 'Aamachya Aamhi Natya Manch' (We are for Ourselves Theatre Forum).[128] The plays made and performed by Aamachya Aamhi Natya Manch include *Baara Gharachya Baara Jani* (1985), *Hum Awaz Uthayeinge* (1986), and *Nari Itihas ki Talash Mein* (1988).

Briefly tracing the histories of the women's movement in Mumbai will help us better understand the wider context and genesis of these plays. On 8 March 1980, anti-rape protests were held in Mumbai, Bangalore, Delhi, Hyderabad, Surat and other cities as part of the nation-wide ferment around the Mathura rape case.[129] Nandita Gandhi

---

[128] This literal translation from the Marathi was provided by Vibhuti Patel (email 2023).

[129] Mathura, a minor tribal girl, was gang-raped inside a police station in Maharashtra's Gadchiroli district. Women's groups organised in protest after the Supreme Court exonerated the rapists. Upendra Baxi, Vasudha Dhagamwar, Raghunath Kelkar and Lotika Sarkar wrote an open letter (Baxi et al. 1979) to the Chief Justice of India on the Mathura rape case judgment, noting that the acquittal of the policemen was a travesty of justice and a denial of human rights.

(2011) recalls, 'Women from alternative groups, teachers, students, professionals converged together to protest' in Mumbai. Many women met for the first time at the protest and bonded. Several of them, including Sonal Shukla, Sujata Gothoskar, Sandhya Gokhale, Vibhuti Patel, Nandita Gandhi, Pamela Philipose, Aruna Burte, Flavia Agnes, Rohini Hensman, Hasina Khan and Ammu Abraham,[130] kept meeting to discuss salient issues, and soon they set up the Forum Against Rape. Within six months, they renamed it the Forum Against Oppression of Women, to signify the wide range of their concerns.

Sujata Gothoskar (2017) who has worked with trade unions and various left formations, says, '[T]hose were magical times... There was a feeling that revolution was around the corner.'

Jagriti (Awakening)

The group realised that women's movement activists must come together to effectively fight patriarchal social structures. FAOW therefore organised the (First) National Conference on Perspectives for Women's Movement in November 1980.

---

[130] Ammu Abraham, an activist for women's rights and civil liberties, has been engaged with Women's Centre for over four decades (Desai 2019).

Aruna Burte works on women's health at the Centre for Enquiry into Health and Allied Themes (CEHAT), a research centre dedicated to strengthening people's health movements.

Flavia Agnes is a lawyer, writer, and co-founder of Majlis, an organisation providing legal support to women.

Hasina Khan is founder-member of the Bebaak Collective, set up in 2017, which works for gender just laws and the abolishment of all discriminatory personal laws.

Nandita Gandhi co-founded Akshara Centre in 1995, with Nandita Shah. They are co-authors of a comprehensive early account of the women's movement in India (1992).

Pamela Philipose is a journalist and a writer, and has worked with *The Indian Express* and the *Women's Feature Service*.

Rohini Hensman is an independent scholar and activist who writes on workers' rights, feminism, minority rights, globalisation and imperialism.

Sandhya Gokhale is an electrical engineer, and a long-time activist concerned with women and labour issues as well as being involved with FAOW.

Sonal Shukla (1941-2021) was a Gandhian educationist, women's movement and trade union activist. In 1990, she co-founded Vacha to empower adolescent girls, and was active with it to the end.

Sujata Gothoskar is a long-standing activist with labour in the unorganised sector, and a member of the Non-Traditional Livelihoods Network.

Vibhuti Patel is former Head of Economics Department, SNDT University and Professor, Women's Studies, Tata Institute of Social Sciences, Mumbai.

As part of the preparations for the conference, a number of activists decided to depict women's life-cycles through folk songs. They gathered women's folk songs from different Indian languages, and prepared a dance-drama called *Jagriti.*

Some 200 women attended the conference. They engaged in lively conversations and debates, discussing ground realities and consolidating their feminist perspectives. They put in place fledgling strategies to bring about a change in the laws and policies on rape, dowry, domestic violence and abuse.

On the last day of the conference, *Jagriti* was performed. This musical ballet was very spirited, and included folk songs in Kannada, Tamil, Malayalam, Telugu, Konkani, Marathi, Hindi, Gujarati, Bengali and Bhojpuri. The commonalities in women's lives, despite the distinctive flavours of different regions, were well depicted.

Actors in *Jagriti* who had also researched and contributed folk songs included Lalitha Dhara, Sonal Shukla, Ujjawala Mhatre, Padma Prakash, Jaya Menon, Kamala Ganesh and Vibhuti Patel. The main singers were Lalitha Dhara, Kamala Ganesh and Vibhuti Patel. Lalita Dhara also handled the English narration while Vibhuti handled the narration in Hindi.

Rekha ki Kahani Usi ki Jubani (Rekha's Story in Her Own Words) and *Pyramid*

Nari Sangharsh Samiti's engagement with women workers was throwing up a whole host of issues, and inspired their performance of two short street plays, in 1982.

Rekha ki Kahani Usi ki Jubani dealt with sexual harassment at the workplace, and also touched upon several related issues which women workers were confronting. Trade unions usually subsumed women's issues within the rubric of 'labour' issues, thus neglecting important concerns such as differential wages, the lack of toilets for women, sexual harassment, abuse and rape. The play *Rekha ki Kahani Usi ki Jubani* brought out the urgent need to deal seriously with this range of issues. The lived experiences of women workers were depicted.

While the typical trade union considered capitalism the enemy, socialist feminist perspectives brought to awareness the interaction between capitalism and patriarchy. Thus women workers suffered the double burden of exploitation within the workplace as well as at home.

Rekha ki Kahani Usi ki Jubani was written by Vibhuti Patel, and directed by Shanta Gokhale. Shanta Gokhale was especially invited to direct the play since she was a skilled dramatist. The actors were Sandhya Gokhale, Nandita Shah, Kamakshi Bhate, Ujjawala Mhatre, Vibhuti Patel and Sonal Shukla. Nari Sanghash Samiti facilitated the workshop.

Nari Sangharsh Samiti also facilitated a workshop to rehearse the play *Pyramid.* Vibhuti Patel wrote *Pyramid* for 8 March 1982 (International Women's Day) under the auspices of Jagruti Kala Pathak. Music for its songs was based on the Gujarati Bhavai style. The play drew links between women's unpaid household labour and capitalist exploitation in the workplace. This social structure was shown by forming a pyramid, women at the base, men at the center, and one person, the capitalist, at the top. The play culminated in women breaking the shackles of household oppression, women and men uniting 'from mill, dock, shed, in spite of police dread... from fields, from factories... to end capitalism.'

Pyramid, Kriti festival, Aurobindo Ashram, Delhi, May 1983. Actor at top of pyramid: Suhaila Abdulali.

Pyramid was directed by Shanta Gokhale and the actors were Sandhya Gokhale, Nandita Shah, Kamakshi Bhate, Ujjawala Mhatre, Sonal Shukla and Vibhuti Patel. It was performed by FAOW at the Kriti festival in Delhi, in 1983. *Pyramid* proved to be a very effective play, and it continues to be performed to date by college students.

Women's Centre was set up in September 1981. Many women had been approaching FAOW for help in situations of domestic violence, rape, harassment and abuse. Ammu Abraham, Sujata Gothoskar, Flavia

Agnes, Rohini Hensman and Vibhuti Patel were among those who started Women's Centre (Patel 2011), to support such women. Both FAOW and Women's Centre were initially run from Sonal Shukla's home (Punwani 2021: 5).[131]

In January 1984, Women's Centre moved to a dedicated space in Santacruz East. Most women who came with problems needed legal aid, counselling, and support to heal and rebuild their lives. Women's Centre, with very few full-time activists and several part-time volunteers, was besieged with 'cases'. It felt like fire-fighting: even if the flames were doused in one home, they still blazed in thousands. Where did all the violence come from? It seemed necessary to dig deeper into the family, where our psyche is formed and attitudes are nurtured.

Baara Gharachya Baara Jani *(Twelve Women from Twelve Homes)*

Women's Centre activists realised that to address violence at its roots, reflection and change had to be stimulated across society. They decided to set up a street theatre group to make plays which could reach out to many sections of society. That is how Aamachya Aamhi Natya Manch was set up. It was composed of Centre activists and a few women who had initially come to it for help.

Aamachya Aamhi Natya Manch met daily between October and November 1985. It included Lata Pratibha Madhukar (Lata PM), Nirmala Sathe, Sandhya Gokhale, Chayanika Shah, Nandita Shah, Vandana, Bharati, Meena, Kunda PN, Kamakshi Bhate, Preetha, Leena Najiani and Swatija Manorama. Participants collectively directed, and acted, in the play. The workshop was facilitated by Lata PM, Nirmala Sathe and Vibhuti Patel; Lata PM wrote the script (Patel, email 2023).[132]

The group members probed violence within families, including their own. People opened up and began articulating deep concerns.

[131] Chayanika Shah notes that FAOW and Women's Centre, both simultaneously housed in Sonal Shukla's home, provided an unusual feminist space, in 1982: 'Survivors could come, stay there—the home was open to them. This was a very gutsy thing to do, very imaginative. Laws weren't there, organisations weren't there; it was just a feeling that one must reach out!' (Sonal Shukla Memorial meeting, 10 September 2021). We recall, from Chapter 6, that Chayanika Shah acted in *Om Swaha* in 1983, with fellow students from IIT Mumbai.

[132] Vibhuti Patel (email 2023) provided information on the actors, writers, and workshop facilitators for all the plays discussed in this chapter.

Spending time together, sharing collectively, they got to know each other better and found the process very enjoyable. A number of questions came up for discussion, for instance: 'Should a street play always present clear, undiluted feminist perspectives, or should we compromise, to avoid alienating the audience? How much dilution is acceptable?' (Jagori Samooh 1988, 32). Given the wide range of audience backgrounds, such questions are important, though there may be no fixed answer. While it would be nice to say exactly what one thinks, it is often strategically better to present a less radical perspective, so as not to scare off the fence-sitters, and leave space open for dialogue.

The play carried a ring of authenticity; it was based on experiences gathered within Women's Centre. Stories of 'twelve women from twelve homes' were fictionalised to create a collective biography, portraying oppression, and sparks of resistance. Together, women of different ages and from different stages of life presented a stark indictment of the patriarchal family and society. The play indicated the double or triple burden many women bear, battling intimate partner violence in addition to carrying out many other tasks that ensure basic survival.

Even as hidden experiences were made visible, there were intimations of solidarity, based on shared sensitivity, and a solid politics. Recognising the power of street theatre, the actors were enthusiastic and confident about making a difference.

The Play

The opening song sets the wider context, placing the women's movement alongside a rich stream of oppositional, liberationist social movements, from Jyotiba Phule, Savitribai Phule, and Pandita Ramabai to Ambedkar and others.

Twelve women stand in a semi-circle; their lives different, yet similar. Four are young, unmarried, 'kumara'; four are married, 'saubhagyavati', fortunate because they have husbands! Four were elders, some widowed, inauspicious.

The Sutradhar probes for more details. The women claim to have no names, no addresses; they are women who look after their homes, families, who cook, clean, work, earn, feed husbands, fast for them. Their husbands curse, abuse and batter; life passes by without love, or respect!

Sutradhar: You tell the truth, sisters! But you must not speak of private matters in public!

A man rains blows on his wife. Their daughter tries to intervene, but he continues, undeterred.

Chorus: Don't tell anyone, keep quiet! Suffer, within four walls!

A woman files for divorce: her husband beat her and burnt her with cigarettes.

He defends himself: I love her. Look at her—could anyone beat such a beautiful wife? All day I'm at work. Who knows who she meets?

The judge asks her what she does all day! She answers: Housework. I go out to buy groceries.

The judge rules that the husband doesn't beat his wife, ignoring the wounds and burn marks on her body. He orders them to live together, and advises her: Remain quiet. Men get angry sometimes, they can't help it!

Another woman: My husband wanted a fair bride, but married me, for dowry!

She tries to win his heart, does all the housework, bears him a son; but finally, he abandons her.

Different women from different homes.

A 50-year-old woman asks the Sutradhar to read out a letter from her husband. He informs her: Sister, he has given you talaq!

Her husband had been threatening to bring home a young wife! She is devastated—where will she go? How will she survive?

Vidya comes forward—a woman who took the decision to divorce, after trying for years to manage within a violent marriage. She finds a job and focuses on looking after herself and her child. She feels enormous relief.

A girl runs home: Ma, five-six boys harassed me in the shop!

Neighbors turn on the mother and daughter: This girl talks to everybody! Why did you send her alone to the shop?

She snaps back: Those boys harassed me. Why do you blame us?

A woman wishes to apply for a job; her husband is furious: You get these ideas because you sit with Stree Mukti women! They break up homes!

She reminds him: When you were out of a job, you wanted me to work! Now, I will work because I want to!

A woman laborer: I've been listening! I thought such things happen only to poor women.

Her husband drags her away, saying: These are women from big houses. You have nothing in common with them!

She asks, defiant: What do I have in common with you?

The women come together, singing: We are different women, from different homes, we demand our rights; women of a brave new era, we will smash the walls of patriarchy!

Performing

The group performed *Baara Gharachya Baara Jani* at the Second National Women's Movements Conference, hosted by FAOW in late 1985.[133] There were around 400 participants, an atmosphere of solidarity and strength, creative learning, and plural sources of feminist knowledge construction (Vibhuti Patel 2011). The play was much appreciated and sparked off lively discussions.

The actors felt greatly encouraged by the positive response and were keen to perform at various venues in the city. It proved difficult, however, to find a time convenient to all members. Those engaged in full-time jobs were free only in the evening. Some performed essential household chores in the evening; several were unable to stay out late. Finally, the lack of a mutually conveninent schedule made it impossible to continue doing the play.

Thus, the play was performed only two or three times. This was sad indeed, for while an understanding of women's issues was growing

---

[133] National Women's Movement Conferences, organised by the autonomous women's movement, were held in Mumbai (1980 and 1985), Patna (1987), Calicut (1990), Tirupati (1994), Ranchi (1997) and Kolkata (2006).

Baara Gharachya Baara Jani, Mumbai, 8 March 1985: Singing during the play. (Left to right) Preetha, Leena Nanjiani, Lata PM, Sandhya Gokhale, Swatija Manorama, Meena Thomas.

Closing with movement songs. (Left to right, back row) Bharati, Vandana, Nandita Shah, Vibhuti Patel, Sonal Shukla, Kunda PN; (front row) Lata PM, Meena Thomas. Banner reads *Nari Atyachar Virodhi Manch*—Forum Against Oppression of Women.

fast within the movement, dialogue with wider society was relatively slow. For women directly associated with movement groups, the lenses through which they looked at their lives and society had altered. They experienced the movement as a refuge, a network, platform, and place where they belonged, to which they contributed, and which added depth and meaning to their lives. Outreach, through theatre and other means, was of critical significance. Yet because of the constraints which activists faced, in common with most women, they were not always able to reach out sufficiently.

A few months later, in 1986, Aamachya Aamhi Natya Manch made a new play on personal laws. It had a smaller cast, trying to ensure from the start that each actor would be able to commit to a longer performance schedule.

Hum Awaz Uthayeinge (We Will Raise Our Voices)

The play *Hum Awaz Uthayeinge* showed women from different religious backgrounds raising their voices against discrimination, demanding justice, and asserting their right to live with dignity.

The Second National Women's Movements Conference (November-December 1985) focused on personal laws, especially debating the feasibility of a Uniform Civil Code (UCC). Shehnaaz Sheikh[134] of Mumbai, whose husband had divorced her using triple talaq, had filed a case in the Supreme Court challenging Muslim personal law. Conference participants discussed the pros and cons of two possible scenarios to work towards—either a UCC or gender-just but different personal laws.

The conference passed a resolution on 'Women and Personal Laws' which noted that equality and justice are not available to women in India, regardless of the religion they practice. It argued that personal laws further institutionalise inequality. The resolution underlined the need for a civil code under which all women are afforded legal rights equal to men in matters of marriage, divorce, maintenance, custody, inheritance, property, adoption, and other such matters. A minority opinion, included in the resolution, felt that any move for reform must come from within communities. The resolution unequivocally and unanimously condemned communal designs which threaten minorities.

---

[134] Shehnaaz Sheikh later studied law and founded the feminist Muslim organisation, Aawaz-e-Niswaan.

'Justice for Shah Bano' had become a rallying call in the women's movement: Shah Bano, an elderly woman in Indore, was in dire straits after her husband divorced her and threw her out of the house. The Judicial Magistrate had awarded her a paltry maintenance, not sufficient to subsist on. The High Court increased the amount, but her husband challenged this in the Supreme Court. In April 1985, the Supreme Court upheld the maintenance awarded to Shah Bano, noting that the provisions of Section 125 of the Criminal Procedure Code were applicable to women across religions; it was a husband's responsibility to provide maintenance for a divorced wife unable to support herself.

Aamachya Aamhi Natya Manch decided to engage with discriminatory personal laws. The Shah Bano case exposed discrimination against women in Muslim personal law, but as the women's movement pointed out, there was discrimination in the personal laws and customs of all religious communities. Rising fundamentalism was further enforcing discriminatory norms.

Hum Awaz Uthayeinge was produced in a workshop facilitated by Women's Centre. Participants were Lata PM, Nirmala Sathe, Vibhuti Patel, Bharati, Meena Thomas and Flavia Agnes. All of them co-directed, as well as acted, in the play, which was written by Lata PM. It showed that, despite women having many common problems, they were divided along communal lines. Men of each community took it upon themselves to enforce discriminatory practices. Through the play, activists sought to take these issues to the people, encouraging them to reflect on and reinterpret religious injunctions in light of democratic norms.

We will raise our voices!

In the play, men of Hindu, Sikh, Muslim and Christian faiths praised their religions sky-high. Women, on the other hand, pointed out injustices, and questioned why their welfare was less important than some religious directive. They came together, crossing community lines, and realised they confronted some similar issues in their lives. Religious patriarchs and personal laws might divide them, but when women met, they found they weren't very different from one another. They decided to work to end exploitative practices like sati and triple talaq, and to demand a uniform civil code with personal laws based on equality and justice. The play urged everyone to reflect upon their beliefs, rather than blindly follow religious injunctions. Religion, it asserted, should help everybody lead humane, happy lives.

The play began with a song; and several songs, full of vigour, were woven into the play, interspersed with dialogues declaring women's intentions to unite and resist.

The Play

Entire cast (a rousing song calling for united struggle): *Mil ke chalo, mil ke chalo...!*

Hindu man: Our religion is humanist. Its personal laws should be the laws of all religious communities.

Sikh man: We want our own laws!

Muslim man: We will not tolerate any interference with the Shariat!

Christian man: We accept no change in Christian laws, even if the laws were made hundreds of years ago.

Woman 1: Which laws are you talking about—divorce, maintenance, marriage...?

Woman 2: These laws directly affect women.

Woman 3: You play with women's lives, under the pretense of religion!

Mary seeks a divorce, on grounds of adultery.

Padre: Marriage is a sacred union. Behave well, your husband will return to you!

Judge: Christian personal law does not allow a woman to divorce her husband on grounds of adultery only; there should be cruelty or abandonment.

But a man can divorce his wife on grounds of adultery only!

Razia is given talaq unilaterally by her husband; she returns to her parental home.

Sakina and Fatima (Razia's sisters): We must at least demand maintenance from such men!

Men of the family: Shariat doesn't grant maintenance to women!

Razia, Sakina, Fatima: The Shariat says no alcohol! Do you follow such injunctions? We bring up children, but when the son grows up, we have to give him to his father!

An Adivasi household; Laadkibai (to her father): My husband gave you a bride-price when he married me. I have to give him that amount to be free of him. He harasses me, beats me. I work all day!'

Laadkibai's father: I sold you to him. That money is mine!

Laadkibai: Bapu, you are stealing my money!

He pushes her roughly and goes out.

A Hindu household; Uma (to her husband): I will go to court if you bring home another wife. Bigamy is a crime under Hindu law!

Uma's husband: I will do as I wish! You can leave, if you want.

Uma goes to her brother's house, but he doesn't let her stay there.

Uma: I too grew up in this house! Surely I have some rights here!

Uma's brother: Father did not leave any will. Under Hindu law, daughters have no right to paternal property.

Religious leaders try to intervene, but the women want no more of their injunctions! They take action—one battles for custody of her son, another puts her name on a school form as the only parent... and so on!

Chorus: We fight for reform in all personal laws! We want equal rights in property, marriage, divorce, guardianship, maintenance... equality, dignity, and justice. We will be silent no more!

Women come together: *Dharam kahe hum anek, par hain hum auratein sab ek.* (Religion says we are different, but we women are alike.) We speak up, raise our voices, together!

Performing

Hum Awaz Uthayeinge was first performed on 8 March 1986, at a large gathering organised by several women's groups. Women and men from various social strata were present. The powerful play drew everybody in with its intensity and the extremely relevant concerns it raised. The show went well and was followed by serious discussion.

Many social organisations invited the group to perform in different neighbourhoods. The play got women thinking about their own status within their communities, looking deeper into the discrimination inherent in so many customs and the law. Watching the play began a process of introspection and exploration.

Some people in the audience disagreed with the play's point of view and were enraged to find women questioning the strictures of organised religions. They put forth obscurantist views and defended the status quo. Sometimes there were heated arguments, while at other times there was thoughtful reflection and a feeling of solidarity.

Nari Itihas ki Talash Mein (In Search of Women's History)

Among the street plays associated with Women's Centre and FAOW was *Nari Itihas ki Talash Mein*, made in 1988. Written by Vibhuti Patel, it was produced in a workshop facilitated by Sonal Shukla. The play was directed by Madhusree Dutta, the talented dramatist who had earlier worked with women's movement theatre in West Bengal.[135]

Nari Itihas ki Talash Mein was a pageant on women's history. Its actors included Meenal Patel, Chayanika Shah, Sandhya Gokhale, Vibhuti Patel, Flavia Agnes, Odile D'Mello, Sonal Shukla, Sandra and Susan Mathai. Dineshwari Thonse, who joined FAOW in 1986, acted in some shows of *Nari Itihas ki Talash Mein*, and found it a transformative experience.[136]

Twenty-five performances of the play were sponsored by UNICEF. It was performed in schools, colleges and other venues. In addition, the group held three shows of *Nari Itihas ki Talash Mein* to help raise a corpus fund for Sahiyar, a women's group based in Vadodara.

Street theatre is difficult to sustain, because of the intense commitment and enormous time input it requires. While Aamachya Aamhi Natya Manch did not perform plays beyond 1988, it was active for another year or so. Lata PM and Nirmala Sathe kept it alive with programmes

[135] Two plays from West Bengal are detailed in Chapter 19. In 1991, Madhusree Dutta directed *Aaj Pyaar Bandh Hai* (*Today Love is on Strike*), an adaptation of Aristophane's *Lysistrata*. She co-founded Majlis with Flavia Agnes in 1990, to further women's rights and cultural activism. The same year, Madhusree curated 'Expression—A Women's Cultural Festival' in Mumbai, bringing together theatre, art, songs, storytelling, critical pedagogy and activism. The festival was a milestone in feminist cultural activism.

[136] Around the same time, Dineshwari Thonse, Nina Haeems, Sonal Shukla and others set up Vacha, a library for women, which soon developed into a centre for empowering adolescent girls.

that narrated stories and sang songs on the theme of women's rights movements. They used Marathi folk tunes and the folk narrative styles of storytelling Katha Kathan and Jagar.[137] Through these they spread the word not only about Indian movements, but also those across the rest of the world.

[137] Jagar literally means consciousness-raising or awakening.

16

Agar Mariam Hoti
Reclaiming Symbols, Myths and Dreams

ASTHA, a department of the Xavier Institute of Communications, Mumbai, created two street plays as part of a project titled 'Stree Katha'. Stree Katha examined and re-imagined stories about women in mythology, tradition, dance, art, cinema, television and other media. Its members realised that many social norms seemed to be guided by religious tradition and customs, rather than constitutional principles of justice, equality, liberty and fraternity. Within tradition, a lot was positive, but much of it was getting eroded and distorted due to communal and patriarchal forces. The group took up popular stories, symbols and role models from Hindu, Christian and Islamic traditions, and attempted to reinterpret them from women's points of view.

The ASTHA team began with the question, 'How does one make inroads into the lives of ordinary women for whom faith is everything?' (Viegas 1988, 46). They realised that deeply-ingrained symbols need not be uprooted, but could instead by reclaimed and represented as positive, active images which would inspire and strengthen contemporary women, in tune with contemporary situations and needs.

They thus decided: 'Through a creative and dramatic enactment of the woman's world (and the symbols which form part of it) we would invite women to reflect on alternative ways of seeing both themselves and their religious models. And we would encourage them to organise themselves around new symbols, positively rather than negatively as communal groups tend to do.' (Pereira 1988: 6)

Agar Mariam Hoti

The play *Agar Mariam Hoti* reinterpreted the figure of Mother Mary from a feminist perspective, presenting her as a possible role model for contemporary women. The initiative imagined her as a strong, thoughtful, and socially active woman. Mary is an archetypal figure, held in deep reverence and therefore very influential. By presenting her as a woman who actively questions the status quo, this legacy could be strategically used to support women who speak up, question discrimination, and intervene in contexts of communal tension.

In the early months of 1988, ASTHA staff member Christabel Neelakantan conducted an attitudinal survey on faith among 25 Catholic women. It confirmed that women drew solace from the image of Mary; specifically, the strength to bear their daily 'crosses' (Viegas 1988: 45). The survey was conducted at the popular shrine of Mary, Mother of Perpetual Help, Mahim. Many of the women interviewed had been worshipping at the shrine for decades and continued to do so whether or not they were granted the favours they sought.

The influence of Mother Mary as a role model was found to be pervasive. Girls were taught to emulate the Blessed Virgin: to walk, talk, think like her, and behave 'properly', so that even natural bodily functions and desires could feel polluted, terrifying, and traumatic. Menstrual taboos placed on Hindu girls, as the play *Aurat aur Dharm* showed, were comparable here; girls in households across religions were being socialised thusly. And as *Ehsaas* showed, schools reinforced similar modes of behaviour.

Making the Play

Savia Viegas and Jyotsna Kapur, both of who were in ASTHA,[138] together wrote the first version of the script of *Agar Mariam Hoti*. While writing the script they shared their own experiences of religion and communalism, and discussed how to structure the script. They wished to raise significant questions through the play: why do women bear the brunt of violence, whether domestic or communal? In what ways can women intervene to check the spiral of communal

[138] Savia Viegas is a historian, writer, and painter. She has worked at the Research Centre for Women's Studies at SNDT University, Xavier Institute of Communications, and has taught Art History at the University of Mumbai.

We were introduced to Jyotsna Kapur in Chapters 9 and 10, as a DU student who was part of *Ehsaas* from 1982 to 1986.

violence? What are women's rights? Can social violence be halted without weeding out domestic violence, and ensuring equal rights for women?

The script suggested that, for as long as domestic violence carried on, women would be unable to contribute as equals in the public domain. It made a reasoned appeal for changing gender roles and ingrained attitudes. Violence against women in the family was shown to be closely connected with social and communal violence. If women could play an active public role, they were likely to promote peaceful ways to resolve conflicts, preventing communal conflagration.

Once the play group formed, the script became the basis for lively, and sometimes heated, discussion. The group included several volunteers, along with ASTHA members. Some of the male participants denied any links between women and communal violence, and argued that it made no sense to show women intervening in issues of communalism. Instead, they suggested that the play focus on the nexus between religious leader and politicians, who were responsible for creating communal tension. Some participants said, 'Catholics have rarely been violently communal.' Others noted that while women may not usually be actively violent, they become proponents of communal thinking and regressive traditions. Everyone agreed it was true that women were among the worst victims of communal conflicts, and that in the aftermath of violence, they were often active in processes of relief, rehabilitation and the rebuilding of lives.

Discussions within the group led to reworking the script. Dialogues were improvised, sequences reframed. Integrating various perspectives and ideas, Savia and Jyotsna finalised the script, drawing clear links between women and communal violence. *Agar Mariam Hoti* presented Mary as a woman involved in social issues, holding strong opinions and making her presence felt in public life. The opening scene began with a group of men breaking down a big wooden cross, in a frenzy of rage, born of communal discord.

Men from two communities, involved in the conflict, pushed women aside, telling them to keep quiet, that these were 'men's issues'. The women put forward a series of arguments, trying to calm the men, but they were repulsed. Eventually, the women restored the cross, and brought the warring men together. Through song and movement, women asked a number of pertinent questions about gender roles in society and religion. The play deftly brought out a continuum: from women's containment within the household to their exclusion from leadership, or even participation in social and community decision-making.

The group[139] worked with zeal and dedication, although some had lingering doubts about the messages that they were trying to convey throught the play. Strong reassurance came from a participant who had initially been extremely skeptical about the script. His thinking changed during rehearsals and he said, 'I am participating in the play because I believe in what we are trying to put across. The script makes sense!'

The Play

The rousing beat of a kettledrum. Actors stand in a circle, around a cross. The tempo quickens, men move, increasingly frenzied, then hit out, knock over and break the cross.

The Sutradhar comments: Luckily it's just a play. Had it been reality, there might have been bloodshed. If somebody tampers with our religious symbols by throwing a cow's tail into a temple or pig's meat into a mosque or by breaking a cross, we get so worked up that we are ready to fight and kill.

Bipin, Prakash, Ramesh, Venkat, Augustine: We have to show our strength! Either they die or we die!

Jyotsna, Christabel, Poonam, Savia: Has any good ever come out of fighting, even killing, in the name of religion? Religion means a lot to us, but why should we forget our humanity? Men will die, families will be destroyed. Just think, who benefits from fighting and killing?

Men: Go home. We men will protect you... protect our homes... from danger.

Women: Is there no danger at home? This fire you light will reach our homes too. Walls, divisions, killing are all the result of your decisions. How long will you take decisions about our lives? How can society move ahead, leaving women, half the world, behind?

The women move towards the cross; the men warn them not to touch it, not to interfere in matters of religion. Men cover their faces with masks depicting a cross ending in a sword.

Women challenge them, bringing up Mary, who gave birth to Jesus, and Mary Magdalene, his follower. Mother Mary broke orthodox traditions

[139] The actors were Augustine Fernandez, Vipin Nadkarni, Sanjeev Kumar, Prakash Gaekwad, Martin D'Souza, Ramesh Shah, Venkatesh Raghavan, Christabel Neelakantan, Poonam Chawla, Savia Viegas and Jyotsna Kapur. The songs were composed by Christopher and Kush Gupta.

and fought alongside Jesus, for the sake of a new society! Did she fight with her head covered? Did she fight hiding at home?

The men attempt to refute them, but the women, singing, set the cross straight.

Women in chorus: I am Mary, Mary of this age! For truth I fight! I was buried in the earth, but seek to reach the sun. I am Mary of this age! I know my duty and my rights. I will not remain in men's shadow... I look after my home, and children. In the shadow my powers fade. I peep into many homes, and find the same!

Savia, Jyotsna, Poonam: Alcohol, philandering, battering! We followed the rules, wept, took refuge in religion, but the abuse did not stop. Why should we honour religious symbols?

Yes, I am Mary! Mary of this age!

Christabel: Though religion is being misused, for us it is an essential part of life. That is why religious symbols are sacred to us.

Women: The cross was broken in a frenzy of violence; violence has to stop—it can destroy homes, and relationships... Men's crooked ways have to stop, their power smashed. Women must have rights!

Sanjeev: How will society change just because women get rights?

Women: As long as violence and inequality continue in our homes, how can we bring about peace and equality in society? We should think on this together, and devise new ways... There is anger in your eyes. We too are angry, about violence, poverty, unemployment... How long will we tolerate all this, silently?

Men (agreeing): Some have nothing, others have too much of everything...Who knows what will happen, in an atmosphere of murder and mayhem? What guarantee is there that we'll survive...? So many are unemployed, and wander about aimlessly.

They have understood that it is a mistake to take out their anger on others, who might belong to a different religion, but are actually

Women Demand Our Rights!

equally helpless, vulnerable and miserable!

Men: Our neighbours become sheep brought to slaughter! Instead, if we come together, we can be a strong force!

All (chorus): Today, we ask some questions, of you, ourselves, everyone. Who said god is a man and woman a lowly creature? When it is the mother who gives birth, why is the child's name the father's? Is religion more important than the right to life? If religion offers us contentment and peace, why has it become an intoxicant? What is the point if by walking on these paths we become half-human, hardly human...? Today we ask a few questions...

Performing

Agar Mariam Hoti was performed for the first time on 17 September 1988 at the Bandra Fair, a week-long medley of entertainment, commerce and religion, organised annually around the shrine of Mount Mary. Every day, crowds of devotees flocked to the shrine and the fair. Four performances of the play were held during that week.

People saw the play and were engrossed. Women seemed to be the most receptive, but men spoke much more. These were the views put forward: It is important for people to co-exist peacefully. Blind faith can be damaging. Religion should teach love for humankind. A 70-year-old woman who joined mid-way during a performance stayed up to the end, and exclaimed with feeling: 'You are right. It is only when women have equal rights in society that any change for the better can take place!'

The play was performed in a few colleges. During post-performance discussions, students described their experiences of religion and society quite sensitively. In a mixed college, some commented that the play was unusual and thought-provoking because it linked two issues—gender dynamics at home and gender vis-à-vis communal conflict—

which they had earlier seen as being separate. In a women's university, the play evoked a different line of thought: students discussed the restrictions they faced at home, how religious teachings always promoted male privilege and sexist attitudes.

Women's groups invited the play group to diverse venues. Women's movement activists found it a powerful play. One criticism was that the two themes, of gender at home and in conflict situations, should not have been combined because the message gets too complicated for audiences on the street. Some people thought that the use of religious symbols was not a very secular approach.

The play group felt that this ploy helped them communicate with believers, rather than only non-believers or secular activists. They were interested in reaching out to the widest possible section of society, rather than restricting their message to the already converted.

Ek Thee Achhi Ladki (There Was Once a Good Girl)

A group of girls made a street play called *Ek Thee Achhi Ladki* based on their own experiences. The ASTHA team facilitated this, through workshops held during January and February 1988. The girls examined popular culture as it impacted them, re-imagined scenarios and presented their perceptions. In particular, they began to question various stereotypes of what it means to be a 'good' girl (Kapur 1988).[140]

The three-week workshop was held in Chuim, an urban slum in Khar, Mumbai, in partnership with the Chuim Community Centre. Eight girls, aged 9 to 16, participated: Ameena, Anasuya, Anju, Hemlata, Pratima, Pushpa, Rohini, and Vaishali. All eight laboured in their own homes—fetching water, cooking, serving, washing, cleaning, and caring for siblings and ill family members. Six of them worked outside too, as domestic helpers, or vegetable sellers. All of them had attended school, but some left midway. They came to the community centre daily, for a sewing class, which provided a respite from their regular chores and a potential source of income.

To participate in the theatre workshop, the girls had to take time off from their sewing. Sessions would be intensive: daily, for 90 minutes. They carefully weighed the pros and cons. Their families also had a

[140] This section is largely based on Jyotsna Kapur's (1988) 'Behind the Scenes: Putting a Street Play Together'.

say: stitching was a proper thing to learn, but theatre? The girls, excited by the prospect of doing a play, decided to join. After the first day, Hemlata's brother and Ameena's uncle objected. Hemlata and Ameena fought it out and continued with the workshop.

Jyotsna Kapur, the facilitator, had prior experience in street theatre, especially as an actor in *Ehsaas*. She saw the objective of the workshop as building girls' self-confidence and awareness of issues affecting their lives—the process was more important than the product.

The girls knew each other to some extent, and got to understand one another better during the workshop. In the beginning, they were constrained. So accustomed were they to work, that simply relaxing and enjoying body movements was a challenge. Trained to feel guilty about their bodies, they held back, giggling and confused. Jyotsna encouraged them to simulate everyday activities—washing, sweeping, kneading, mopping—and then make larger movements. Washing morphed into beating, with vigourous arm movements. Mopping built up into concentrated waist movements, until they grew giddy. Vaishali recalled seeing a neighbour possessed by the goddess, and joked: *Hamein Devi aa gayi!* (We are possessed by the goddess!) Gradually, inhibitions disappeared, and dresses flew as their bodies swayed, jokes were cracked, tensions loosened, and there was a tremendous release of energy.

They frequently sang together, improvising on popular lyrics and tunes. During voice training sessions the girls were initially embarrassed by the loud sounds projecting from their throats and abdomens, which carried to the room below, a crèche. Nine-year-old Pushpa, the youngest participant, was the only one without inhibitions—she experimented freely, screaming when needed. Miming, music, games and exercises created an atmosphere of spontaneity and team work, and helped build self-confidence and life-skills. If girls learned to project their voices, perhaps they would speak back effectively when harassed on the streets, at home or at work.

The group was very taken by the idea of writing a play. Jyotsna told them about young Roop Kanwar, who had recently died by sati in Rajasthan. The girls wondered what led her to die on her husband's pyre.[141] They tried to imagine her childhood, and this in turn led them to reflect on their own experiences of childhood. Soon, immersed in

[141] 18-year-old Roop Kanwar died on her husband's pyre a day after his death in Deorala village, Rajasthan.

a pool of collective experiences, they decided to make a play on their own lives.

A plot emerged as the girls opened up and spoke of overworking at home, lack of attention in school, drudgery in the workplace, harassment on the streets, and pressures to marry. They felt like they were being trained to become martyrs, for the sake of the men in their families. They saw their mothers suppressed, bossed around by fathers and brothers. Defiance shone through and they asserted that, come what may, they would *not* become satis. Rather than trying to live up to everybody's expectations, they would learn to look after themselves.

The Play

Roop Kanwar is portrayed as an obedient daughter, docile sister, submissive wife and daughter-in-law. This portrait segues into the question, 'What does it mean to be a "good" girl?'

Girls sing and dance garba but then Vaishali rushes off to work, Rohini to wash utensils, Anu to wash clothes, Anju to make tea for her employers, Hema to cook, Ameena to sell vegetables, and Pushpa to grind masala.

Anu: Roop Kanwar was a good girl. On 4 September 1987, 18-year-old Roop Kanwar died on her husband's pyre. Men stood around with swords, shouting, "Sati Mata ki Jai!" People worship her.

Pushpa: Why did she let herself be burnt? She was brought up with love, like all of us!

The girls wonder: Will we too become satis one day?

Their school-teacher scoffs at their ambitions to be teachers, doctors, sportswomen, and rebukes them: Nobody in your family is educated... Learn to make rotis like your mother!

They recite, in sing-song chant: I am a good girl, never loud, never angry... obedient, quiet, I do the housework, go to school, to work, and nowhere else!

Pramila weeps. Her mother is ill, yet works too much, at home and outside. The other girls sympathise. Back at home, she helps her mother. Her brother complains she's only interested in fashion, and attracting boys.

Pramila: Your friends whistle at me—why don't you stop them?

Mother: This happens in every home...! Pramila, I'll do all the housework... I want you to study.

The girls watch *Chhaya Geet* on TV—romantic songs with macho men, docile women.

The girls, going home, chant:

Yeh sheher—ek jungle,
Baahar baitthe bhediye
khatarnaak, khuunkvaar,
Parchhaiyaan, lambi
parchhaiyaan...
Vo pakad leinge chheen leinge
Utthaa leinge daboch leinge...
Ghar ke baahar, ghar ke andar.

(This city—a jungle,
Wolves prowl, dangerous,
ruthless,
Casting long shadows,
They pounce upon me, grab,
harass, assault, abduct
On the streets, and inside
homes.)

'This city, a jungle, wolves prowl...'

Hema: Good girls don't complain!

Anu: I heard my marriage is fixed, to some boy... Who knows how they will treat me... When my friend got married, they gave her lots of work, and very little food... He might beat me. I feel frightened. Maybe they will burn me... No! I will study! I will stand on my own feet. I will not give in.

Pramila: My brother will help with the housework. I will study, do something I want!

Anju: We will go out, and deal with the men there together. The street is not their private property!

Vaishali: We'll change many things!

Hema: We'll weave a new story, make a fresh start.

All: We will live, with dignity and courage. We tell you a story, a true story, our own story!

Performing

Every year, the Chuim Community Centre organised a one-day fair, Anand Mela. As 7 February 1988 drew closer, the girls prepared, rehearsed, and were nervous. They performed at the Anand Mela.

During the performance, they missed cues, forgot some lines, faced wrong directions, yet managed to convey their message, feelings and thoughts. The audience, largely local, was appreciative. Local girls were especially moved, seeing their own lives mirrored in the play. Eyes glistened with tears when Pramila wept for her ill mother and sparked with anger when her brother scolded her. They felt a stirring in their blood when Pramila, Vaishali, Hema and the other girls in the play decided to struggle for a better future.

Nobody from the actors' families came to see the play. The girls weren't surprised; their parents generally had little time for them. The organisers had hoped the play would encourage the families to reflect, and begin paying more attention to their daughters. The girls felt hurt, but also relieved, because the play might anger their families, leading to unpleasant consequences, and curbs on future activities!

The group performed several times during subsequent weeks. Within Chuim and other working-class localities, some girls and women in the audience identified with the characters and shared their own experiences. They performed for a few women's organisations as well. As they grew in confidence, they became aware of their responsibility to the audience. They remembered dialogues, projected louder, spread out, faced and made eye contact with the audience.

An elderly woman asked Anju and Pushpa, 'How come you understand all this so clearly although you are so young? It took us a long time to see these connections.' Anju replied, 'We worked out some things while making the play; others, we are learning from you!' For the young performers, understanding of wider social realities was growing exponentially.

ASTHA had earlier tried working with women in Chuim, discussing sati and the portrayal of women in Ramanand Sagar's *Ramayana,* a TV serial that was a big hit at the time. But the women were uncomfortable about confronting cultural beliefs; they seemed to fear retribution—human and divine. Engaged in domestic and wage-labour, they were hard-pressed for time. Some of them brought up experiences of domestic violence, which ASTHA did not really feel equipped to deal with.

The work with adolescent girls proved to be far more effective. Chuim Community Centre staff realised that along with skills like stitching, girls need life-skills like critical thinking, self-expression, communication and teamwork, all of which were honed during the workshop.

ASTHA felt satisfied with this experiment. The group that made the play—eight girls and one facilitator—had grown close to one another, through honest sharing. Jyotsna reflected, 'It was this honesty which communicated itself to the audience and was the strongest element of the play.' (Kapur 1988: 29)

17

Sinister Games
Stories of Change from Gujarat

A group of women students from Maharaja Sayajirao University (MSU), Vadodara set up Sahiyar Stree Sangathan in 1984. An organisation by women, for women, they soon became a strong pressure group for justice, peace, and social change. Intent on creating public awareness on gender issues as they intersect with class, caste, and religious fundamentalism, Sahiyar adopted street theatre as one of its modes of outreach.

Their plays included one on dowry and another, done very innovatively, on gender socialisation and invisible crimes against women. These themes were in accord with the motivation behind starting Sahiyar. Conscious of the secondary status of women, the group perceived the need for an autonomous women's organisation in Vadodara which would understand the gravity of women's issues. 'Sahiyar' in Gujarati means 'woman friend'; female friendships have traditionally been very important for women and feminist organisations reinforced this by adopting names like Sahiyar, Saheli, and Sakhi.

Trupti Shah[142] was a steady driving force behind Sahiyar. While studying in MSU, she participated in left activism, and got involved in the nation-wide anti-rape campaign that built up around the Mathura rape case. Trupti attended the first National Women's Movement Conference in Mumbai in 1980, perhaps its youngest delegate. After that, she decided to set up a women's organisation in Vadodara. She

---

[142] Trupti Shah (1962-2016) was an economist and Academic Coordinator of the MSU Women's Studies Research Center. Strongly conscious of the capitalist paradigm, Trupti's left leanings remained strong. One of her last public engagements was a presentation on women and gender at a national meeting of Radical Socialists in 2014 (Marik 2016).

subsequently co-founded Sahiyar with friends and fellow students (Sahiyar Team 2016; Shah 2011a).

Sahiyar worked consistently on violence in the family, including individual case-work, public awareness campaigns, and lobbied for changes in law. In 1985, anti-reservation agitation among middle-class youth turned into communal violence. With like-minded groups, Sahiyar organised a Street Play Festival in riot-affected areas of Vadodara.

In 1986, Sahiyar intervened in a case of gang rape by police of an Adivasi woman in Bharuch district. Sahiyar's fact-finding report became the base for a mass movement in that area, which had a high Adivasi population. Due to this, the CBI launched inquiries. This campaign sharpened the organisation's understanding of rape, and the myths perpetuated by the media and upper-caste society. Sahiyar's intervention was critical in getting the culprits punished.

Dahej ka Danav (Dowry Monster)

Sahiyar made a street play in 1986 in response to an invitation from some progressive members of the Parihar caste. The caste was known for its practice of high dowries, and progressive sections were keen to reform it from within. They requested Sahiyar to perform an anti-dowry play at a caste conference, thinking that a good play would educate people and spark off meaningful discussion. Sahiyar asked Manthan, a youth group, and Parivartan, a cultural group, to join in making and performing a street play. The three organisations held a workshop in which they shared experiences over a few days, improvised, and evolved a script. They rehearsed the play and were soon ready to perform (Jagori Samooh 1988: 58).

The play was called *Dahej ka Danav*. 'Dowry' in those years had become symbolic shorthand for a range of women's issues, a focal point, reinforcing as it did the devaluation of girls and the exploitation of women. Divided into eight short scenes, the play tells the story of a battered woman, a stock situation, and shows several alternative courses of action that she could take.

Scene 1:

A young woman, surrounded by flames, screams for help: 'Who is bothered if a girl dies...? She is alone, has to suppress her pain, confusion, sorrows. If she speaks, a volcano erupts...!'

Scene 2:

A married woman asks some questions of her husband.

Wife: Do you love me...?

Husband: Love? What are you saying?

Wife: Would you have married me if my father hadn't given dowry? He took loans, works day and night.

Scene 3:

Wife: I'm a human being, not a robot or rubber doll, a toy which is wound up to sweep, clean, wash, cook, and be available to you at night if you want.

Husband: Shut up!

He slaps her.

Scene 4:

There is to be an office picnic, but Mr Patel will not go; he has three daughters and is obsessed with saving money for their dowries.

Colleague: You keep your daughters at home. You are not living your life. In gathering dowries, not only you, your whole family is getting burnt to ashes.

Scene 5:

A young woman enters her parental home: They are asking for another 50,000 rupees. I will not go back to that house. I work from morning to night, do all the work of the house! How badly he beats me!

Father: We spent 2 lakhs on your marriage. A girl looks good only in her sasural. So what if he slaps you now and then?

Mother: If there is a family, there will be some conflict. You can handle it!

The woman returns to her sasural.

Her brother gets the news and announces: My sister has been burnt to death!

Scene 6, an alternative scenario:

Wife: I will not ask my parents for even one paisa!

Husband: If you don't do as I say, you can get out of this house!

Wife: But this is my home, I have done everything for it! ...From childhood, I was told I belong to another family. Where is my home, where I can live as I like? I used to imagine that marriage is based on mutual love... But for you and your society, marriage is a business. I have had enough. I am leaving!

The woman goes to a friend's home.

Friend: What happened, Ranjana? Have you finally decided to leave?

Wife: Yes! Now I will stand on my own feet, earn, live with independence and dignity!

Friend: Good! Your new life is starting! I think you should file a case, so those people learn a lesson!

Scene 7, another alternative scenario:

A group of girls discuss the fact that their friend Sangeeta is refusing to take a dowry despite her parents being willing to give it! They come to realise that rather than a dowry, women should get equal rights to property.

Girls, together: Not dowry, we want equal property rights!

They sing a song, about gender equality.

Scene 8, a third alternative scenario:

Several boys come to see a girl, Bela. She rejects them, and tells her sahiyar:

Shadi ke bazaar mein khada hokar sahiyar mori,
Daktar aaya sahiyar mori,
Tukur-tukur roop dekha ree sahiyar mori,
Padhai na poochhi likhai na poochhi,
Kya-kya doge poochha sahiyar mori.

(I stood in the marriage market, my friend,
A doctor came,
Peered and leered at me,
Asked not about my education or interests,
But only, what dowry will be given!)

Another boy wants to marry a working woman, who will run their household and supply capital to begin a business.

Finally, a young man who believes in love and understanding turns up, he wants no dowry. Bela likes his attitude and is willing to accept him as a suitor.

Performing

The team performed *Dahej ka Daanav* at the Parihar community function. It led to a lot of discussion. Parihars are Rajputs and the men take pride in being protectors of their womenfolk. At the same time, the women must conform to an ideal and maintain family and community honour. Women questioning norms, arguing with their husbands, walking out of their marriages, was not acceptable to some present, and they became defensive. Some others were shaken out of their complacency. Several conversations began that day.

Subsequently the team was invited by a number of organisations, especially women's groups, to perform in different parts of Vadodara. Post-performance, people invariably wanted to talk about oppressive social customs, and some women expressed an interest in joining Sahiyar in its activities.

Achko Machko Kareli (Sinister Games)

Sahiyar made another play in 1986—short, power-packed, with a fierce, tight script and lines set to a special rhythm, familiar to most people. Called *Ackho Maçhko Kareli,* the play was adapted from a popular children's game, in which two children stand opposite each other, hold hands, making a gateway. Other children pass through this doorway one by one, in a continuous loop, interrupted only when a child gets 'caught' in the doorway, and is out of the game. The rest of the children then resume walking through the gateway.

There are different versions of this game. Some of us have played it with the chant: 'Oranges and lemons, sold for a penny, All the schoolgirls are so many..., Remember me till I am dead, dead, dead, dead, dead.' At this point, the child in the doorway gets 'caught'. Finally, only one child is left 'alive'—the winner.

This sinister game served as a template for the play *Achko Machko Kareli.* The words were changed to bring up some of the most brutal crimes against women. One by one, women get 'caught' in the trap of male violence.

> Children: *Rakshak bane bhakshak, aadhi raat ko aaye thhe, aaye thhe, police chauki le gaye, le gaye (Protectors became abusers, they came at midnight, took me to the police station)*
>
> A girl gets caught.

Children's games: getting caught!

Mathura: I am Mathura, 14 years old, what shall I say? At night in the police station, they raped me...

Game resumes: Bahurani, bride, of Ahmedabad, the stove took her life, took her life.

A girl gets caught.

Varsha: I'm Varsha of Ahmedabad, my in-laws killed me.

Game resumes: Young woman from Baroda, her in-laws threw her out, threw her out.

A girl gets caught.

Arti: I'm Arti of Baroda, trapped by my in-laws. See what happens in a big house!

Two groups face each other and sing, the tune based on a popular Gujarati folk-dance.

Group A: We ask Hemant Vaid, why did you throw out Artiben? Achko machko ķareli.

Group B: We wanted gold and 3 lakh Rupees... We threw her out, we fear nobody!

Group A: You don't know Hemant bhai, women are strong. They light lamps of protest now, Sahiyar is with them. Come women of Baroda! Come, we fight for women's rights today!

All the women: We will shatter male domination, light lamps of women's liberation! The flame will rise, high, atrocities burn to ash, Come let's go to every lane, give a call to every home, every woman!

> The game resumes: Protectors became abusers, took her to the police post, and trained their guns...
>
> Gunata: I am Gunata, of Saagbari, Don't talk of that dark night, me alone, soldiers four. Who will hear my agony?
>
> Gunata sings, based on a folk tune: We will fight, we will fight today. One atrocity doesn't end, ten more are committed. Sahiyar, we will fight all atrocities... Night of terror... police caught me... They stripped me, tied me with rope, beat me black and blue. Sahiyar, we will fight... Dragged me into a truck, raped me, took me to the police station, and still more, they raped me.
>
> The women in chorus: One crime followed by another, endless... We will delay no more, We fight today against such atrocities, this is just the start, we fight today, this moment, to end all crimes against women, all humiliation and atrocity! We fight back, no more abuse, no more violation! Today, right now, right away, we fight back, we resist, stop this abuse, today!

The play was imaginatively conceived and performed with great energy. The testimonies of Mathura, Varsha, Arti, and Gunata drew the audience into the horror; they had no option but to take a stand. This was a very effective way to reach out and draw in more people, especially young women, to women's movement campaigns and actions against violence and sexual assault.

Through the decades, Sahiyar incorporated street plays, songs, garba dances, poster exhibitions, wall paintings, film shows, and other creative media into their work. Through these media they were able to address people across social strata. Students, NGO workers, trade unionists, teachers, lawyers and government personnel got involved in their campaigns, group discussions, workshops, trainings and seminars.

Sahiyar publishes training material, a newsletter, booklets, and leaflets on issues concerning women. The Sahiyar library has resources in Gujarati, English and Hindi, on gender, patriarchy, the history of the women's movement, songs, street plays, women and development, women and law, and documentation on women's issues across economic, social and political domains (Sahiyar website).

In later years, Sahiyar focused on building area-based awareness programmes, and training grassroots women as community leaders. This helped make it an organisation rooted among the people. It survived over the decades without big funding, relying on the strength of the collective (Shah 2011).

Dahej ka Savaal (The Question of Dowry)

We now turn to a third play from Gujarat, *Dahej ka Savaal,* made by Udgaar, a youth group in Surat. *Dahej ka Savaal* was designed to be performed for children, and addressed their teachers too. The idea was to influence socialisation processes by inculcating gender-equitable perspectives and respect for girls and women.

The word 'udgaar' means outpouring, a rush of expression and emotion. The group was committed to strengthening the stree-mukti andolan. Realising that awareness must begin from childhood, their play touched upon gender roles, stereotypes, dowry, marital violence, rape, unequal wages, discriminatory inheritance rights and laws, and oppressive customs (Jagori Samooh 1988, 81). The play emphasised the struggles of girls and women, and contributed to building awareness and resistance.

Dahej ka Savaal is a short play, with fast-changing scenes, vignettes, and an abundant use of chorus. The opening scene brings alive the feel of the grassroots women's movement, with a rousing song:

> 'Come sisters, women who labour, millions of women, do not bow or bend, let us march ahead together, step by step... One sky, one world, our blood one colour, women, come as one from villages and cities...'
>
> Next scene:
>
> Girls keep a five-day fast, Gauri vrat, foregoing various foods for five days as is customary during Shravan, the rainy season; but many girls do not like to do so! After puberty, they continue the fast. Its name changes to Parvati vrat.
>
> A girl asks why she can't eat while her brother does. She is told, 'It is written in the Puranas that Parvati fasted to secure Lord Shiva as her husband. That's how Parvati got such a magnificent husband! All girls must fast, and they will get good husbands.'
>
> Girls, nervous and scared, line up.
>
> Grooms' parties: We want a beautiful bride, wealthy, earning yet homely, an efficient housewife.
>
> A boy selects a girl, the others are disappointed. He demands cash, and many items of dowry.
>
> Chorus: A doctor, to get married, demands a car, An engineer demands money... A pig is matched with a virgin bride!
>
> The bride's mother conducts a puja for her prospective son-in-law's welfare and long life. The wedding takes place.

Women's intelligence, thoughts, personalities, burn to ashes in the marital fire.

To the sacred fire is offered the sacrifice of a woman's whole being:
Her intelligence – Om Swaha
Thoughts – Om Swaha
Voice – Om Swaha
Personality – Om Swaha
Courage – Om Swaha
Liberation – Om Swaha
Everything – Om Swaha....

The chorus comments on the sorry state of women, despite performing Gauri vrat, Parvati vrat: endless daily tasks, taunts, working non-stop like a machine, neither grumbling nor falling sick. When she is ill, her husband alleges she's putting on an act...

Goddess of justice: This society is a jungle for women. Justice is only for the powerful!

A woman: We will fight for our rights, we will live free!

Sutradhar: Come, let us spread this message to every house, in every street; we will suffer no more, nor bear your insults in the name of family, religion, customs and rituals! We will wipe out sorrow, confront rather than cry; together we will live our dreams, become the river flowing free...!

The play was performed in a number of schools. Children were attracted by the play's fast-paced action, rhythmic chants and movements, meaningful words and tantalising ideas. During discussions, Udgaar members were surprised to find boys more outspoken than girls.

Perhaps the girls did not feel comfortable speaking openly,

especially in mixed-sex schools. Their socialisation within the school and home trained them to remain silent, while allowing boys the freedom to speak as they like.

Maybe the girls feared ridicule and criticism if they spoke up. Possibly, also, the strength of their feelings made it difficult for girls to open up. They might have been torn by emotions of confusion, shock, guilt... they felt virtuous when they fasted, were praised for being good girls. Yet some seeds were sown, for a new perspective to take shape.

Reaching out to teachers was important. So long as they remained steeped in patriarchal thinking, they would continue to reinforce unequal gender norms. Teachers responded positively to the play, but there was discomfort too. Some said: 'Customs have to be followed. Everybody does so!' Several women teachers quietly acknowledged that customs were unfair, and ought to be changed. There was a churning of emotions, here too.

Aditi Desai: *Stree Savdan (Women Beware)*

When Ahmedabad Women's Action Group (AWAG), an autonomous women's group, was founded in 1981, they asked Aditi Desai to make a play. She had begun acting at the age of 14, in plays directed by her father, an active member of the Indian People's Theatre Association (IPTA). In 1984, she made another play with AWAG, a street play called *Stree Savdan.* During her association with AWAG, her understanding of women's theatre developed (Mangai 2015: 69).

In the Adivasi areas of Sabarkantha and Panchmahals, Aditi involved people in transformative theatre, trying to empower them to struggle for their rights in health, education and governance. Initially she was wary of doing theatre with local village women, most of whom had no literacy. Fusing feminist perspectives and the Theatre of the Oppressed[143] with local cultural motifs and practices, she soon discovered that there was a great advantage in working with villagers since they already sang and danced with ease. Improvising and performing in unusual settings such as under a moonlit night sky, her plays clicked with local audiences and led to practical results, such as farm workers fighting and winning proper wages, and women standing for Panchayat elections (Ahuja 2001: 20-21).

[143] Theatre of the Oppressed (TO) is a form of interactive theatre credited to the Brazilian dramatist Augusto Boal (1931-2009).

Aditi has held many theatre workshops to facilitate self-expression and storytelling. She muses: 'Anger, frustration, hatred have to be relieved in some way. My experience has been that performing arts is the most powerful medium of bringing out those emotions...' When she held theatre workshops with women survivors of the 2002 anti-Muslim pogrom, she found that dark experiences of violence were engraved on their souls, and that the workshops helped them express some of their anxiety and anger. She had a similar experience when conducting workshops in a jail with female prisoners.

Interestingly, Aditi Desai notes that many young women today wish to enter the performing arts and make a mark, but their parents are not very supportive. This is because theatre 'is a group activity and parents have an impression that their daughters might get "spoilt" or "maligned" if she enters this profession.' (Pandya 2014)

Theatre has often been perceived as a subversive space where 'good' girls might get 'spoilt', become self-willed and rebellious. There is more than a grain of truth in this perception, especially when it comes to the feminist street theatre. Girls (and women) find support here to speak up, explore their emotions and think for themselves. They might challenge status quo, break oppressive rules and do their level best to smash the patriarchy! (Ibid.).

SECTION SIX

MANY PLACES, MANY PLAYS: FOR VOICE AND CHOICE

> We sing and dance at festivals and marriages.
> Now we have developed the confidence to sing and act for our activist work too.
>
> – *Rashmi (Priya 1995: 170)*

> Whatever speech we give will not be as powerful as drama... We find the medium very enriching personally, and for spreading movement ideas. Mahila Sanghams, rural women collectives, make street plays, with traditional song and dance forms.
>
> – *Amal (Priya 1995: 172)*

> We travel across MP and adjacent states, compose songs on land and forest rights, and improvise skits and plays... In two years Ekta Parishad has spread like wildfire, across the state.
>
> – *Kasturi (Priya 1995)*[144]

The street plays discussed in the first four chapters of this section, all made in the 80s, deal with different forms of gender-based violence, and women's resistance. Each reflects something specific from the local culture—of Chhattisgarh,[145] West Bengal, Rajasthan and Uttar Pradesh (UP). Most of these plays were made and performed by strong women's organisations including Chhattisgarh Mahila Jagriti Sangathan, Sachetana (West Bengal), Sakhi Kendra and Mahila Manch

---

[144] All three of these quotes are from my article 'Reflections on the Use of Culture' (Priya, 1995). They are based on conversations and participant observation undertaken during the workshops described in this chapter.

[145] Chhattisgarh was part of Madhya Pradesh at the time, but had a distinct identity due to its high proportion of indigenous people. It became a state in 2000.

Chhattisgarh Mahila Jagriti Sangathan, 1994: Women produced plays with songs, accompanied by dholak and tambourine.

(UP). The fifth chapter describes street plays made in 1995 during a series of cultural workshops with women grassroots activists in six regions of the country: north, south, east, west, central, and north-eastern.

The play *Teri Meri Kahani*, from Chhattisgarh (Chapter 18), showed women trapped in predatory family relationships, and indicated that female solidarity and mutual support can help prevent tragedies. Formal devices which worked well in the play included popular children's games, adapted to signal the grim reality lurking beneath the make-believe.

Two plays from West Bengal (Chapter 19) brought out the dehumanisation of relationships within capitalist society, manifested in the institution of marriage. *Bandor Khela*'s short, hard-hitting story was told through the ploy of a popular street entertainer and his pair of monkeys. *Meye Diye Sajiye* was longer, a swirl of mythological, literary and historical references knit into the script. It showed unscrupulous marital and parental families and a young woman, treated shoddily by both, who eventually took charge, and wreaked her vengeance.

From Rajasthan, the play *Dahej* (Chapter 20) showed a brave young woman who called off her marriage at the last moment. The entire village supported her move. Set in a rural context, the play brought out the extreme inequality between girls' families on one side, and boys' on the other. Another play, *Intezaar*, was about sati, and here, too, the woman refused to succumb to pressure. Even as the religious establishment geared up for her sati, she rose, and walked away into the unknown.

The play *Teen Behenon ki Atmahatya* (Chapter 21) fictionalised a tragedy: three sisters from Kanpur had died, in 1988, of suicide. The play indicated that for many women, circumstances remained terribly grim and death sometimes seems preferable to life. It was a clarion call to unite for radical change.

Chapter 22 describes several diverse plays, made by grassroots women activists in cultural workshops held across the country in 1995. This unique endeavour carried forward the spirit of Indian feminist street theatre, taking it across borders too: three plays, made and rehearsed in the final workshop, brought issues from India to a global audience of women activists.

18

Teri Meri Kahani
A Ghost of a Chance, in Chhattisgarh

The autonomous women's organisation Chhattisgarh Mahila Jagriti Sangathan (CMJS) was founded in 1979. A booklet describes its genesis and concerns:

> Women's issues were hardly discussed in public at the time, in Raipur and surrounding areas; even social organisations had no real perspective on women's issues; opposition parties were silent. The Sangathan began raising issues of women's inferior status, violence and denial of decision-making; women workers' problems, especially in the unorganised sector; discrimination against women in laws—on rape, dowry, divorce, maintenance, guardianship and inheritance; objectification of women in media and consumer culture (Chhattisgarh Mahila Jagriti Sangathan 1994, inside back cover).

Social worker Shashi Sail[146] steered CMJS through the decades, along with scores of women in Raipur, Mahasamund, and other parts of Chhattisgarh.

A particular case in Raipur sparked off much introspection and discussion among CMJS members. This led them to make the street play *Teri Meri Kahani (Your Story, and Mine)*. On 19 February 1981, 25-year-old Gayatri suffered severe burns and was taken from her sasural to hospital, where she breathed her last. Gayatri had been married for two and a half years, and left behind a seven-month-old child.

---

[146] Shashi Sail (1946-2021) and her co-activists supported the education, livelihoods and empowerment of women and young people, especially those from Adivasi, Dalit and minority communities. She was active in the civil liberties movement, as was her husband Rajendra Sail.

Members of CMJS knew that Gayatri's was not an isolated incident. From their work with many women, and experiences within their own families, they were well aware that domestic violence was considered a private matter, not open for discussion. The air bristled with stories, which people half told one another, half withheld. CMJS members were deeply disturbed and went through a process of soul-searching, asking themselves, 'Who knows how many women are suffering, even dying, unknown, invisible in dark corners of ordinary homes?' (Jagori Samooh 1988: 62).

They realised there was a crying need to do something to end the violence. They asked themselves whether they were ready, understanding that their peaceful lives may be shaken up should they plunge into such tangled issues. They got together and shared incidents from their own circles, and from the media. They knew of the play *Om Swaha*, which took such issues out onto the streets. Street theatre appealed to them, it seemed an effective way to generate awareness. They decided to create a campaign, with a street play.

CMJS activists made *Teri Meri Kahani* through a collective workshop process, in June '81.[147] The play took off from Gayatri's death, and portrayed a very ordinary family, carrying the tenor of everyday routines. Women prepared food, served guests, discussed saris and slippers. They had little control over the big questions, which loomed large. The play made common cause with countless women, underlining how pervasive domestic violence was—'your story, and mine'. It showed the complicity of women who have internalised patriarchy, the rampant neglect and disregard of girls, mothers oppressing their daughters, grooms' families talking down to brides' families, and gender-based violence, all intertwined into the fabric of normal life.

Teri Meri Kahani deftly used a range of devices to startling effect: a woman rose from her grave and spoke truths which no living woman dared utter. In its own way, the play disrupted the 'normal' and broke the vicious cycle of silence. In the end, the audience was urged to think about what is to be done.

---

[147] I observed some of the workshop, a lot of colourful dupattas flying about, the actors serious and involved. I was in Chhattisgarh during June 1981 as part of a 'Gaon Chalo' programme that Shashi and Rajendra Sail ran, with the aim of introducing students from various parts of India to Chhattisgarh's life and society.

Teri Meri Kahani (Your Story and Mine)

Sunita's wedding is to take place in a couple of days. Her dowry is spread out, on display. Neighbourhood women gather, and comment upon the various items. Sunita's mother tells them the family has taken a loan, to meet the wedding expenses and dowry demands.

Sunita sits quietly. Into this milieu, a ghost enters—Shobha's ghost.

Shobha (to Sunita's mother): Are you bribing them with these things? To ensure they do not scold or fight with your daughter, taunt her, trouble her endlessly, beat, scratch, drag her by the hair... That they do not place hot coals to burn her body, or strangle her until she stops breathing? ...And what if, despite you giving them all this...?

Sunita (day-dreaming): Imagine... I'm sitting on the terrace in a pink silk sari, kohl lining my eyes, flowers in my hair, sindur in the parting. A soft breeze kisses me. Two unknown eyes come towards me, slowly.... A pure wave of emotion flows in my heart...In that moment, I will learn to live. I will love him. The unknown will become known. He will be mine.

Shobha (to Sunita): You are the bride? ...Engaged already, even though it is not yet two months! ...You met him four days ago, but my relationship with him is deep, as deep as death... They gave you this sari! I know it well. It still carries the fragrance of my body. It has a small burn—see, here.

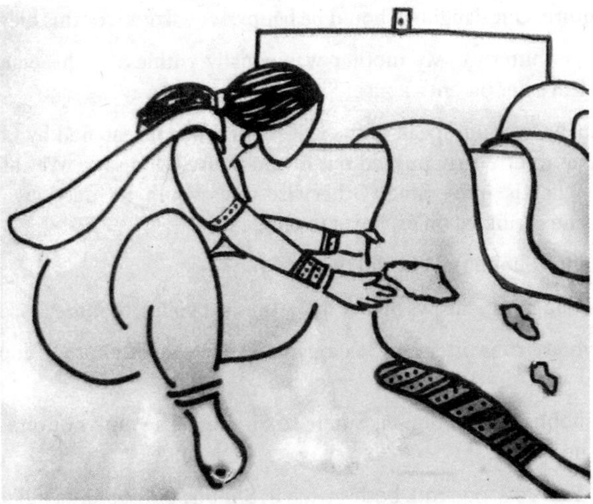

Sunita finds the burn mark on Shobha's old sari. Shobha was burnt to death. Her ghost warns Sunita... or is it Sunita's own sub-conscious mind?

Sunita: What are you saying? You mean he was married earlier?

Shobha: Yes, but... I died... Now you will live there, sleep in my room, place your head on my pillow. You will be my husband's new wife, my child's stepmother...I have come to talk to you... Do you feel scared? All they will do is force you to taste acid, burn your body with acid, pour acid in your eyes. That's all, nothing to be scared of!

Sunita (rushes to her mother): Why didn't you tell me? He was already married... He has a child? ...His first wife was called Shobha. She was killed, burnt with acid.

Neighbour (to Sunita): Come, sit here, don't worry... See here, this is your wedding sari... We are embroidering it with gold gota on the border...

Bhabhi (Sunita's sister-in-law): ...Even if it's true, how does it matter? This will not happen to you. In your destiny you have only happiness, and more happiness.

Sunita: Doesn't it matter to you that somebody burnt to death? You sit, like machines, stitching tinsel onto saris, filling your emptiness with lies... How come you all were not shocked to hear that a woman was burnt to death?

Neighbour: I kept quiet. But we all know that a woman died of burns some days ago...

Sunita's mother: Whatever happened is in the past! We should look to the future. Our daughter should be happy, we ask god for this blessing.

Shobha (bitterly): My mother was equally ruthless... The daughter must leave her parent's house! She must be sent away!

Gradually, women speak of their lives. One was threatened by her in-laws, another nearly pushed out of the house. One says: We tolerate even what is intolerable. Otherwise, we would be dead by now, kerosene sprinkled on us, burnt to cinders!

Sunita (to Shobha): Why did they kill you?

A girl (laughing, throws up her dupatta): Is it yours, or mine?'

Everybody runs after her. It's a game. They snatch another dupatta. Throw it.

All: Shobha said to Sunita, Sunita to Shobha, it's yours not mine, it's mine not yours...!

One: Two cats, one roti, both snatch it, Shobha pulls, Sunita pulls, one alive, one dead.

Two: Wait, here comes the monkey, a groom, he gets the roti...

Boy: You, come with me!

Girl: Why?

Boy: I'm your groom, you're my bride.

Girl: Wait, let me think... It's a matter of life and death. No, I'll make my own destiny!

Mother: Marry him!

Three: If she gets older you won't find a groom. The dowry will increase!

Mother: Bhabhi, Masi, Dadi, don't let our girl run away! Catch her!

Two women face each other, arms raised, hands interlaced, forming a gateway. The others queue up and pass through the gate, singing. As the song ends, one person gets caught.

'Poshampa bhai poshampa, What've they done, Ma and Pa?
They found her a man, She's to go, that's the plan!'[148]

Shobha gets caught.

The game carries on: *Poshampa bhai poshampa...*

A girl gets caught.

Boy: Come with me. I'll take you on a trip to heaven.

Girl: Heaven? What's going on?

Sunita: Two days to my wedding! Tell me, what should I do...? Nobody answers, I keep asking... Let's play a game, I will throw a handkerchief behind someone, that person has to answer.

Sunita runs, everyone chants *Koda jamaal shahi...*[149]

She throws the hanky, but the girl who gets it refuses to speak, to advise Sunita on what she should do.

One: What will Sunita do?

Two: Sunita will do whatever her mother tells her to.

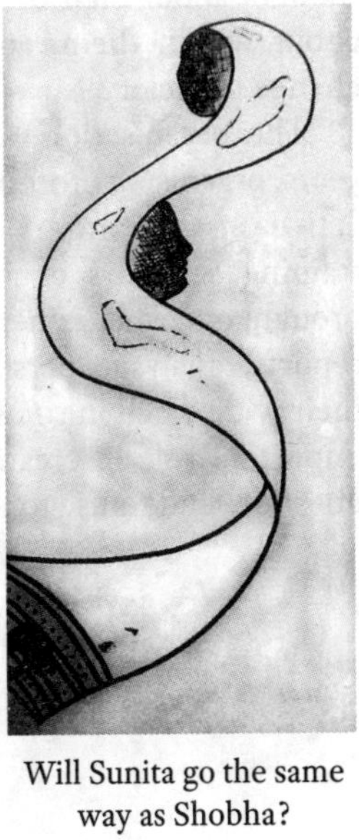

Will Sunita go the same way as Shobha?

[148] This is similar to the game in Sahiyar's play *Achko Machko Kareli*, discussed in Chapter 17. The language and verse differ.

[149] This was adapted from a popular children's game, including the verse.

Three: Will Sunita do whatever her mother tells her to?

Sunita (to everybody, the audience as well): I am to be married in two days. What should I do?

Shobha (walking into the audience, challenging them to take a stand): I am dead. Will Sunita, too, go the same way?

Performing

The CMJS team performed the play in various places. It was open-ended: there was no ready solution to Sunita's dilemma. The play got people involved, and of course they told Sunita not to marry the man. This would at least save her from one particular hell-hole. But, long-term solutions would need to go deeper into the psyche of the family and the structures of power which give very limited choice to women. Nobody seemed to know how to go about it; it's as if everyone, including Sunita, was stuck in quicksand.

Audiences watched the play intently, were sad, shocked. They took in the analysis and wondered what could be done. They must have thought about their own lives too. As these ideas and feelings jostled about within them, attitudes could change, resulting in a gradual change in society.

The organisation, CMJS, campaigned ceaselessly over the next years, organising protests, sit-ins, legal action, and boycotts. CMJS was active on many fronts of women's empowerment: work, education, training, seminars, counselling, legal aid, livelihoods, housing... They brought out a magazine, *Awaz Aurat Ki (Women's Voice)*, which carried reports, analysis, personal portraits, and news of struggles. With their wide reach in rural and urban Chhattisgarh, the group played an important role in creating a climate where women began to openly question, and refuse to tolerate the intolerable.

19

Giving Away the Girl and *Monkey Dance* in Bengal

Two street plays by the women's group Sachetana, *Meye Dile Sajiye (Giving Away the Girl)* and *Bandor Khela (Monkey Dance),* dealt with the commodification of women within a corrupt family system. Both plays, as well as a proscenium play named *Eto Rakto Keno (Why So Much Bloodshed),* were written by Malini Bhattacharya.[150] Bhattacharya was a co-founder of Sachetana, an organisation set up because: 'a number of Kolkata-based academics and intellectuals, deeply interested in women's issues, felt that their academic work in this area needed to be supplemented by an active engagement with the movement.' (Bhattacharya 2003: vii) Sachetana was pioneering in many ways, being the only women's organisation in West Bengal at the time to produce full-length plays on issues the movement was throwing up.

Meye Dile Sajiye was written in 1982, *Bandor Khela* in 1984 and *Eto Rakto Keno* in 1987. Madhusree Dutta, who directed both street plays, notes that Malini Bhattacharya wrote all three plays within a space of five years—'The early 1980s—the euphoric beginning of the contemporary women's movement in India which re-examined every text, every form and every structure and helped in making borders of all kinds more fluid, all identities less rigid, all expressions more multicultural.' Thus, these plays are documents of a period when distinct attempts were made to develop a language and a form that

[150] Malini Bhattacharya is a scholar, playwright, retired Professor of English and Director of the School of Women's Studies at Jadavpur University, Kolkata. She has been a Member of Parliament (1989-96), a member of the Communist Party of India (Marxist) and the National Commission for Women, as well as Chairperson of the West Bengal State Commission for Women.

would adequately represent women's experiences. This birthed a spate of magazines, posters, songs, plays, and 'an avalanche of women's narratives.' (Dutta 2003: xxii)

Meye Dile Sajiye (Giving Away the Girl)

Madhusree Dutta found *Meye Dile Sajiye* to be 'a rollercoaster ride through Euripides, Bankimchandra, early IPTA productions, the Phoolan Devi myth, wife murders, the metaphor of Tushu the desired daughter, the ever-vacillating chorus of the epics, and a musical form to incorporate all these.' (Dutta 2003: xxiv)

Sachetana members were initially not confident about acting: 'Few of our members had histrionic or performance talents.' (Bhattacharya 2003: vii) The Jadavpur Drama Club stepped in to perform *Meye Dile Sajiye,* but the actors lacked the technical skills required for street theatre. Their singing was lackluster. And being almost all male, they weren't able to identify deeply with women characters.

Production quality picked up when Madhusree, freshly graduated from Delhi's National School of Drama (NSD), returned to Kolkata in 1984, and agreed to direct the play. Initially apprehensive about directing a play being produced by a women's group, Madhusree found that the experience strengthened her feminist commitments. She, along with the actors of her theatre group Anarya,[151] brought discipline to the production. They created nuanced movements, ensured that sequences flowed and links were clear. The play had fast-paced action, and melodious singing accompanied by the harmonium and tabla. Props included a rope strung with mango leaves for the marriage scene, and a half-mask for Debi Choudhurani.

By and large, students of Jadavpur University took part in Sachetana plays. Most joined for short periods of time, so there were continuous reshuffles, each play being prepared anew many times. At times the cast was all-female, at other times it was mixed. A series of competent actresses carried off diverse roles. Tista Bagchi acted in *Meye Dile Sajiye* as the bridegroom's father, and later painstakingly prepared a musical score for the play. Ranjabati Sircar acted in *Meye Dile Sajiye* and later composed a short play on sexual harassment and assault, involving mime and movement, which was performed at Jadavpur University

---

[151] Anarya was a short-lived theatre group which produced a Bengali version of Brecht's *Mother Courage.*

and elsewhere. A number of actors were the daughters of Sachetana members. The organisation was unique in accommodating several teacher-student, mother-daughter, and aunt-niece combinations.

Sarmistha Datta Gupta joined Sachetana in April 1984 and began acting in May; she first heard of Sachetana from an aunt who was a founder-member. She was a teenager at the time, just about to enter Jadavpur University. Gupta (2003: xxvi-xxvii) muses, 'My initiation into the movement and a basic understanding of gender issues, is inseparably linked to being part of the cultural squad of Sachetana.' She participated in 'play readings, rehearsals, endless debates and *addas*,' and joined a peace rally. Her family was alarmed, apprehensive that feminist ideas would make it difficult to ever find her a good husband. They imposed a curfew: she must reach home by 6 pm. But rehearsals began only at 5 pm, so she would perform her role and rush off. Rehearsals were mostly in Ratnabali Chatterjee's[152] house on Rashbehari Avenue, and sometimes in Malini Bhattacharya's house on Golam Hossain Road.

The Play

The chorus sings a parody of the nursery rhyme 'A Marriage of Two Dolls':

The bride is decked, the cash is checked,
Dear father, now why do you bawl?
The girl was bred, the girl was fed,
And then she grew so high,
A thorn in the flesh did she become,
So you bid her now goodbye!
You checked the bridegroom's pedigree,
But does he have a human heart?
You failed to check...

Bride's father (to groom's father): I've given the boy his watch and diamond buttons, but haven't yet been able to arrange the motorcycle...

Groom's father: Our prestige is at stake—you should have thought of that.

The bride's father promises to send over a motorcycle. She is to leave soon with her husband and in-laws.

[152] Ratnabali Chatterjee was Professor of History at the Department of Islamic History and Culture, University of Calcutta.

Chorus: You brought me to the market place, you led me, roped and tied!

The bride's father visits his daughter's marital home.

Groom's father: Your girl's too dumb to make a good wife. Haven't you taught her how to please, to cook, clean, the senses to tease?

Bride's father: Give her one more chance, to your tune she will dance.

Groom's father: Let the delicate darling rest at your place. Don't bring her back!

Bride's father (taking her back): A golden girl, who'd laugh and play. And look at what I brought away! She doesn't talk, just sits and cries. Is this that same little girl of mine?

The bridegroom and his father begin to arrange another marriage, another fat dowry. But suddenly, Debi Choudhurani, the much-adored dacoit queen, arrives on the scene armed with a gun.

Debi Choudhurani (to the groom and his father): You ruin a girl's life and want the law to protect you?

Jolted out of their smug skins, they grovel at her feet. Debi asks some more hard questions, then with long thick ropes, ties and gags the two recalcitrant men.

A courtroom, Debi Choudhurani is in the judge's chair.

Groom's father: Why should I suffer, when bigger criminals run loose?

Chorus: A stove bursts each day, as part of the game; greed hangs out its tongue of flame.

The groom and his father agree to take back the bride.

Debi Choudhurani (to the bride's father): She needed a BA degree for the marriage market, isn't that so? Today, if she's unable to think beyond living like a parasite, you too are responsible for that.

The father pleads that he did what every father does, the best for his dear daughter.

Debi Choudhurani: Should a father buy poison for his daughter then, and plead innocence when she writhes in pain?

Debi Choudhurani unmasks herself, and is revealed to be the bride! The men are enraged: their daughter/wife/daughter-in-law made a fool of them! How dare she question family norms, and even punish the patriarchs?

Bride's father (raises his hand to hit her): She's no innocent little girl!

Groom: She's a real spitfire.

Bride (to groom): All this time I silently bore your beating, to save the "relationship"!

She informs them that she will not return to her marriage. In fact, she has already secured the job of a schoolteacher.

Chorus: In spite of all this fairy-tale stuff, is it all that easy to get a job? Where are the jobs?

Bride's father: Can our daughters really become Debi Choudhuranis? Until they allow themselves to be crushed without a murmur, there's bound to be trouble.

Groom (to bride): Stop talking big and come home with me.

Chorus: Is there no other way?

Bride: Do we have to return to the same life yet again?

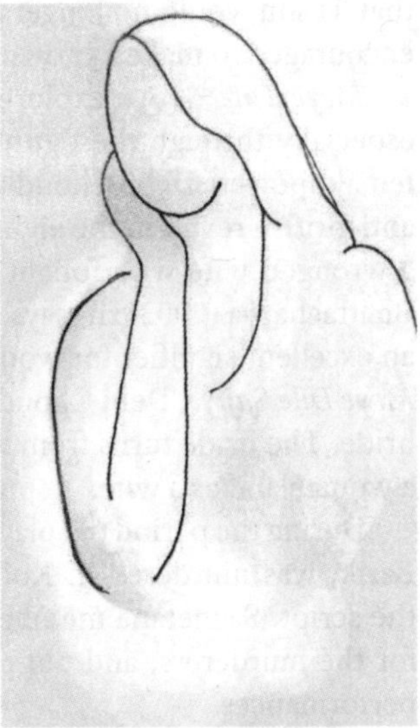

An obedient daughter, a crushed wife, a parasite, a spitfire, or Debi Choudhurani? Who am I?

Chorus (singing): *Tushu's my girl, my piece of the moon, I shall not get her married soon...*
Should a proposal come her way, "Choose for yourself" I would say,
Let her not marry with a dowry soon, Tushu my girl, my piece of moon.

The play ends with two possibilities, leaving the choice to the audience: will the young heroine be able to strike out on her own, facing brass-tack practicalities, or will she return to the same rotten life yet again? The two alternative endings create an opportunity for dialogue with the audience.

Performing

Meye Dile Sajiye was performed in college halls, neighbourhoods, and various open areas. In response to suggestions from the audience, Malini Bhattacharya changed a couplet in the final song. The original version said that if Tushu were to be given away, let her be given away without gifts of money and jewellery. These lines were removed, so that Tushu would no longer be 'given away'. Instead, Tushu would be encouraged to make her own decision, to 'choose for herself'.

Meye Dile Sajiye explored resources of strength within culture, especially through the figure of Debi Choudhurani, who symbolised female power. Debi Choudhurani, a legendary dacoit queen, led an anti-British revolt in the eighteenth century; at the same time, she was a wronged wife who fought for her marital rights.[153] Thus as Malini Bhattacharya (2003: xii) says, 'The icon of Debi Choudhurani provided an excellent signifier for women's status even in a modern context.' In *Meye Dile Sajiye*, Debi Choudhurani becomes a kind of alter-ego of the bride. The bride turns from victim to survivor and fights for justice as a woman and as a wife.

During the period the play was performed, a young woman, Debjani Barik, was murdered in Kolkata. This prompted further changes to the script. Sachetana members made posters demanding punishment for the murderers, and put the poster panels up alongside their play performances.

A performance of *Meye Dile Sajiye* at Gandhi Bhavan, Jadavpur University, sparked off heated debates on dowry and gender roles. Lines such as 'Just gold, no cash please' and 'What remains unseen, not a visible mark is a woman's unpaid work' sparked off thinking on the hidden dimensions of dowry, property relations, and women's unpaid work. In post-performance discussions, Sachetana would stress that reality was not reducible to a game of villains and victims: the entire family structure was implicated.

Sarmistha, with Antara Dev Sen and some other students, members and non-members of Sachetana, formed an Anti-Dowry Squad: they sang songs from *Meye Dile Sajiye* and organised debates on gender issues in several colleges such as Dinabandhu Andrews College and Murlidhar Girls' College.

Sarmistha notes that most of her college-mates were curious but dismissive of the autonomous women's movement; those in leftist students' wings regarded it with suspicion, as Western and elitist, or 'anti-male', joyless, and detrimental to family harmony. Being branded a feminist was a serious deterrent to heterosexual relationships. Sarmistha recalls that her reading of feminist novelists such as Virginia Woolf, Rokeya Sakhawat Hossain and Sulekha Sanyal

[153] Devi Choudhurani is acknowledged to be a historical figure, although she is known to us largely through Bankim Chandra Chatterjee's novel *Debi Choudhurani* (1884).

was entirely outside class. It was when Professor Jasodhara Bagchi[154] linked Romantic poetry with the women's movement that feminism, sexuality, and related issues suddenly entered classroom discourse. In 1988, the School of Women's Studies, Jadavpur University, was set up.

Bandor Khela (Monkey Dance)

Malini Bhattacharya wrote *Bandor Khela* at Madhusree's behest, and it was first performed on 8 March 1984. Short yet multi-layered, its intent was similar to *Meye Dile Sajiye*. Both plays presented arguments seldom found in 'anti-dowry' plays of the time, such as a daughter's greed for commodities, acquiring class, and callousness towards her own parents. Though seemingly linear, *Bandor Khela* had sharp melodramatic graphs: each sequence began with a popular reference, and ended with an emotional and ethical shift. There was lots of scope for improvisation, such as in the particular film songs sung and the names of contemporary superstars mentioned.

Madhusree recalls the excitement of performing the play: 'So much traffic, a major junction, and in the middle of all that we had to perform, no mikes, nothing! Such was the euphoria that we didn't mind...' (Dutta cited by Mangai 2015: 55).

Bandor Khela combined two modes of popular entertainment—the monkey dance and the street play. A popular entertainer, the bandar-wala, with a pair of monkeys balanced on his cycle was not an uncommon sight in those days: one monkey decked up in a frock, the other in a shirt and knickers. The ensemble would park in a residential colony or busy marketplace, the bandar-wala calling out *'Bandar ka naach dekho!' (See the monkey-dance!)* If a troupe arrived in one's neighbourhood, children and adults rushed to the site. The troupe settled down, the damru going diga-diga, monkeys prancing around as far as their chains allowed, childlike yet ancient-looking, eyes twinkling, tails emerging from lithe bodies, holding out little paws to shake human hands.

An audience would gather, and enjoy the well-rehearsed enactment: the man asking questions, the monkeys responding. Role-playing anthropomorphised the simians, usually as a romantic/ married couple.

[154] Jasodhara Bagchi (1937-2015) was a professor, author, activist and founder-director of the School of Women's Studies, Jadavpur University, as well as Chairperson of the West Bengal Women's Commission.

Malini Bhattacharya skillfully used this genre, which was in itself a satire on social mores. This intermeshing of forms was accompanied by an interlacing of content. Formulaic romance and marriage tropes were already embedded in the monkey-dance repertoire: into this template, the play injected another strand of thinking. The only speaker in the play is the bandar-wala, while the monkeys nod and shake their heads, dance, run, grimace.

The Play

> The play opens with the bandar-wala promising that his monkeys will act just like humans—walk on two legs, eat at a table, even marry. He breaks into a ditty, and introduces the monkeys as Rajesh Khanna and Hema Malini. He asks whether they are ready to marry. Hema is unsure whether Rajesh is earning a good income. Rajesh, it turns out, is a big official and will keep her in comfort. She happily agrees to the match.
>
> Rajesh hesitates. How can he marry without the certainty of a handsome dowry?
>
> The bandar-wala quips: Wow—human company has made him pretty sharp!
>
> Rajesh demands cash, a TV, almirah, a double bed, and utensils. Hema assures him that her father will provide these as well as ornaments and clothes. Rajesh demands a car, but Hema's father cannot afford this. For Rajesh, no Maruti means—no wedding!
>
> Hema breaks into heartrending wails. Her father offers more cash; the match is fixed. Hero and heroine dance à la Hindi movies. Love is up for grabs, pledged to the highest bidder!
>
> They get married, and 'taking many gifts and a big dowry, the bride leaves for her in-laws with a smile.'
>
> In her sasural, matters take a turn for the worse. Hema accomplishes prodigious amounts of housework, but Rajesh complains that she's lazy, and kicks her. She works with greater vigour, fetches him drinks and devotedly presses his legs.
>
> Bandar-wala (to Rajesh): Tell me what's wrong with her.
>
> Rajesh's grouse is he was cheated out of a car!
>
> Rajesh threatens to divorce Hema. The bandar-wala advises her: Try to please him...! Remain quiet, whatever he says.
>
> He croons, to set the atmosphere: 'O please, give me love, love me!'

Hema behaves obsequiously as advised, but the situation doesn't improve one bit. Rajesh is determined to divorce her.

Bandar-wala: Her dad won't take her back. She can't live alone. What will the poor girl do?

But Rajesh is adamant.

Monkey tricks.

Bandar-wala (to Rajesh): Get kerosene and a box of matches. Set her on fire, at night, while she sleeps. That'll take care of your troubles. You can marry again, get a car and whatever else you want.

Surely this is a logical conclusion. Rajesh, however, cannot bring himself to kill her. The bandar-wala springs the final ironic twist.

Bandar-wala: He says he can't set fire to his wife! Such a small thing! Tell me, ladies and gentlemen, would it be a problem had he been a man? Rajesh, you better stick to your monkey-dance! You'll never ever be a human!

He says this with relish and emphasis, as befits the climax, and sings a little ditty, as street entertainers do: *Naach meri bulbul, To paisa milega... (Dance, my birdie, money you'll get...)*

Performing

Bandor Khela was performed on 8 March 1984 at a joint women's rally, and several times thereafter at different venues. The play brought to the fore some less-explored issues—women's enforced financial dependence, the centrality of marriage to their lives, and also, how beasts don't kill their partners, but many men do!

Wherever it was performed, the play at first evoked delight in the audience; soon, however, entertainment morphed into a disturbing, grim denouement. Madhusree recalls that people would initially be quite cool, and then, at the end, there used to be pin-drop silence. The punch-line, the notion that humans are more 'brutal' than animals, gave people a bit of a jolt, even stirred their conscience.

The Long Haul

With both *Bandor Khela* and *Meye Diye Sajiye*, audience members were often deeply moved. Others felt uncomfortable or embarrassed, from a sense of the 'unmentionable' being mentioned. Malini Bhattacharya (2003: xviii) notes that 'vague discomfort is not the same as becoming aware of an issue... So I am really not sure to what extent the "awareness-raising" project was successful.'

Sachetana performed *Meye Diye Sajiye* for Doordarshan, and produced an audio cassette of the play. Its script was published in *Group Theatre*, a Bengali journal, while *Bandor Khela's* script appeared in one of Sachetana's newsletters. Both the plays became quite popular, and several groups performed them, sometimes informing Sachetana, sometimes not. While Sachetana was glad about the plays being performed, they were concerned about the quality of production, particularly regarding the music. They felt it was unfair to expect audiences to sit through a shoddy production, even if it is on the streets.

Malini Bhattacharya's proscenium play, *Eto Rakto Keno (Why So Much Bloodshed),* dealt with gendered violence in synchrony with rising political violence in the name of caste and religion. The play was jointly directed and produced by Sachetana members, and staged twice, in Basanti Devi College on 8 March 1988 and in Jadavpur University.

In 1987 Madhusree left Kolkata for Bombay, and in 1989 Malini Bhattacharya was elected as a Member of Parliament. Sachetana tried to keep up the play, with Sarmistha and others collectively directing. They performed it at Basanti Devi College and Jadavpur University. By the close of the 80s decade, however, Sachetana's cultural committee became defunct; the plays were never again performed in any consistent manner.

Members of Maitree, a network of women's organisations and activists, continued to sing songs from *Meye Diye Sajiye* on several occasions.

In Delhi in 1986-87, Kalindi Deshpande, who was active in the Janwadi Mahila Samiti (JMS),[155] wrote a play on dowry, using the monkey-pair ploy. It is likely that the play, called *Main Hoon Ek Ladki Kunwari* (*I Am a Virgin Girl)*, was partly adapted from *Bandor Khela.* Clearly, ideas and modes of outreach were circulating across regions, within autonomous and left women's groups. *Main Hoon Ek Ladki Kunwari* was performed by Buland Natya Manch, an all-women theatre group set up by Kalindi; the actors were Moloyashree Hashmi, Nandita Das, Shikha Trivedi, Rajni, Anusha, Savita behenji and Kalindi herself (Moloyashree, interview 2017).[156]

Malini Bhattacharya, meanwhile, was an MP until 1996. She made critical interventions in establishing the National Commission for Women, laws against pre-natal sex determination, and raised several issues relating to economic liberalisation.

Bhattacharya (2003: vi) explains why she wrote no more plays after 1986: 'The conjunction of circumstances which had acted as an incentive for writing plays had already disappeared', that is, the vigorous phase of the women's movement which peaked with events like the campaigns around the Mathura rape case, Roop Kanwar's sati, and the passing of the Muslim Women's Act.

For Sarmistha Dutta Gupta, translating the plays into English 'was like reliving those heady days of bonding and constant questioning of our selves and our work'. She feels that the plays continue to be relevant, even increasingly so, for the issues they dealt with are still with us. As Madhusree Dutta puts it: 'After all, the times which we claim had made Malini a playwright are still prevailing, though they have travelled through many refractions.' (2003: xxv)

---

[155] Kalindi Deshpande was active in women's and left causes, as President of JMS, an office bearer of AIDWA, and Delhi state committee member of the CPI(M).

[156] Moloyashree acted in one other play by Buland Natya Manch, also written by Kalindi Deshpande. Buland Natya Manch lasted for a few years and did at least two more plays.

20

The Brave Bride of Rajasthan, and *'I'm Not Your Sati Mata!'*

Two plays with a rural ambiance were produced in workshops in the early 80s, by women as well as men who worked with communities in various parts of the country, though predominantly in North India. Both plays were set in Rajasthan, though they could just as well have been set in Bihar, MP, or UP, which form a cultural continuum. Situated in the Hindi-speaking cow belt, these four states have been dubbed the 'Bimaru' states, signifying low socio-economic indices, including those associated with gender.

In *Dahej,* made during a workshop held in Manaklav, Rajasthan in 1982, a brave bride refuses to marry into a patently greedy family. *Intezaar*, made during a workshop in Mirzapur, UP in 1983, portrays a woman who is pressured to commit sati, but refuses. These were radical acts indeed, particularly given the contexts.

Dahej (*Dowry*, or *The Brave Bride*)

A 12-day theatre workshop held at Sucheta Kripalani Shiksha Niketan, Manaklav, Rajasthan situated at the edge of the Thar Desert, had 35 participants, of which only eight were women. They were all trainees in a six-month programme for grassroots development workers; most were from Bihar and UP, some were from Odisha, there was one each from Assam and Maharashtra, and four from Rajasthan. Most had never acted; several had never even seen a play. Their interest was in learning 'community theatre', with the aim of (variously) motivating people to give up the purdah system, helping strengthen the anti-deforestation Chipko movement, motivating mothers to send their children to school, and resolving conflicts (Sharma and Krishnamurty 1982: 3-7).

The group engaged in theatre exercises, discussions and improvisations. Wishing to do something relevant to the local context, they created two plays: *Dahej*, on dowry and marriage customs, and *Paani*, on water scarcity due to which women were walking vast distances to fetch water (Sharma and Krishnamurty 1982: 14-15). *Paani* had a straightforward script, showing people getting together to challenge sending water away via a huge pipeline to Jodhpur city.

Producing the script for *Dahej* was a more complicated process. As the group discussed issues around dowry, marriage and relationships, there were several disagreements. Some justified dowry demands as helping families resolve their financial problems. Others felt that dowry was not the right way to deal with financial problems. Men's frustrations were being borne by women, dowry victims were isolated and suffering. Somebody said that consumer items flooding the market had aggravated dowry issues. A local participant related a true story that had occurred a few days earlier, in a nearby village. A marriage was to take place and the groom, his male relatives and friends all turned up, but at the last minute they demanded a higher dowry. The bride's family had already given a substantial dowry, which they could ill afford. The bride rose to the occasion—she opposed the wedding. The entire village stood by her. This real-life incident became the seed idea for the play *Dahej*. The play was in Hindi, with a Sutradhar explaining scenes in the local language, Marwari (Jagori Samooh 1988: 69).

The Play

The play begins with a bhajan, sung with the dhol-manjeera. It morphs into mourning. Radha, a lively young girl from the village, died a few days after her marriage.

A villager: I sing because I cannot bear the pain! This pain is not just mine, we all feel it... we should all think about it.

Sutradhar (agreeing): One person's concern should become everybody's concern. When a problem becomes collective, it's the first step towards resolution.

Lalaji (a cloth merchant): It is the wedding season and we can make a bit of money. But you are doing a play against dowry!

Sunar (a jeweler) and Naujavan (a young scooter agent) join forces with Lalaji.

Sutradahar: For these people, dowry is nectar, but what about those for whom dowry is poison?

Next scene: Radha's home. Father Bheekhu is depressed. The mother speaks of their younger daughter.

Mother: Neighbours are asking about Lachhiya—when is she getting married?

She asks Chacha (Bheekhu's younger brother) to find a groom for Lachhiya. Chacha and Pandit (a priest) set out to locate a groom. They search high and low, and finally arrive at the house of Ramji Sahu.

Ramji Sahu agrees to wed his son, Ganpat, to Lachhiya, on the condition of a hefty dowry. Ganpat is an immature brat, yet Ramji Sahu behaves as if he is doing Lachhiya's family a huge favour, and demands a grand wedding feast.

Chacha (worried): We are poor people. How will we spend so much?

But he agrees, and the wedding date is fixed.

Lalaji, Sunar, Naujavan, and Choodiwali (a bangle-seller) crowd into Lachhiya's house, trying to sell their wares at exorbitant rates. Lachhiya's mother tells them she does not have the means to buy expensive goods.

Lachhiya (filled with foreboding): It's to be the bond of a lifetime. Life is long... or perhaps mine will be short, like Radha's! (Wedding songs, the baraat approaches.) They are coming, these strangers. Are they interested in me, or the merchandise that is to accompany me?

Upon arrival, Ramji Sahu demands additional cash, gold and a scooter, claiming that Chacha promised all of this. Bheekhu is distraught. He feels his hand is being forced: he will have to beg and borrow to meet these demands, reducing the family to penury.

The bride—supposed to be quiescent and voiceless—speaks up, clear and no-nonsense.

Lachhiya: Mother, tell these people to go back the way they came!

Pandit: Ignore her! Lachhiya is just a child.

'Whether I am a child or an adult, I will not suffer Radha's fate. I will not go with these deceitful people!'

Lachhiya: Whether I am a child or an adult, I will not suffer Radha's fate. I will not go with these deceitful people!

Mother: But what will people say?

A villager: Ramji Sahu, your demands are outrageous. You do not know us. This is Khuhar village! We dislike such greed. We will not accept you or your son. Leave at once! Do not even ask for water to drink, nobody will give you one drop! Go, now!

Ramji Sahu (shouts): Nobody can stop this marriage!

Villagers (surrounding him): This marriage will not take place!

Some lift their laatthis, threatening Ramji Sahu and his baraatis. Ramji Sahu starts running away; his son and the rest of the baraatis run away too. Villagers chase them, for quite a distance.

Performing

On Day 10 of the workshop, the group performed *Dahej* and *Paani* in Chaupasini village, 10 kilometers from Manaklav. The shows were in the evening; arrangements for lighting had been made. Props—water pots, vessels, and a broom—were collected from local homes. Nearly 200 people gathered and the performance space got reduced to a smallish circle.

People watched both plays attentively. When invited to describe their response, a young man (of the Thakur caste) came forward and said, 'Everybody faces the problem of dowry. We all need to think about it...' Some others agreed with him, saying dowry demands should not be made. However, on the water problem, upper-caste Thakurs in the audience said they faced no water problem, since they had tubewells. On the other hand, Dalits[157] suffered greatly from water shortage, but they did not speak up in the mixed gathering. In fact, the Dalits here were free of the dowry problem, since bride-price[158] was prevalent in their community.

When they were debriefing the next day, the team concluded that plays which portray social conflict might need to be performed

[157] The term used for Dalits in the source (Sharma and Krishnamurty 1982) was 'Harijan'. The term Harijan, coined by Mahatma Gandhi to replace the earlier term 'untouchables', was in common use during the 80s. The term Dalit (literally broken, oppressed), coined by Jyotirao Phule in the nineteenth century, came into use later.

[158] Bride-price is prevalent in some Adivasi and Dalit communities. This involves the groom's family giving a sum of money or quanitity of goods to the bride's family.

differently for different social strata. It is meaningful to present in a mixed group only when the oppressed sections feel strong enough to speak and present their points of view. The group felt it was important to involve the audience for a play to lead to meaningful change. Knowledge of the local language, songs, stories, and ethos would have strengthened impact of their performances.

On Day 12, the group performed at an open spot between two villages, lit by petromax and their jeep headlights. The small audience was intensely interested, even inching closer to better watch and hear the performers. There was not much time, however, for discussion.

For the participants, the workshop and performances were significant experiences. Workshop sessions helped open up knots within; they found ways to release anxieties and aggression, to express themselves uninhibitedly. Everyone enjoyed the creative, democratic atmosphere and gained confidence in improvisation, role-playing, devising situations, and performing. They hoped to use theatre within their communities of work, to spark discussions and arrive at solutions.

Intezaar (*Waiting*): A Play on Sati

Alarippu held a theatre workshop in Vanvasi Seva Ashram, Mirzapur, in January 1983. Nine women participated: including Runu Chakraborty, Maya, Nandini, Rashmi, Chitra, and the facilitators, Tripurari Sharma and Lakshmi Krishnamurty; and about 20 men. During the first few sessions, the women felt they could not open up and speak freely, so they decided to meet separately late in the evenings. They created a few plays in these sessions, in addition to the plays made jointly with the rest of the group.

During discussions in the all-women team, participants zeroed into two issues. One was purdah, which, whether the veil, ghunghat or burqa, symbolised restricted mobility and constricted lives. The second issue was sati; a male participant in the workshop, Poonam Bhai of Rajasthan, had mentioned that his wife was revered as a Sati Stree in his area. She had vowed to commit sati, should he die. After constructing a temple in their village, a sadhu had asked for a woman volunteer to take the vow. Many women wanted to take the vow, so lots were drawn, and Poonam Bhai's wife won. She took the vow to commit sati in that very temple, accompanied by celebrations and felicitations. Because of this, she was held in high regard and he felt proud and happy.

Women participants were aghast. Most hadn't realised the practice of sati was still alive, they thought of it as a nineteenth-century phenomenon. Sati was perhaps being revived, in the climate of growing religious bigotry accompanied by reactionary attitudes towards women. The issues of sati and purdah became points of departure for the play they made.

The play *Intezaar* recreates an ethos of blind faith, in which religious leaders systematically misinform people to control them, particularly making use of women. A pandit and his disciple try to bamboozle villagers, telling them that the goddess will reward whichever village has a woman ready to commit sati. However, the woman they pick refuses to submit to their machinations.

The Play

Scene: A temple. The priest and two disciples discuss how to attract people.

Disciple 1: Why can't somebody become sati, for the sake of this temple? Let's declare that this temple is awaiting a sati!

Disciple 2: Imagine, if it happens, how many people will come, and make offerings!

Disciple 1: People will earn, selling tea, food!

Disciple 2: Shoes, slippers, purses, bedding, clothes, jewellery.

Disciple 1: Every year there will be a mela. Our ancient culture, values, will be reborn!

They announce that the temple is calling for a Sati Mata.

Chorus: Sati Mata is hiding somewhere, drag her out, she will burn on the pyre, countless images will be made of her, seek her, or make her!

Women say: From amongst us, one is to be a Sati Mata... The poor woman will be caught unaware!

Women (in long odhnis): *Teen gaz ki odhni, odhni ke kone chaar, chaar dishaon ka sansar... Deewar bani hai ghunghat, ghunghat andar hai ghutan, ghutan bhari hai zindagi, odhni hai zindagi, zindagi hai odhni.* (My veil of three lengths, has four corners, the world stretches in four directions, the veil has become a wall, we suffocate inside, the veil is our life, our life the veil.)

A family scene: Four women, all veiled, work—grinding flour, washing clothes, cleaning lentils, cooking. They are Saas, Chhoti Bahu, Badi Bahu, and Nanad.

Chhoti Bahu: I used to be full of life. But seven years of marriage, and he hasn't been with me for even seven hours! Yet everybody taunts me, because I haven't had a child.

Saas: We shall have a child here, soon! Seven years ago my son went away, but he is to return.

Nanad: My brother will come!

Chhoti: What is he to me? Someone who has hardly seen me, doesn't recognise me?

Nanad: Seven sacred steps you took around the fire, with him.

Chhoti: Relationships are made by living together, sharing joys and sorrows.

Nanad: Bhaiya is coming, he has sent word!

She dresses up Chhoti, mehndi on her hands, and bangles.

There is a commotion outside; they are told that Chhoti's husband has died in an accident.

Chhoti (stunned, empty-eyed): Somebody has died...But what was he to me?

Nanad: He was your husband...These bangles have to be broken!

Chhoti: No! You put them on me so lovingly. I like the colour green...

Male voices from outside: She has the Devi upon her! She will become sati!

Women (to Chhoti Bahu): You will become sati! You will be worshipped as Sati Mata.

Chhoti: But I want to live!

Voices: The village will become a pilgrim spot, shops will come, roads, electricity! You will be venerated as a Devi!

Chhoti: You all want me to burn, to death? What sin have I committed?

Voices: Sati Mata ki jai! Sati Mata amar rahe! Sati Mata will live forever!

'I will live!'—she walked out.

Nanad: Tomorrow at dawn...

Chhoti: I have to die, to be burnt! ... Is this what the seven sacred steps are about?'

Chhoti cries herself to sleep.

Chhoti (at dawn, lifts her ghunghat and looks out): The sun's first rays... This is to be my last morning! No, I will not let this happen... There is a road, outside. People walk on that road. I too will walk.

She leaves the house.

Voices: Sati! Sati! Where is Sati Mata? Where is she? How could she vanish?

(There is a commotion, there are people all over.)

Nanad (holds up her odhni like a flag): She said, "I will live! I will not die, I will not be burnt!"'

(The voices are silenced.)

Impact

Intezaar proved to be a prophetic play in some ways. About four years later, a young woman named Roop Kanwar died by sati, immolated in a concremation on her husband's pyre, in Deorala, Rajasthan. A temple was devoted to her and people thronged to pay obeisance.

Roop Kanwar was unable to protect herself as Chhoti in the play did. *Intezaar* showed a woman who simply resisted all the pressures put upon her. She questioned what was accepted as normal in a marriage, in relationships, and the final, terrible sacrifice that a sati makes.

After the Roop Kanwar sati in 1987, the women's movement took up cudgels against the practice of sati, launching campaigns with in-depth investigations and analysis of the phenomenon, holding protest demonstrations, mobilising public opinion, and demanding that the state law and order machinery make necessary interventions.

Intezaar ultimately proved to be the most important play to emerge from the Mirzapur workshop. Seeing the need for just such a play, to help stir thought and discussion, Alarippu brought it out of hibernation. The Alarippu team rehearsed and performed it several times, at different spots (Katyal 1998-99b: 114).

21

Teen Behenon ki Atmahatya
Sisterhood in Kanpur, UP

Triple Suicide: A Tragedy Unfolds

On 3 February 1988, a tragedy unfolded in Kanpur city: three sisters died by suicide. They were educated, college-going young women. Newspapers reported the event, but not the reasons behind it. Members of Sakhi Kendra and Mahila Manch, Kanpur-based women's organisations, felt it was important to understand why this had happened. What were the issues involved?

Sakhi Kendra and its sister organisation Mahila Manch were autonomous women's groups, set up in 1982. They were very active in Kanpur and surrounding areas of UP. Sakhi Kendra was designed as a grassroots organisation that provided counselling, legal aid, shelter and support to women survivors, while Mahila Manch focussed on campaigns and awareness-building across the state. In mid-February 1988, Neelam Chaturvedi,[159] the founder-director of both organisations, met the family of the three deceased sisters. I accompanied her on this visit, as a participant observer.[160]We pursued the investigation further, meeting neighbours, friends, relatives, college principals, and school-

[159] Neelam Chaturvedi is Sakhi Kendra's General Secretary and President of Mahila Manch. She is also Treasurer and a founding member of the National Alliance of Women's Organisations (NAWO).

[160] I was in Kanpur at the time, researching the UP women's movement for my PhD. I carried out participant observation with Mahila Manch and Sakhi Kendra in Kanpur during February and March 1988. Some of their activities during that period included the retrieval of dowry from the marital home of a domestic abuse survivor (who was a medical doctor, as was her husband), a Jan Sunvai or people's hearing on domestic violence in a working-class neighbourhood, and regular counselling and legal aid work.

teachers. This enabled an understanding of their motivations and the possible sequence of events that led to their deaths.

We had intense discussions to piece together what may have happened in the ill-fated home. It was situated in a bylane of Coolie Bazar, a residential-cum-market area in central Kanpur, densely packed with narrow two- to three-storey buildings. Up a staircase, grey paint peeling from its walls, was the first-floor flat where the desolate parents continued to live, with their two younger daughters and son. The father worked in the Life Insurance Corporation. He had been keen to educate all his children and arrange good marriages for them.

The three girls helped their mother in the kitchen, went to college by rickshaw and after class, returned straight home. Shobha, 22, had completed an MA and was pursuing a stenographer's course at a Women's Polytechnic. Komal, 20, was pursuing an MA in Education at DAV College. And Seema, 18, was doing a BA at Johri Devi College.[161] Teachers recalled them as being serious, hard-working, quiet girls who were never involved in any trouble.

Neighbours praised the three sisters, saying they walked with their eyes downcast, didn't wander about, talk loudly, or draw attention to themselves. Their mother hardly left the house. It was their father who did the shopping: he bought the rations and groceries, and even daily vegetables on his way back from office. The girls never went out with friends. Shobha and Komal had no friends; they didn't even converse with the girls sitting next to them in class. Seema had one childhood friend, Renu, who told us that Seema was very angry about customs like dowry; that she was interested in detective stories, and had no fear of death, but if a boy on the street passed a comment, she would never answer back, thinking he may harass her further.

Shobha applied for jobs, but didn't get any, despite being qualified. Her father had encouraged her to work and earn and the whole family felt disappointed when she failed to secure a job. Marriage, too, proved elusive. Five or six grooms' parties had been to 'see' Shobha, but negotiations floundered on the shores of dowry. The father prepared to spend his entire savings on this one marriage. To a family from Allahabad, he agreed to give Rs. 50,000 in cash, besides jewellery and household items. Shobha kept a fast every Thursday, praying for this

---

[161] To maintain privacy, the girls' names were changed for the play, and I continue to use these altered names.

proposal to come through. After a few months, in January 1989, the Allahabad family sent word that they had arranged their boy's marriage elsewhere. Shobha was devastated by this rejection and said to her parents, 'Don't look for more boys for me. I will find a job, stand on my own feet. Look for boys for Komal, then Seema.'

The three sisters were very close. They studied together on the terrace and shared confidences. They had discovered that jobs were not easy to find and marriage too seemed out of reach; and if they did marry, the family finances would plummet. Hemmed in, they felt like a burden on their parents, an obstacle in the path of their three younger siblings. The thought of suicide reverberated from one to the other and metamorphosed into a common decision. In early February, there was a wedding in the extended family; they excused themselves, pleading the need to study. At 6.30 am, the rest of the family stepped out, leaving for the railway station.

The trio wrote suicide notes, asking their parents to forgive them. They changed into fresh clothes, took old, strong cotton saris and tied them into nooses—one attached to the ceiling fan, the other two to a couple of solid metal knobs on the living-room ceiling. Climbing onto stools, each one put a noose around her neck, and let go. The family returned in a couple of days and, getting no response, broke open the door to discover three corpses.

Theatre Workshop: Making the Play

Members of Sakhi Kendra and Mahila Manch were deeply affected. The sheer *ordinariness* of the situation was disturbing: what these young women faced was commonplace, rather than unusual. Layers of oppression, confusion, and finally desperation, seemed to have enveloped the three young women. To initiate a public discussion on the underlying issues, Sakhi Kendra and Mahila Manch decided to make a street play, and to perform it around 8 March 1989.

Around ten women volunteered to participate in the play. As daily workshop sessions began, a couple of members dropped out, finding the time commitment impossible. Eight came regularly, and thus the play group crystallised. There was young Rani, a factory worker; Meena, a lawyer and Christian; Bhuri, elderly and working-class; Sheela, a middle-class activist and housewife; Rashmi, a middle-class singer and activist; Meera Sharma, young and working-class; Neelam, mentioned above; and myself.

Several others came by now and then, observed, offered suggestions for the evolving storyline, and feedback on rehearsals. Nobody in the Kanpur group had prior experience of doing a street play, but they were talented and lively—Rashmi was a brilliant singer, Neelam and Meena were fearless orators, Sheela and Rani were full of ideas, Bhuri was a compassionate soul, and Meera was full of energy.

In the workshop, participants shared emotions and experiences, and an atmosphere of trust built up. Each one felt an empathetic link with the three sisters. A participant shared that she had once had suicidal thoughts during a crisis in her life. Gradually, we learnt that almost everyone in the group had, at some point or the other, contemplated suicide. Participants touched sadness, vulnerability, in themselves, in each other. They realised that Shobha, Komal and Seema, lacking connections to a wider world, of solidarity, of alternatives, had given way to despair.

The group's intense involvement coupled with their hard work resulted in a skeletal plot. Roles were taken up spontaneously. Sharing within the group had brought the participants closer and lent depth to both the plot and its enacting. Within a week, the play was ready. I penned the script based on our discussions and, truth be told, adapted some dialogues and sequences from earlier plays I was familiar with—*Om Swaha* and *Ehsaas,* and movement songs.

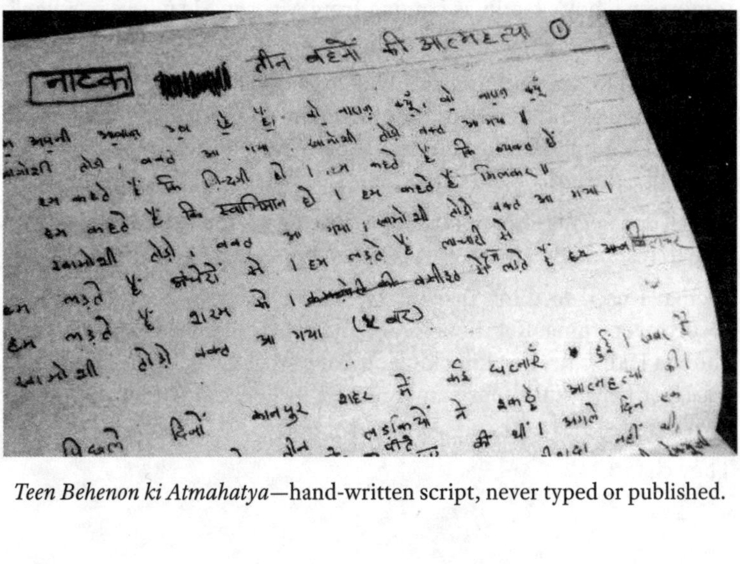

Teen Behenon ki Atmahatya—hand-written script, never typed or published.

The Play: *Teen Behenon ki Atmahatya* (*The Death by Suicide of Three Sisters)*

The play begins with the song:

> *Hum apni awaz uttha rahe hain, vo naraaz kyun, vo naraaz kyun?*
> *Khamoshi todo, vakt aa gaya!*
>
> (We lift our voices high, why are they angry, why are they angry?
> Break the silence, it's time!)

Sutradhar: In Kanpur, on 3 February, three sisters died by suicide. The next day, two more girls died by similar means. (He briefly relates the facts of several recent incidents.)

A young woman: This can happen to me too! Often, when I am very troubled, I feel like ending everything!

Home scene: Shobha, Komal, and Seema do puja in the morning, clean the house, serve breakfast to their younger siblings, pack their father's lunch-box, then leave for college. In the evening, they study, do more housework...

Seema: I want to go for my friend's birthday party, for just an hour, with my classmates.

Father: No Seema, girls who wander around get spoilt! I'm so fond of my daughters! You are capable, intelligent, good-looking... Shobha, tomorrow a boy's family is coming from Meerut. He works in a bank. Dress well!

Seema and Komal enthusiastically help Shobha dress nicely. The boy's family comes, and demands an exorbitant dowry. Parties come from Kolkata, Kanpur, Bareilly, Shahjahanpur, and later send word that they didn't like the girl.

Komal and Seema ask Shobha not to lose heart: the Allahabad family is sure to respond positively. But they too reject her.

Seema: I used to think that my two elder sisters accept everything, absorb everything. But there is despair in their silence, not acceptance. Shobha Didi is tired of knocking on doors that never open. There's no place for her in this house any more. A girl becomes a burden to her own parents!

They chant:

Groping in the dark, for light, for life, for a way out.

Ek ghera hai, isi mein rehti hain hum,
Udne ke sapne chhodo...

(There is a cage, in which we live,
Give up your dreams of flying...)

Komal is sad, Shobha depressed, Seema angry.

Shobha: In getting me married, Pitaji will spend all his savings. What will happen to my sisters?

Seema: I feel really angry! In college, they are taking out a rally against sati. I wish I could join, but I'm scared! I do not fear death, though; and I no longer have faith in God.

Komal: We were speaking about feeling suffocated... I cannot bear it anymore!

Seema: Is there really no place for us in such a big world? A little corner, where we could live?

Shobha: You're crazy—always asking questions. Have you ever received any proper answer? Be quiet, like us. You and I don't have the power to change the world. We can leave it, though.

Komal: Leave? But Ma-Pitaji... they love us so much!

Seema: Let's run away, the three of us!

Shobha: Yes, let's run away, far away, together.

Komal: There's nothing in life, no direction... It's best to leave!

Seema: But how...?

Shobha: That's not too difficult, once the decision is taken.

Next Scene

Father: Girls, we're going to Lucknow for your cousin's wedding.

Shobha: Yes Pitaji. We'll catch up on our studies.

Father: Alright. Once we return, I'll take everyone to see a film.

Seema: Pitaji, what if we go on our own, to see a film?

Father: What are you saying? You can't go alone!

Komal (to herself): Pitaji, we will go. You'll see!

Father (leaving): Girls, stay home, keep the door shut. We'll return in two days.

Shobha, Komal, Seema (soft chant, with actions): Write letters for Ma-Pitaji, Take off our gold earrings, our sisters can wear them, stand on stools, tie saris from ceiling fan and kundas, act with courage, act with courage!

Their bodies go stiff and sway from side to side.

Sutradhar: No screaming, no storms! Just a weird silence spread everywhere... These three, so scared in life, didn't hesitate to embrace death. They passed from one silence to another...

Woman 1: But, is suicide the only solution? Is there no other way?

Woman 2: At times I want to break everything! If I had poison, I would drink it! But each time something stops me, gives me strength. I glimpse a facet of life which is dear to me and a way to live opens up.

Woman 1: These girls weren't able to find such a way... They wanted just a little space in this vast world. Why couldn't we, the world, provide a tiny corner where they could dwell peacefully?

Woman 2: Are we responsible for their suicides then?

Woman 1: Who is responsible? The girls, who embraced death? Their parents? Or the dowry-seekers? Or society, the whole of society, and the social prejudices which pervade everything and contaminate everyone?

All (to the audience, voices rising in anger and grief): Who is responsible for the deaths of Shobha, Komal, and Seema? Who is responsible for their deaths?

Sutradhar: Please, tell us—who is responsible? What do you think?

Performing

The first show of *Teen Behenon ki Atmahatya* was held on 8 March 1988, International Women's Day. It was performed in the courtyard of Meera Sharma's home in Dadanagar, a working-class settlement. The audience of 30 to 40 women was attentive, concerned. Shades of empathy flickered across many of the gathered faces. When the three sisters died, Bhuri, in the mother's role, spontaneously wept. This happened in every show: Bhuri was simply unable to check her tears.

A somber mood persisted as the plot unravelled, the atmosphere heavy with questions. Several women observed that they understood the situation of the three sisters well. One said: 'I feel suffocated in my life, just like Shobha, Komal and Seema. In fact, most women feel a sense of suffocation. Somehow I keep myself from suicide. But these three sisters reached a point of no return!'

For a fortnight, we performed the play at several places in Kanpur. Everywhere, women felt deeply connected to the theme. In Lakshmanpurva, a working-class area, women asserted: 'Parents must bring up daughters with a spirit of freedom. Girls must grow up fearless!'

In Raipurva, a middle-class neighbourhood, a woman sobbed as she shared:'Those who suffer realise what suffering means. I educated my daughters, and married off two, but one of them is desperately unhappy! I am trying to settle my third daughter, but boys demand a huge dowry!' In Miriampur, a resident named Shanti related several instances where girls were over-sheltered and later suffered for it. In Vishnupur, a semi-rural settlement, a woman said:'If parents give them freedom, girls grow up brave, walk fearlessly in the world, stand on their own feet, but if they're kept in purdah, within four walls, they are unable to look after themselves when they grow up.'

The play was performed in Rani's house in Vishnupur. Rani had been working in a factory, supporting her younger siblings and aged parents with her wages (Rs. 400). When 30 women workers were unjustly retrenched, she went on strike, was ruthlessly harassed by factory managers, and had to leave the job. She related the story, very angry and anxious. Another woman related how she used to work in Kanpur's Nari Niketan, and really liked working there; but after she married, her husband made her leave the job.

The day the play was performed in Rani's house in Vishnupur, just two lanes away a 14-year-old girl burnt to death. That morning, her father had beaten her up for talking to a boy. A few days earlier, Bijoya from Bengali Colony died similarly; she was in love with a boy and planned to marry him, but neighbours called her shameless and threw stones at them. Another girl in Kanpur killed herself the day after newspapers carried the story of the triple suicide, 'inspired' by the three sisters.

The play was performed in colleges and parks too. People asked, 'Why are so many young women dying by suicide?' Some said, 'What else could they do?' Another asked, 'Is this the only way to overcome our sorrow?' Someone replied, 'There must be other possibilities. Let's find and discuss them...Step out and make better lives!'

Some young women were outspoken, even rebellious, though confused and scared. Elderly women said: 'Our lives are what they are! But our daughters should not suffer like us!' In its own way, the triple suicide was a wake-up call for society.

The Long Haul

For Sakhi Kendra and Mahila Manch, this first experience of street theatre proved meaningful. It stimulated introspection and discussion across different classes of society, wherever they performed. In subsequent years they honed their theatre skills and integrated street theatre into their work. This complemented Sakhi Kendra's counselling, legal aid, emergency help line, and shelter home services, which provided support to hundreds of survivors of rape, mental torture, murder attempts, abandonment, acid attacks and so on.[162]

By 2008, they had a cultural team of 12 members, staging 15 to 20 street play shows per month. The plays dealt with acid-throwing, sex-

[162] For instance, from April 2006 to September 2008, the Sakhi Kendra helpline handled 1,587 cases, the counselling centre 345 cases, in addition to 329 legal cases, and sheltering 154 inmates (Mehrotra and Jha 2009: 39).

selective abortion, domestic violence, unemployment, corruption, and other issues which came up during Sakhi Kendra's intensive work in the communities. The plays tried to reflect women's lived realities and struggles. All the scripts were thoroughly discussed with core staff before their finalisation. Two plays, *Budhape ki Laatthi* (*Support for the Elders*) and *Garbar Ghotala* (*Big Mess*)[163] showed incidents of wife-beating and individual protest building up into collective struggles.

Budhape ki Laatthi and *Garbar Ghotala* were performed in Ahirwan and Gadariyapurva, both working-class neighbourhoods, and the audiences responded positively: 'Such plays are useful. Women start speaking out, and refuse to accept wife-beating or male alcoholism. The perpetrators feel ashamed.' (Mehrotra and Jha 2009: 19). From some areas, a reduction in alcoholism and an absence of acid-throwing incidents were reported as an impact of the play performances. The theatre interfaced with thousands of people and seemed to help the process of public awareness at large.

At the same time, it was observed that some audience members laughed during scenes of wife-beating. The plays tended to relapse into stock depictions, a kind of caricatured portrayal, although the politics was fortunately clear: the women did not remain silent victims, rather they questioned, challenged, and took action to change the situations they were trapped in.

The cultural team was the only wing of Sakhi Kendra that included men along with women. One of the actors, 20 years old, had lived in Sakhi Kendra's shelter home from the age of 12, after years of being repeatedly raped by her father. She fought and won a legal battle, attended school, grew up, found a job, and joined Sakhi Kendra in many activities: she was very lively, and a good actor.

The male members of the team were fairly sensitive and concerned about issues such as violence against women. They too were struggling. Some faced family pressures to earn better. In mixed teams, with something like street theatre, a gender balance has to be proactively maintained, otherwise there's a tendency to lapse into the normative: slanted towards male energies, with less evidence of the female. Sakhi Kendra was trying to keep a watchful eye, to prevent this from happening (Mehrotra and Jha 2009: 20).

---

[163] I saw the plays performed, on 6 and 8 December 2008, as part of field research towards an external evaluation of Sakhi Kendra's work on women's empowerment (Mehrotra and Jha 2009).

22

Women's Drama
Across the Country and Beyond

Street theatre, as we have seen, was inseparable from the women's movement of the 80s. It was on the frontlines of feminism, expansive rather than exclusive, idealistic and unconnected to the market. By the 90s, while the early spontaneity of the movement morphed into institutionalised silos, some of this spirit carried forward. This spirit was apparent in a series of cultural workshops, held between March and August 1995 and facilitated by Alarippu.[164] A cross-section of women participated, especially from Dalit, minority, working-class and indigenous backgrounds. They articulated concerns, role-played, made street plays, and performed locally as well as at the World Conference on Women, held in Beijing, China (September 1995). Activists from around the world shared experiences at the Beijing conference, and discussed agendas for the future.[165]

---

[164] This series of cultural workshops was facilitated by Tripurari Sharma of Alarippu, and co-facilitated by Bhanwar Gopalji and Shiv, seasoned artistes rooted in the Tilonia Social Work and Research Centre, Rajasthan; they too were part of Alarippu. This chapter draws largely from my memories, notes and a journal article, 'Reflections on the Use of Culture' (Priya 1995). The article was based on participant observation and process documentation of the workshops.

[165] The United Nations organised several world conferences on women, in Mexico City (1975), Copenhagen (1980), Nairobi (1985), and Beijing (1995). Over 17,000 participants attended the Fourth World Conference on Women in Beijing, including 6,000 government delegates, 4,000 accredited NGO representatives, 4,000 media representatives, and international civil servants. A parallel NGO Forum drew 30,000 participants. The 'Beijing Declaration and Platform for Action' was adopted by 189 countries, and remains a key policy document, with a global agenda for gender equality and empowerment.

Six regional cultural workshops were held, in Uttar Pradesh (UP), Madhya Pradesh (MP), Rajasthan, Odisha, Andhra Pradesh (AP), and Assam, and a final workshop was held in Delhi. These intensive residential workshops encouraged participants to mingle, develop trust, discuss issues, immerse themselves in theatre, improvise, script and rehearse. Street plays were performed in villages, bastis, at traffic junctions, colleges, and even in an auditorium on 8 March 1995 in Kanpur. At the Delhi workshop, three plays were prepared and rehearsed for performance in Beijing.

Gumraah (Astray): In North India

Participants in the workshop in Kanpur, UP, made a play named *Gumraah*. The participants included 15 women from Sakhi Kendra-Mahila Manch, two from Disha, Saharanpur, three from Nari Vikas Seva Samiti, Padrauna, and five from Ekta Manch, MP. Together, they identified a theme of common interest: anti-alcoholism.

The play began with a rousing Alha, a popular oral ballad style that traditionally extols brave male warriors. Here, it told of young men falling prey to addiction to alcoholism, gambling, gutka or drugs, and

Gumraah, Kanpur, March 1995. Actors (from left): Seema, of Mahila Manch, Kanpur, and Kasturi, of Ekta Manch, Madhya Pradesh.

the impact this had on women, children, and families. Seema, a Sakhi Kendra-Mahila Manch member, portrayed her own reality: she had been married to an alcoholic and had suffered torture and abuse. She acted with conviction, tears glistening in her eyes and hope shining through the words of the songs she sang so melodiously. Like others in the group, she had learnt folk songs while growing up, powerful genres such as Alha, Kajri and Hori. Rashmi, of Sakhi Kendra-Mahila Manch, remarked: 'We sing and dance at festivals and marriages. Now we have developed the confidence to sing and act for our activist work too.' (Priya 1995: 170)

Kaushal and Roshan, from Saharanpur, recalled the anti-alcoholism struggle waged by them and thousands of women in 1993, picketing for months in the summer heat. Though they faced threats and police lathicharges, they refused to budge until the government agreed to stop licensing liquor shops in and around their villages. In *Gumraah*, the two women depicted experiences from the anti-alcoholism movement; their theatre skills were strong, since they had previously performed street plays in the course of their work.

Ekta Manch participants, too, were adept at street theatre. Kasturi, from the Ekta Manch cultural troupe, explained: 'We travel across MP and adjacent states, compose songs on land and forest rights, and improvise skits and plays. These are important means of mobilisation.' (Priya 1995: 172) Steeped in vibrant folk traditions, all five Ekta Manch participants were brilliant actors, singers, and dancers. Kasturi added: 'In two years, Ekta Parishad has spread like wildfire.' No doubt part of the reason for this was its deep roots in local culture.

Gumraah was performed at several venues in Kanpur. Women's eyes glistened with tears when Seema expressed her pain and conveyed the indignity of her situation. Some men looked weighed down by guilt and the enormous kohl-lined eyes of children expressed intense involvement. In the intimate circle, onlookers ringed around actors, the play was like a mirror, reflecting the contradictions and quirks of the onlookers. Ordinary lives took on a new poignancy. Alcoholism was seen to be an individual aberration as well as a social issue. It could be examined collectively, and strategies towards resolution devised.

The day the group performed in Palhepur village, Seema was on top of the world. It was where she grew up and where she returned after separating from her husband. She now worked in Palhepur and surrounding areas, taking up women's and other social issues. Sakhi Kendra-Mahila Manch distributed a pamphlet among its audiences

Gumraah, Kanpur, March 1995, performed by workshop participants, in a working-class basti.

and passers-by: 'We find men take to alcohol to escape from their troubles, but few women do so! The question is, should a troubled human being take to addiction—alcohol, lottery etcetera—or seek creative, collective ways to a better life? The challenge today is to stand firm on the stage of life, kick aside false dependencies, and bring about transformation in society.' (Priya 1995: 170)

Sakhi Kendra-Mahila Manch continued performing over subsequent months, to build a concerted campaign against alcoholism in and around Kanpur. A few days after the workshop, they created another play, on women and governance, specifically Panchayati Raj, and performed 40 shows within a month; they were now comfortable using the language of street theatre.

Play on Women's Issues Across South India

Twenty-two activists participated in the southern region workshop, hosted over five days in the rural campus of the Society to Train and Educate for People's Participation (STEP), Ankushapur, Ranga Reddy district, AP. The meals were simple, using locally-grown ingredients. Participants came from people's groups in AP: Ashraya, Asmita, Beedha Prajala Iluja Sangam (BPIS), Prajvala, Stri Vimukti and STEP, including eight women from surrounding villages, as well as Tamil Nadu's Swati, Ekta, and Association of Rural Education and Development Service (AREDS), Karnataka's Pragna Trust, and one young dramatist from Kerala. The workshop began with a diya-lighting and a collective pledge: 'Accepting each of us is different, we will work together for the betterment of women's lives.' Vanaja, from TN, felt this helped build team feeling and got the group off to a good start.

The workshop generated a street play which depicted the common concerns of women across all four southern states—basic needs, price rise, violence against women, anti-arrack agitations, political participation, corrupt bureaucracy, and state violence. The workshop was conducted by the participants, with games, exercises, rich discussion and in-depth sharing. Amal of STEP mused: 'Whatever speech we give will not be as powerful as drama... We find the medium very enriching, personally, and for spreading movement ideas. Mahila Sanghams, rural women collectives, make street plays, with traditional song and dance forms. Sometimes men and women make plays together, on common issues of landless labourers and marginal farmers.' (Priya 1995: 172, 175-76)

Clare, one of four participants from TN, explained: 'In the South, most groups have a cultural team. Rural or urban, we do street theatre as a means of conscientisation. I am a resource person with NGOs, to impart necessary skills and confidence. Through group spirit, we generate a play and when we perform the spirit shines through. We even relate our life histories in front of people, going beyond drama.' (Priya 1995: 172)

Participants discussed the difficulties in building women's struggles. Jayamani, from Kolar, Karnataka, lamented that with several television channels, women were addicted to the one-way box and spent lots of time in front of it. Mariamma, a health worker from Bengaluru, added that women and girls in urban slums wanted to dress like the women they saw on TV. But their economic conditions were precarious and the options for earning were very limited.

The play was performed on the last day of the workshop, in Kondapur village, where local groups had not worked previously. The team sang songs, presented the play, mimed and danced. About 800 villagers gathered from Kondapur and nearby villages. The programme made a strong impact and evoked an emotional response. People said:

'This is the first time somebody has come and shown us our life like this.' (Priya 1995: 173) Discussions continued for over an hour, and people were keen to have a video of the play, as well as more plays, jathas and cultural workshops.

Central India: Role-Playing

Some 20 women participated in the central India workshop, hosted by the Chhattisgarh Mahila Jagriti Sangathan (CMJS) in a green campus in Pithora village.[166] Most of the participants were from CMJS. In addition, there were two from Friends Association for Rural Reconstruction (FARR), Rourkela, Odisha, and four from Mahila Jagriti Kendra, Gomia, Bihar. CMJS had been doing street plays since its first play in 1981, titled *Tere Meri Kahani (Your Stories and Mine)*. The tranquil, natural atmosphere of the Pithora campus was ideal for a workshop. In their free moments, participants relaxed in the shade of huge banyan trees, helped kitchen staff pluck 'barbattas', local beans, or stepped out to visit nearby potters.

Morning exercises began around six in the morning, and the last session continued post-dinner. Games such as acting-out-the-meaning-of-one's-name proved to be good ice-breakers: participants had evocative names like Asha (hope), Chanchal (restless), Basanti (associated with spring), Prem Shila (reservoir of love), and Zarina (treasure). Friendships were worked out, overtures were made. In a restful moment between hectic sessions, Harbhajan (from Bihar, who was extraordinarily mobile despite having lost her fingers in a childhood accident) had Pratibha's head resting on her lap. Pratibha, from Odisha, was desperately missing her two little daughters. Pratibha said, 'She [Harbhajan] is my mother,' which Harbhajan acknowledged, adding, with feeling, 'Every woman in this land is a mother for all other women. Don't you think so?' (Priya 1995: 174).

A special sensitivity and caring manifested in these workshops. In one session, each person was to speak loudly. Harisun Nisha's voice was so low that everybody burst into spontaneous laughter. The circle was repeated and Harisun Nisha's voice was low again, but this time nobody laughed at this shy person. Mutual appreciation and enjoyment built up, participants were surprised to be sharing so much: '*Pehle sharam*

---

[166] The campus belonged to another local NGO, active in the release and rehabilitation of bonded labourers.

lagti thee, ab bahut achha lag raha hai!' ('Earlier I was inhibited, now I feel very good!') (Priya 1995: 174)

Humour helped keep spirits up and achieve group cohesion. Playing 'Follow the Leader', Naseema turned everyone into donkeys carrying piles of clothes, then vigorously washing them—all the dirty clothes of all the people in the world! In piercing high-pitched tones, this diminutive young woman kept everyone busy, and in splits of laughter. Perhaps, symbolically, the women were getting prepared to wash dirty laundry in public!

Participants, most of whom were working-class women, spoke of domestic violence, unequal wages, overwork, and rural-urban migration. Role-playing led to the making of a play, which was performed near the workshop venue. The rural audience was attentive and identified with the issues, which the CMJS planned to take forward in subsequent work.

Workshops in East, West, North-East India

Workshops in Odisha, Rajasthan, and Assam were short yet dramatic! The eastern India workshop took the form of a two-day Tribal Women's Meet, with over 500 women from different parts of Odisha. A number of creative activities were organised simultaneously—theatre, singing, painting, photography, screen-printing, marble painting, toy-making, clay-modelling, pottery, and outdoor games. After some initial hesitation, women enjoyed participating in these activities. They created skits, songs, and artwork, which they presented in the evening, along with traditional dances celebrating nature, festivals, and human life.

In the Urmul Trust's spacious campus in Lunkaransar, Rajasthan, over 1,200 women gathered for the western India workshop, from villages near and far. They were warmly welcomed and, dipping their hands in paint, they placed bright hand-prints on large cotton sheets, their unique signatures, registering the presence of each woman.

Participants chose from a range of creative activities—theatre, writing, photography, painting, screen-printing, clay-modeling, science-through-magic, skipping, cycling, and tractor-driving! They displayed tremendous talent in song and dance, and sharp analytical skills during discussions on the themes of health, livelihoods, education, and Panchayati Raj. Everybody ate simple, delicious local

Cultural workshop, Sanskriti Kendra, Delhi, August 1995. Hundreds of hand-prints by women grassroots workers being displayed, in rehearsal for the Fourth World Conference on Women, September 1995.

food in the mess, and scoured their brass thalis clean with dry sand. It was summertime, and water was scarce in the Thar Desert. The campus was a swirl of vibrant colour, with embroidered lehanga-odhnis, tie-and-dye, and appliqué-work. Song and dance kept spilling over, from the stage to the centre of the arena, pathways, or just anywhere. At one point, a thousand women were dancing, a moment of indescribable exuberance. After the workshop ended and everybody left, the campus truly looked deserted!

The workshop in Guwahati, Assam, covered two activity-packed days. Most participants were from Assam, while a few were from Manipur, Nagaland and Meghalaya. Women brought up some of their problems, constraints, and struggles. They practiced agriculture in tough mountainous terrain and cared for households and children. Many bore primary responsibility for agriculture and trading in the local markets. In addition, militarisation had created immense stress for the women of Manipur and Nagaland. They spoke of suffering atrocities committed by armed forces. The workshop was too short to create a street play, but they brought these issues to the final cultural workshop, held in Delhi.

In Delhi: Actor-Activists from Across India

Twenty-two women, from a dozen or more states, participated in the final workshop in Delhi's beautiful Sanskriti Kendra, Anandgram. Participants included Amal and Ambika from AP; Clare, Vanaja and Christi from Tamil Nadu; Kasturi, Babita, Janaki and Manju from MP; Sanjitha from Kerala; Malti from Karnataka; Sharda, Chandrakala and Shaila from Maharashtra; Ambika and Rabia from Gujarat; Chaobi Devi and Ramani Devi from Manipur; Shanti from Delhi; Norti Bai from Rajasthan; Sabina from Goa; and Kishwar Shirali from Himachal Pradesh.

Cultural workshop, Sanskriti Kendra Delhi, 1995. Participants include Norti Bai from Rajasthan (standing, second from left), Ramani Devi from Manipur (sitting, first left), Tripurari Sharma, workshop facilitator (sitting, third from left, wearing spectacles).

Participants embodied diverse experiences and ideological orientations. Amal worked with rural women in a church-based organisation. Ambika was part of the Progressive Organisation of Women, which had a membership of 60,000 peasants and workers. Clare was a radical nun, and Vanaja was active with students in and around Madurai. Christi worked with women in 300 villages, and

Sanjitha was part of a women's theatre group. Malti worked with Dalit women, especially Devadasis. Sabina was founder-member of a women's collective called Bailancho Saad. Kasturi was a full-time cultural activist, and Babita, Janaki and Manju worked on livelihoods and health. Sharda belonged to a state-wide women's network, Chandrakala was active with earthquake-affected people, and Shaila was involved with integrated rural development. Ambika and Rabia were community organisers with Sanchetana, Ahmedabad. Norti Bai was a grassroots activist in the Tilonia Social Work and Research Centre, and Shanti a seasoned activist from Delhi.[167] Kishwar was a feminist psychologist. Ramani Devi and Chaobi Devi were Meira Paibis—women protecting their communities from alcoholism, drugs, and army atrocities.

The group discussed possible themes and decided on three plays to cover a gamut of issues. Translations back and forth into English, Hindi, and Tamil were arranged, though this did not fully meet the needs of all participants, the Manipuris for instance. The group worked, from morning to late at night; the atmosphere was relaxed and friendly, food delectable, and rooms comfortable. As Janaki said during a restful moment, one starry night, with a rehearsal underway, '*Aisi hi zindagi honi chahiye...na naukri ki fikr, na khane ki chinta!*' (This is what life should be like... no tension about jobs, no worry about food!) (Priya 1995: 177).

During the second week of the workshop, all three plays took shape: they were scripted, movements blocked, and performance spaces designed. Everybody was gripped by a passion, to act their parts well, to make plays that would communicate their views and experiences to the world. A marvellous repertoire of songs was composed, a whacky Telugu anti-arrack number, melodious Marathi women's movement ditties, thunderous Tamil chants, lilting Chhattisgarhi and Bundelkhandi rural women's struggle songs, Konkani, Kumaoni, and Gujarati folk songs. Women readily picked up the words and tunes of each other's songs, creating a remarkable multilingual medley.

During the last two days, final rehearsals were held. They gathered again in Delhi the following month to travel to Beijing. At the women's conference, they put up the following three plays.

---

[167] Shanti's story was recounted in Chapter 10.

Cultural workshop, Sanskriti Kendra, Delhi, August 1995. Images of diversity and dissent, in the play on the Indian women's movement which was performed at Beijing, September 1995. (Left to right) Kishwar Shirali from Himachal Pradesh, Sanjitha from Kerala.

One: On New Economic Policies

This play dealt with the impact of the new economic policies on women. Since the early 90s, India had begun opening its doors to neo-liberalisation and globalisation. Most Indians were adversely affected. The play showed intensifying poverty, deteriorating conditions of subsistence labour, and spiralling inflation. Through masks and movement, the nexus of multinational companies with politicians, land acquisition, and GATT (the General Agreement on Trade and Tarriffs) were imaginatively depicted. These were damaging for most women, workers, craftspeople, farmers, indigenous communities, environments, and cultures. Observations from across India lent a unique piquancy to the play.

Scene by scene, the play spelt out the larger picture, interspersed with people's lived experiences. It was a sharp indictment of the neo-liberal policies being thrust upon the nation. The play suggested that people's basic needs ought to be fulfilled, as a priority; any expansion of the economy should not be at the cost of the poor. Women's work was rendered ever more precarious, even while the costs of basic goods rose exponentially.

Two: On Peace and Conflict

The second play depicted women's experiences in the face of armed conflict. In Manipur, some other parts of north-east India, and Jammu and Kashmir, armed forces were granted 'special powers', under the cover of which incidents of torture, rape and extra-judicial killings were taking place with impunity. The play expressed the fear, sorrow and anger felt by ordinary people. It showed women getting together as citizens, mothers and respected elders, to actively oppose violence, whether by military and paramilitary forces, insurgents, or misguided youngsters.

The play critically examined state policies in the realm of peace and conflict. Rather than negotiate, instill good governance and attempt to solve problems faced by common people, cycles of violence were being generated in the name of counter-insurgency. The play suggested that the laws granting special powers to armed forces be withdrawn, as a precondition to the process of restoring peace. Moreover, attention must be given to issues of education, health, livelihoods, and agricultural support, which are people's real needs.

Three: On the Indian Women's Movement

The third play presented significant women's struggles from twentieth century India in tableau form. These ranged from women's participation in the freedom movement and the Telangana armed struggle, to movements for access to resources–water, land, forests, the Chipko, Narmada and fisherpeople's movements. It provided glimpses of women's protests against rape, sexual harassment, domestic violence, communalism, and religious bigotry, and their struggles for livelihood, in fields and factories.

Overall, the play afforded glimpses into the panorama of the Indian women's movement. It was a powerful collage of images, of discrimination and dissent, oppression and the potential for transformation. The play mentioned some challenges facing the movement. Its class-caste base, leadership, and hegemony were questioned. Certain issues such as mental illness were identified as having barely been touched upon. Moreover, most issues that had been previously identified by the movement still required immense amounts of attention and action.

During the Delhi workshop, the class-caste nature of women's movement groups had come up for discussion. Malti stated that Dalit women's issues were by and large ignored in mainstream women's movements. Shanti pointed out an increasing domination by middle-class women in NGOs that were hierarchically structured, with working-class women being relegated to being employees rather than fellow-activists on an equal footing. She said bitterly: 'They are the ones who pay us and they are the ones who make us dance like monkeys,' (Priya 1995: 179)—a pithy comment on self-appointed leaders who controlled the purse-strings of various organisations. It was a sharp observation, critiquing the movement from the inside.

The Plays at Beijing

All three plays were well received. Most of the issues taken up held relevance in different parts of the world. Women discussed and presented alternative priorities and agendas for economic well-being, as well as for conflict transformation and peace building.

The play on the women's movement got the maximum audience, being staged in the main arena where one slot was reserved for each country. Dense movement histories were packed into half an hour of charged performances. As the play ended, the actors unfurled a long cloth, several sheets stitched together, which carried (in paint) the handprints of all the women who had participated in the cultural workshops: an emotional climactic moment which proved very effective dramatically too.

It was an interesting juncture for India's feminist street theatre. The form had gained a certain stature and was now travelling to places as an integral part of the movement. At the same time, it was reflecting on the movement, providing thoughtful critique, inviting introspection. Had it been widely performed back in India, this play could have been a powerful means of generating critical debate and self-reflection, within and on Indian feminisms. Sadly, there was very little formal follow-up; if the group wanted to perform in India, they would have needed financial and organisational support, which probably wasn't forthcoming.

So one wonders, did the theatre of grassroots women activists travel out to an international arena only to be buried in obscurity back home? Or did feminist street theatre continue to thrive in the hands of these activists, and others? We know that some women's groups, such as Sakhi Kendra-Mahila Manch (Kanpur), sustained their engagement with street theatre over the decades. But what about the broader scenario?

SECTION SEVEN

FEMINIST STREET THEATRE AS CONTEMPORARY HISTORY

What still seems to be of value about the plays is their close association with a very important phase of the women's movement in India... [which emphasised] the particularity of women's oppression across class and caste lines. From the 1980s it was perceived that even while maintaining its links with broader democratic movements, the women's movement needed to highlight issues like dowry, rape and fundamentalist attacks on women's rights. At this point, a cultural group foregrounding such issues was really doing pioneering work. It was trying to create an audience that would give some thought to these issues.

– *Malini Bhattacharya (2003: xx-xxi)*

It didn't compete with the market because of course it didn't belong there.

– *Tripurari Sharma (2013: 146)*

The immediacy of a street play is the strongest—it reaches out across socio-economic barriers because of the nature of the beast. There is no taking away from that. You tell a story that is true. People talk about the impact even after years. There's a lot of interesting street theatre happening... However, I've never come across a woman-intensive play group quite like *Om Swaha* or *Ehsaas*.

– *Sanjoy Roy (interview 2017)*

Thank you for showing us how women were thinking all those years ago. I wasn't even born then! We think that all this thinking began recently, so it's wonderful to know how it was.

> Today one tends to feel terribly isolated. It's so necessary to have a sense of community, but it's missing...
>
> – *Shreya Tiwari (conversation, 2016)*

This section takes a look at the legacy of the feminist street theatre of the 80s: the difference it made. Feminist street theatre has gone through ups and downs. There have been ruptures, continuities and discontinuities. While street theatre is an established genre today, its role and function have by and large altered. Yet there is a radical edge today too, in the hands of several directors, actors and activists.

When considering the legacy of feminist street theatre, we identify some implications for education, epistemology, and pedagogy. We also describe some of the theatrical work undertaken by different groups which bears kinship to that of traditional theatre, embodying similar intent, passion, and methods.

Finally, we describe an experiment presenting some popular feminist street plays of the 80s in a new form. A programme of expressive readings, *Zindagi ke Natak, Natakon ki Zindagi,* was prepared and performed, a sister venture to the writing of this book. This is a fitting conclusion: a looking back that simultaneously moves ahead, creating new scripts from the archives, melding with contemporary feminist-democratic impulses.

23

Legacies: The Difference It Made

From the late 70s, radical political vision coincided with rich theatrical imagination to create extraordinary feminist street theatre. That widespread, exuberant conjunction of art and activism lasted only a few years, thinning out by the late 80s and through the 90s. But its legacy is still alive amidst us.

Once Kanchan walked out, she could never be pushed back in, however hard the patriarchy tried and still tries. Stepping into the unknown, many women have experimented with alternatives in infinitely nuanced ways—these would have been impossible without that first decisive act, the letting go of the known.

The 80s opened up the field, breaking many silences around gender, family and women's lives: the sphere of the personal and its implications for the political. The feminist street plays communicated women's perspectives in unique ways. They were intimate yet collective; engaged with power in its many dimensions, dealing with macro-issues and structures as well as the minutiae of daily phenomena. The relational element—dynamics of sharing, mirroring, and empathy—was essential to this theatre.

Deep Learning: Collaborative Processes, Critical Pedagogies

The Feminist Theatre Workshops

The workshop methodology foregrounded theatre as a process and 'workshopping—as an empowering activity' (Katyal 1998-99a: 2). Collaborative processes began in feminist theatre workshops, a creative furnace in which women spoke of experiences long-concealed, desires, pain and anger. Participants turned inwards and towards one another, feelings and identities melted, morphed into new metal, individuals grew stronger even as camaraderie and solidarities were forged.

The theatre engaged the whole person: physical, intellectual, emotional. Bodies, habitually held tense and tight, stretched, enjoying the release of energy. Chronic shoulder pain dissolved, someone who worked in the fields felt her calf muscles relax. Defenses dropped, boundaries became fluid, channels opened up for wider communication.

As Katyal (1998-99a: 2) notes, 'For women who, in our society especially, are not encouraged to develop an intimacy with their bodies, who are conditioned to be ashamed or uncomfortable about their physicality, the process of focusing on the body, on exercises which change the awareness of and relationship with and deployment of one's body offers an additional benefit, opening up a dimension of physicality which is normally out of bounds.'

Actor-activists of the 80s often recall these theatre workshops as liberatory. Theatre exercises encouraged playfulness, spontaneity and camaraderie. A strong team spirit would build up, with mutual appreciation and support. Workshop processes helped develop self-confidence, and encouraged self-discovery and communication.

Tripurari Sharma (2013: 143) muses: 'As inhibitions dissolve, so do many physical and emotional knots... The flow then is easy. There is a state of readiness, a harmonious flow of energy wherein a creative give and take happens without much ado. The play begins to develop—words, images, objects get woven into a pattern.'

Women told their own stories and spontaneous improvisations generated the material for play scripts:

> True they had suffered and you did not have to provoke them to tell their story. Touch a woman and the skin sheds itself. They wanted to talk, to share, to discuss.... Simple things—like wanting the glass of milk that the brother gets, or being allowed to sit by the window, or that the advertisements of washing soap would really be true and the scrubbing of utensils would cease, or that men would become angels and give at least half their earnings for the home, that schools would not insist on clean uniforms for their children.... There was no end to such wishful thinking. Yet they talked of larger issues too—like rape in the fields, murder in the house (either for dowry or other reasons), burning of brethren during riots, being beaten black and blue, bored children sitting idle without work.... Again the list is endless (Sharma 2013: 142, 144).

Role-playing enabled the enactment of deeply personal experiences and emotions, even things otherwise impossible to express. There were discoveries made and embodied learning: sensory stimulus, emotions, ideas and interactions woven together with visions of a radically changed world.

The theatre has enormous relevance for education at several levels. The participatory, holistic way in which plays were made involved the whole being, incorporating cutting-edge learning-teaching, awakening compassion, awareness, reflective and critical thinking, cooperation and collaboration. These are missing pieces in mainstream education.[168]

It was critical pedagogy in practice. A force built up during workshops, performances and discussions, which could ripen into thoughtful action. Women observed their own fears, started questioning and realising how patriarchy controlled their lives and minds. So, the learning went deep, helping decolonise the mind, refashion the self. Such workshops are used extensively to date with women and vulnerable groups, such as transgendered persons.

Agitprop or Participatory and Dialoguic

Rather than try to provide a complete ideological resolution of problems, feminist street plays were slanted towards praxis and conscientisation: educating, motivating viewers to engage in exploring the conditions of their lives and, together, change what needs to change.[169]

Media scholar Ranjini Mazumdar observed that street plays were often performed with a vanguardist attitude and failed to set up dialogue with the people or to respect other forms of popular resistance (*Seagull Theatre Quarterly* 1997a: 51). Her observation dovetails with Safdar Hashmi's view that the function of street theatre, 'a militant political theatre of protest', was 'to agitate the people and to mobilise them behind fighting organisations.' (Hashmi 2007: 13)

The feminist street plays were a militant political theatre of protest. However, it is important to state that they did not mobilise women behind fighting organisations, so much as they evoked women's strength to fight exploitation in myriad ways—creatively, individually, collectively, in organisations and outside. They respected women's

---

[168] The importance of such learning is widely recognised today; see for instance UNICEF, *Comprehensive Life Skills Framework*, UNICEF India, 2019.

[169] This is in sync with Paulo Friere's formulation of 'critical pedagogy', described in his influential book *Pedagogy of the Oppressed* (1970).

agency and autonomy and made efforts to set up dialogues and help build solidarities so as to strengthen popular resistance. Therefore, 'The tone of the plays was not didactic, but experiential.' (Sharma 2013: 144) This theatre was participatory, more than vanguardist.

Mangai (2015: 68) describes her journey from didactic to participatory feminist theatre. She directed four plays on female infanticide/feticide (in Tamil).[170] The fourth, *Pacha Mannu (New Earth)* in 1993-94, marked her transition to feminist theatre. *Pacha Mannu* was produced in a workshop facilitated by Rati Bartholomew, under the aegis of Voicing Silence, which was set up by educationist Mina Swaminathan to facilitate women's self-expression. *Pacha Mannu* used powerful imagery, local idiom and life-cycle rituals which reinforce patriarchal norms. Audiences, especially women, participated actively in post-performance discussions, but sometimes there was an uneasy silence, as in Rakkiampatti village where infanticide had recently taken place.

Mangai notes (2013: 207-208) that *Pacha Mannu* may be classified as street/agitprop/political/developmental theatre, even while it defied all these descriptions. Doing such theatre prompts those involved towards democratic modes of functioning. It draws them away from advocating easy, fixed solutions, a didacticism activists can easily slip into. Voicing Silence continued producing feminist plays, including *Pani-t-thee* (on courageous women from mythology) and *Avvai* (remagining the Sangam poet), both of which were written and directed by Mangai.

Uma Chakravarti (interview 2015) muses that agitprop existed in the left, to speak to crowds, to workers, urging them to join the proletarian revolution. In feminist theatre too, women spoke to crowds, wanted them to think and engage in radical change, but because some very fine theatre-persons were involved, they transformed street theatre into something very creative.

Feminist street plays were invariably open-ended, and invited audiences to feel involved, speak their minds and take a stand. As such, the feminist street theatre is close kin to Augusto Boal's 'Theatre of the Oppressed' which aims to transform lives by inviting members of the audience to think actively about the conditions of their lives, and the

---

[170] The first three were *Yaar Kutravali? (Who Is Guilty?)*, staged by the All India Democractic Women's Association (AIDWA) in 1986, *Karpathin Kural (Cry of the Womb)* performed by Sakthi (AIDWA's women's cultural troupe) and Chennai Kalai Kuzhu, and *Thoppuzh Kodi (Umbilical Cord).*

lives of others in society. In TO, the spectators become spect-actors, they join the play and begin acting out solutions to individual and social problems. By enacting a particular action in a play, one is strengthened to implement similar action in life.

Collaborative and participatory modes of learning-teaching, theatre production and circulation have percolated into diverse educational programmes. Such modes elicit student engagement and knowledge construction in the classroom, drawing in everyone's experiences and insights; here, the teacher is a facilitator rather than an instructor. Conventional teaching on the other hand is like proscenium theatre: students are fairly passive, as they sit in rows and file out after the lecture; the transaction is unidirectional, top-down. David Devadas, who acted in *Om Swaha* (interview 2016) says, 'Perhaps my street theatre experience helps me when I teach. I very often ask my students to form a circle, and encourage them to respond, ask questions, discuss. There's eye contact, I tend to gauge responses, and react, adapt to that.'

Theatre and Theory

'Theatre' and 'theory' have a common root in Greek, meaning 'a way of seeing'. The feminist movement and street theatre offered ideas, the seeds of new theory, heralding increasingly comprehensive understandings of gender, human society, and life.

Actors narrated and *showed* stories—ethnographic material transmuted into docu-drama. Sharing personal histories, researching ground realities, they pointed to the intricate links between social norms and subjectivities. Incidents and events, dramatised, laid bare some of the underlying dynamics within relationships. Viewers found their circumstances mirrored, but not naturalised—rather, patterns of hierarchy and power were questioned. Even as the plays destabilised myths relating to 'normal' families, relationships, religion, law and the nation-state, stories came in from the audience, 'data' that further enriched the understanding that was building up.

The feminist theatre combined multiple narratives and perspectives. Feminist ethnography similarly seeks to build a picture of the way things are, the 'truth' or 'truths' about something, respectfully listening to many testimonies, juxtaposing and sifting through diverse voices.[171] When some audience members opposed the actors, arguing

[171] See for instance *Feminist Epistemologies* (Alcoff and Potter 1993).

for instance that 'women are women's worst enemies,' a measured response had to be formulated. Over time, actor-activists became sophisticated in their thinking about what they were doing, and how to articulate their positions. All of this helped strengthen as well as widen their perspectives.

Street plays often articulated complex analysis, highlighting the dialectical nature of culture as a site of women's oppression and creative resistance. Pithy one-liners and dialogues captured complex ideas and deconstructed patriarchy. Masculinist fixities were disrupted and the roots of inequality exposed.

David (interview 2016) recalls a palpable impact when, as the bride's father in *Om Swaha*, he intoned, '*Ladki to paraya dhan hoti hai.*' Daughters as 'wealth that belongs to another,' a clichéd cultural norm tightly interwoven into the belief system was suddenly challenged. The very familiarity of these words shocked the audience when juxtaposed with murder. Insights were conveyed and found their mark: onlookers could not help but identify, examine, and rethink their own positions.

The larger impact of the feminist theatre was undeniable. Feminist scholarship developed in tandem with it. Many women's movement issues first gained visibility in the 80s through street theatre. The women's movement and its theatre were forerunners of Women's and Gender Studies, which gradually entered institutional academics. Several pioneering feminist scholars were activists.[172] They built up theory with an ear to the ground, strengthening relevant disciplines and interdisciplinary work. Activist-academics' writing is frequently more lucid than the 'pure' intellectuals': it respects its subjects, understands dialectical links between theory and practice, and avoids over-jargonisation.

If knowledge production is concentrated in academia, it will inevitably fall short. The latter typically abstracts from others' experiences, examines from a vast distance, and is unable to provide intimate knowledge as the immersed, organic intellectual might: one whose senses and feelings are involved, as much as the intellect. The feminist street theatre afforded an opportunity to collectively engage in such a holistic experience. Often, a performance evoked knowledge which one already had an inkling of, but which lay buried deep within.

---

[172] Uma Chakravarti, Vina Mazumdar, Malini Bhattacharya, Sudesh Vaid, Ilina Sen, Amrita Chhachhi, Chhaya Datar, Gail Omvedt, A. Mangai, and many more names come to mind.

> A performance takes one to another level of "knowing". What may be lurking within one in an incoherent shape, when echoed externally, comes sieved through a collective experience and changes its dimensions altogether. From the personal it becomes common knowledge—something that exists outside one—and being out in the open can be assuring as well as disturbing, if it challenges even a speck that lies dormant within. (Sharma 2013: 146)

The feminist street theatre sharply articulated a plethora of issues that were undeniably significant and rendered these visible in the public sphere so that they became common knowledge. The feminist movement and this theatre thus impacted media, law, policy and programming, and helped to bring gender to the mainstream. Feminist understandings of the nature of the Indian state developed through advocacy and confrontation and influenced popular consciousness.[173] Of course, there remain huge grey areas, gaps in theory and understanding.

Solidarities: Sakhis, Sisters, Comrades

Feminist street theatre strengthened the women's movement internally, giving it a visible public presence. Engaging dramatically with large numbers of people, it impelled society to begin to *see* from women's perspectives.

Post-performance discussions were often intense and people spoke up. Performances of *Om Swaha* for instance evoked overwhelming demands for practical support; this was the impetus behind forming Saheli and Karmika in Delhi. In Mumbai, Stree Mukti Sanghathana started counselling services in response to urging by some of those who saw *Mulgi Zali Ho*.

The theatre group Janam, which identified as left but not, at the time, feminist, made *Aurat (Woman)* in 1979, portraying working-class women's struggles. Later they made *Yeh Bhi Hinsa Hai (This Too is Violence),* decrying violence against women in Hindu mythology, and *Voh Bol Utthi (She Spoke Up),* depicting a girl enjoying simple pleasures which patriarchy denies. These are powerful plays, with important

---

[173] In the mid-80s, the official establishment considered women's issues apolitical, but by the late 80s feminist groups came under the radar of intelligence agencies. For instance, Sabla Sangh-Action India actors recall police deployments and intimidation when performing *Zimmedar Kaun* in the early 90s.

insights. Dia Da Costa (2013: 166, 171) underscores one way in which they were different from feminist plays: 'What is missing in Janam's plays is perhaps the fact that women do build collectives among peers and friends... The power of laughter and humor is undeniable in the making of collectivities and collective struggle. And yet these are rarely represented in Janam's plays.'

In feminist plays, female friendships were common, usually essential to the story, taken for granted and built upon. When walking out of an oppressive situation, it was another woman who would understand, empathise, and offer refuge. Women's groups gave themselves names like Saheli, Sakhi, Sahiyar, signifying female friendship. The theatre contributed to forging these new solidarities. Its core methods afforded a means for strengthening collaborative feminist politics. Sometimes, of course, the camaraderie of workshops and productions was episodic, event-based and short-lived.

Sexuality was a sub-text in the women's movement and the feminist street theatre. Heterosexuality was interrogated along with its attendant baggage of violence and power, 'sexual politics' within patriarchy. The right to choose one's (heterosexual marriage) partner was a favoured trope, projected as liberatory. The right to leave an abusive partner was similarly championed. Sexuality was seldom addressed directly, and hardly ever in relation to pleasure; same-sex relationships, even less so. Understanding and openness evolved over the years.

The treatment of caste was similar. Caste, in left and women's movements of the time, was generally subsumed within class. Gradually, awareness grew. The street theatre group Jagriti made and performed a play on inter-caste marriage in the late 80s, after a team member, Anand Kumar, insistently brought up the significance of Dalit issues. The Dalit feminist activist Rajni Tilak[174] kept up sustained efforts to educate feminist groups in Delhi on caste and made headway slowly but surely. In 2010, Saheli's[175] street play *Kaun Jaat (What Caste)*

---

[174] In her autobiography, *Apni Zameen Apna Aasmaan* (2017: 116-17), Rajni Tilak (1958-2018) describes joining Aahwaan, a Dalit theatre group, in the mid-80s and acting in the play *Devadasi* as the Devadasi's mother. Aahwaan was set up by Sujata Paramita and *Devadasi* was its first play. Other actors included Amar Ramteke, Tara Ramteke, Hemant, Karmsheel Bharati, Ashok Lokhande, Yashwant Nikaase and Anand Bharati, and the director was Dinesh Khanna. The play was staged in the Shri Ram Centre auditorium and was well received.

[175] Saheli made a play on hazardous contraceptives, *Norplant*, in the early 90s, in which the actors included Kalpana Mehta, Nilanjana, Suhas, Jaya Mehta, Hari, Sunita, Davi, Deepak, Dimple, Asha Kachru and Anita Srivastava. Around 2000, Saheli made a play

depicted the interconnections between sexual violence, caste and communal violence, with the narratives of Surekha Bhotmange from Khairlanji, Manorama Thangjam from Manipur and Bilkis Bano from Gujarat woven into the script (Saheli 2010).

The Long Haul: The Women's Movement and Its Moving Images

During the 80s, the figure of the rebellious new woman made its way into media, academia, and homes; theatre and the movement contributed to this changing consciousness. The new woman was expressive rather than silent, leading change, not acquiescing to injustice. Defiance, dissent, and struggle embodied an alternative, desirable way of being. This image addressed woman qua woman, on the basis of imputed commonalities of experience within patriarchy, across class, though relatively undifferentiated by caste or alternate sexualities.

Within a few years, the image of the new woman lost some of its shock value. Tropes of the independent woman, valiantly battling, walking out to make a better future, were by the 90s taken up by TV serials, soap operas, movies, print and digital media. While this extended outreach, it led to appropriation, distortion, dilution, the figure spread thin, caricatured. Moreover, with media expansion, the proliferation of crude, commercialised images has resulted in numbing and inattention on the part of viewers.

Sheba Chhachhi (interview 2015) perceived the image of the militant struggling woman turning into a stereotype. One day at a demo in the late 80s, she found press photographers making women pose, placards raised, resembling candid shots she'd taken at some of the earliest protests. It shocked her: 'It's like you start by countering a stereotype, and end up creating a new stereotype.' By the early 90s, she felt the need for a different exploration and moved into more complex art, staged portraits, installations, bringing to them the same feminist inquiry and concerns.[176]

Within the movement was a kind of exhaustion, with continuous fire-fighting and crisis management, particularly around sexual violence. She says,

---

on sexual harassment at the workplace titled *Mahaul Badalna Hai (We've Got to Change the Environment)*.

[176] Sheba Chhachhi, photographer, installation artist and filmmaker, has made unique interventions at the intersections of art and activism.

> Sexual violence, violence against women has an unprecedented presence in the public domain today. It has increased massively. There is a backlash, which has to do with the slightly more emancipated figure of woman that emerged in the 90s and beyond. So while the conditions and nature of patriarchal forces are somewhat different, the violence is mutations of the same. Yet the discourse around it doesn't seem to draw on our history of experience, so this puzzles me—how can it not? There is some disconnect.

Part of the reason for this disconnect seems to be the absence of a popular women's medium that communicates widely, impacting public perceptions as feminist street theatre once did to an extent. The plays communicated women's perspectives and their aspirations to society at large; there is still a need for such communication.

Safdar Hashmi (20013: 17) noted that street theatre became popular at a time when various forms of community entertainment were fast disappearing; a living theatre was needed, that would be in sync with people's aspirations. While Janam has continued over the decades, performing and connecting with its audience, few feminist theatre groups have managed to do so.

As the women's movement institutionalised in the 90s, much of its activism became project-based, and theatre began to settle into being a mode of functional communication and mobilisation, rather than a site of exhilarating discovery and praxis. Old hands dropped out, either to do other work, or from sheer fatigue and burnout. Some of the seasoned street theatre actor-activists continued doing street plays now and then: such as Runu from Delhi, Rashmi from Kanpur, Kasturi from Chhattisgarh, Trupti Shah from Gujarat, and others elsewhere.

As gender concerns were mainstreamed, terms like 'empowerment' entered policy domains, and mechanisms such as the National and State Commissions for Women were created, generally with more rhetoric than authentic commitment. Practical support was required; the women's movement floundered on the shore of an ocean of needs. Women needed more employment options, daycare services, counselling centres, legal aid, and shelter homes. The state lacked sufficient political will, and women's groups lacked sufficient funding.

Women's movement agendas diversified with new generations of feminists, but there was inevitably overwork, overburdening, too much pressure; and conflicts surfaced, of caste, class, age, authority. The putative sisterhood of the 80s faded like a dream. Moreover, patriarchal backlash tried to undo whatever gains the movement had made. Rightist forces have been ascendant, and women's, workers', and minority rights are under siege. Nonetheless, feminist ideas have continued to spread, struggles are increasingly inclusive and intersectional. Radical interventions are being made through art, media, law, politics, literature—and theatre.

24

Threads of Continuity, and Kindred Theatre

Today, the power of street theatre is well recognised, though it has lost some of its radical thrust. By the turn of the century, street theatre became so common that Habib Tanvir (2013: 70-71) wondered whether to call it India's mainstream theatre. Nukkad Natak, an established genre today, is useful as a competitive event in colleges and schools, and has been appropriated by businesses to advertise products as well as by sundry social advertising and political-mobilising entities. Protest has partly moved online, on-screen rather than face-to-face.

The need for oppositional media has never been more urgent. Most media today is driven by profit-motivated conglomerates using technology and algorithms to fuel disinformation, create hatred and fear. Filipino journalist Maria Ressa, a Nobel Peace Prize winner, speaks of the need to design independent media initiatives to build communities of action: 'it is time to build the world we want... a world of peace, trust and empathy—bringing out the best we can be.' (Nobel Prize 2021)

Feminist street theatre was, at its root, absolutely independent, and sought to build collective action towards a world of equality, justice, and peace. This vision is not lost and dissent is alive and well. In theatre, there are new possibilities and cutting-edge experiments. We can trace threads of continuity with the radical street theatre of the 80s.

Sanjoy Roy (interview 2017) notes: 'The immediacy of a street play is the strongest—it reaches out across socio-economic barriers because of the nature of the beast. There is no taking away from that. You tell a story that is true. People talk about the impact even after years.' His company, Teamwork Arts, has recorded hundreds of plays performed in out-of-the-way places, including street plays. He finds a lot of interesting street theatre happening, such as MK Raina's work with adults and kids in Kashmir,[177] and a group in Odisha that does 'cycle street theatre'—travelling on cycles, with props and so on. 'However,' adds Sanjoy, 'I've never come across a woman-intensive play group quite like *Om Swaha* or *Ehsaas*.'

Feminist Theatre Directors: Street, and Stage

Some of the contributions of the feminist street theatre of the 80s are with us today in the form of ideas that have seeped into popular consciousness, and methods that have shaped practices in amateur as well as professional theatre groups.

Theatre professionals, who contributed immensely to street theatre with plays such as *Om Swaha* and *Ehsaas*, moved on to different spaces of experimentation. Anuradha Kapur and Madhusree Dutta co-founded Vivadi in 1989 with painter Nilima Sheikh, singer Vidya Rao, and writer Geetanjali Shree, with the aim of presenting authentic images of women in theatre, music, and painting. Madhusree (2003: xxiii) describes the 80s as a formative period for young writers, actors and directors, who, by the 90s, were skilled enough to attempt complex narratives of women's experience.

Mangai (2015, 36-37) notes that women dramatists during the 90s unpacked patriarchy in history, nationalism and neo-liberalism, along with delineating personal and political journeys. Kirti Jain (2013) identifies abundant imagery, an acceptance of ambiguity, and a refusal to push towards a climax as unique strengths of women directors. Similarly, Anuradha Kapur (in Subramanyam 2013b: 116) reflects: 'Together we do invent a feminist language which will not converge, where parts are not blended into one another, which will have breaks and distortions and where the play is episodic in nature.'

Anuradha Kapur's collaborative proscenium theatre bore the mark of her street theatre years: there was no one authorial voice, standard plot or climax, the plays were episodic rather than linear, and evolved collectively during rehearsals. There was an abiding concern with gender and representation; for instance, in her play *Sundari: An Actor*

[177] Dramatist MK Raina has been working with Bhand Pather, a traditional travelling theatre in Kashmir. Tripurari Sharma has worked with traditional forms such as UP's Nautanki theatre, and Neelam Mansingh works intensively with the Naqqal artistes of Punjab.

Prepares which represented the life of Jayshankar Sundari, a popular female impersonator on the Gujarati stage.

Maya Rao improvised a powerful solo piece, *Walk,* soon after the December 16, 2012 rape-cum-murder of Jyoti Singh ('Nirbhaya'). She first performed it amid protesting students at Jawaharlal Nehru University and it has been evolving ever since. It is a searing interrogation of abuse, harassment, freedom, consent, power, relationships, intimacy, friendship, sexuality, voyeurism, and a fervent plea for justice, safety, law and order that respects the rights of every woman: to walk, go out, lie in the park, to be fearless even in the dark. It spells out the costs, yet absolute necessity, of resistance. *Walk* powerfully voices what women began to collectively assert in the 80s: the need and desire to break out and walk free. Despite all these struggles, the streets still remain dangerous, as does the world.

Maya (interview 2015) muses: 'By some kind of detour, today I do *Walk*, which is what? Definitions have all blurred, who knows the difference between dance and theatre, between street theatre and anything performed out in public: is that street theatre? Not that I want to define, but maybe *Walk* is like a solo street performance.'

Sushama Deshpande performs her 75-minute-long solo play titled *Vhay Mi Savitribai (Yes, I'm Savitribai).* She identifies deeply with Savitribai, the radical 19th century women's rights activist, educationist and anti-caste reformer whom she sees as a figure of enormous contemporary relevance. Often, she arrives at the venue early with her costume, and chats informally with the audience about Savitribai, even as she turns herself into the iconic figure. The audience might be rural or urban, the venue open-air or enclosed. Her solo performance is electrifying and the audience is invariably deeply moved.

Sushama Deshpande sees theatre as a great medium of change (Gahlot 2019). She wrote *Vhay Mi Savitribai* and staged its first performance on 3 January 1989, Savitribai's 158th birthday. After the 2,500th show in 2004, she stopped counting (Sharma 2014). She performs it in Hindi too, and is putting together an English version. She maintains no copyright and many others have performed the play in different languages.

Sushma Deshpande's oeuvre includes plays with Stree Mukti Sanghatana, LGBTQ activists, sex workers and Tamasha dancers, as well as stories about women poet-saints and the struggles of Dalit women. Most of these plays were performed outside the proscenium, as street plays or in other informal spaces.

Street Theatre: By Women's Groups

Women's groups in various parts of the country continue to use the street theatre medium, usually evolving new plays during intensive workshops. These workshops are a hallmark of the feminist street theatre methodology. The participatory empathetic workshop space creates a feeling of safety, enabling participants to express and enact deeply personal experiences. Such enactments are often carried forward and knit into plays, with personal stories being 'fictionalised' to some extent. Fictionalisation may add dramatic power. It may also help to preserve confidentiality, especially if the individuals involved are uncomfortable with the public disclosure of their personal stories when linked to their own names.

Often the stories that women recount during these theatre workshops are of abuse and suffering, one's own or that of one's mother, sister or friend. The articulation itself becomes part of a process of healing and resistance. Tripurari Sharma (2013: 145) observes that, '[T]he moment one is not passive but begins to articulate and question, one ceases to be a victim. Over the years the number of survivors has increased and so these stories have taken over. But those who are no more are the foundation. Suffering and strength do not exist in an either/or relation. Shades of both, along with a vibrant desire to live and laugh, make every story a complex one.'

Swayam's Theatre Troupe, Kolkata: Survivor Stories

In 1997, the Kolkata-based women's group Swayam tied up with Sima and Sanjoy Ganguly,[178] practitioners of Theatre of the Oppressed (TO), to make plays based on survivor experiences.[179] Survivors of abuse learnt the TO forum method, in which spectators are invited to become spect-actors. They made a play showing one of them, Rekha,

[178] Sanjoy Ganguly set up Jana Sanskriti in 1985, inspired by August Boal's Theatre of the Oppressed (TO), and took this theatre to various constituencies. Jana Sanskriti developed 30 satellite theatre teams in West Bengal, nine of which are all-women teams. The organisation also developed teams in Tripura, Jharkhand, New Delhi, Odisha, Maharashtra, Gujarat, UP, Rajasthan, and Karnataka. These teams reach at least 2,00,000 spectators every year through their performances (Jan Sanskriti website). Another practitioner of TO, Delhi-based Jaya Iyer, works with NGOs and movement groups across the country; for more, see Jaya Iyer (2006).

[179] The Swayam-Jana Sanskriti workshops were conducted by Sanjoy Ganguly, Sima Ganguly and Satyaranjan Pal.

being harassed by her in-laws and contemplating options—she could adjust, run away, retaliate, call for help, commit suicide, or protest.

Researcher Sameera Iyengar (1998-99: 20) describes the first performance, on 7 March 1997, at a Women's Day function at Triangular Park off Hazra Road:

> [W]e were charged up, and our energy definitely carried over to the audience who sat so close to us. People put in performances as never before, and with each appreciative response from the audience, the energy level rose higher, the actors became freer, their stage presence became stronger—it was wonderful to watch the dynamic and the changes that it wrought.

The story paused at a freeze—Rekha's husband hitting her, neighbours and social workers on the margins. At this point the play was opened up to the audience, who were invited to complete its story. Women were so eager to participate that Sima literally had to make them wait their turn, and regulate the time spent on stage with each solution. A man too came up, acted as Rekha's brother and took her away to their parental home. Swayam actors were elated at the overall response, particularly by men: 'While we all knew that it was only in a play, that it was still a far cry from that "joining in" becoming a reality, that moment still gave one hope and an even stronger belief that change was possible.' (Ibid.)

Swayam's theatre troupe continues to make and perform street plays, and plays a vital role in raising awareness on women's rights. Survivors of violence explore creativity and self-expression, write plays and songs, and perform in neighbourhoods, schools, and colleges. Between 2019 and 2020, the group held 53 street play performances.

Soumi Jana, who heads Swayam's theatre troupe, is a survivor. Swayam supported her rehabilitation, through healthcare, legal action, and further studies. 'Theatre helped her express her feelings, regain confidence and move on in life; she now extends the support she got, to other women' (Swayam 2024).

Anuradha Kapoor of Swayam[180] notes (De 2020) that theatre is the most powerful medium in their effort to end violence through community outreach. India has laws against domestic violence, but their implementation is poor. There is no easy end to violence, but

---

[180] Anuradha Kapoor is the Founder and Managing Trustee of Swayam. She set up Swayam in 1995. Note: Anuradha Kapoor is not the same person as Anuradha Kapur—the Delhi-based theatre director who was part of Theatre Union.

efforts are underway. When women come to the organisation for support, they are already going against the grain, and are ready to change their lives.

Since 2016, Swayam has a mobile van which opens up into a stage, with a sound system and microphones. Travelling across Kolkata, it parks in strategic locations, and the troupe gets into the act—theatre, songs, poster exhibitions, films and leafleting. The van has an inbuilt counselling room, where women can come to talk to a feminist counselor, in seclusion, with confidentiality.

Kislay's Street Plays, Delhi: Tackling Community Issues

Kislay, a community-based organisation in Vikaspuri, Delhi, began using theatre as a vehicle of social change soon after its inception in 1992. Several of its field organisers were trained in Theatre of the Oppressed (TO) and began using it in their work. Through this medium, they inspired people to get involved and take action to resolve community issues.

In the early years of the twenty-first century, Kislay created street plays on local issues, based on the problems people were facing. The plays questioned policies affecting the urban poor, corruption in the Public Distribution System, dowry and discrimination against the girl child. A performance lasted two to three hours. Members of the audience would get involved, some even wept when they saw persons like themselves being exploited.

People became spect-actors, intervened and enacted possible solutions. Several women treated the issues, whether ration or dowry, as their own, and portrayed strong characters. Audiences found that the plays addressed issues connected with their own lives, which no other media did. The play sessions were invigorating and motivated people to take relevant action (Ramachandran 2003, 65-72).

In 2017, a dozen more members from Kislay were trained in a theatre development workshop in Kolkata. They subsequently trained other members of Kislay as well as youth and women from the communities in the use of theatre for social change (Kislay 2018). Plays on various issues continue to be made and performed, to raise issues and mobilise social action.

In 2021, awareness programmes were organised in 21 slum clusters on the rights of informal sector workers. Domestic workers prepared a play on their employment situation and experiences during the lockdown due to the Covid-19 pandemic. Women construction workers prepared a play on issues such as accidents at work sites, their experiences during the pandemic, wage discrimination and poor working conditions.

The domestic workers' play discussed their rights to notified wages, leave, health security, pension and other social security provisions. They also prepared posters on these issues and put them up in their communities. Community walks and street corner meetings were organised, where they answered people's queries and held discussions.

On 10 March 2021, more than 500 women workers participated in the International Women's Day programme. This was a platform on which to enhance their leadership qualities and share the problems they faced due to the pandemic. Domestic workers and construction workers performed their plays. They spoke and performed poetry as well as stories based on daily problems and struggles (Kislay 2024).

For over three decades, Kislay has been making sustained efforts to empower informal sector working women. Plays made by Kislay address gender oppression at home and in the workplace. Kislay's efforts have contributed to a more aware and articulate public, as well as to some policy changes. For instance, in situ rehabilitation of slum dwellers and workers was accepted in principle by the DDA (Delhi Development Authority) in 2019.

Vanangana, UP: Rural Women's Theatre for Change

Vanangana, set up in the Banda and Chitrakoot districts of Bundelkhand, UP in 1993, is a frontrunner in the strategic use of street theatre to help deal with women's issues, domestic violence in particular. Vanangana initially worked to strengthen the livelihoods of the most marginalised women (Dalit and Adivasi), but soon discovered that the everyday violence they suffered continued to disempower them. Violence against women was commonplace, including wife-beating, sexual assault and murder.

Vanangana made its first street play *Mujhe Jawab Do (Answer Me!)* in which the chief protagonist Mantoria is battered, tries to escape to her parental home but is sent back to her husband who ultimately kills her. Even while her corpse lies on the stage, the police and the sarpanch accept bribes, and Mantoria's family and neighbours display apathy. Towards the end of the play, Mantoria rises up and asks the audience to tell her who was responsible for her death.

Within the first few months from its creation in 1998, the Vanangana theatre team performed the play in more than 50 villages, many of which had lost their daughters or daughters-in-law to domestic violence. The performance was 'accompanied by songs, marches, poster exhibitions, and open public discussions where emotionally charged women and men passionately discussed the themes of the play.' (Nagar 2015: 63)

Earlier, when Vanangana had tried to discuss the same issues, hardly anybody would show up. But the play evoked a lot of discussion. In response to a scene where Mantoria and her husband fight for the custody of their son, in Rehuta village, women in the audience commented that when it's the mother who gives birth, how does a father have first claim? In Laudhiya village, women discussed the ways in which the murders of women are covered up in their village, for instance a a woman was burnt by her family but the police were told she got burnt accidentally while cooking (Uppal 2016: 16, 29).

The play *Badalti Tasveer (Changing Scenario)* showed Sampatiya, a survivor of violence who gathered the courage to strike out on her own, set up a shop and run her household as a single mother. Another woman, Sukhiya, was on the verge of dying by suicide. To her, Sampatiya said: 'Listen, I faced many difficulties. I took my decisions. You must do the same. I started my shop, educated my children. Now you have the Domestic Violence Act to protect you: go to court, fight for your rights!' Sukhiya took her advice: she decided to live and struggle, rather than give up (Uppal 2016: 17, 26).

The Vanangana theatre team, many of whose members were themselves survivors of violence, devised the plays based on real-life stories. When women in the audience saw protagonists in the play take positive action to transform their lives, they felt a new sense of hope. After seeing the play, several women would call Vanangana to share issues of domestic violence, often it was mothers requesting help for their married daughters. Vanangana is committed to provide counselling, temporary shelter, legal aid, skills training and training on women's rights. Many women who approached Vanangana in distress now lead dignified lives, supporting themselves and their children. Pushpa, from the Vanagana theatre team, reflected that the police and judges behave as if 'The family should not break, let the women break. But we at Vanangana firmly believe—Let the family break—the first priority is to protect the woman!' (Uppal 2016: 27).

By enacting the stories of their lives and tapping into rural idioms and folklore, grassroots workers have touched the hearts and minds of villagers, women and men, from different castes and age groups. They have bridged the divide between private and public realms: 'Activism for these campaigners could no longer be contained within "women-only" groups. It had to flood the streets and compounds of the villages and the walled spaces of the state administration.' (Nagar 1995: 62)

For the women in the Vanangana theatre team, it has been deeply satisfying to share their experiences of empowerment. Surajkali, a team member, notes, 'Nukkad natak is an effective medium to engage with women, and men. We have managed to shift the focus of domestic violence from a husband-wife issue to a larger canvas.' (Misra 2017: 4) However, women public performers might still be held in disdain by some sections of society. Kes Rani is nervous whenever she performs in a village where her extended family members reside, because they might criticise and spread rumours about her. But Kes Rani carries on, saying, 'Once I start performing my nervousness disappears and then I don't care anymore.' (Uppal 2016: 38)

Sabitri Heisnam to Mallika Taneja: The Body as a Site of Protest

Sabitri and Kanhailal Heisnam's theatre has expressed pain and rage in response to militarism and violence in Manipur. In 2000, Sabitri portrayed Draupadi, based on Dopdi Mejhen in Mahasweta Devi's short story *Dopdi* (2014), written in 1978. In it, Dopdi refuses to be cowed down, even by brutal gang-rape, and fearlessly confronts the culpable military officer with her battered nude body. In that fierce subversive act, this indigenous revolutionary exudes power while her violators are terrified. Sabitri Heisnam enacted this on stage in an exceptionally powerful portrayal.

Sabitri Heisnam's stage act was enormously difficult, for nudity on stage makes demands at odds with female socialisation. Minakumari, an actor withthe Sagolsem Theatre, Manipur, notes the following about wearing skin-revealing costumes: 'I have some cultural shyness about showing my body... I cannot really completely shake off my cultural and traditional inhibitions' *(Seagull Theatre Quarterly* 1997b: 141). Sabitri Heisnam's act was severely criticised by orthodox society.

In 2004, 12 elderly Manipuri activists, Meira Paibis (literally 'women with burning torches', who form vigilance squads to protect people from atrocities) staged a congruent protest at the gate of Kangla

Fort, Imphal: they stripped, while displaying a huge slogan, 'Indian army, rape us!' These elderly women activists were outraged by the gang-rape and murder of a young woman, Thangjam Manorama, the latest atrocity committed under cover of the Armed Forces Special Powers Act (AFSPA). Security forces, granted impunity under AFSPA, had perpetrated countless fake encounters, tortured, raped, and orchestrated the disappearance of ordinary citizens. The Meira Paibi's dramatic protest, in full public glare, was very tough to enact. And it was effective, drawing attention to the situation in Manipur, shaking up the administration, which yielded to some of the legitimate demands the Meira Paibis were making (Mehrotra 2013).

The Delhi-based actor Mallika Taneja drew inspiration from Sabitri Heisnam and the Meira Paibis: 'It is from those women that I learnt about the naked body being used as a site of protest. That incident has stayed in my head, deeply affecting all I do.' The solo performance Mallika first did in 2014 was equally brave, and political. In the short play *Thoda Dhyan Se (Be Careful)*, she wore and divested herself of clothing. For several minutes, she stood near-naked, silent, locking eyes with the audience, then said: '*Thoda dhyan se rehna chahiye, aapko pata hai na zamana kharab hai?' (You should be a little careful—you know the world is a bad place?)*. Dripping with sarcasm, the actor re-exposed entrenched norms which exonerate perpetrators of rape, harassment, and abuse. Before stepping out onto the street, she donned layers of clothing, even a helmet—self-protective gear which can never be protective enough.

She performed the play hundreds of times, in multiple venues. Forty years ago, the mother in *Ehsaas* remonstrated—'*Time par ghar aa jaya karo beti, tumhe pata hai zamana kharab hai.*' *(You should come home on time, daughter, you know the world is a bad place.)* The subtext reveals a world where men violate with impunity, while women are hurt, humiliated, broken in body and spirit. Mallika Taneja makes clear the brutality of victim-blaming, holding women responsible for crimes committed against them. In 2015, about a year into her performance, she broke the final taboo: she stripped completely. Recalling her first performance of this version at a theatre festival in Zurich, Mallika says: 'It was terrifying even though Europe is used to nudity on stage. But even there, audiences were uncomfortable, they are not used to a nude body looking at you looking at it.' This version she has performed only to small audiences, with no mobile or camera allowed. Her challenge is fierce, as she pushes boundaries in a deep questioning of entrenched attitudes and mindsets (Nair 2017).

A Street Play on Manipuri Women's Resistance

In May 2010, cultural activists in Kerala, led by Professor Sara Joseph and Civic Chandran made a street play, *Meira Paibi,* dealing with the resistance of Manipuri people, especially Irom Sharmila, who had been fasting since 2000 seeking the withdrawal of AFSPA. The play was performed in Kerala (in Malayalam) some 50 times; then performed (in English and Hindi) as part of the Hind Swaraj Peace March, which wended its way through Bangalore, Chennai, Vijayawada, Pune, Bhopal, Delhi, Kolkata, Guwahati, and Itanagar. Wherever *Meira Paibi* was performed, people were keen to join the campaign to repeal AFSPA.

Soon after the cross-country peace march, Ojas SV, a young activist from Pune who acted in the play, adapted it as a solo performance, and continued performing it. She called it *Le Mashalein (Holding Flaming Torches).* With enormous commitment, she travelled across the country doing hundreds of shows over three to four years. She performed for instance, in 2011, in Jaipur at the Police Training Academy, cultural centre Jawahar Bhavan, several schools and colleges in shows arranged by the People's Union for Civil Liberties, and at nearby towns Bhim and Beawar in shows arranged by the Mazdoor Kisan Shakti Sangathana.[181] This powerful, radical street theatre brought a whole new world to the attention of people, many of whom had known hardly anything about Manipur.

Collaborative Theatre with Women in Prison

Through collaborative theatre, dramatist and activist Smita Bharti (2005) explored trauma, taboos, and human rights issues both in and outside prison. During a series of workshops in Delhi's Tihar jail and in a college, in 2004, she encouraged women to redefine 'security', to break out of vicious circles of fear and actively reimagine their futures. The women prisoners and college students became co-explorers and self-expressive, interrogated social norms and made critical choices. A unique co-production between jail inmates and students of Bharati College was performed in the jail in December 2004.

This 'docu-theatre' indicated human rights violations were taking

[181] The Mazdoor Kisan Shakti Sangathan is a leading people's organisation which has spearheaded democratic movements for the Right to Information, Right to Work, and Right to Food.

place in and outside jail. All the participants had experiences of abuse, which they were able to speak, weep, and express rage about, within the safety of the workshop space and then together, in the production.

Exploring Sexual and Gender Identities: Pushing the Boundaries of Theatre

A number of plays featuring non-normative sexualities have pushed the boundaries of theatre, articulating complex perspectives. These plays re-pose questions about gender and performance, challenging audiences to reconsider their own sexual and gender identities, and processes of embodiment which are actually performative (Mangai 2015, 239-42).

Avanthi Meduri (1999: 28), a bharatnatyam dancer and scholar, crafted a play on silenced histories of the Devadasi, collaborating with the Chennai-based experimental theatre group Koothu-p-pattarai.

In 2003 Mangai (2015) made a play called *Manasin Azhaippu (Call of the Heart)* with Aravanis and transgender people, on issues of citizenship and identity. She also crafted *Uraiyatha Ninaivugal (Unsettled Memories),* which interrogated the idea of a birth-based family versus an Aravani adopted family. Mangai also worked with LesBit, a Bangalore-based group, evolving *Musical Chair* (2008)—stories of love and loss enacted by intersex and transgendered individuals, Hijras, lesbians, and sex workers, all playing each other's stories.

In 2006, the Veshya Anyay Mukti Parishad (VAMP, Council of Sex Workers for Freedom from Injustice) partnered with the NGOs Sangram and Point of View to make a play named *My Mother, the Gharwali, Her Maalak, His Wife.* Directed by Divya Bhatia and Sushama Deshpande, the actors in the play are women in sex work from Sangli, Maharashtra. They have participated in theatre workshops and use theatre as a means of resistance. An actor explains: 'We have staged this play to ask society not to enforce its rules on us.' (Mangai 2015: 223-31) VAMP has made another play directed by Sushama Deshpande, named *Hum Aur Tum Sab (We and You, All),* which tells the story of their struggles to organise and fight for their rights. The opening song, 'Just because we're sex workers, don't mess with us' sets the tone. They want people to recognise sex work as work, a source of livelihood which they should be able to practice with safety and dignity. VAMP sees theatre as a means of community storytelling, of including personal narratives of trauma, violence and disease, but also laughter and sisterhood (Mitra n.d.). In Kolkata, the cultural group Komal Gandhar has made plays such as *I Am That Woman,* portraying members' lives, concerns and perspectives. Its members are all sex workers, and the theatre is a critical tool in their movement.

In 2015, transgender activists Living Smile Vidya, Angel Glady, and Gee Imaan Semmalar created, designed, and performed the play *Colour of Trans 2.0.* They tracked their own experiences through monologues, cabaret, and clown theatre, unravelling trans lives, family dynamics, caste, and issues of representation. Living Smile Vidya and Angel Glady are Dalit transwomen from Tamil Nadu. Living Smile Vidya wrote India's first transgender autobiography—*I Am Vidya: A Transgender's Journey* (2013)—and is an actor in Tamil and Malayalam films. Angel Glady has worked with French clowns from 'Clowns Without Borders'—she feels art is the best tool with which to build a revolution, and is co-founder of the trans theatre group Panmai, based in Chennai. Gee Imaan Semmalar is a savarna trans activist from Kerala who has written, directed, and acted in a multilingual docu-fiction film on transmen, and hosted a radio show on 'Q radio', an online LGBTQ radio channel.

Men Against Violence: A Theatre Group

A men's organisation, Men Against Violence and Abuse (MAVA), was set up in 1993 to combat gender violence. It runs a campaign, 'Redefining Masculinity.' In 2016, students from several Mumbai colleges made *Mardangi (Masculinity),* a play challenging popular stereotypes of masculinity, such as: men don't cry, are dominant, strong, and good at earning money. Harsh Sadhani, MAVA's director, notes that society enforces many such expectations on men, putting pressure on them to behave in certain ways, which negate the idea of gender equality and reinforce tendencies to violate and subjugate women.

Mardangi had an impact on young men, beginning with the actors themselves. Post-performance discussions and workshops helped consolidate their learning. Aniket Kamble, a first-year student at Kirti College, notes, 'Through these workshops we realised... there is very little conversation on sexuality and that people can be gay and transgender. A lot of awareness has been generated about the idea of masculinity and how it is extremely skewed. We all need to introspect.' Ravi Jaiswal, a first-year student from the Nirmala Niketan Institute of Social Work, realised that unequal gender roles tend to be taken for granted; but if we are to tackle violence against women, these must be addressed (Bhatkhande 2016).

Shakti Shalini and Pandies' Theatre, New Delhi: Survivors Speak

Shakti Shalini (the shelter home Shahjahan Begum and Satyarani Chaddha ran after its inception in the Delhi women's movement of the 80s) hosted an unusual production on 21 April 2019: the Greek tragedy, *Medea*. Playwright Anuradha Marwah[182] translated and adapted the play into Hindustani and directed it, under the aegis of Pandies' Theatre. The audience consisted of about 50 women and a number of children, from Shakti Shalini and working-class settlements in Nehru Nagar, south Delhi, as well as a few activists and academics.

Medea had fury dripping from her eyes, a set face and scornful lips: she and her children were betrayed and abandoned by Jason, who was marrying again, a political match. Women from Shakti Shalini and the Nehru Nagar basti reacted to the violence experienced by Medea, saying bitterly: 'Men do these things, openly, everyday!' One woman judged Medea for killing her children: 'A good woman would not have done that.' Another countered: 'Her hand shook when she killed them! She loved them, she had brought them up.' They spoke of the anger women feel when betrayed by men they love, a common enough experience, and said, 'It is a good play! Show it to many people!' *Medea* was also performed at Nithari, a village in Noida where a number of children were brutally raped and murdered between 2005 and 2006. These performances were a part of Pandies' Theatre's intention to take classical theatre beyond auditoria and directly to the people.

Between 27 and 29 November 2020, Pandies' Theatre organised a deeply disturbing event, entitled *Home and the World.* Shakti Shalini survivors, migrants in Nithari village, and Afghan refugees took the stage for about 90 minutes each, and shared real-life stories of abuse and exploitation at the hands of husbands, fathers, brothers and boy-friends.

On 14 and 21 March 2021, Shakti Shalini survivors performed a play they had made named *Ubermensch: Masculinity from the Lens of Women,* exploring what leads to gender-based violence, such as the phenomenon of son preference, unequal distribution of domestic

[182] Anuradha Marwah is a novelist and scholar, and Professor of English Literature at Zakir Hussain Delhi College, Delhi University.

work, and ideologies of toxic masculinity. Both these events were held online, during the COVID-19 lockdown.

Anuradha Marwah (2021) found the survivors' messages direct, simple, and 'inspired by 1960s second-wave feminism: the personal is political; gender equality begins at home; silence and powerlessness go hand in hand.' They performed gender in a way that made it clear that things are changing within women; but masculinity is a hard nut to crack, tenacious. They noted that during the COVID-19 pandemic, domestic violence increased exponentially. Yet there was joie de vivre in their performance, as they reflected upon their own nuanced negotiations with patriarchy, and had fun spoofing several men! There was anger too, but also the demonstration of courage: they had walked out of the worst situations, and were intent on rebuilding their lives. The performance represented an unambiguous challenge to patriarchy and the violence it spews. The audience of some 300 viewers watched intently and participated in the discussion, turning a virtual space into a site for building collectivity.

It is noteworthy that Pandies' Theatre group, set up in 1993 by Sanjay Kumar,[183] has collaborated with Shakti Shalini since 1995, holding theatre workshops which help survivors find the strength to deal with their trauma. Pandies' Theatre focuses on empowering marginalised people, through workshop-based theatre. A workshop commences with a play by Pandies' Theatre and proceeds to inspire the participants to create and present a play before their community. The plays are on issues that are important to the participants: gender biases, LGBTQ rights, rights of prisoners, child rights, communalism, caste and so on, and include possible modes of rectification. Pandies' Theatre has partnered with many social rights groups in Delhi as well as Haryana, Punjab, Jammu and Kashmir, Rajasthan, Uttarakhand, Karnataka, Odisha and Maharashtra.

Taking Back the Streets: Gender-Ventions and Pinjra Tod

In 2014, a series of public performances titled 'Gender-Ventions' took place in Anand Vihar, Patparganj, Malka Ganj and other crowded public places: 'Delhi's nerve centres which are usually left out of the mainstream culture circuit, saw such plays pop up on the streets.' (Puri 2014) Male actors enacted sexual harassment, ogling at women in a

[183] Sanjay Kumar is a playwright, director, teacher in Delhi University, and Founder-President of Pandies' Theatre.

packed bus, making passes and uttering lewd comments. Audiences were invited to become spect-actors, to step into the shoes of any of the actors and behave as they would, or should. With a young team of 15 actors, activists and students, conceptualised and directed by Niranjani Iyer, supported by Goethe Institut/Max Mueller Bhavan, Gender-Ventions was performed for a few weeks in September 2014, in four to five locations each day.

The actors sought to establish the streets, a public space, as a woman's right. As Iyer put it: '...women don't really have any space in the city... You are always planning your day... wondering about by what time you'll be safe home... If you want to have some kind of ownership over the city, you can't go through spaces as if you were being hunted.' (Puri 2014)

Pinjra Tod, literally 'Break the Cage', is a feminist women students' group that came up in 2015 in Delhi University and Jamia Millia Islamia, and soon spread to other campuses in Delhi as well as other cities and towns. The feminist collective opposed misogyny and discrimination on campuses and took up cudgels against regressive gender-based hostel rules, practices like dress codes, curfew timings, CCTV surveillance, and the lack of sexual harassment committees. Pinjra Tod organised protest action and public hearings, drew up a charter of demands and made representations to the Delhi Commission for Women (Barua 2020). It was strong in its anti-patriarchal, anti-caste, and anti-communal politics.

Of the countless actions taken by Pinjra Tod, we look at one: a night march titled 'Women Claim the Streets', dated 3 October 2016. Sexual harassment was rampant in colonies adjoining Lady Shri Ram College, where many women students from Gargi, Kamla Nehru, LSR, Deen Dayal, and Deshbandhu College lived in PG (paying guest) accommodation: 'These streets and lanes have been filled with stories of fear and harassment for decades.' (Pinjra Tod 2016) Police patrolling was a partial solution; more important was for women to occupy the streets, gallis, and mohallas in large numbers, and assert their right to these spaces:

> Let us occupy the roads and re-define them, the very roads where we are catcalled, humiliated and abused. Let us fill these streets characterised by fear and abuse, with the power of our desires and dreams.
>
> Let us refuse the patriarchal "protection" that cages us in the name of "safety" and demand empowering mechanisms that do not undermine women's autonomy... We do not need to be caged for

> our "security," we need infrastructure such as street lights and safe public transport around our campus areas... We do not need more "survelliance" through CCTVs, but need the police and the legal system to be supportive and accountable. We need more affordable university hostels so that we do not have to live in exhorbitantly priced unregulated PGs (Pinjra Tod 2016).

The march saw large numbers of women marching from the back-gate of LSR, through Kailash Colony, Amar Colony and National Park, from 5.30 pm. After a couple of hours, the 'loud and exuberant' group reassembled at the LSR back-gate park and there was a session of open sharing, of experiences, poetry and songs, winding up with a rousing street play by Pinjra Tod (Kalita 2016). Among the songs was Pinjra Tod's signature song:

Din bhi hamaara, raatein bhi hamaari, sadkein bhi hamaari chauraahe bhi hamaare!
Pitrisatta ki khol de pol, pinjra tod! Pinjra tod!
Jhootthi suraksha ka khol de pol, pinjra tod pinjra tod!
Chalo mahilaon ki svatantrata ki ore, pinjra tod, pinjra tod!
(Pinjra Tod 2016)
(The day is ours, nights too are ours, the roads are ours and the crossroads too!
Expose the dark secrets of patriarchy, break the locks! break the locks!
Expose the shameful reality of false security, break the locks, break the locks!
Come walk towards women's freedom, break the locks! break the locks!)

Reflections on Women's Theatre

At the Women Playwrights' International Conference, Mumbai in 2009, actors, playwrights, directors, and critics reflected on women's theatre. The overall theme was 'The Democratic Stage'. In a discussion on 'future hope in theatre', young panelists including Sanchi Jeevani, a teenaged playwright from Nagpur, spoke of the difficulties that women writers and directors face: the field is still male-dominated, and biased towards commercially successful rather than meaningful theatre.

Anju Uppal of Media Matters collaborates with social organisations to hold workshops, and make and perform plays. She said she finds the experience most rewarding when the audience is involved, and the script is reworked to integrate their views. Kanchan Sontakke, of Natyashala Charity Trust, emphasised the therapeutic effect of theatre, particularly on troubled children. Cultural critic Anjum Katyal suggested the need to review whether social theatre is too strident: does it preach to the converted, and do aesthetics get sidelined by the message?

Pushpa Bhave, a scholar, critic and teacher, wondered whether, when women are directors, perceptions of pain and pleasure change from the dominant. Actor-director Mita Vashisht spoke of sensitive, self-confident aesthetic representations of the female, as opposed to viewing women as bits of anatomy, or puerile caricatures of the 'modern woman'. Mita herself has written *Lal Ded*, a play on the life of the eponymous mystic Kashmiri poet-philosopher. She has performed it solo many times, in many places. Such plays respect women's dignity, rather than focussing only on suffering; they exemplify the female gaze, which emphathises with rather than objectifying women.

Senior director-actor Usha Ganguli expressed satisfaction that women directors have had the fortitude not to compromise their voices and values in the face of market forces. On the contrary, they have retained and expanded their space (Stree Mukti Sanghatana 2012).

In 2010, the Indian Association of Women's Studies (IAWS) and IP College, Delhi University, organised a workshop titled 'Cultures of Resistance: Women's Movements As Performance' (8 to 10 September). In the morning, old-timers Gouri Choudhury, Kamla Bhasin, Runu Chakraborty and Jaya Srivastava sang songs from the women's movement of the 80s, while the afternoon session was devoted to 'Journeys with Street Theatre', recalling the powerful cultural resistance posed by street plays. The venue being IP College made it all the more evocative since this was where the first ever performance of *Om Swaha* had taken place (in 1979). Younger people enjoyed seeing, listening to, and learning about some of these rich histories. Professor Uma Chakravarti (interview 2015) notes that the feminist street plays of the 80s were a very powerful intervention, and one that hasn't completely gone away. In 2020 she organised a similar recall of cultural resistance by the women's movement, with theatre, music, songs and films (described in Chapter 25).

Clearly, feminist street theatre and the women's movement have contributed to wider shifts, in culture and politics. They have stimulated alternative imaginaries in terms of gender, work, identity, politics, and the meaning of freedom. The current flows strong today, as new generations join the older ones, to dream and act anew.

25

Zindagi ke Natak, Natakon ki Zindagi
Plays of Life, the Life of Plays

When conceiving this book, I imagined inviting some old-time actors to come together, reminisce, and also perhaps perform one of the vintage feminist plays. This dream-idea, of bringing history alive through actual performance, developed in unexpected ways. Getting a whole group together proved impractical; instead, a programme of immersive play readings came about, taking shape with the involvement of three actors—Shanti,[184] Indira Mukherji,[185] and myself.

Shanti had been very much a part of the 80s street plays. We became friends in the feminist movement, and in 2000 set up Sampurna Trust, a women's collective through which we held gender workshops in colleges, published stories, prepared creative communication material, and ran a counselling and health centre and creative worshops for children in Dakshinpuri, south Delhi. Sampurna was an enabling space, although with barely any funds, and our inputs were part-time. We worked elsewhere to run our households.

India Foundation for the Arts offered Sampurna Trust an organisational grant, wherein I would work on a book, and others would join in to create a theatrical performance.[186] It was a small grant,

---

[184] Shanti's journey is described in Chapter 10.

[185] Indira Mukherji is a storyteller, researcher, teacher, and writer. She trained and worked as a political scientist before giving it up to follow her passion, storytelling as a form of healing, and communicating.

[186] Initially, India Foundation for the Arts offered an individual grant to work on this book, but I was simultaneously awarded a research fellowship by the Nehru Memorial Museum and Library, making it technically impossible to receive an IFA individual grant. IFA suggested converting it into an organisational grant, which worked very well, helping to broaden the ambit, and enabling a tiny honorarium for each participant.

spread rather thin, but it allowed Shanti to give it some time too. Of the play scripts I'd gathered, it turned out that between us, we'd acted in five of the plays: Shanti in *Aurat aur Dharm*, *Parivar ki Gaadi,* and *Intezaar,* and I in *Ehsaas* and *Om Swaha*. We began reading scripts together. As we read them, memories were stirred and shared.

One day I read out the script of *Ehsaas* to my storyteller friend, Indira Mukherji. She liked some of it, but found some parts outdated. Around the same time, that is December 2015, a family friend, Shailaja Dixit, got in touch. She had moved to California, where she was executive director of Narika, a non-profit for survivors of domestic violence, mostly Asian-origin women. When I mentioned the plays, she was extremely interested, so much so that I read out a few excerpts from *Ehsaas* for her. She was deeply moved. 'I'm tearing up, hearing this,' she said. 'I hear the same thing around me every day.'

Shailaja explained why *Ehsaas* resonated with her experience. Asian women came to Narika with specific issues of overwork, unreal pressures and expectations to do with gender socialisation and particular kinds of stereotypes, which usually came from wider family and culture, but were expressed as conflict and violence within couple's relationships. Cultural assumptions got carried across continents, tenaciously. She asked me to read the excerpts again, so that she could take a short video and share it with her colleagues.

This encounter suggested that many forms of violence these plays dealt with are still with us: there was shock value in the realisation. This lends the plays the capacity, perhaps, to subvert what Bharucha (2000) calls 'our conditioned complacency—the biggest violence of our times.'

We picked up the scripts with new-found confidence: the plays were still relevant. The three of us, Shanti, Indira and I, began reading together. We zeroed into *Aurat aur Dharm,* which Shanti recalled vividly, and *Ehsaas,* which I loved. It was great fun to swap stories, of making and doing these plays. We spontaneously took up roles. Each play was 40 to 45 minutes long. As we read, we edited parts which were not so relevant today, or which required more actors.

Reading aloud organically evolved into a performance, and snowballed into a production which we had not really imagined or envisaged. Tanveer Asji, of IFA, egged us on once he visited Delhi and heard us read. We weren't sure it would work as a formal performance, it was experimental and new. Tanveer buoyed up our confidence: he had a strong feeling it would work. We were enjoying meeting, rehearsing;

our neglected performer-selves were delighted and began—although with some trepidation— looking forward to doing the readings in front of an audience.

We rehearsed once a week from January to February 2016, taking up (multiple) roles, doing final edits, working out cues, firming up our coordination. We met on either Saturday or Sunday at one of our homes, ate a potluck meal, chatted awhile, then settled down for three to four hours of intensive rehearsal sessions, practising reading, singing, and commentary. Luckily, Shanti and Indira are both gifted singers.

Carefully selected excerpts, with crisp new commentary, formed a patchwork script, stitching together the past and the present, a new production. The commentary briefly introduced each play, its evolution, contexts, the people involved, and the conditions of its production and performance.

Performing the Old Plays in New Ways

At some point, we gave our production a name: *Zindagi ke Natak, Natakon ki Zindagi* (Plays of Life, the Life of Plays). We felt that just as these plays are based on real lives, so too does each play have a life of its own!

The enactment echoed remembered intonations, facial expressions, and gestures. The actors interacted with one another and there was eye contact with the audience. Street theatre morphed into a novel form, adapted from and mimicking the original. It preserved the spirit, idiom, drama, words and some of the body language, minus a large cast and spatial movement. A fresh wrapping of history was added *qua* commentary.

We performed six times between March and May 2016, for small audiences. The programme, including audience interaction, took a minimum of one and a half hours, and sometimes up to three or four hours. The three of us performed at the Delhi School of Social Work (DSSW), the Foundation for Contemporary Indian Art (FICA) Reading Room, and in Downstairs@47, Tejeshwar Singh Memorial Trust's Basement Studio. Indira had committed to two performances, but managed to stay for three. Only Shanti and I performed at Action India and Studio Safdar, doing the plays *Ehsaas* and *Aurat aur Dharm*. At the Delhi School of Economics, I went solo, since Shanti couldn't get leave from her job. In 2017 we performed again at Studio Safdar, joined by the activist Savita Sharma.[187] In 2020 there was a final performance at the All India Women's Studies (AIWS) Conference; Shanti's job again prevented her participation, so Savita took on some more roles. We included *Om Swaha* in the last two performances, both Savita and I having acted in *Om Swaha* during the 80s.

At the Delhi School of Social Work (DSSW), 5 March 2016

Shanti arranged the first performance at DSSW, Delhi University. She had met three DSSW students during their fieldwork in east Delhi's Seelampur basti, and had held a session on gender for them. They felt greatly inspired, and invited her to their college; she offered to do the play there, and they were happy to accept.

The performance was held in a large classroom, with maybe 50 students and five teachers. Indira, as the Sutradhar, greeted everybody, and related how these plays were created and performed hundreds of times. We began with a song, then read *Ehsaas:* becoming a teacher disciplining little girls, then women preoccupied with housework and wifehood, moving to a mother-daughter sequence, dialogues between brother and sister, a young woman and her fiancée, a husband and wife, college girls and their principal, harassment on the street and in buses, and women who finally strike out on their own, struggling towards independent identities, alternative lives.

After the reading, I briefly explained the circumstances in which *Ehsaas* was scripted in 1979, and performed during the 80s. The play was made in this very university, and was even sometimes rehearsed in the DSSW lawns, as well as performed there for a sizeable audience of students and teachers.[188]

Our programme continued. Shanti began reading *Aurat aur Dharm*: men ridicule women's claim to equality; Rukma and her jethani refute misogynist customs and menstruation taboos, and celebrate the birth of a girl; a woman, widowed during the anti-Sikh killings, asserts her rights, and struggles to educate her daughter. Shanti described the circumstances in which the play was written in 1985, and performed over a few years. We then opened the floor for discussion.

---

[187] Savita has been a counselor at National Commission for Women, Delhi Commision for Women and Saheli, as also an actor with Alarippu in the 80s and early 90s.

[188] We held some rehearsals of *Ehsaas* in DSSW during 1982-84, when Jyotika Virdi studied at DSSW, and performed it there at least once, if not twice.

A DSSW teacher said, 'Street theatre is such an effective, powerful medium. Our students did it a lot, but not lately. They should do it!' Another teacher added that it is important to record and share testimonies, as these plays did.

A student spoke about her younger brother now laying the table at meal-times and taking up small household tasks, a big change for their family. Another student disagreed—he said that such small individual changes don't matter; the overall structure has to change.

A teacher was inspired to share: 'I don't like to cook; my husband finds cooking cathartic. My saas objected so I tried to hide it at first. But now she too has accepted it. I haven't cooked for years, my husband cooks regularly. My sons cook too, they enjoy it. This is the first time I am sharing this in college. I have been teaching here for 25 years!' After this marvelous story of role reversal, a student remarked: 'In my village in east UP the women, including my mother, dadi, sister, have the same age-old problems; when will the women's movement reach them?' And a teacher suggested, 'You have shown the problems very well. But you should also bring out some of the possible solutions.'

There was lively discussion, everyone pitching in. The programme carried on for some two hours.

At the Foundation for Contemporary Indian Art, 19 March 2016

A motley audience of artists, photographers, curators, theatre-persons, activists and journalists gathered at FICA's reading room, to watch and listen to the vintage play readings.

Post-performance, a young photographer asked: 'During the December 16, 2012 anti-rape protests,[189] I saw many street plays. Most seemed to be thought out in English, and performed in Hindi. Was that how your plays were written?' We explained how most women's street plays in the 80s emerged in local, spoken languages—from their conception in workshops, development through improvisation and discussion, to their scripting and performance. For plays like *Aurat aur Dharm* and *Ehsaas*, this language was Hindi.

Mangai, theatre director and scholar, mused: 'Women didn't invent street theatre, but they brought something new, developed a different aesthetics.' She found the readings very evocative, and appreciated the history-telling, noting that it was important whenever possible

[189] On 16 December 2012, a young woman was gang-raped and fatally assaulted in a public bus in Delhi. The 'Nirbhaya' case sparked off major anti-rape protests.

to present a roll-call of the entire cast, all those who took part, for the record.

A middle-aged gentleman felt that the plays gave him a sense of what Delhi was like 40 years ago—'A big village, compared to today!' But the sense of insecurity was strong for women even then, and has only grown stronger over the years. Actor-activist Ponni Arasu, from Tamil Nadu, shared: 'When I studied in LSR, Delhi University, in 2001, we did a play after a girl was raped in the university. We did that play 100 times all over the city.' Ponni affirmed that there exist rich, complex histories of feminist street theatre, with many players—unless we consciously document these histories, they will vanish without a trace.

David Devadas, who had acted in *Om Swaha* in the 80s, commented on how powerful the readings were. He had always been struck by the power of street theatre, but its reach was limited. Mass media on the other hand was spewing junk, yet reaching millions. He suggested combining the power of street plays with mass media, by putting plays onto a website so that they could reach more people.

A young woman came up to us later and asked, quiet desperation in her voice, 'Nothing has changed for me, my mother, khala, nani, the things you show in the play still happen. When will things change? And how?' She was an art historian, and had studied in the west. Sadly, the old plays still reflect contemporary reality.

At Downstairs@47, Tejeshwar Singh Memorial Trust, 20 March 2016

This performance was held in a beautiful basement space, its wooden floors gleaming, and we had an empathetic host in Brinda Singh,[190] an old-timer in Delhi's social movements. People trickled in, and we enjoyed performing!

Parvin Sinclair, a senior academician,[191] asked about the impact of these plays. Shreya Tiwari, a young educationist at the Mahatma Gandhi Institute for Peace and Sustainable Development, felt she

[190] Brinda Singh is a Managing Trustee of the Tejeshwar Singh Memorial Trust. She was the CEO of Mobile Creches in the 1990s and has been a very committed social activist over the decades.

[191] Parvin Sinclair was Professor of Mathematics at the Indira Gandhi National Open University (IGNOU) and later Director of the National Council of Educational Research and Training (NCERT).

Vintage Play Readings programme, Downstairs@47, Panchsheel Park, Delhi, 2016. A diverse audience. Actors: Shanti, Indira Mukherji.

gained a sense of the continuity of feminist struggle over generations: 'We think that all this thinking began recently, so it's wonderful to know how it was... Today one tends to feel terribly isolated. It's so necessary to have a sense of community, but it's missing.'

Actors Ratna Pathak and Naseeruddin Shah were in the audience. He commented: 'The performance was fantastic! If the words are relevant, then good simple reading like this is bound to be very effective!' College student Vivek Lohia remarked: 'I recently saw 15 street plays at a college fest, on environmental issues, women's, and other issues. Those plays didn't have so much punch as the ones you have shown us today. These plays are so relevant; I can't believe they were written 35 years ago. It feels like they were written last week!'

Manmohan Singh, director of Kaivalya Educational Foundation, commented on how rigid perceptions of gender continue to be: 'We gave a lift to a street boy the other day, and he said to me, "How come you allow your wife to drive your car?" Fact is, it's her car, and she's the one who drives.' He also recounted that, at a recent meeting, a high-level government official kept harping on about how 'We should empower women to become good housewives.' Nobody, except Manmohan, raised any objection to this.

At the Sociology Department, Delhi School of Economics, Delhi University, 30 March 2016

Sociology professor Janaki Abraham, who saw the programme at the Tejeshwar Singh Memorial Trust, invited us to perform for her MA students. Neither Shanti nor Indira could make it on a weekday, so I went solo. It was a two-hour session, with approximately 30 students, and the performance was held during their Social Stratification class. Professor Tulsi Patel joined in briefly.

My reading focused on *Ehsaas,* with detailed commentary and a broad introduction to other plays. The students were interested. After the reading ended, one woman student immediately said, 'Everything you have shown in this play is still relevant. Everything in the play is still happening in our lives.'

Ehsaas has a sequence on the harassment of women during Holi and university authorities' apathetic attitude towards this. Several of the Sociology MA students had a strong response to this sequence, and described the contemporary situation. Before Holi, which was on 24 March that year, the Vice-Chancellor had sent a circular to all five women's hostels on campus, banning women from stepping out. In case a woman went out, she would not be allowed back in. 'We have a really bad time during Holi,' the students said. 'If it is for our protection, then they should at least let us return to our rooms, in case we happen to be outside!' Janaki commented, 'Women are locked up to control women's sexuality. It's the same ideology carrying on!'

One student said as young adults, they should be allowed much more freedom. She described how, when she was in hostel at Jamia, girls were on the first floor, and boys were on the ground floor. During Holi, 'The boys came up to the girl's common room, and we all played Holi. It was really nice. It was my best Holi!'

Another student brought up the class character of the women's movement of the 80s and 90s, and we had a long discussion on that. We also spoke of how the LGBTQ movement unfurled in the wake of the women's movement in the 80s and 90s.

After the class dispersed, one student lingered, to share with me, 'In the metro recently, a man masturbated in front of me. I slapped him and took him to the metro police at Kashmiri gate. The policeman refused to register a case, said, "*Kal aapki shaadi ho jayegi, kya court ke chakar kaat-te rahoge*?" (You will get married tomorrow, will you keep doing rounds of the courts?) When I told my mother, she agreed with me that we should register a case, but my father said, "No, it is a very bad idea." This is how things ended.'

At Action India, Jangpura, 8 April 2016

We responded to a request from Action India, to perform at their office. The setting was conducive, with posters all around celebrating forty years of Action India, redolent of the rich history of autonomous grassroots women's movements. *Aurat aur Dharm* was made by Action India-Sabla Sangh, which Shanti was part of in the 80s.

The 40 or so Action India members present watched with rapt attention. After it ended, Gouri Choudhury said: 'This is the history of the women's movement! It can't happen again, but it's very important for us to recall. People don't even know these things. It was a journey of ideas. Action India is 40 years old this year and we include this programme in our 40-year celebration!'

Susheela, Manorama, Ramzan, and Gyanvati, who had made and acted in plays during the 1980s and 90s, recalled some of their experiences. Younger members said hearing the plays made them yearn to be part of a movement!

Vintage Play Readings programme, Action India office, Jangpura, 2016. Audience constituted by social activists on the staff of Action India. Susheela (top left photo, white-haired) was an actor in feminist street theatre during the 80s and 90; so were Ramzan and Manorama (bottom left photo, front row second and third from left) and Gouri Choudhury (seated on chair). Actors (top right photo) Deepti, Shanti.

Susheela reminisced, 'We made *Aurat aur Dharm* after working with survivors of the 1984 riots, Sikh widows. At that time, we used to go in juloos, jathas, protests, with every sangathan. Today, there is none of that. I miss those days!' She said that earlier she was house-bound, since in her caste women don't go out to work. When she stepped out, all hell broke loose. But she gained a lot from the decision, and there was no question of stepping back. Gradually, her husband supported her. Now, she is on the verge of retirement.

Manorama shared:

> With my sisters in the movement I did a play on communalism, *Zimmedar Kaun,* a hundred times, at every crossroad. I feel the movement is still on, and we can take it further, forward... Years ago, in Sunder Nagri single women came together and developed an understanding, that we are single, but we are sampurna, whole. Living with a man, you suffer. If a wife eats before him, if she says anything, she is beaten. Single women live without being beaten, and we run our own homes. Single women have become free, very strong, due to the women's movement. Society says, widows cannot put on a bindi. I began wearing bindis during a theatre workshop in Saharanpur, many years ago. My brother opposed it, society opposed it, but I persisted... Earlier I couldn't speak, today I stand in front of anybody and put across any matter!

Ramzan shared how everybody at home tried to stop her from working, scared that it was not safe for her to travel, go out, and meet different people. She wanted to earn, was worried about her three daughters, their dowries, their weddings. Once she began working, her perspective changed. Joining women's groups, she learnt so much, acted in plays, went everywhere: 'I got courage and confidence. I realised the girls have to be educated. Marriage was put on the back burner. Today, my daughters are standing on their own feet. In my neighbourhood, and family, everybody comes to me for advice!'

Kriti said: 'The plays could seem outdated to me, because I experience lots of freedom. But recently, a girl's family came to see my brother, and kept saying, "Our girl has been entirely at home, absolutely under our control!" Finally I said, "We don't want that."' She added that, whether 40 years ago or today, there is so much violence against women—murders, rapes, dowry deaths, and emotional abuse.

Mridula mused: 'When the British ruled our country, we were slaves. I feel, we women are still slaves. Some found a way to struggle, and they show a way to younger generations, so we are able to breathe freely a bit at least.' She dreams that her daughter will live her life with freedom, the way she wants to: 'For this, I, her mother, will always support her.'

Shameem shared: 'What we saw in *Ehsaas* today, we heard all the time—"Girls are made for the home, men for outside."I used to listen, and remain quiet. Later I learnt, whether man or woman, one has full rights to see the whole world. I took these ideas home, and changed things there too.'

Gyanvati recalled many movements, camapaigns, and scores of plays she has been a part of. Her family was orthodox: 'I made many changes, in myself, my family, my children, and earned respect... So many things have happened—there is not enough time to recount them.' Two of her children had inter-caste marriages; one of her daughters, Manju, has a job in a bank, and lives on her own. She was in Chhoti Sabla, the girls' group, from the age of seven, so she has courage, and confidence.

Gouri Choudhury felt that the play readings had created a movement atmosphere, and that many more such sessions were needed! She remarked, 'Talking about our lives was an important dimension of our work, earlier. It was part of building feminist understanding. Today, like other NGOs, we are caught up with projects, targets, figures. We don't talk about our lives anymore!'

At Studio Safdar: 13 May 2016 and 23 June 2017

The vintage play readings were performed twice at Studio Safdar, Delhi's quintessential space for radical, activist theatre.[192]

Both times, there were academics, theatre-persons, students, artists, and activists in the audience. Manohar Khushalani of Theatre Union, who acted in *Om Swaha* in the 80s, said with excitement: 'You have done it exactly as it was done then! It was such an important play. Because of it, laws changed, people grew aware: there were protests against dowry and dowry deaths!'

There were questions about patriarchy, then and now, quite intricate discussions on capitalism as linked to patriarchy, and the role of radical culture such as this. The impact of the plays and the movement came up, as well as the backlash women were facing, and

---

[192] Studio Safdar is an independent, non-funded space for arts and activism, established in 2012 by Janam.

Vintage Play Readings programme, Studio Safdar, 2016. A diverse audience, including members of Janam. Actors: Deepti, Shanti.

the current state of women's movements. Dr Swati Pal, the principal of Janki Devi Memorial College, a women's college, wanted to know where scripts could be accessed—it would be good to introduce students to the plays. The Indian Cultural Forum arranged to video-shoot the entire programme, and NewsClick later edited the two-hour footage, making two 10-minute videos, one on *Ehsaas*, and the other on *Aurat aur Dharm.*[193]

The second performance at Studio Safdar was, in tandem with Jana Natya Manch (Janam), 'An Evening on Street Theatre in Delhi'. This included our presentation of *Ehsaas* and *Om Swaha*, and Janam's enactment of scenes from *Aurat*, *Voh Bol Uthi*, and *Yeh Bhi Hinsa Hai.* Moloyashree Hashmi described Janam's journey with street theatre since the late 70s,[194] while we shared memories and histories, providing a sense of the legacy of feminist street theatre, born of a vibrant women's movement. It was a powerful confluence of two important streams of Delhi's street theatre.

[193] The two short videos are available online, as part of an article on the Indian Cultural Forum website titled 'Feminist Street Theatre: Plays as Contemporary History' (Mehrotra 2016).

[194] Janam had by then completed over 8,500 performances of nearly 75 street plays and 15 proscenium plays, in 140 cities across India.

At the Indian Association of Women's Studies Conference, 29 January 2020

We were invited to perform at the Indian Association of Women's Studies' conference at the National Law University in Dwarka, Delhi.[195] The programme, held in the evening, was part of the cultural events coordinated by Professor Uma Chakravarti,[196] and was witnessed by a few hundred participants, academics, and activists. We read from *Ehsaas* and *Om Swaha*, interspersing the readings with brief narrative histories, and we sang songs. Some old-timers in the audience enjoyed this so much that they spontaneously joined in, and several couldn't resist getting up from their seats in the auditorium and dancing! Younger people in the audience were enthused and touched by this spontaneous dancing, the spirited enactments and evocative songs.

An IAWS conference poster shows Sheetal Sathe, Sumangala Damodaran (bottom row), Deepti, Shanti, among others.

For younger academics, such as those from Savitribai Phule Pune University, the play readings programme was a coming-alive of histories they had glimpsed in courses and texts on the Indian women's movement. One said: 'We have heard and read about the plays of the 80s and it was wonderful to see. We look forward to the book, to reading more details.'

---

[195] It was the XVIth IAWS national conference held from 28 to 30 January 2020. The tentative conference schedule is available at iwwage.org/wp-content/uploads/2020/01/Tentative-Conference-Schedule.pdf (accessed 20 March 2023). The conference theme was 'Constitutional Principles in 21st Century India: Visions for Emancipation'.

[196] Cultural activists Bindhumalini, Sumangala Damodaran, Sheetal Sathe, Moloyashree Hashmi, and Vidya Rao also made musical or theatrical presentations during 28 and 29 March 2020. Since Shanti was sadly unable to take leave from her job to rehearse and perform, Savita Sharma joined me at the readings programme.

Nalini Nayak,[197] an eminent academic-activist from Kerala, said to us, 'Really, on stage you looked like you are 20 years old, when you acted as young students in *Ehsaas*! Down south we still face the same issues that you have shown.' Young research scholars from JNU buzzed around, wondering if we could do more such play-readings.

The old plays are powerful today too. Read against the shifting background of women's lives, political consciousness, society and state, they interrogate and extend the inherent possibilities of feminist activism. The plays and songs help nurture hope and courage, providing a sense of the intensity and continuity of women's struggles, joyous even when desperately serious.

Together, we sang movement songs that are etched into our memories, each song belonging to all of us, reclaiming our collective histories, helping free our imaginations and strengthening us to build the future of our dreams:

Tod tod ke bandhanon ko
Dekho behenein aati hain!
Aayeingi zulm mitaayiengi
Vo to naya zamana laayeingi
Naacheigi gaayeingi vo fankaari dikhaayeingi,
Haan meri behna vo fankaari dikhaayeingi,
Ab vo sisak sisak ke na royeingi,
Ab vo sisak sisak ke na royeingi!
Tod tod ke bandhanon ko
Dekho behenein aati hain!

(Breaking barriers, see the women are coming!
They will come and end injustice,
Bring about a new world,
They will sing and dance and skillfully craft
Yes my sisters will craft new wonders,
No more will they sob and weep,
No more will they sob out their hearts,
Breaking barriers, see the women are coming!)

[197] Nalini Nayak has been actively involved with coastal communities and fishworkers' movements for over three decades. She is founder-member of the International Collective in Support of Fishworkers, and co-founder and general-secretary of the Self-Employed Women's Association, Kerala.

Acknowledgments

Maximum gratitude to Sheba Chhachhi for her wonderful photographs. They have enriched the book immeasurably, bringing a visual dimension to life, with finesse and acute sensitivity. These, and more, will soon be accessible in a digital archive of the women's movement that we are together working on.

Illustrations by Ashma Singh resonate with the play scripts, enactments, as do the illustrations from ASTHA, Stree Mukti Sanghatana and Chhatisgarh Mahila Jagriti Sangathan. Most sketches are hand-drawn, powerful and communicative.

Professor Vibhuti Patel shared precious information concerning a number of plays, photographs and a play script, and was unstinting in her endorsement of the historical value of this work. Jyoti Mhapsekar cheerfully answered sundry queries, vetted the chapter on *Mulgi Zali Ho*, and took keen interest in the progress of the manuscript. Their solidarity has helped extend the scope of this book.

Interspersing the text with varied images and snippets from the 1980s and 90s not only reflects the zeitgeist of the women's movement of the time, its aesthetics and politics, it also conveys a sense of shared visions, a camaraderie that has miraculously survived the ravages of time.

Thanks to Siddhartha of Sidhbari, who supported the processing of visuals into print-ready matter.

Much gratitude to each of the street play actors, activists, directors, theatre professionals, amateur comrades-in-arms who shared your memories, reflections, thoughts and feelings. It was a delight to interact, listen, chat, interview, converse—a pleasure-filled research process. This book is yours as much as it is mine.

I would like to thank India Foundation for the Arts (IFA) and the South Asia Women's Fund (SAWF) for their support. Sampurna Trust received a grant from IFA under its Arts Research programme; the grant was partly supported by SAWF. The eighteen-month grant (during 2014 - 2016) helped me research and write the first draft of the book. It also helped us in Sampurna Trust (a non-formal feminist collective), to put together an experimental programme of dramatised readings from feminist street plays. Special thanks to Tanveer Asji, IFA, for his strong belief in this work, perceptive comments on the first draft, and for arranging some of the early performances; and to Arundhati Ghosh for her support throughout. A residency in 2019 at the Bellagio Centre, Rockefeller Foundation, provided me with quiet reflective space, helping move towards writing of the second draft.

The participation and involvement of Shanti, Indira Mukherji and Savita Sharma, helped make our programme—*Zindagi ke Natak, Natakon ki Zindagi*—a success. These have been the best saathis, the most fun to work with, creative, energetic and adventurous. Their brilliant singing and expressive reading transmuted the programme into a living, breathing creature. Thanks to those who hosted the performances (Delhi School of Social Work, Foundation for Indian Contemporary Art, Tejeshwar Singh Memorial Trust, Sociology Department Delhi School of Economics, Action India, Studio Safdar, Professor Uma Charkravarti and the Association of Indian Women's Studies), and the audiences at each venue for their kind attention, warm response, comments and questions.

I would like to thank everyone at Zubaan Books, especially Urvashi Butalia for her expert editorial comments through three book drafts, and unflagging support; Zara Ismail for meticulous copy-editing (and for letting me know how much she enjoyed the matter); and Melissa Fernandes, for detailed attention to the publication.

And now, dear reader, the book is in your hands. Your responses will complete the circle.

Photo and Illustration Credits

Photos

Sheba Chhachhi – photos on page numbers 4, 5, 23, 32, 34, 39, 43, 55, 60, 61, 63, 71, 72, 74, 125, 130, 136, 139, 143, 144, 156, 162, 171, 183.

Note: Photos on pages 5 (second pic), 43, 72 (first and fourth), 74 (first) were cropped only for the present publication.

Ehsaas Group – photos on page numbers 87, 104.

Vibhuti Ramachandran (2003) – two photos on page number 160.

Stree Mukti Sanghatana – two photos on page number 175.

Amar Jesani, Vibhuti Patel – two photos on page number 188.

Deepti Mehrotra – photo on page number 251.

Alarippu – photos on page numbers 259, 261, 265, 266, and 268.

Tanveer Asji, India Foundation for the Arts – photos on page numbers 308, 313.

Kriti, Action India – photos on page number 310.

Illustrations

Ashma Singh, *Nukkad Nukkad Aangan Aangan* (Jagori Samooh 1988) – illustrations on page numbers 20, 25, 27, 87, 88, 115, 138, 148, 153, 186, 190, 212, 215, 225, 227, 233, 237, 242, 246, 253.

ASTHA (1988) – illustrations on page numbers 22, 108, 199, 200, 204.

Stree Mukti Sanghatana (2010) – back and front cover illustrations on page numbers 168, 172.

Chhattisgarh Mahila Jagriti Sangathan (1994) – illustration on page number 220.

Indian Association of Women's Studies (2020) – poster on page number 314.

Bibliography

Books, Chapters in Books, Play Scripts, Dissertations, Papers, Articles, Reports, Archival Memoirs

Aamachya Aamhi Natya Manch (Mumbai). 1988. 'Baarah Ghar Ki Baarah Auratein', in Jagori Samooh (ed.). *Nukkad Nukkad Aangan Aangan*, pp. 32-39. New Delhi: Jagori.

Aamachya Aamhi Natya Manch (Mumbai). 1988. 'Hum Apni Awaz Uthayeinge', Jagori Samooh (ed.). *Nukkad Nukkad Aangan Aangan,* pp. 108-13. New Delhi: Jagori.

Aggarwal, Shobha. 2022. 'Introduction: Reminiscing ABVA's Struggle for Gay Rights', in Arun Bhandari, JP Jain, Jagdish Bhardwaj, Lalitha SA, Dr PS Sahni, Shalini SCN, and Siddhartha Gautam, *Less Than Gay: A Citizens' Report on the Status of Homosexuality in India,* pp. 21-90. New Delhi: AIDS Bhedbhav Virodhi Andolan.

Agnes, Flavia. 1984. *My Story, Our Story of Rebuilding Broken Lives.* Bombay: Women's Center.

Afzal-Khan, Fawzia. 2000. 'Street Theater in Pakistani Punjab: The Case of Ajoka, Lok Rehs, and the (So-Called) Woman Question'. In Fawzia Afzal-Khan and Kalpana Seshadri-Crooks (eds). *The Pre-Occupation of Postcolonial Studies*, pp. 171-199. Durham: Duke University Press.

Ahuja, Chaman. 2001. 'Diverse Activists', *Theatre India,* 3: 20-21.

Alarippu (Delhi). 'Intezaar', in Jagori Samooh (ed.), *Nukkad Nukkad Aangan Aangan,* pp. 102-107. New Delhi: Jagori.

Alcoff, Linda and Elizabeth Potter (eds.). 1993. *Feminist Epistemologies.* New York: Routledge.

Aneja, Anu. 2019. *Women's and Gender Studies in India: Crossings.* Abingdon Oxon and New York: Routledge.

Aneja, Anu. 2023. *Feminist Theory and the Aesthetics Within: A Perspective from South Asia*. Abingdon Oxon and New York: Routledge.

Ancy, Anita, Asha, Deepti, Fatima, Seema, Sanjeevani, Ruth, Madhu, and Tripurari. 1979-80. 'A Women's Theatre Workshop', *Manushi,* 4: 24.

Anonymous.1983. 'Kriti: A Creative Workshop for Women', *Manushi,* 16: 34-35.

ASTHA. 1988. *Two Street Plays for Women: Ek Thee Achhi Ladki, Agar Miriam Hoti.* Bombay: Xavier Institute of Communications.

ASTHA. 1988. 'Agar Mariam Hoti', in ASTHA, *Two Street Plays for Women,* pp. 31-44. Bombay: Xavier Institute of Communications.

ASTHA. 1988. 'Ek Thee Achhi Ladki', in ASTHA, *Two Street Plays for Women,* pp. 9-23. Bombay: Xavier Institute of Communications.

Aston, Elain. 2020. *Restaging Feminisms.* London: Palgrave Macmillan.

Banerjee, Sumanta. 2019. *The Parlour and the Street—Elite and Popular Culture in Nineteenth Century Calcutta.* Kolkata: Seagull Books.

Banerjee, Trina Nileena. 2021. *Performing Silence: Women in the Group Theatre Movement in Bengal.* New Delhi: OUP.

Bartholomew, Rati. 1988. 'Nukkad Natak ki Aitihasik Prishtthabhumi', in Jagori Samooh, *Nukkad Nukkad Aangan Aangan,* pp. i-v. New Delhi: Jagori.

Barua, Anoushka. 2020. 'Pinjra Tod: A Contemporary Feminist Movement', *The Armchair Journal,* 9 August. armchairjournal.com/pinjra-tod-a-contemporary-feminist-movement/ (accessed 22 January 2023).

Baxi, Upendra, Vasudha Dhagamwar, Raghunath Kelkar, Lotika Sarkar. 1979. *An Open Letter to the Chief Justice of India.* pldindia.org/wp-content/uploads/2013/03/Open-Letter-to-CJI-in-the-Mathura-Rape-Case.pdf (accessed 21 September 2020).

Bhargava, Simran. 1985. 'St Stephen's Colleges Girls' Lockers Burglary Incident Creates Hoopla in DU', *India Today,* 28 February. www.indiatoday.in/magazine/indiascope/story/19850228-st-stephens-college-girls-lockers-burglary-incident-creates-hoopla-in-du-769815-2013-11-27 (accessed 8 May 2022).

Bharti, Smita. 2005. *Beyond Silences: Docu-Theatre in Jail and Outside,* New Delhi: WISCOMP.

Bharucha, Rustom. 2000. 'Documenting Culture: Prejudices and Possibilities', *Humanscape,* VII(4): 31-34.

Bharucha, Rustom. 2003. *The Politics of Cultural Practice: Thinking Through Theatre in an Age of Globalization.* New Delhi: OUP.

Bhatia, Nandi. 2004. *Acts of Authority/Acts of Resistance: Theatre and Politics in Colonial and Postcolonial India.* New Delhi: OUP.

Bhatia, Nandi. 2010. *Performing Women/ Performing Womanhood: Theatre, Politics and Dissent in North India.* New Delhi: OUP.

Bhatkhande, Ankita. 2013. 'College Students Join Hands to Redefine "Mardangi"', *Mumbai Mirror,* 9 January. mumbaimirror.indiatimes.com/mumbai/other/college-students-join-hands-to-redefine-mardangi/articleshow/50505040.cms (accessed 22 January 2023).

Bhattacharya, Malini. 2003. *Giving Away the Girl and Other Plays.* Sarmistha Dutta Gupta and Paramita Banerjee (trans.). Calcutta: Seagull Books.

Bhattacharya, Malini. 2003. 'Giving Away the Girl', in Malini Bhattacharya, *Giving Away the Girl and Other Plays.* Sarmistha Dutta Gupta (trans.). pp. 1-26. Calcutta: Seagull Books.

Bhattacharya, Malini. 2003. 'The Monkey Dance', in Malini Bhattacharya, *Giving Away the Girl and Other Plays.* Paramita Banerjee (trans.). pp. 27-33. Calcutta: Seagull Books.

Bhattacharya, Malini. 2003. 'Why So Much Bloodshed?', in Malini Bhattacharya, *Giving Away the Girl and Other Plays.* Sarmistha Dutta Gupta (trans.). pp. 35-57. Calcutta: Seagull Books.

Butalia, Subhadra. 2002. *The Gift of a Daughter—Encounters with Victims of Dowry.* New Delhi: Penguin.

Chakraborty, Runu. Undated. 'O What Kind Of A Foreign Land Is This?', *Living Feminisms Archive.* Jagori. www.livingfeminisms.org/story/pakistan-travelogue (accessed 19 August 2023).

Chakravarti, Uma. 2013. 'Cultures of Resistance: Women's Movement as Performance', in Kavita Panjabi and Paromita Chakravarti (eds) *Women Contesting Cultures,* pp. 58-71. Kolkata: Bhatkal and Sen.

Chhatisgarh Mahila Jagriti Sangathan (Raipur). 1988. 'Teri Meri Kahani', in Jagori Samooh (ed.). *Nukkad Nukkad Aangan Aangan,* pp. 62-68. New Delhi: Jagori.

Chhatisgarh Mahila Jagriti Sangathan. 1994. *Yadi Saans Lene ki bhi Jagah Mile To Mein Naya Rachoongi Naya Gaaungi....* Raipur: Chhattisgarh Mahila Jagriti Sangathan.

Costa, Dia Da. 2013. [2007]. 'Mirrors of Value? Advertising and Political Theatre in the Hegemonic Construction of Women in India', in Sudhanva Deshpande (ed.), *Theatre of the Streets,* pp. 149-77. New Delhi: Janam.

Costa, Dia Da. 2016. *Politicizing Creative Economy: and A Hunger Called Theatre.* Champaign, IL, University of Illinois Press.

Dahej Virodhi Mahila Manch. 1988. 'Om Swaha 2', in Jagori Samooh (ed.). *Nukkad Nukkad Aangan Aangan,* pp. 52-61. New Delhi: Jagori.

Dalmia, Vasudha. 2006. *Poetics, Plays and Performances: The Politics of Modern Indian Theatre.* New Delhi: OUP.

Das, Manini. 1979. 'Women Against Dowry', *Manushi,* 3: 15-17.

Dasi, Binodini and Rimli Bhattacharya. 1998. *My Story and My Life as an Actress.* New Delhi: Kali for Women.

Datar, Chhaya. 1989. *Waging Change: Women Tobacco Workers in Nipani Organise.* New Delhi: Kali for Women.

De, Hemchhaya. 2020. '#ActAgainstAbuse: Meet Anuradha Kapoor, Founder of Kolkata's Swayam', *Femina,* 16 May. www.femina.in/trending/actagainstabuse/meet-anuradha-kapoor-founder-of-kolkatas-swayam-157969.html (accessed 22 January 2023).

Deepti and Shobha. 1982. 'Women Lecturers Mobilize Against Dowry Death,' *Manushi,* 12: 46-47.

Desai, Rajvi. 2019. 'Do Not Go Gentle: Lessons from Four Decades of Fighting for Women's Rights', *The Swaddle,* 13 May. theswaddle.com/lessons-from-four-decades-of-fighting-for-womens-rights/ (accessed 5 October 2020).

Deshpande, Sudhanva. 1997. 'The "Inexhaustible Work of Criticism in Action": Street Theatre of the Left', in *Seagull Theatre Quarterly,* 16: 2-21.

Deshpande, Sudhanva (ed.). 2013. [2007]. *Theatre of the Streets: The Jana Natya Manch Experience.* New Delhi: Janam.

Devi, Mahasweta. 2011. *Five Plays.* Samik Bandopadhyay (trans.). Kolkata: Seagull Books.

Devi, Sabitri. 1997. '" My Acting Is Almost Entirely My Life"', *Seagull Theatre Quarterly,* Number14-15: 52-61.

Dewan, Saba. 2012. 'Of Chick Charts, Hen Charts and Other Such Women's Stories', *Kafila,* 8 May. kafila.online/2012/05/08/st-stephens-college-the-class-of-85-saba-dewan/ (accessed 12 December 2016).

Dharwadker, Aparna Bhargava. 2005. *Theatres of Independence: Drama, Theory and Urban Performance in India since 1947.* Iowa City: University of Iowa Press.

Donkin, Ellen and Susan Clement (eds). 1993. *Upstaging Big Daddy: Directing Theatre As If Gender and Race Matter.* Ann Arbor: University of Michigan Press.

Dutta, Madhusree. 2003. 'A Director's Note', in Malini Bhattacharya, *Giving Away the Girl and Other Plays,* pp. xxi-xxv. Calcutta: Seagull Books.

Dutt, Bishnupriya. 2022. *Maya Rao and Indian Feminist Theatre.* Cambridge: Cambridge University Press.

Dutt, Utpal. 2009. *On Theatre.* Kolkata: Seagull Books.

Ehsaas Group. 1988. 'Ehsaas', in Jagori Samooh (ed.). *Nukkad Nukkad Aangan Aangan,* pp. 2-11. New Delhi: Jagori.

Erven, Eugene van. 1992. *The Playful Revolution: Theatre and Liberation in Asia.* Bloomington: Indiana University Press.

Gahlot, Deepa. 2019. 'Theatre Is A Great Medium of Change, Says Sushama Deshpande', *The Hindu,* 19 September. www.thehindu.com/entertainment/theatre/theatre-is-a-great-medium-of-change-says-sushama-deshpande/article29458968.ece (accessed 30 March 2023).

Gandhi, Nandita and Nandita Shah. 1992. *The Issues at Stake: Theory and Practice in the Contemporary Women's Movement in India.* New Delhi: Kali for Women.

Gandhi, Nandita. 2011. 'Feminist Thoughts from Here and There', *Poster Women—A Zubaan Project,* 4 August. www.posterwomen.org/?p=5488> (accessed 17 March 2022).

Gautham, Leila. 2014. 'Something Is Rotten in St Stephen's: An Ex-Student Speaks Out!', *Youth ki Awaaz,* 19 November. www.youthkiawaaz.com/2014/11/st-stephens-college-rules-for-girls-hostel/ (accessed 20 June 2022).

Ghosh, Arjun. 2012. *A History of the Jana Natya Manch: Plays for the People.* New Delhi: Sage.

Glenn, Susan A. 2000. *Female Spectacle: The Theatrical Roots of Modern Feminism.* Cambridge, Massachusetts: Harvard University Press.

Gokahle, Shanta (ed.). 2014. *The Theatre of Veenapani Chawla: Theory, Practice, Performance*. New Delhi: OUP.

Gokhale, Shanta. 2020. *One Foot on the Ground: A Life Told Through the Body*. New Delhi: Speaking Tiger Books.

Gothoskar, Sujata. 1997. *Struggles of Women at Work*. New Delhi: Vikas Publishing House.

Gothoskar, Sujata. 2011. 'Sujata Gothoskar', *Poster Women—A Zubaan Project*, 17 August. www.posterwomen.org/?p=5773 (accessed 12 September 2020).

Government of India. 1974. *Towards Equality: Report of the Committee on the Status of Women in India*. New Delhi: Ministry of Education and Social Welfare, Department of Social Welfare.

Gupta, Sarmistha Dutta. 2003. 'In Search of the Right Words', in Malini Bhattacharya, *Giving Away the Girl and Other Plays*, pp. xxvi-xxx. Calcutta: Seagull Books.

Hashmi, Mala. 1997. '"Drama Has To Be Created and Crafted, Even on the Streets"', *Seagull Theatre Quarterly*, 16: 58-71.

Hashmi, Safdar. 2013. [2007]. 'The First Ten Years of Street Theatre', in Sudhanva Deshpande (ed.), *Theatre of the Streets*, pp. 11-17. New Delhi: Jana Natya Manch.

Heble, Ayesha. 2017. *Third Person Singular*. New Delhi: Tara India Research Press.

Iyengar, Sameera. 1998-99. 'Theatre as a Magnifying Lens', *Seagull Theatre Quarterly*, Issue on *Theatre for Change*, Number 20-21: 10-23.

Iyer, Jaya. 2006. *Healing through Dialogue: Theatre of the Oppressed and Beyond*, New Delhi: WISCOMP.

Jagori Samooh (ed.). 1988. *Nukkad Nukkad Aangan Aangan: Mahila Andolan ke Dauran Ubhre Nukkad Natakon ka Sankalan*. New Delhi: Jagori.

Jain, Kirti. 2013. 'In Search of a Narrative: Women Theatre Directors of the Northern Belt', in Lakshmi Subramanyam (ed.), *Muffled Voices*, pp. 151-64. New Delhi: Har Anand.

Kagal, Ayesha. 1986. 'Performing "A Girl Is Born"', *Times of India*.

Kapur, Anuradha. 2019. 'Genealogy and Overwriting', in *Marg*, Issue on *Staging Change: Theatre in India*', 70(3): 16-23.

Kapur, Anuradha. 2021. 'Rati Bartholomew: 4 January 1927–23 September 2021', *Indian Cultural Forum*, 23 September. indianculturalforum.in/2021/09/23/rati-bartholomew-4-january-1927-23-september-2021/ (accessed 24 September 2021).

Kapur, Jyotsna. 1988. 'Behind the Scenes: Putting a Street Play Together', in ASTHA, *Two Street Plays for Women*, pp. 24-30. Bombay: Xavier Institute of Communication.

Kapur, Jyotsna. 2013. *The Politics of Time and Youth in Brand India: Bargaining with Capital*. Delhi: Anthem Press.

Katyal, Anjum. 1998-99. 'Editorial', *Seagull Theatre Quarterly,* Issue on *Theatre for Change*, 20-21: 2-9.

Katyal, Anjum. 1998-99. 'Playwright, Director, Activist: Interview with Tripurari Sharma', *Seagull Theatre Quarterly*, 20-21: 99-132.

Katyal, Anjum. 2022. 'The Badal Sircar Workshop: Towards A Collective Growth', in Tripurari Sharma (ed.) *Theatre India: Number One,* pp. 77-85. New Delhi: National School of Drama.

Katyal, Anjum. 2024. *Safdar Hashmi: Towards Theatre for a Democracy.* Hyderabad: Orient Blackswan.

Kaushal, JN (ed.) 2005. *Sheila Bhatia.* New Delhi: National School of Drama.

Krishnamurty, Lakshmi. 1983. 'Diary of a Theatre Workshop', *How,* January-February, pp. 5-10.

Kumar, Radha.1993. *The History of Doing: An Illustrated Account of Movements for Women's Rights and Feminism in India 1800-1990.* New Delhi: Kali for Women.

Kumar, Sanjay. 2023. *Performing, Teaching and Writing Theatre: Exploring Play.* Newcastle upon Tyne: Cambridge Scholars Publishing.

Lakshmi, C.S. 2000. *Body Blows: Women, Violence and Survival.* Calcutta: Seagull Books.

Lal, Ananda. 2020. 'Usha Ganguli, A Theatre Artiste Who Stood Apart from the Norm,' *The Wire,* 27 April. thewire.in/the-arts/usha-ganguli-tribute (accessed 22 January 2021).

Laughlin, Karen and Catherine Schuler. 1995. *Theatre and Feminist Aesthetics.* Madison: Fairleigh Dickinson University Press.

Maitreya, Yogesh. 2021. *Singing/Thinking Anti-Caste.* Nagpur: Panther's Paw Publication.

Mangai, A. 2015. *Acting Up: Gender and Theatre in India, 1979 Onwards.* New Delhi: Leftword Books.

Mangai, Padma V. 2013. '"Let Me Live": Cry the Baby Girl, in the Cradle and in the Womb, *Pacha Mannu*—An Interventionist Theatre Experience', in Lakshmi Subramanyam (ed.), *Muffled Voices,* pp. 193-208. New Delhi: Har Anand.

Manushi Collective. 1987. *Roshni.* New Delhi: Manushi Collective.

Marik, Soma. 2016. 'Trupti Shah (1962-2016): Remembering A Comrade and a Loving Sister', 30 May. *International Viewpoint.* internationalviewpoint.org/spip.php?article4529 (accessed 25 June 2022).

Marwah, Anuradha. 2021. 'Setting the Stage: Performing Gender in the Time of Covid', *India Writes Network,* 28 June. www.indiawrites.org/2021/06/ (accessed 26 March 2024).

Meduri, Avanthi. 1999. 'A Feminist Retrieval of a Silenced History--God Has Changed His Name: By Way of Introduction...' in *Seagull Theatre Quarterly,* 22: 27-29.

Mehrotra, Deepti Priya. 1995. 'Issues, Ideologies and Forms of Protest:

Women's Groups in Contemporary Uttar Pradesh'. Unpublished Ph.D. dissertation, Political Science Department, University of Delhi.

Mehrotra, Deepti Priya. 2001. 'Nav Srishti: Community Based Education and Health Intervention with Muslim Adolescent Girls in Nangloi, Delhi: Review and Strategy Planning.' Unpublished report, National Foundation of India: New Delhi.

Mehrotra, Deepti Priya. 2006. *Gulab Bai: The Queen of Nautanki Theatre.* New Delhi: Penguin.

Mehrotra, Deepti Priya and Dharmendra Jha. 2009. 'External Evaluation of Sakhi Kendra, Kanpur: Creating Awareness and Empowering the Women in Kanpur', Unpublished report, Christian Aid: New Delhi.

Mehrotra, Deepti Priya. 2010. 'From Kerala to Manipur: Playing for Peace', *Boloji,* 3 August. www.boloji.com/blog/172/from-kerala-to-manipur-playing-for-peace (accessed 20 May 2020).

Menon, Jisha. 2006. 'Rehearsing the Partition: Gendered Violence in "Aur Kitne Tukde"', *Feminist Review,* Issue on *Postcolonial Theatres,* 84(1): 29-47.

Mhapsekar, Jyoti. 2010 [1986]. *Beti Aayi Hai.* Vasant Dev (trans.). Bombay: Stree Mukti Sanghatana.

Mhapsekar, Jyoti and Shubha Khandekar. 1994. *A Girl is Born!—An English Translation of the Marathi Play Mulgi Zali Ho.* Bombay: Stree Mukti Sanghatana and Granthali.

Misra, Savvy Soumya. 2017. 'Mobilising Women in Marginalised Communities to End Violence Against Women and Girls'. *Oxfam India,* 5 April. www.oxfamindia.org/oxfam-in-action/mobilising-women-marginalised-communities-end-violence-against-women-and-girls (accessed 21 May 2021).

Morcom, Anne. 2014. *Courtesans, Bar Girls and Dancing Boys: The Illicit Worlds of Indian Dance.* Gurgaon: Hachette.

Mukerjee, Tutun. 2005. *Staging Resistance: Plays by Women in Translation.* New Delhi: OUP.

Nagar, Richa. 2000. 'Mujhe Jawab Do! (Answer me!): Women's Grassroots Activism and Social Spaces in Chitrakoot (India)', *Gender, Place and Culture: A Journal of Feminist Geography,* 7(4): 341-362. www.tandfonline.com/doi/abs/10.1080/713668879> (accessed 10 April 2022).

Nagar, Richa. 2015. Women's Theater and the Redefinitions of Public, Private, and Politics in North India. *ACME: An International Journal for Critical Geographies,* 1(1): 55–72. acme-journal.org/index.php/acme/article/view/683 (accessed 10 April 2022).

Nagar, Richa and Vanangana. 2002. *Mujhe Jawab Do: Chitrakoot ke Gaavon Mein Vanangana ki Pukar [Vanangana's Cry in the Villages of Chitrakoot].* Lucknow: Asha Prakashan.

Nair, Malini. 2017. '"I was tired of hiding": Delhi-based Actor Mallika Taneja Turns Onstage Nudity into Act of Protest', *Scroll,* 20 March. scroll.in/

magazine/831070/i-was-tired-of-hiding-delhi-based-actor-mallika-taneja-turns-onstage-nudity-into-act-of-protest (accessed 26 January 2023).

National Alliance of People's Movements. 2016. 'Trupti Shah: A Tribute', *Countercurrents,* 27 May. countercurrents.org/napm270516.htm> (accessed 30 March 2020).

Ngangomba, Birjit. 1997. '"The Real Power of Sumang Leela Lies in Its Audiences'", *Seagull Theatre Quarterly,* 14-15: 157-60.

Oldenburg, Veena Talwar. 1992. 'Lifestyle as Resistance: The Case of the Courtesans of Lucknow', in Douglas Haynes and Gyan Prakash (eds.), *Contesting Power: Resistance and Everyday Social Relations in South Asia,* pp. 23-61. Berkeley: University of California Press.

Oldenburg, Veena Talwar. 2010. *Dowry Murder: Reinvestigating a Cultural Whodunit.* New Delhi: Penguin Random House.

Panjabi, Kavita and Paromita Chakravarti (eds.). 2013. *Women Contesting Culture: Changing Frames of Gender Politics in India.* Kolkata: Bhatkal and Sen.

Patel, Vibhuti. Undated. *Pyramid—A Skit.* Unpublished play script.

Patel, Vibhuti. 2011. 'How I Came To Be Involved', *Poster Women—A Zubaan Project,* 5 September. www.posterwomen.org/?p=6007 (accessed 12 September 2020).

Patel, Vibhuti. 2014. 'Campaign Against Rape by Women's Movement in India', *DEP - Deportate, Esuli, Profughe: Rivista Telematica di Studi Sulla Memoria Femminile,* 24: 36-47. www.unive.it/pag/fileadmin/user_upload/dipartimenti/DSLCC/documenti/DEP/numeri/n24/Dep_03_Patel.pdf (accessed 26 January 2022).

Paxton, Naomi (ed.). 2013.'Introduction', in Hamilton et al., *The Methuen Drama Book of Suffrage Plays,* pp. vii-xx. London: Methuen Drama.

Pereira, Myron J. 1988. 'Popular Symbols and Popular Theatre', in ASTHA, *Two Street Plays for Women,* pp. 4-8. Bombay: Xavier Institute of Communication.

Pralayan. 1997. "'Why Do We Choose To Do Street Theatre? The Answer Is Always Political – It Has To Be'", *Seagull Theatre Quarterly,* 16: 73-89.

Pratidhvani. 1995. *Bol Ari O Dharti Bol Va Anya Geet.* Hoshangabad: Eklavya.

Priya, Deepti. 1985. 'Challenging a Masculinist Culture: Women's Protest in St. Stephen's', *Manushi,* 28: 32-35.

Priya, Deepti. 1995. 'Street Theatre Centre Stage: Reflections on the Use of Culture', in *Lokayan Bulletin,* Issue on *Women Towards Beijing: Voices from India,* 12(1/2): 169-79.

Punwani, Jyoti. 2017. '"I've Been Laughing and Crying," Says Woman Who First Challenged Muslim Personal Law in 1983', *Scroll,* 4 September. scroll.in/article/848680/ive-been-laughing-and-crying-says-woman-who-first-challenged-muslim-personal-law-in-sc-in-1983 (accessed 20 June 2022).

Punwani, Jyoti. 2021. 'Sonal Shukla: An Icon of the Women's Movement in India and Across the Globe,' in Jonathan Menge and Isabelle Mischke (eds.), *Icons of Gender Justice: Paving the Way for Women's Rights in Asia,* pp. 65-70. Nepal: Friedrich Ebert Stiftung.

Puri, Nikita. 2014. 'Reclaiming the Streets: Battling for A Woman's "Right to Space"', *Indian Express*, 20 October. indianexpress.com/article/lifestyle/reclaiming-the-streets-battling-for-a-womans-right-to-space/ (accessed 26 January 2020).

Ramachandran, Vibhuti. 2003. 'Street Theatre as a Medium of Development Communication: Case Studies in Four Delhi Slums'. Unpublished M.A. dissertation, Lady Shri Ram College, University of Delhi.

Ramdas, Lalita. 1985. 'Lest We Forget...' *Manushi*, 26: 12-14.

Ramdas, Lalita. 2015. 'Oct 31st 1984 – Dec 6 1992 – March 2002—An Awakening to Reality', *Countercurrents*, 1 November. www.countercurrents.org/lr011115.htm, (accessed 29 January 2019).

Richards, Norah. 1956. *Playwriting and Playmaking*. New Delhi: Ministry of Education, Government of India.

Richards, Norah. 1963. *The Physicians and the Flag: Dramatization of the Passing of Old India and the Day of Partition*. Calcutta: Alpha-Beta Publications.

Roy, Rahul. 2007. *A Little Book on Men*. Delhi: Yoda Press.

Sabla Sangh (Delhi), 1988. 'Aurat aur Dharm', in Jagori Samooh (ed.). *Nukkad Nukkad Aangan Aangan*, pp. 94-101. New Delhi: Jagori.

Sabla Sangh (Delhi). 1988. 'Parivar Ki Gaadi', in Jagori Samooh (ed.). *Nukkad Nukkad Aangan Aangan*, pp. 22-31. New Delhi: Jagori.

Saheli. 2010. 'Breaking Silence. Talking Issues. Singing Perspectives... Evolving New Languages of Resistance', *Saheli Newsletter*, September-December.

Sakhi Kendra-Mahila Manch (Kanpur) and Deepti. 'Teen Behenon ki Atmahatya'. Unpublished play script.

Sai, Veejay. 2007. *Drama Queens: Women Who Created History on Stage*. New Delhi: Roli Books.

Sahiyar (Vadodara). 1988. 'Achko Machko Kareli', in Jagori Samooh (ed.), *Nukkad Nukkad Aangan Aangan*, pp. 114-115. New Delhi: Jagori.

Sahiyar (Vadodara). 1988. 'Dahej ka Daanav', in Jagori Samooh (ed.), *Nukkad Nukkad Aangan Aangan*, pp. 85-92. New Delhi: Jagori.

Sangari, Kumkum, and Sudesh Vaid. 1999. *Recasting Women: Essays in Colonial History*. New Delhi: Zubaan.

Seagull Theatre Quarterly. 1997. '"Street Theatre Is Here and Now"—A Panel Discussion', *Seagull Theatre Quarterly*, 16: 42-57.

Seagull Theatre Quarterly. 1997. 'The Actresses Speak: A Group Discussion', *Seagull Theatre Quarterly*, 14-15: 139-150.

Segal, Kiran. 2012. *Zohra Segal, 'Fatty'*. New Delhi: Niyogi Books,

Segal, Zohra. 2010. *Close-Up: Memoirs of a Life on Stage and Screen*. New Delhi: Women Unlimited.

Sengupta, Debjani. 2005. 'Playing the Canon: Shakespeare and the Bengali Actress in Nineteenth-Century Calcutta,' in Poonam Trivedi and Dennis Bartholomeusz (eds), *India's Shakespeare: Translation, Interpretation and Performance*, pp. 242-59. New Jersey: Pearson.

Sethi, Sunil. 1979. 'Bride-Burning Becomes a Cognizable Blood Sport in Cities like New Delhi', *India Today*, 15 July. www.indiatoday.in/magazine/special-report/story/19790715-bride-burning-becomes-a-cognizable-blood-sport-in-cities-like-new-delhi-822730-2014-03-03 (accessed 26 January 2018).

Shah, Trupti. 2010. 'Religious Fundamentalisms and Communalism: The Case of Sahiyar', in *Key Learnings from Feminists on the Frontlines: Summaries of Case Studies on Women Resisting and Challenging Fundamentalisms.* Association for Women's Rights in Development (AWID).

Shah, Trupti. 2011. 'Memories', *Poster Women—A Zubaan Project*, 25 July. www.posterwomen.org/?p=5215 (accessed 30 March 2022).

Shah, Trupti. 2011. *Nari Andolanno Itihas*, Volumes 1-4. Baroda: Unnati and Sahiyar Stree Sangathan.

Sharma, Aditi. 2014. 'Living With Savitribai'. *Mumbai Mirror,* 8 January. mumbaimirror.indiatimes.com/others/sunday-read/living-with-savitribai/articleshow/28406772.cms (accessed 30 March 2021).

Sharma, Tripurari. 2000, 'Part One: The Process', in Tripurari Sharma and Lakshmi Krishnamurty, *Searching for A Voice,* pp. 3-141. New Delhi: Alarippu.

Sharma, Tripurari. 2013. 'An Unfinished Journey', in Lakshmi Subramanyam (ed.), *Muffled Voices,* pp. 135-150. New Delhi: Har Anand.

Sharma, Tripurari and Lakshmi Krishnamurty. 1982. *Ek Natya Karmshala ki Diary*. Ganesh Pandey (trans.). Unpublished report.

Sharma, Tripurari and Lakshmi Krishnamurty. 2000. *Searching for a Voice.* New Delhi: Alarippu.

Shirali, K.A. 1997. 'Madness and Power in India', *Canadian Woman Studies,* 17(1): 66-71.

Singh, Lata. 2017. *Raising the Curtain: Recasting Women Performers in India.* Hyderabad: Orient Blackswan.

Singh, Tavleen. 1979. 'Married, Marketed, Murdered: All for Love-of Money', *Manushi*, 3: 18.

Sonpar, Shobna and Neeru Kanwar. 2019. *Surviving on the Edge: Psychological Perspectives on Violence and Prejudice in India.* New Delhi: Sage and Yoda Press.

Sucheta Kripalani Shiksha Niketan (Manaklav, Rajasthan). 1988. 'Dahej', in Jagori Samooh (ed.). *Nukkad Nukkad Aangan Aangan*, pp. 69-80. New Delhi: Jagori.

Subramanyam, Lakshmi (ed.). 2013. *Muffled Voices: Women in Modern Indian Theatre*. New Delhi: HarAnand.

Subramanyam, Lakshmi. 2013. 'In Their Own Voice—In Conversation with Anuradha Kapur, Geetanjali Shree and Vidya Rao', in Lakshmi Subramanyam (ed.), *Muffled Voices,* pp. 209-223. New Delhi: Har Anand.

Tanvir, Habib. 2013. [2007]. 'Janam Comes of Age', in Sudhanva Deshpande (ed.), *Theatre of the Streets*, pp. 70-87. New Delhi: Jana Natya Manch.

Theatre Union. 1988. *Om Swaha 1,* in Jagori Samooh (ed.). *Nukkad Nukkad Aangan Aangan,* pp. 42-51. New Delhi: Jagori.

Tilak, Rajni. 2018. *Apni Zameen Apna Aasmaan.* Delhi: Isha Gyandeep.

Thapar-Björkert, Suruchi. 2006. *Women in the Indian National Movement: Unseen Faces and Unheard Voices 1930-42.* New Delhi: Sage.

Udgaar (Surat). 1988. *Dahej ka Savaal,* in Jagori Samooh (ed.), *Nukkad Nukkad Aangan Aangan,* pp. 81-84. New Delhi: Jagori.

Uppal, Ipsita. 2016. 'Ending Violence Against Women – One Play at a Time!: Analysing the Effectiveness of Street Theatre in Combating Violence against Women – A Case Study of Vanangana, A Women's Organisation Based in Rural India'. Unpublished research paper, M.A. Development Studies, Erasumus: International Institute of Social Studies, The Hague.

Vaid, Sudesh, Amiya Rao and Monica Juneja. 1980. *Rape, Society and State.* New Delhi: People's Union for Democratic Rights.

Vanita, Ruth. 1979. '"Women's Safety is Women's Right"', *Manushi,* 2: 21-23.

Vanita, Ruth. 1980. 'Strengthening the "Strong Man Helpless Woman" Stereotype', *Manushi,* 5: 26-28.

Viegas, Savia. 1988. 'Voices from the Crowd', in ASTHA, *Two Street Plays for Women,* pp. 45-50. Bombay: Xavier Institute of Communications.

Vidya, Living Smile. 2013. *I Am Vidya: A Transgender's Journey.* New Dehi: Rupa.

Virdi, Jyotika. 1988. 'Kyon aur Kaise', in Jagori Samooh, *Nukkad Nukkad Aangan Aangan,* pp. vii-ix. New Delhi: Jagori.

Virdi, Jyotika. 2003. *The Cinematic ImagiNation: Indian Popular Films as Social History.* New Brunswick: Rutgers University Press.

Vyas, Neena. 1979. 'Married, Marketed, Murdered: A Mother's Crusade', 3: 19-20.

Women and Religion Group. 1992. *Dharm Hamein Jodta Kaise Hai, Todta Kaise Hai.* New Delhi: Ankur, Action India, Shakti Shalini.

Zurbrigg, Sheila. 1991 [1984]. *Rakku's Story: Ill Health and the Source of Change.* Bangalore: Centre for Social Action.

Videos, Films, Websites, Social Media

Ankur Society for Alternatives in Education. Website. ankureducation.net/ (accessed 16 April 2024).

Alarippu. Website. alarippu.org/ (accessed 19 August 2024).

Chaskar, Vinayak. 2022. *Mulgi Jhali Ho. Video. Doordarshan Sahyadri.* 6 November. www.youtube.com/watch?v=5kxDSubKECU (accessed 16 April 2024).

Erminia Thompson Folsom Collection. Undated. The Movement Comes of Age: Suffrage Plays', Archives and Information Services Division, Texas State Library and Archives Commission. www.tsl.texas.gov/exhibits/suffrage/comesofage/page4.html (accessed 24 August 2021).

Indian Cultural Forum. 2016. *Feminist Street Theatre: Zindagi ke Natak, Natakon ki Zindagi: Excerpts from Feminist Street Plays—Dramatized Readings by Shanti and Deepti, Sampurna Trust, New Delhi.* www.youtube.com/watch?v=aZDtWRxj7Gs&t=3s (Accessed 15 May 2023).

Jagori. Website. www.jagori.org/ (accessed 12 May 2021).

Jana Sanskriti. *About Us.* janasanskriti.org/about-page#the-journey-of-janasanskriti-began-from-a-small-village (accessed 25 March 2023).

Kalita, Devangana. 2016. *Pinjra Tod South Campus Night March.* Facebook Post, 5 October. www.facebook.com/events/1780568978890952/ ?active_tab=discussion (accessed 26 March 2023).

Kislay. 2018. *Kislay Annual Report: April 2017-March 2018.* kislayngo.in/wp-content/uploads/simple-file-list/Annual-report-2017-18.pdf (accessed 26 January 2024).

Kislay 2021. *International Women's Day 2021.* kislayngo.in/index.php/2021/07/03/international-womans-day-2021/ (accessed 26 January 2024).

Kislay. Website. 2024. kislayngo.in/ (accessed 26 January 2024).

Mathur, Vishnu. 2003. *Shahjehan Aapa.* Film. Producer: C.S. Lakshmi, SPARROW (Sound and Picture Archives for Research on Women), Mumbai. www.cultureunplugged.com/play/756/Shahjehan-Apa (accessed 1 April 2015).

Mehrotra, Deepti Priya. 2016. *Feminist Street Theatre: Plays As Contemporary History.* Includes Video *Feminist Street Theatre: Zindagi ke Natak, Natakon ki Zindagi: Excerpts from Feminist Street Plays—Dramatized Readings by Shanti and Deepti, Sampurna Trust, New Delhi.* Indian Cultural Forum. indianculturalforum.in/2016/07/09/feminist-street-theatre-plays-as-contemporary-history (accessed 15 May 2023).

Mitra, Shayoni. Undated. *Theater and Sex Work: VAMP's Performance As Resistance.* Video. Pulkit Datta (Editor and Producer). Barnard Center for Research on Women. bcrw.barnard.edu/projects/transnationalfeminisms/vamp/ (accessed 9 March 2024).

Nobel Prize. 2021. *Nobel Prize Lecture: Maria Ressa, Nobel Peace Prize 2021.* Video. 10 December. Available: www.youtube.com/embed/NsWVb2AUl5Y (last accessed 12 December 2021).

Pandya, Srushti. 2014. *"Emotions need release..." – In Conversation with Director Aditi Desai.* Video. 4 January. Available: www.oowomaniya.com/voices/creative-mediums-for-expression-in-conversation-with-a-theatre-director-aditi-desai/ (accessed 18 March 2019).

Patil, Abhay Shivgounda. 1983. *Om Swaha.* Video. www.youtube.com/watch?v=3C-U2Vk99hc (accessed 12 August 2015).

Pinjra Tod. 2016. *Women Claim the Streets.* Facebook Event, 3 October. www.facebook.com/events/1780568978890952?active_tab=about (accessed 6 March 2023).

Pune Cultural Mapping Team, Sahapedia. 2021. *Vhay Mi Savitribai: A One-*

Woman Play on Savitribai Phule. map.sahapedia.org/article/Vhay-Mi%20 Savitribai:%20A%20One-Woman%20Play%20on%20Savitribhai%20 Phule/2559 (accessed 27 March 2022).

Sahiyar Stree Sangathan. Website: sahiyarstreesangthan.org (accessed 30 March 2024).

Sakhi Kendra. 2020. *DIDI: A Film Dedicated to the Women Who Live for Others*. Video. 22 November. www.youtube.com/watch?v=LvkEIpiKTeA (accessed 23 February 2023).

Shakti Shalini. Website: shaktishalini.org/ (accessed 25 March 2024).

Shakti Shalini. 2022. *Shakti Shalini Annual Reprot 2021-2022*. shaktishalini.org/ annual_reports/Annual%20Report%202021-2022.pdf (accessed 5 March 2024).

Stree Mukti Sanghatana. 2012. Video. *International Women Playwrights Conference Mumbai 2009 (Part 2)*. 29 October. www.youtube.com/ watch?v=vYu7g9kyEXs (accessed 28 February 2023).

Stree Mukti Sanghatana. Website. streemuktisanghatana.org/ (accessed 18 March 2023).

Swayam. Website: swayam.info/ (accessed 25 March 2023).

Swayam. *Theatre Group*. swayam.info/stories-of-change/survivors-as-change-agents/theatre-group/ (accessed 25 March 2023).

Zehtabchi, Rayka. 2018. *Period: End of Sentence*. Film. Producer: Melissa Burton.

Legal Documents

Delhi State vs Laxman Goel & Ors, Supreme Court of India on 23 September, 1985, *Indian Kanoon*. indiankanoon.org/doc/433126/ (accessed 15 February 2019).

Shakuntala & Ors vs The State, Delhi High Court on 3 November, 1983, *Indian Kanoon*. indiankanoon.org/doc/296472/ (accessed 26 January 2021).